I don't like rain.

池田晃久
AKIHISA IKEDA

I heard if you stay holed up inside all the time you get depressed. So I cursed the life of the manga artist. I wanna go out and play!
To head off depression I started taking walks. And you know what? It's fun being able to walk around while everybody else is at work! Now I'm saying, "All hail the life of the manga artist!"
I guess I'm not depressed anymore...

Akihisa Ikeda was born in 1977 in Miyazaki. He debuted as a mangaka with the four-volume magical warrior fantasy series *Kiruto* in 1999, which was serialized in *Monthly Shonen Jump*. *Rosario+Vampire* debuted in *Monthly Shonen Jump* in March of 2002, and is continuing in the new magazine *Jump Square* (Jump SQ). In Japan, *Rosario+Vampire* is also available as a drama CD. In 2008, the story was released as an anime.

Ikeda has been a huge fan of vampires and monsters since he was a little kid.

ROSARIO+VAMPIRE 2
SHONEN JUMP ADVANCED Manga Edition

STORY & ART BY AKIHISA IKEDA

Translation/Kaori Inoue
English Adaptation/Gerard Jones
Touch-up Art & Lettering/Stephen Dutro
Cover/Hidemi Dunn
Interior Design/Mark Griffin
Editor/Annette Roman

ROSARIO + VAMPIRE © 2004 by Akihisa Ikeda
All rights reserved. First published in Japan in 2004 by SHUEISHA Inc.,
Tokyo. English translation rights arranged by SHUEISHA Inc.

The stories, characters and incidents mentioned in this publication
are entirely fictional.

Printed in the U.S.A.

Published by VIZ Media, LLC
P.O. Box 77010
San Francisco, CA 94107

10 9
First printing, August 2008
Ninth printing, March 2015

www.viz.com

ROSARIO+VAMPIRE

2

WITCHES

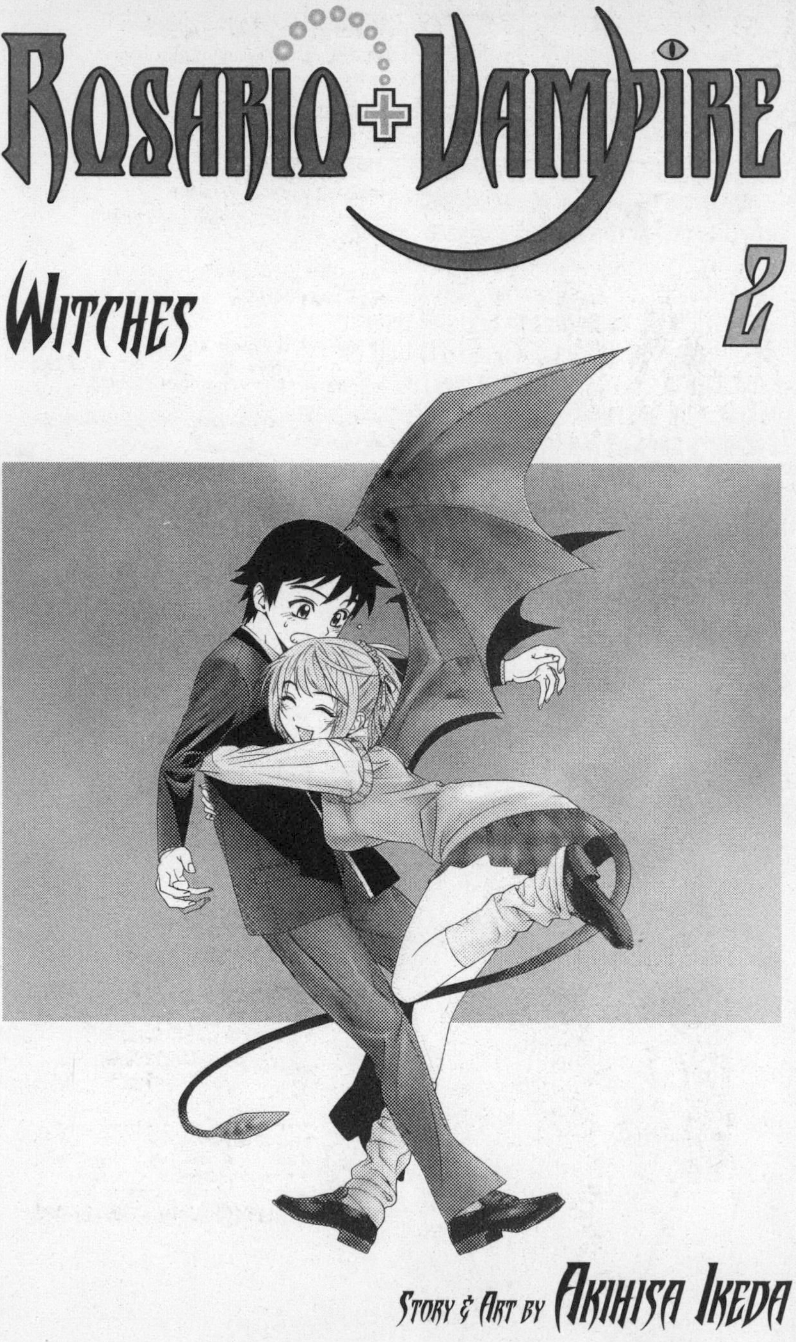

STORY & ART BY AKIHISA IKEDA

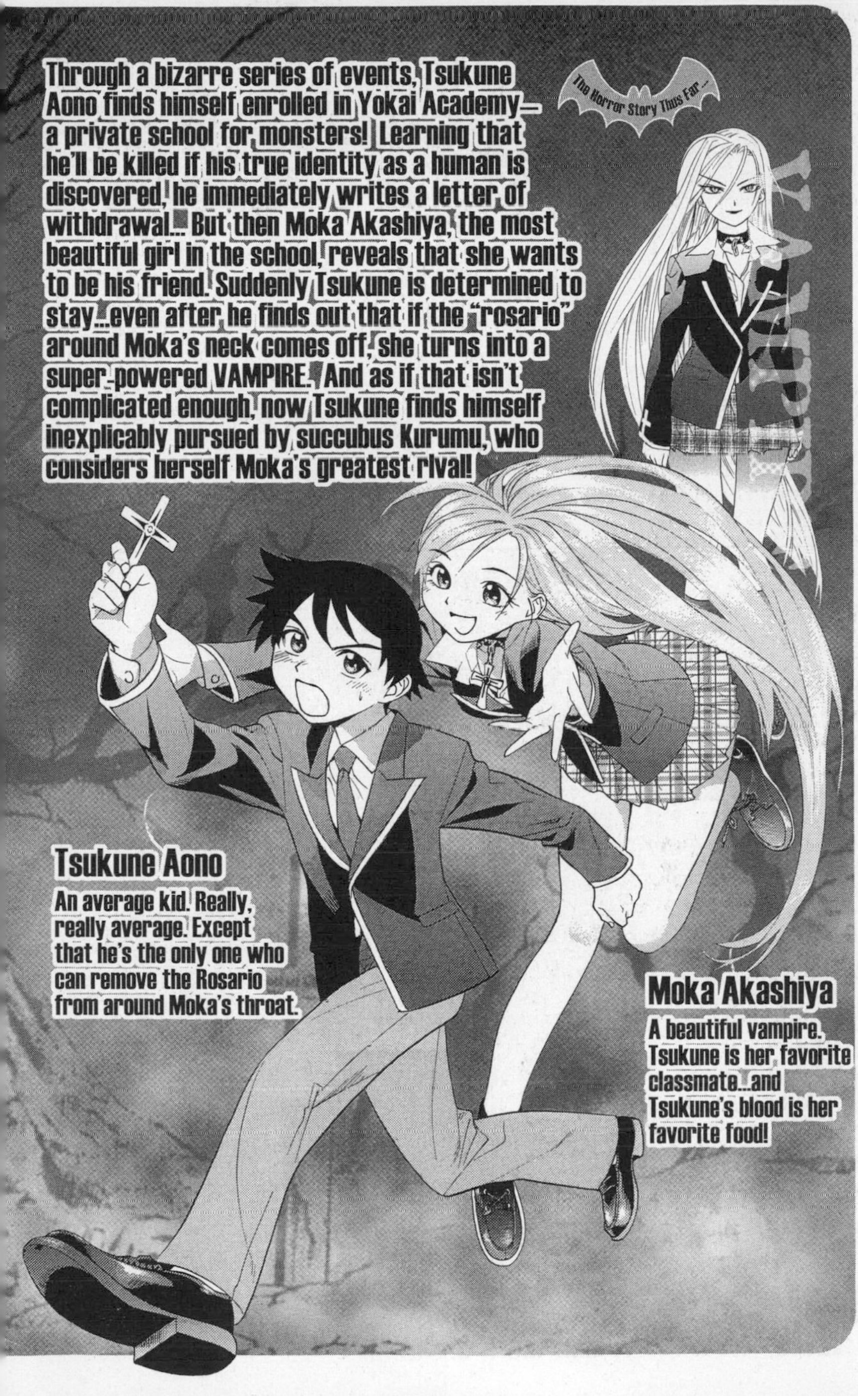
The Horror Story Thus Far...
Through a bizarre series of events, Tsukune Aono finds himself enrolled in Yokai Academy—a private school for monsters! Learning that he'll be killed if his true identity as a human is discovered, he immediately writes a letter of withdrawal... But then Moka Akashiya, the most beautiful girl in the school, reveals that she wants to be his friend. Suddenly Tsukune is determined to stay...even after he finds out that if the "rosario" around Moka's neck comes off, she turns into a super-powered VAMPIRE. And as if that isn't complicated enough, now Tsukune finds himself inexplicably pursued by succubus Kurumu, who considers herself Moka's greatest rival!
Tsukune Aono
An average kid. Really, really average. Except that he's the only one who can remove the Rosario from around Moka's throat.
Moka Akashiya
A beautiful vampire. Tsukune is her favorite classmate...and Tsukune's blood is her favorite food!

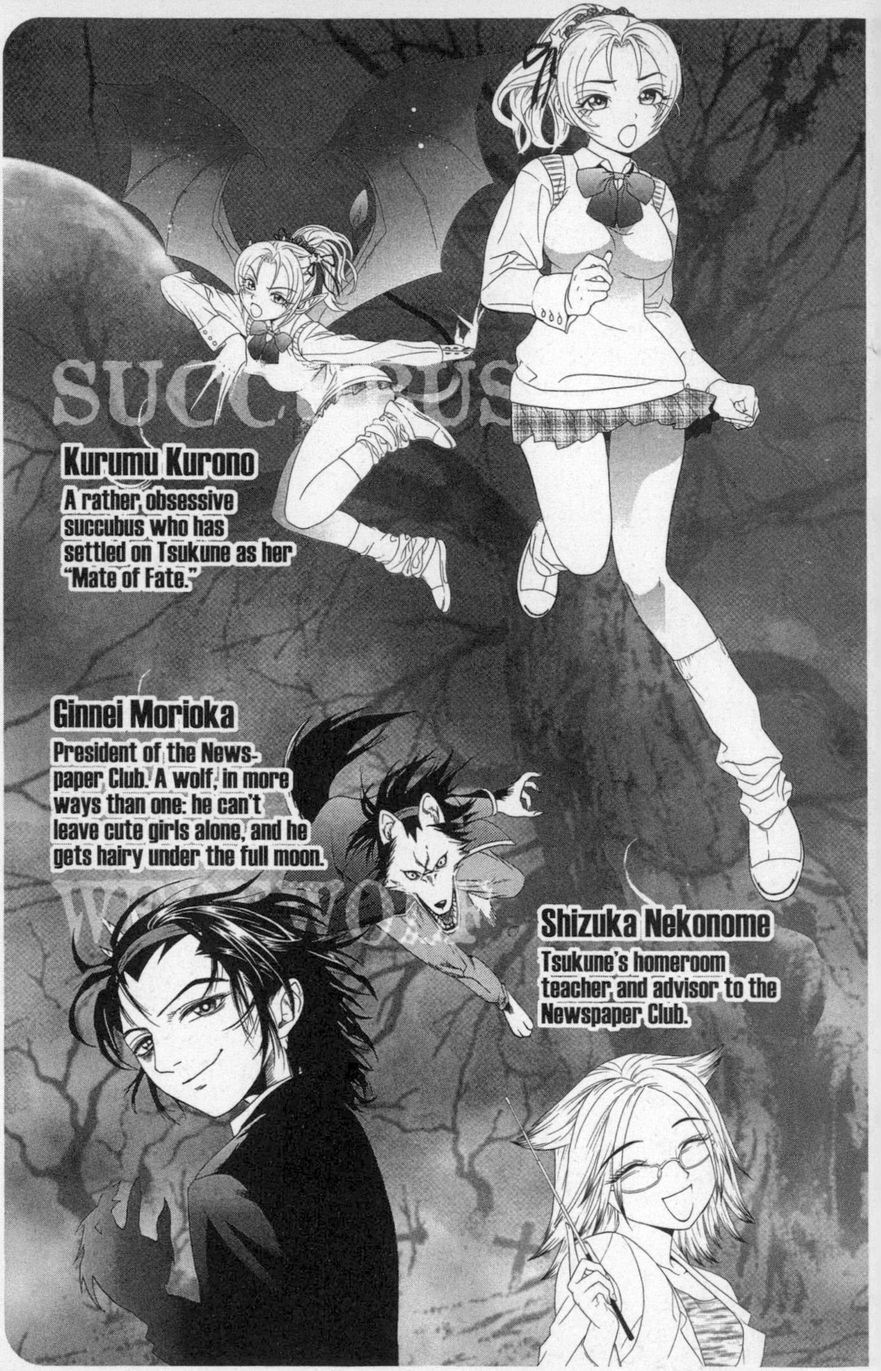
Kurumu Kurono
A rather obsessive succubus who has settled on Tsukune as her "Mate of Fate."
Ginnei Morioka
President of the Newspaper Club. A wolf, in more ways than one: he can't leave cute girls alone, and he gets hairy under the full moon.
Shizuka Nekonome
Tsukune's homeroom teacher and advisor to the Newspaper Club.

CONTENTS

Volume 2: Witches

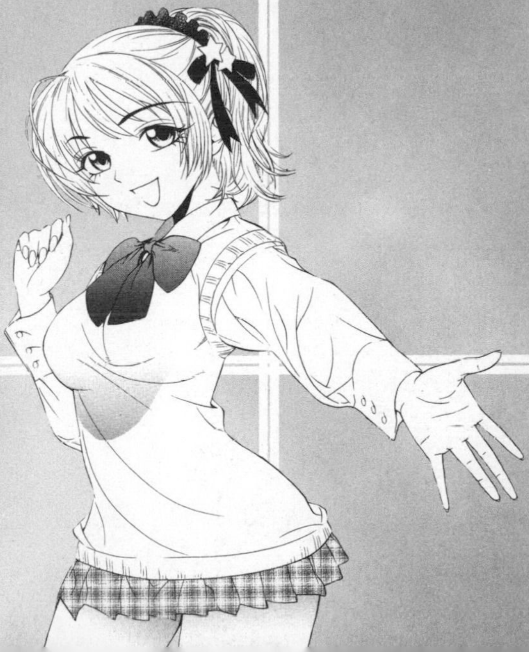

5: Love Is a Witch

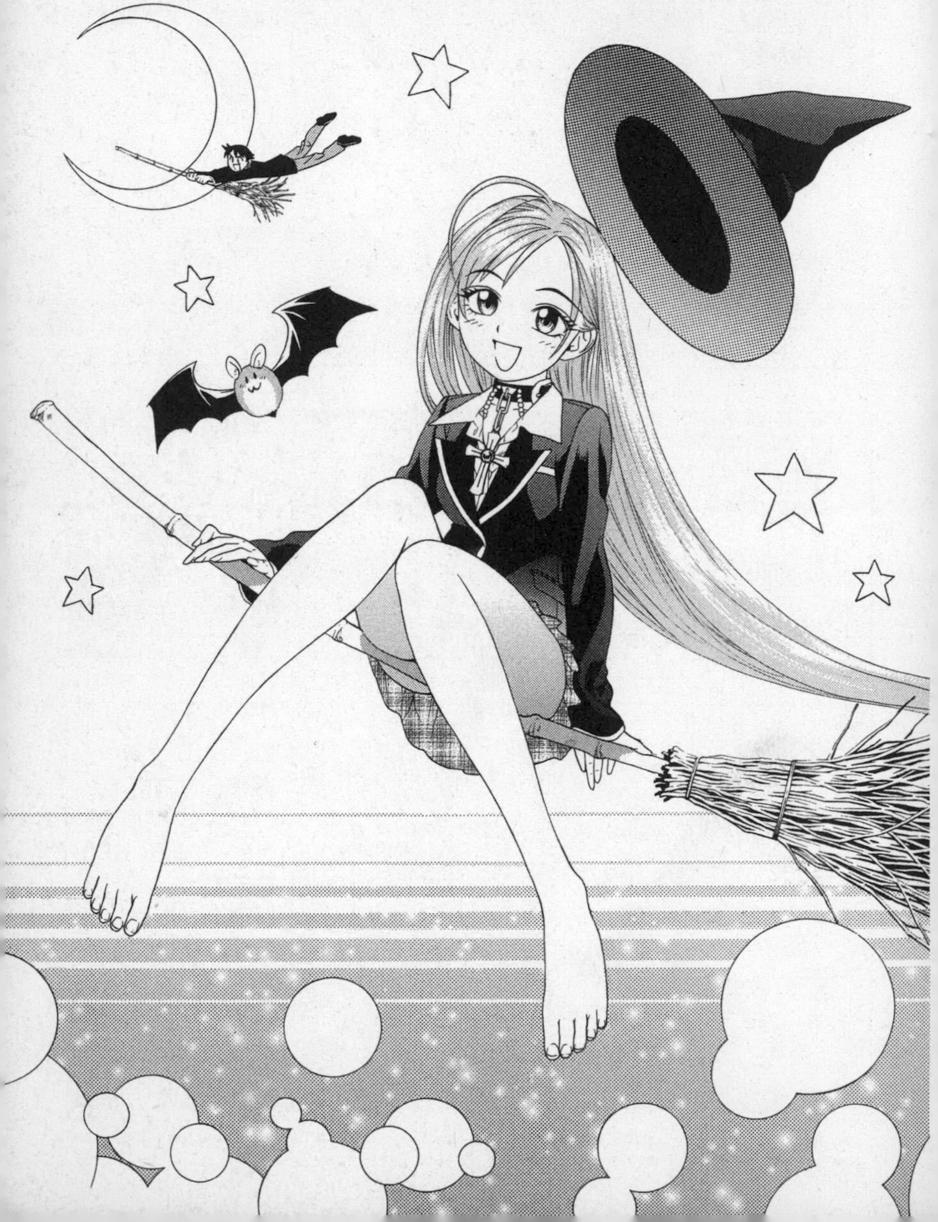

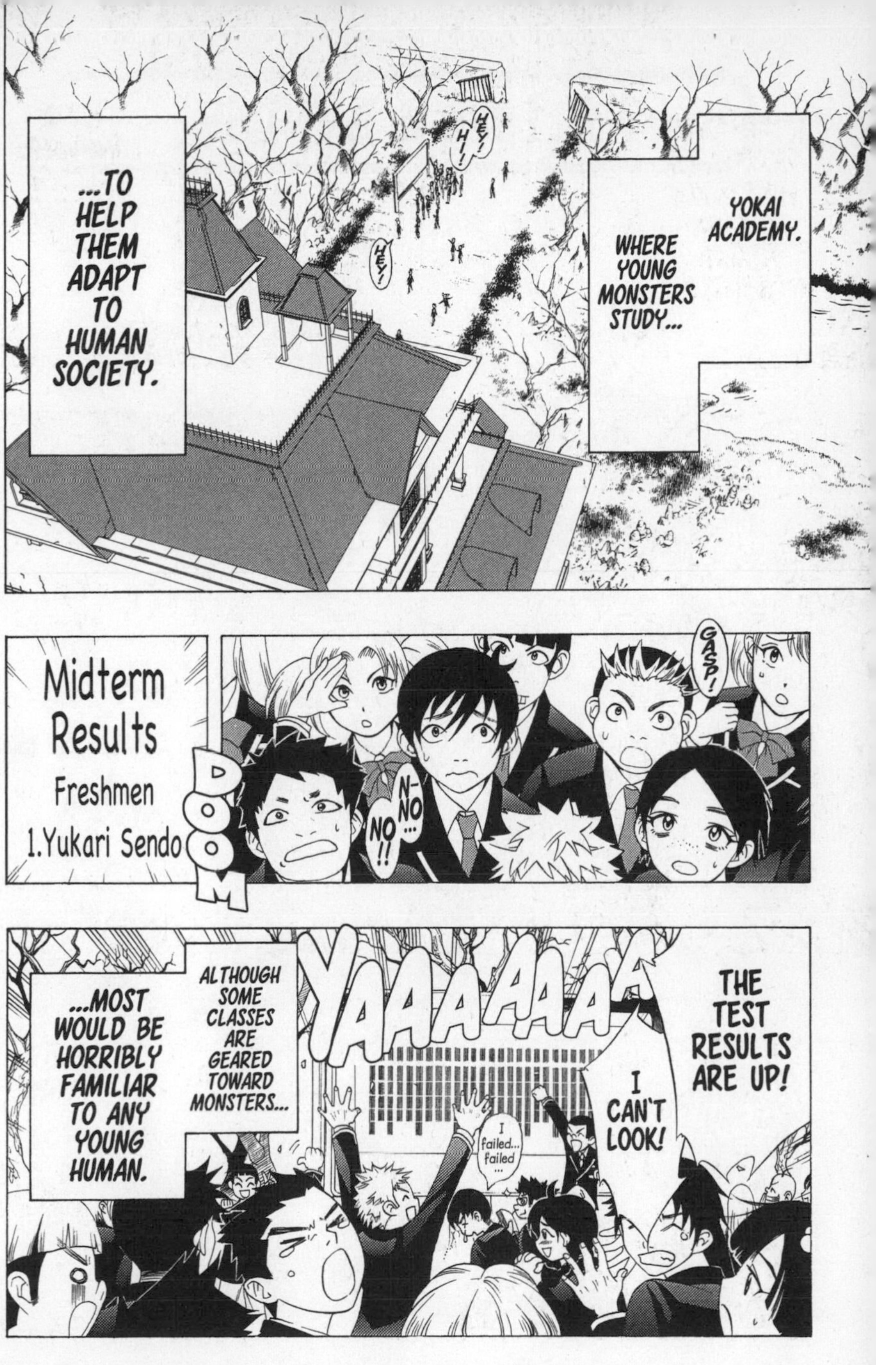
YOKAI ACADEMY.
WHERE YOUNG MONSTERS STUDY...
HEY! HI!
HEY!
...TO HELP THEM ADAPT TO HUMAN SOCIETY.
GASP!
N-NO... NO!!
DOOM
Midterm Results
Freshmen
1.Yukari Sendo
THE TEST RESULTS ARE UP!
I CAN'T LOOK!
YAAAAAA
I failed... failed...
ALTHOUGH SOME CLASSES ARE GEARED TOWARD MONSTERS...
...MOST WOULD BE HORRIBLY FAMILIAR TO ANY YOUNG HUMAN.

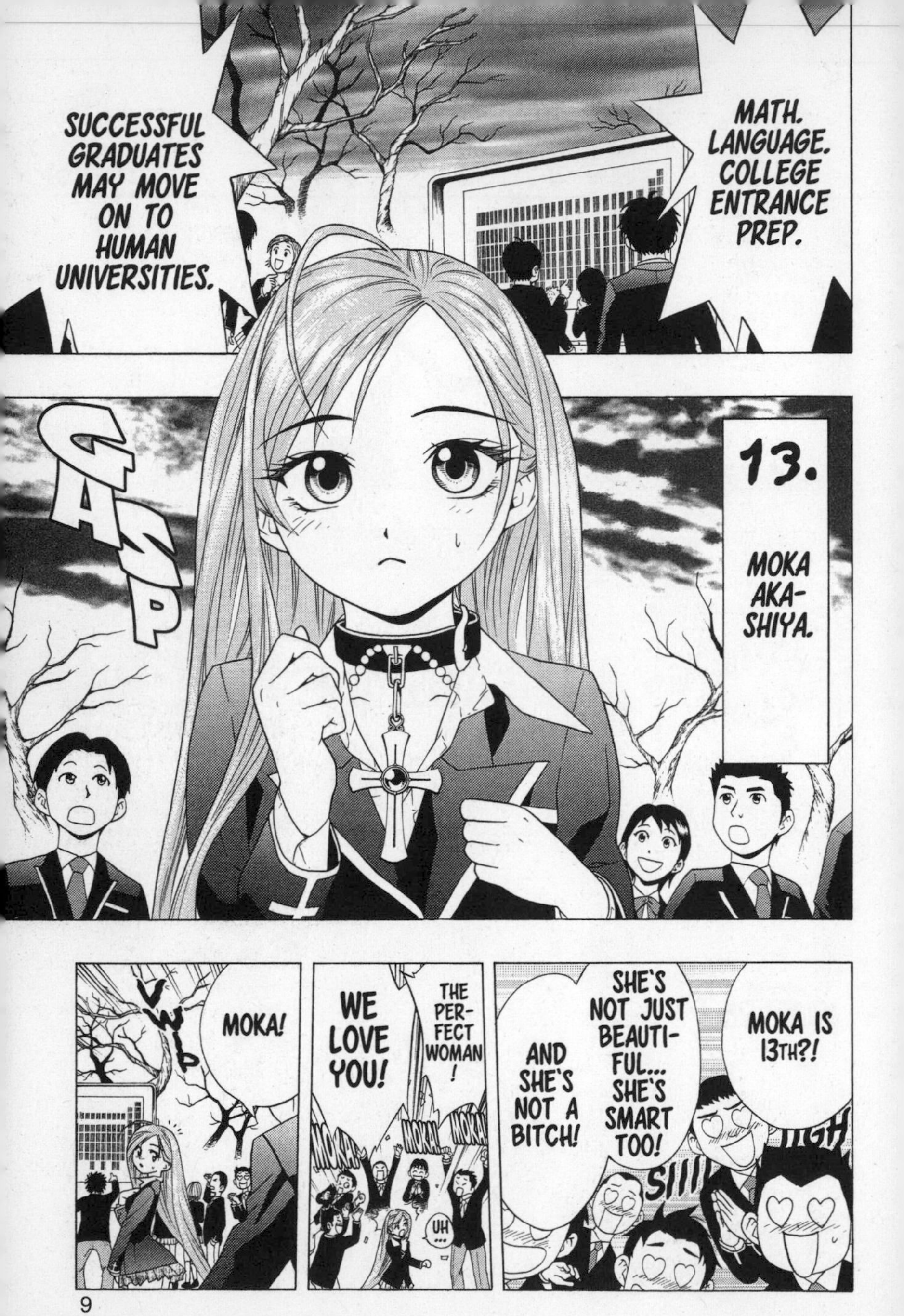
MATH. LANGUAGE. COLLEGE ENTRANCE PREP.
SUCCESSFUL GRADUATES MAY MOVE ON TO HUMAN UNIVERSITIES.
13.
MOKA AKA-SHIYA.
GASP
MOKA IS 13TH?!
SHE'S NOT JUST BEAUTI-FUL... SHE'S SMART TOO!
AND SHE'S NOT A BITCH!
THE PER-FECT WOMAN!
WE LOVE YOU!
MOKA!
MOKA!
MOKA!
UH...
MOKA!

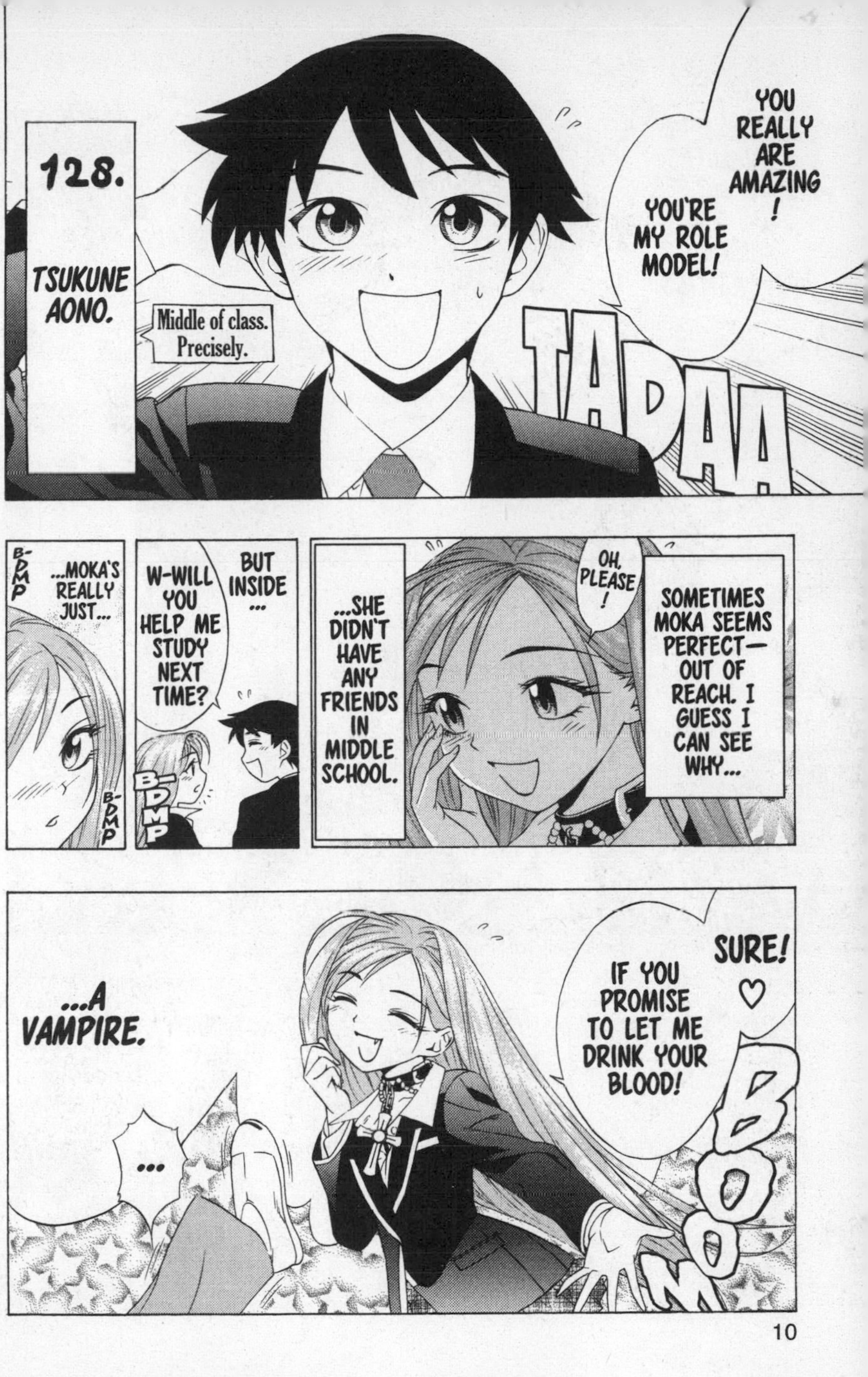
YOU REALLY ARE AMAZING!
YOU'RE MY ROLE MODEL!
TADAA
128.
TSUKUNE AONO.
Middle of class. Precisely.
SOMETIMES MOKA SEEMS PERFECT—OUT OF REACH. I GUESS I CAN SEE WHY...
OH, PLEASE!
...SHE DIDN'T HAVE ANY FRIENDS IN MIDDLE SCHOOL.
BUT INSIDE...
W-WILL YOU HELP ME STUDY NEXT TIME?
B-DMP
...MOKA'S REALLY JUST...
B-DMP
B-DMP
SURE! ♥
IF YOU PROMISE TO LET ME DRINK YOUR BLOOD!
BOOM
...A VAMPIRE.
...

READ THIS WAY

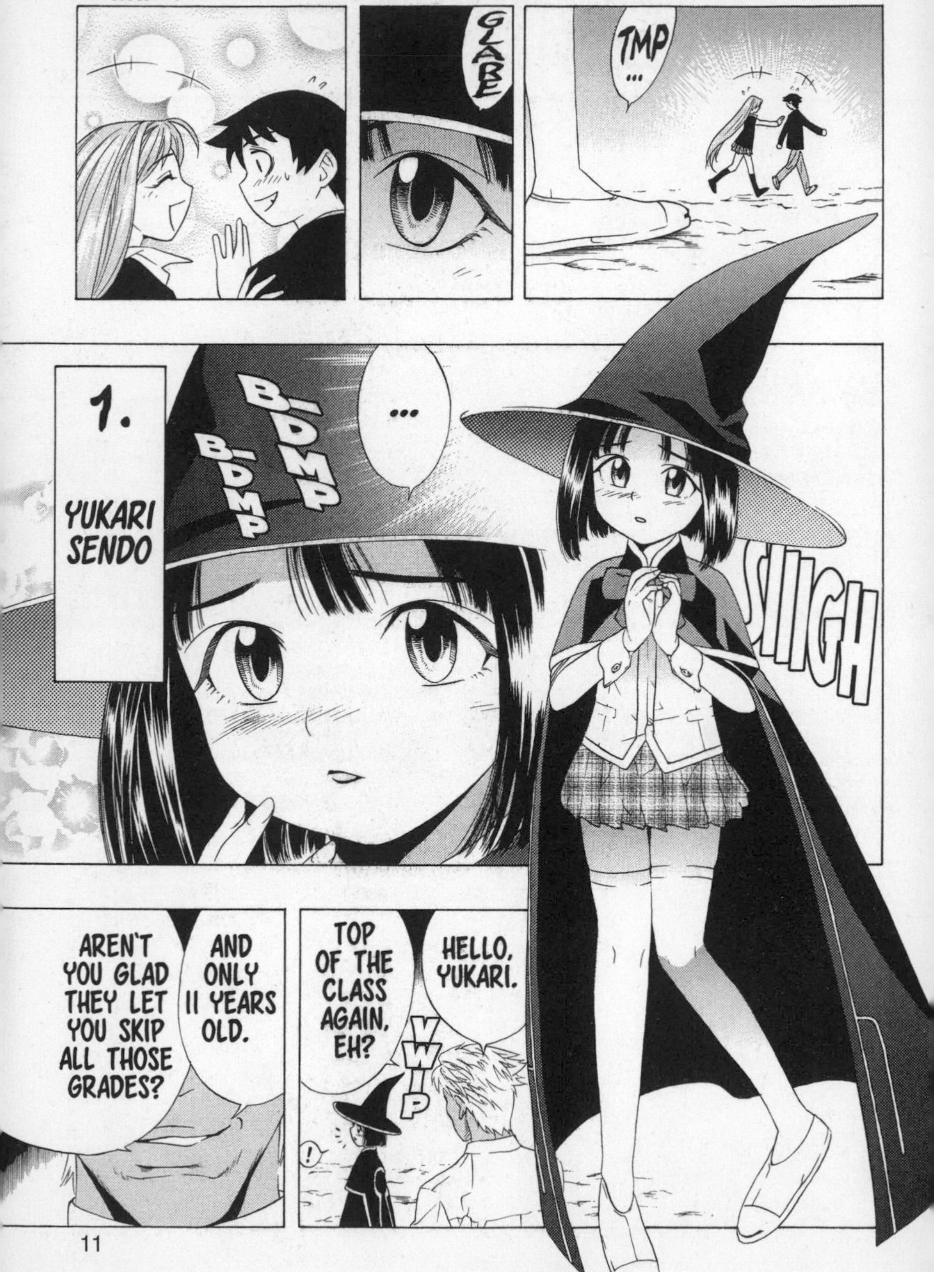
TMP ...
GLABE
...
B-DMP
B-DMP
1.
YUKARI SENDO
SIIGH
HELLO, YUKARI.
TOP OF THE CLASS AGAIN, EH?
VWIP
!
AND ONLY 11 YEARS OLD.
AREN'T YOU GLAD THEY LET YOU SKIP ALL THOSE GRADES?

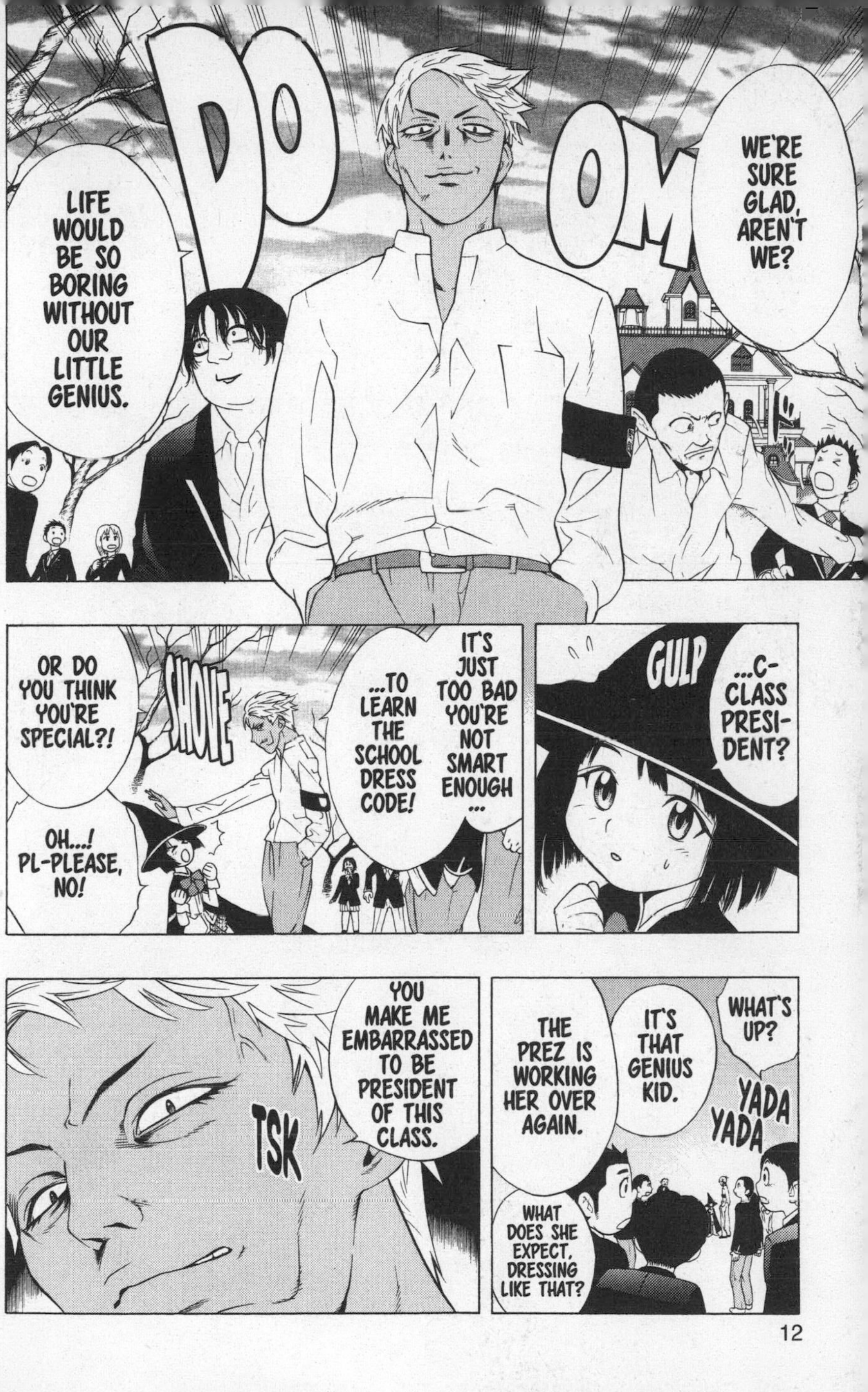

WE'RE SURE GLAD, AREN'T WE?
DO OM
LIFE WOULD BE SO BORING WITHOUT OUR LITTLE GENIUS.
GULP
...C-CLASS PRESIDENT?
IT'S JUST TOO BAD YOU'RE NOT SMART ENOUGH ...
...TO LEARN THE SCHOOL DRESS CODE!
SHOVE
OR DO YOU THINK YOU'RE SPECIAL?!
OH...! PL-PLEASE, NO!
WHAT'S UP?
IT'S THAT GENIUS KID.
THE PREZ IS WORKING HER OVER AGAIN.
YADA YADA
WHAT DOES SHE EXPECT, DRESSING LIKE THAT?
YOU MAKE ME EMBARRASSED TO BE PRESIDENT OF THIS CLASS.
TSK

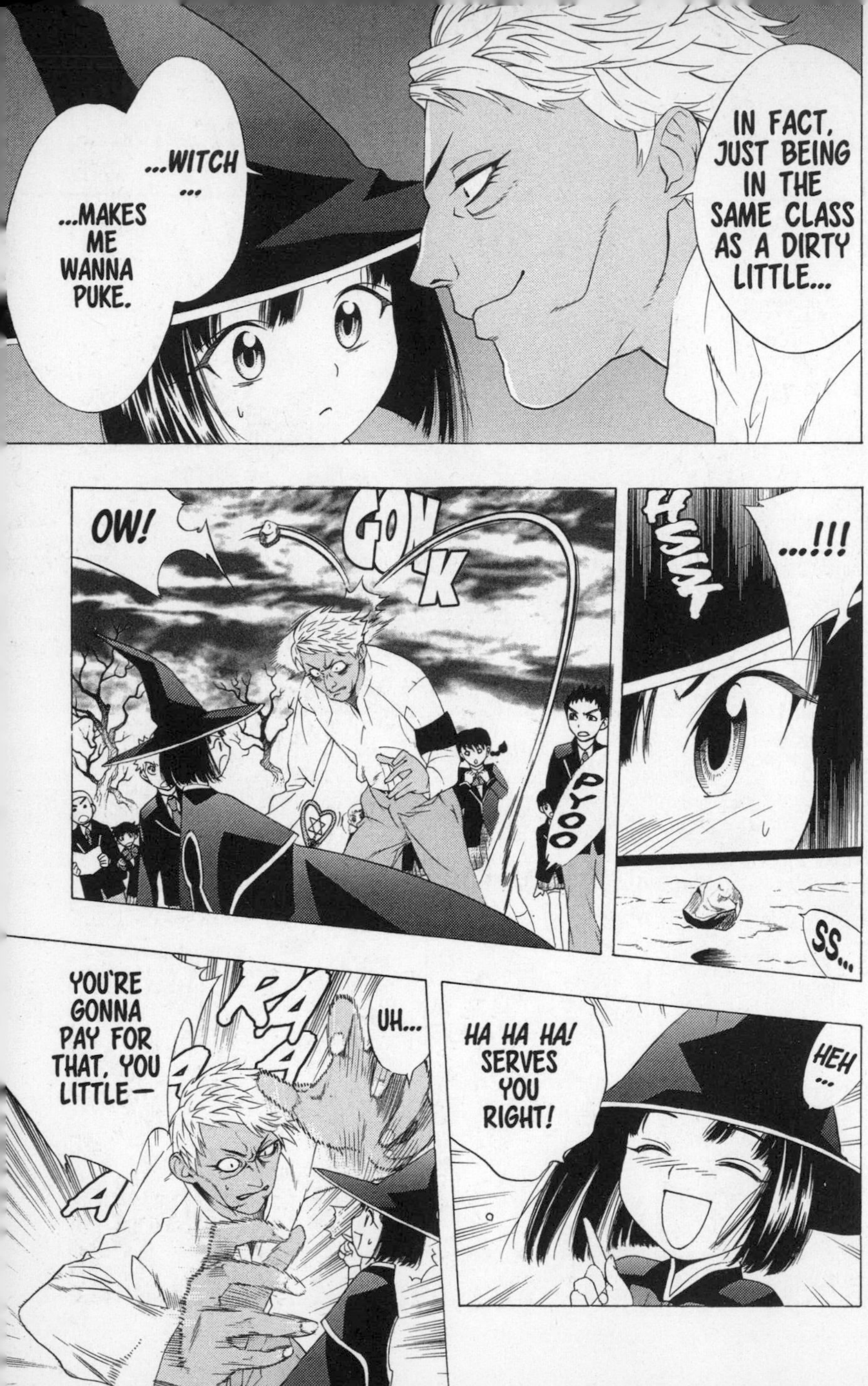
IN FACT, JUST BEING IN THE SAME CLASS AS A DIRTY LITTLE...
...WITCH ...
...MAKES ME WANNA PUKE.
HSSK
...!!!
SS...
GONK
OW!
PYOO
HEH ...
HA HA HA! SERVES YOU RIGHT!
UH...
RAAA
YOU'RE GONNA PAY FOR THAT, YOU LITTLE—

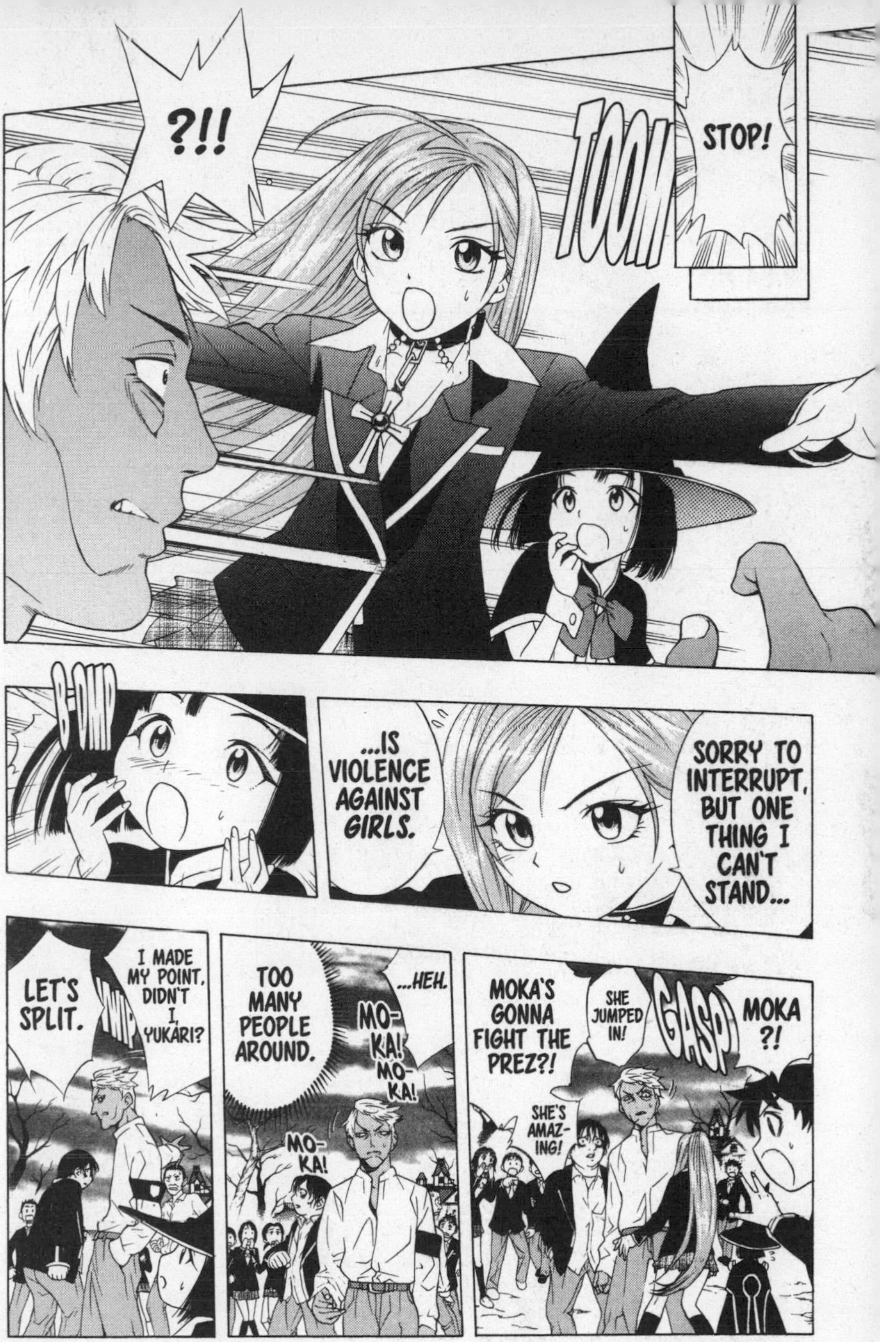
STOP!
TOOM
?!!
SORRY TO INTERRUPT, BUT ONE THING I CAN'T STAND...
...IS VIOLENCE AGAINST GIRLS.
MOKA ?!
GASP
SHE JUMPED IN!
MOKA'S GONNA FIGHT THE PREZ?!
SHE'S AMAZING!
...HEH.
TOO MANY PEOPLE AROUND.
MO-KA! MO-KA!
MO-KA!
I MADE MY POINT, DIDN'T I, YUKARI?
LET'S SPLIT.

READ THIS WAY

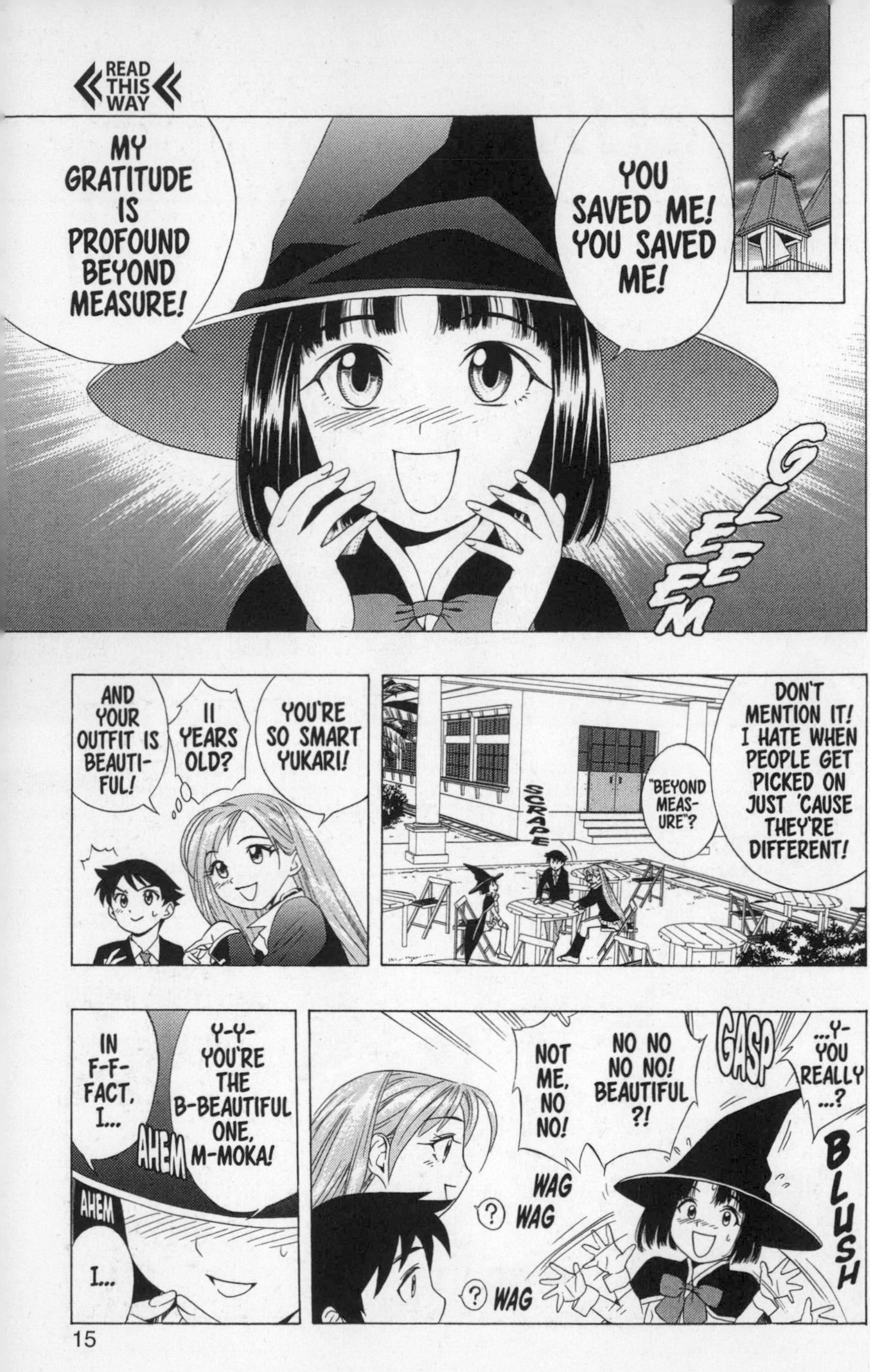

YOU SAVED ME! YOU SAVED ME!
MY GRATITUDE IS PROFOUND BEYOND MEASURE!
GLEEEEM
DON'T MENTION IT! I HATE WHEN PEOPLE GET PICKED ON JUST 'CAUSE THEY'RE DIFFERENT!
SCRAPE
"BEYOND MEASURE"?
YOU'RE SO SMART YUKARI!
11 YEARS OLD?
AND YOUR OUTFIT IS BEAUTIFUL!
...Y-YOU REALLY...?
GASP
BLUSH
NO NO NO NO! BEAUTIFUL?!
NOT ME, NO NO!
WAG WAG
WAG
Y-Y-YOU'RE THE B-BEAUTIFUL ONE, M-MOKA!
IN F-F-FACT, I...
AHEM
AHEM
I...

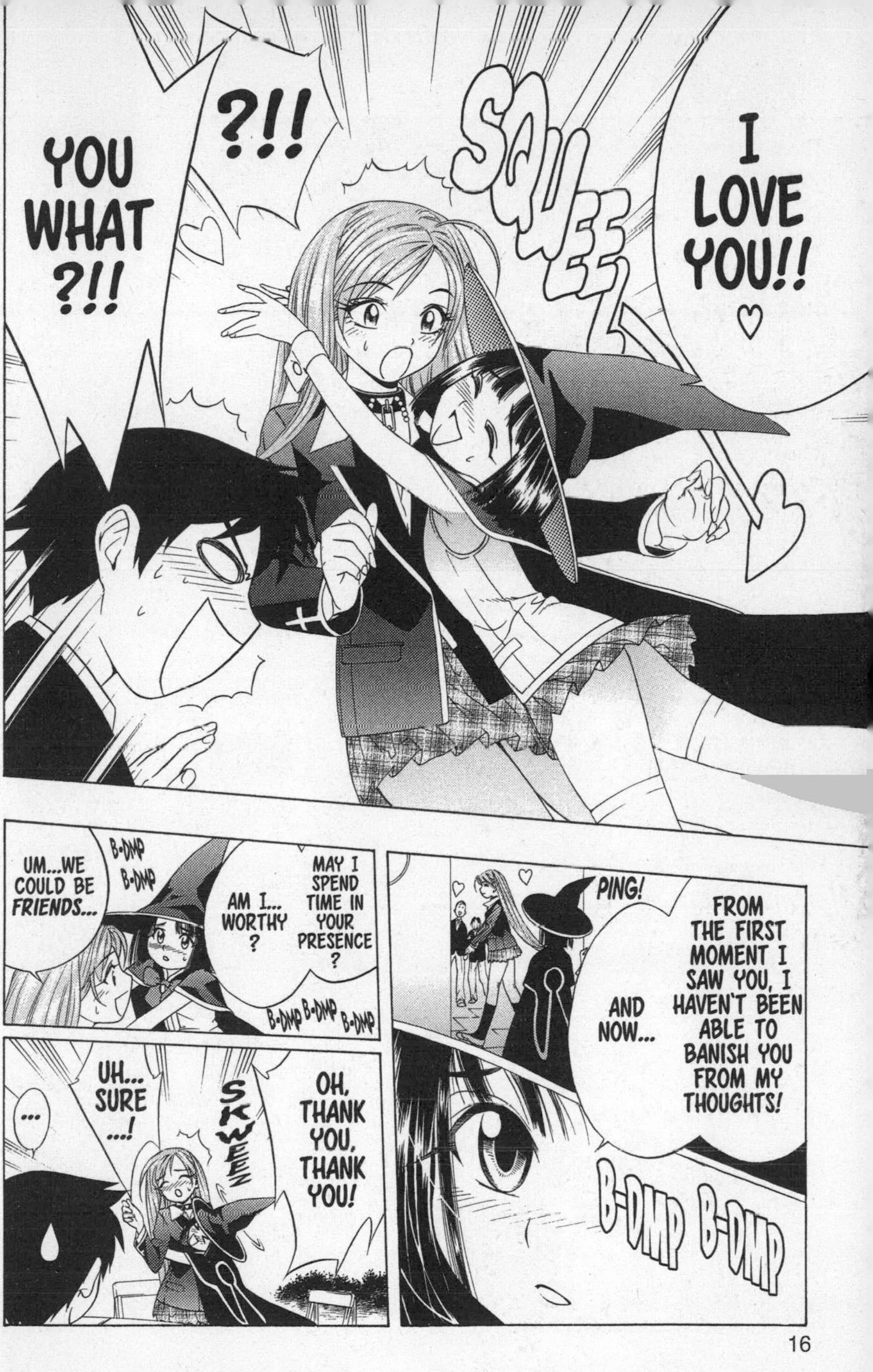
I LOVE YOU!!
SQUEEZ
?!!
YOU WHAT ?!!
PING!
FROM THE FIRST MOMENT I SAW YOU, I HAVEN'T BEEN ABLE TO BANISH YOU FROM MY THOUGHTS!
AND NOW...
B-DMP B-DMP
B-DMP
B-DMP
MAY I SPEND TIME IN YOUR PRESENCE?
AM I... WORTHY?
UM...WE COULD BE FRIENDS...
B-DMP B-DMP B-DMP
OH, THANK YOU, THANK YOU!
SKWEEZ
UH... SURE ...!
...

READ THIS WAY

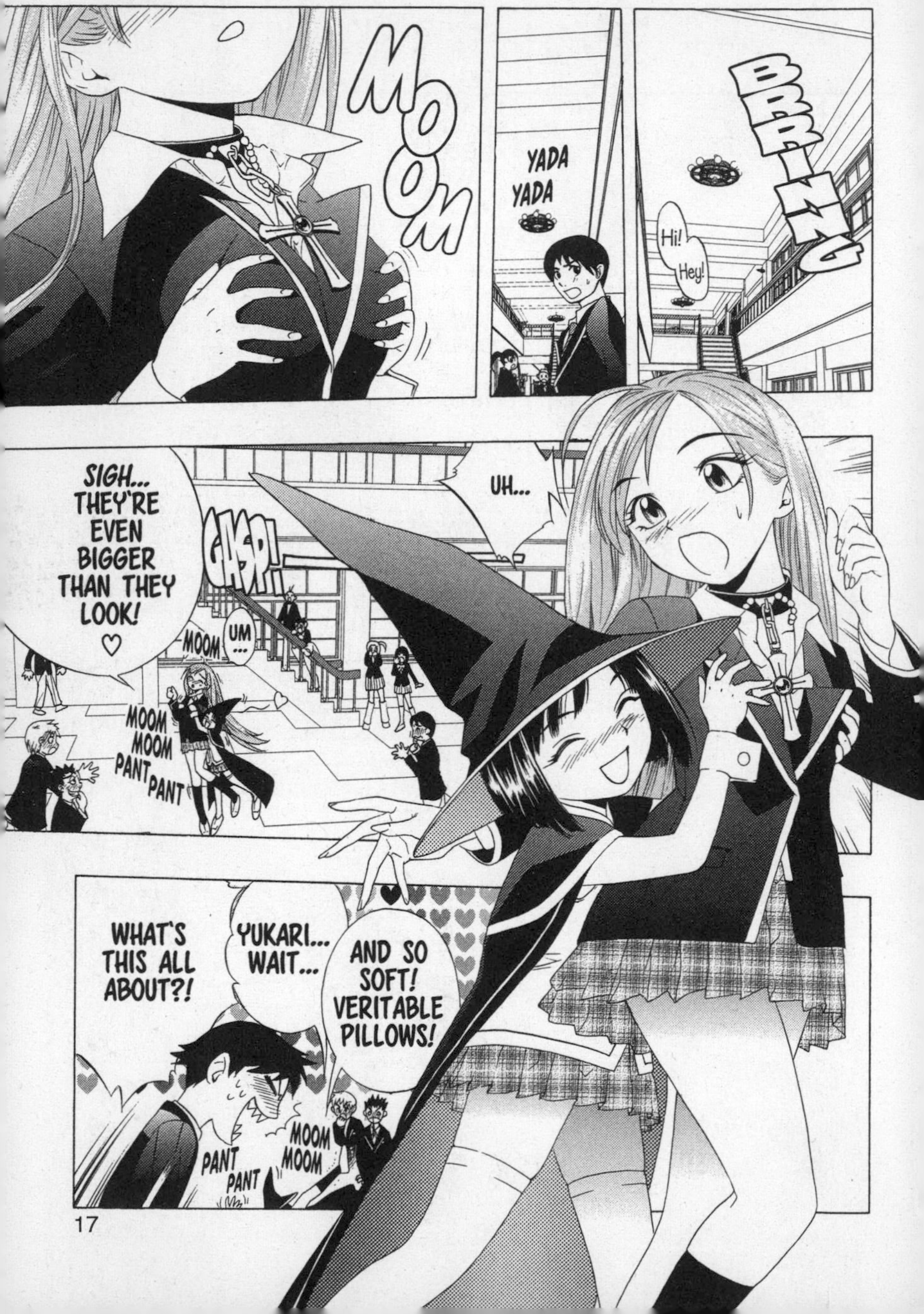
BRRING
Hi!
Hey!
YADA YADA
MOOM
UH...
SIGH... THEY'RE EVEN BIGGER THAN THEY LOOK! ♡
GASP!
UM...
MOOM
MOOM MOOM PANT PANT
AND SO SOFT! VERITABLE PILLOWS!
YUKARI... WAIT...
WHAT'S THIS ALL ABOUT?!
MOOM MOOM
PANT PANT

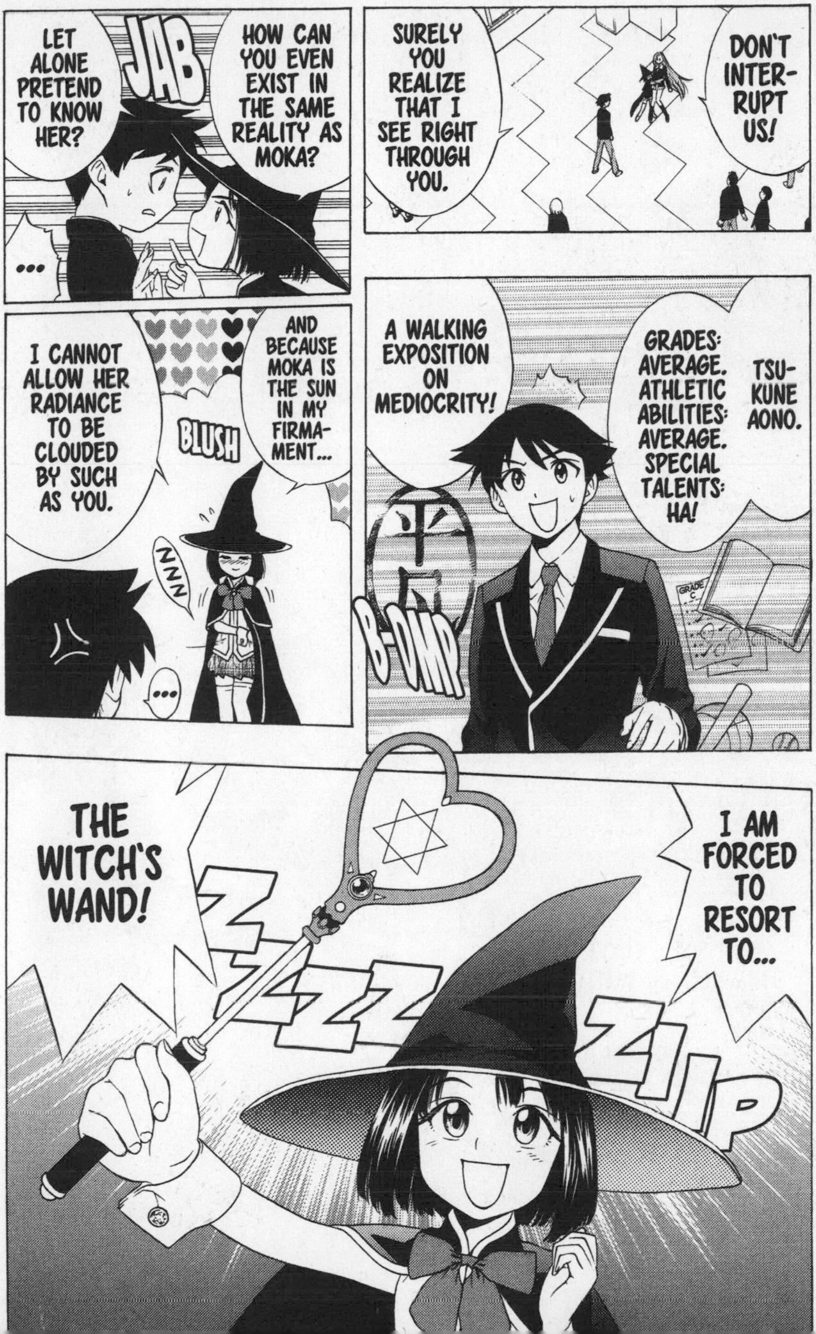
DON'T INTER-RUPT US!
SURELY YOU REALIZE THAT I SEE RIGHT THROUGH YOU.
HOW CAN YOU EVEN EXIST IN THE SAME REALITY AS MOKA?
JAB
LET ALONE PRETEND TO KNOW HER?
...
TSU-KUNE AONO.
GRADES: AVERAGE. ATHLETIC ABILITIES: AVERAGE. SPECIAL TALENTS: HA!
A WALKING EXPOSITION ON MEDIOCRITY!
平凡
B-OMP
GRADE C
AND BECAUSE MOKA IS THE SUN IN MY FIRMA-MENT...
BLUSH
I CANNOT ALLOW HER RADIANCE TO BE CLOUDED BY SUCH AS YOU.
ZZZ
...
I AM FORCED TO RESORT TO...
THE WITCH'S WAND!
ZZZZ
ZIIP

READ THIS WAY

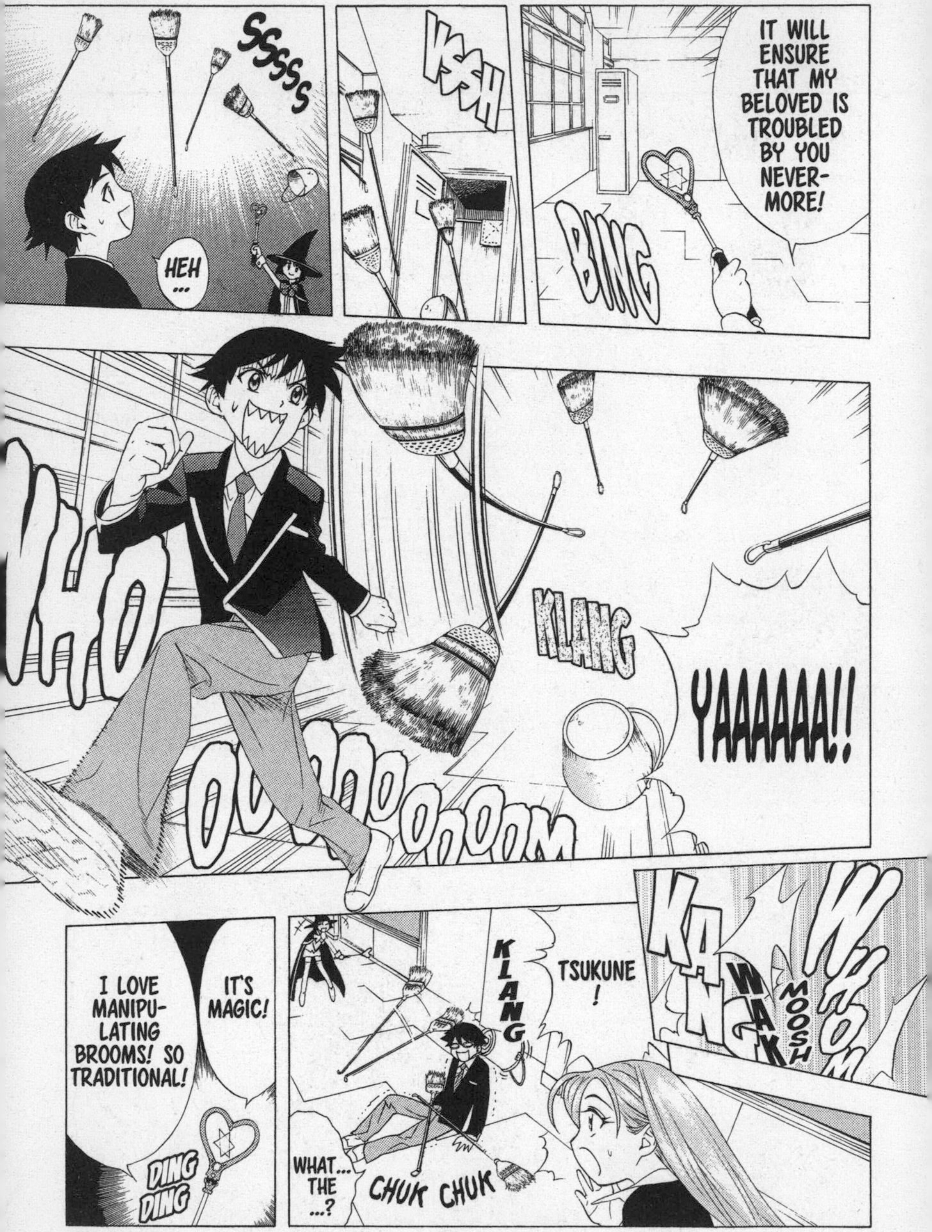

IT WILL ENSURE THAT MY BELOVED IS TROUBLED BY YOU NEVER-MORE!
BING
WSH
SSSSS
HEH ...
YAAAAA!!
KLANG
WHO
OOOOOOOOOM
KANG
WAK
MOOSH
WHOOM
TSUKUNE!
KLANG
WHAT... THE ...?
CHUK CHUK
IT'S MAGIC!
I LOVE MANIPU-LATING BROOMS! SO TRADITIONAL!
DING DING

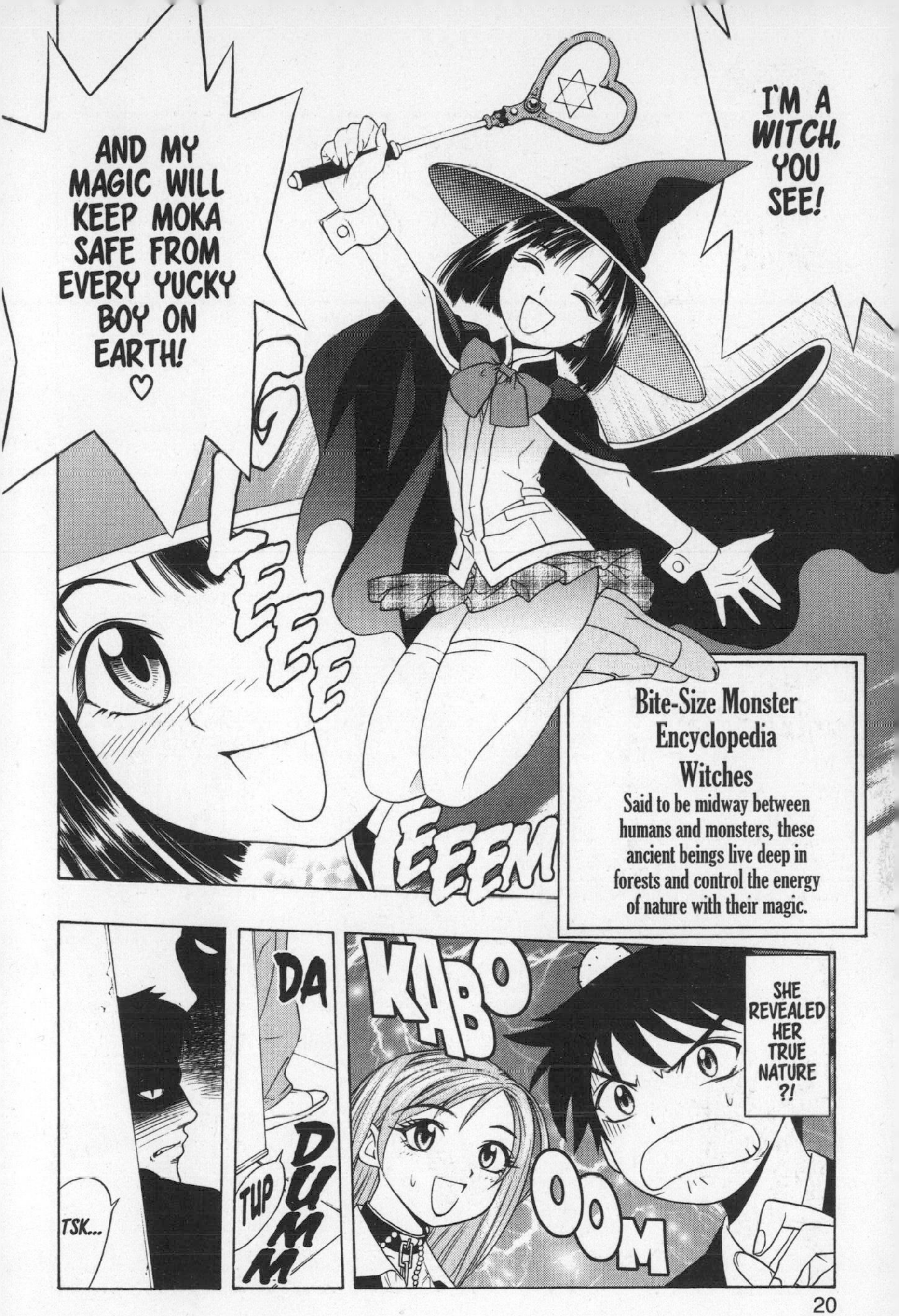
I'M A WITCH, YOU SEE!
AND MY MAGIC WILL KEEP MOKA SAFE FROM EVERY YUCKY BOY ON EARTH! ♡
GLEEEEEEEM
Bite-Size Monster Encyclopedia
Witches
Said to be midway between humans and monsters, these ancient beings live deep in forests and control the energy of nature with their magic.
SHE REVEALED HER TRUE NATURE?!
KABOOOOM
DA DUMM
TUP
TSK...

READ THIS WAY

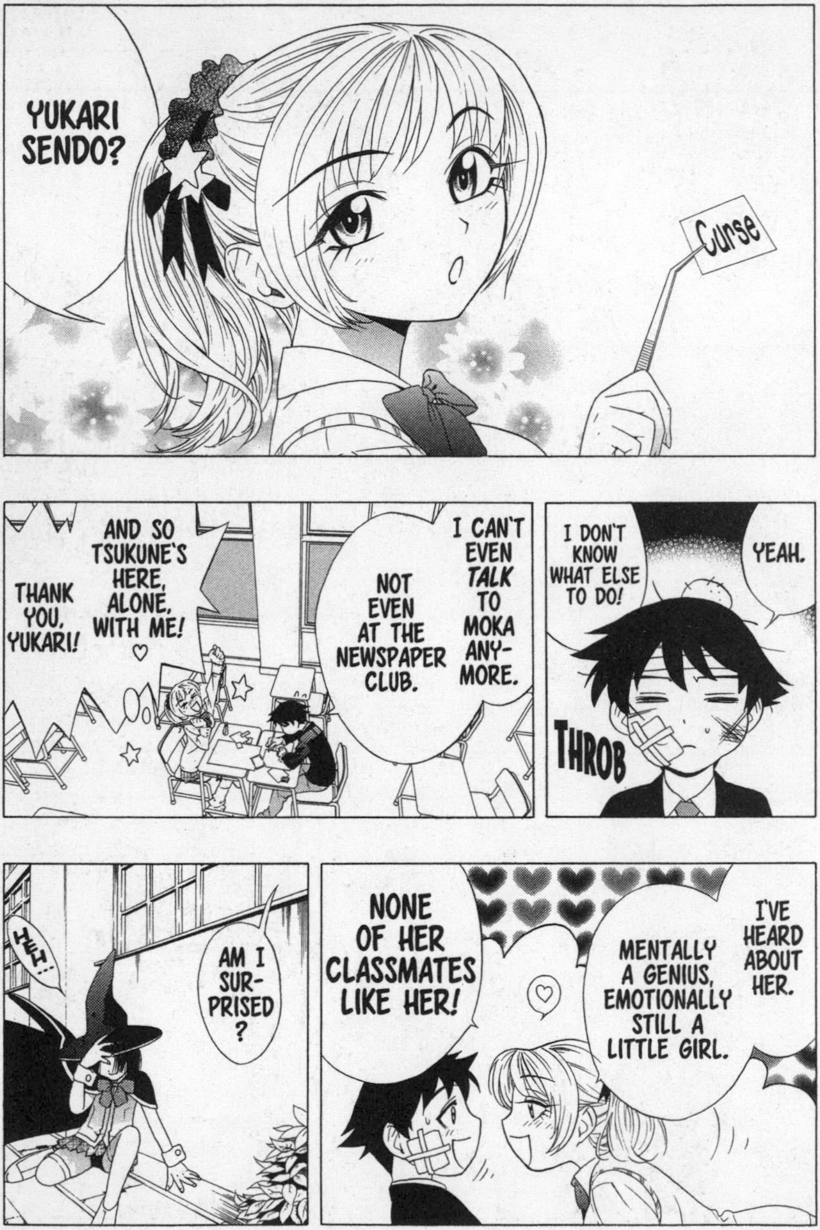
YUKARI SENDO?
Curse
YEAH.
I DON'T KNOW WHAT ELSE TO DO!
THROB
I CAN'T EVEN *TALK* TO MOKA ANYMORE.
NOT EVEN AT THE NEWSPAPER CLUB.
AND SO TSUKUNE'S HERE, ALONE, WITH ME! ♡
THANK YOU, YUKARI!
I'VE HEARD ABOUT HER.
MENTALLY A GENIUS, EMOTIONALLY STILL A LITTLE GIRL.
NONE OF HER CLASSMATES LIKE HER!
AM I SUR-PRISED?
HEH..

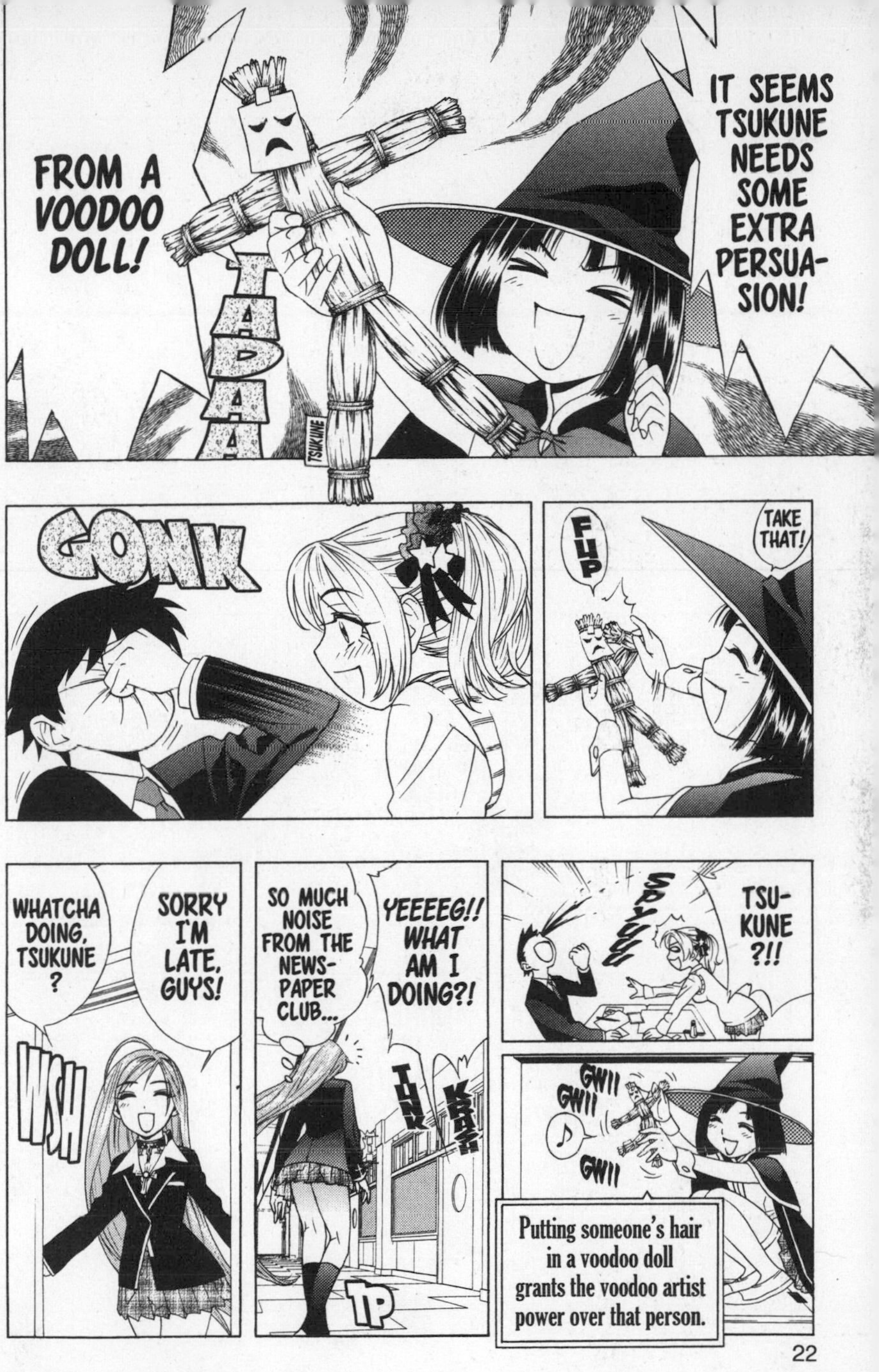
IT SEEMS TSUKUNE NEEDS SOME EXTRA PERSUA-SION!
FROM A VOODOO DOLL!
TADAAA
TSUKUNE
TAKE THAT!
FUP
GONK
TSU-KUNE?!!
SPYUUU
GWII GWII GWII
Putting someone's hair in a voodoo doll grants the voodoo artist power over that person.
YEEEEG!! WHAT AM I DOING?!
SO MUCH NOISE FROM THE NEWS-PAPER CLUB...
TUNK
KRASH
TP
SORRY I'M LATE, GUYS!
WHATCHA DOING, TSUKUNE?
WSH

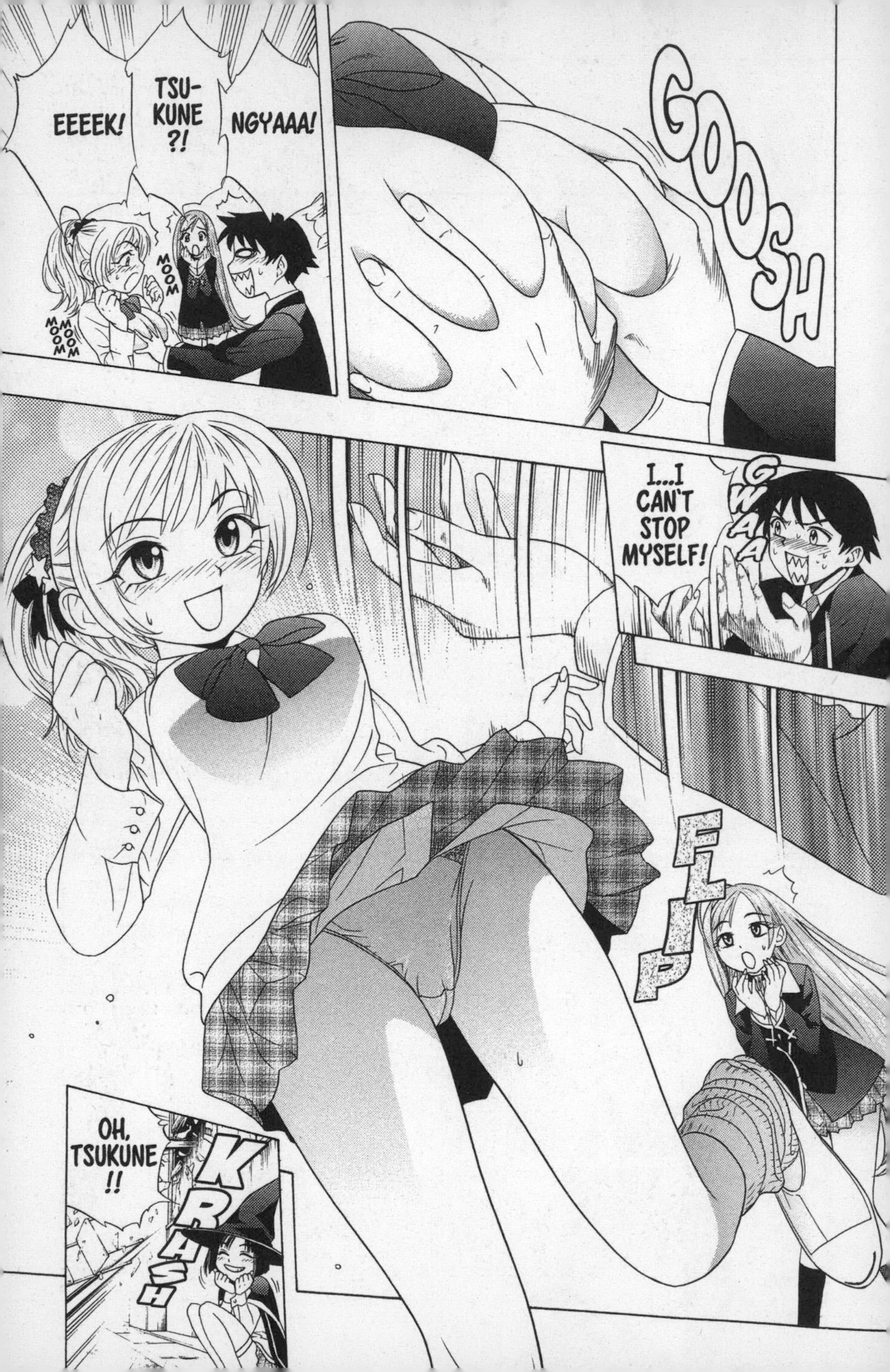
GOOSH
NGYAAA!
TSU-KUNE ?!
EEEEK!
MOOM
MOOM MOOM MOOM
GWAA
I...I CAN'T STOP MYSELF!
FLIP
OH, TSUKUNE !!
KRASH

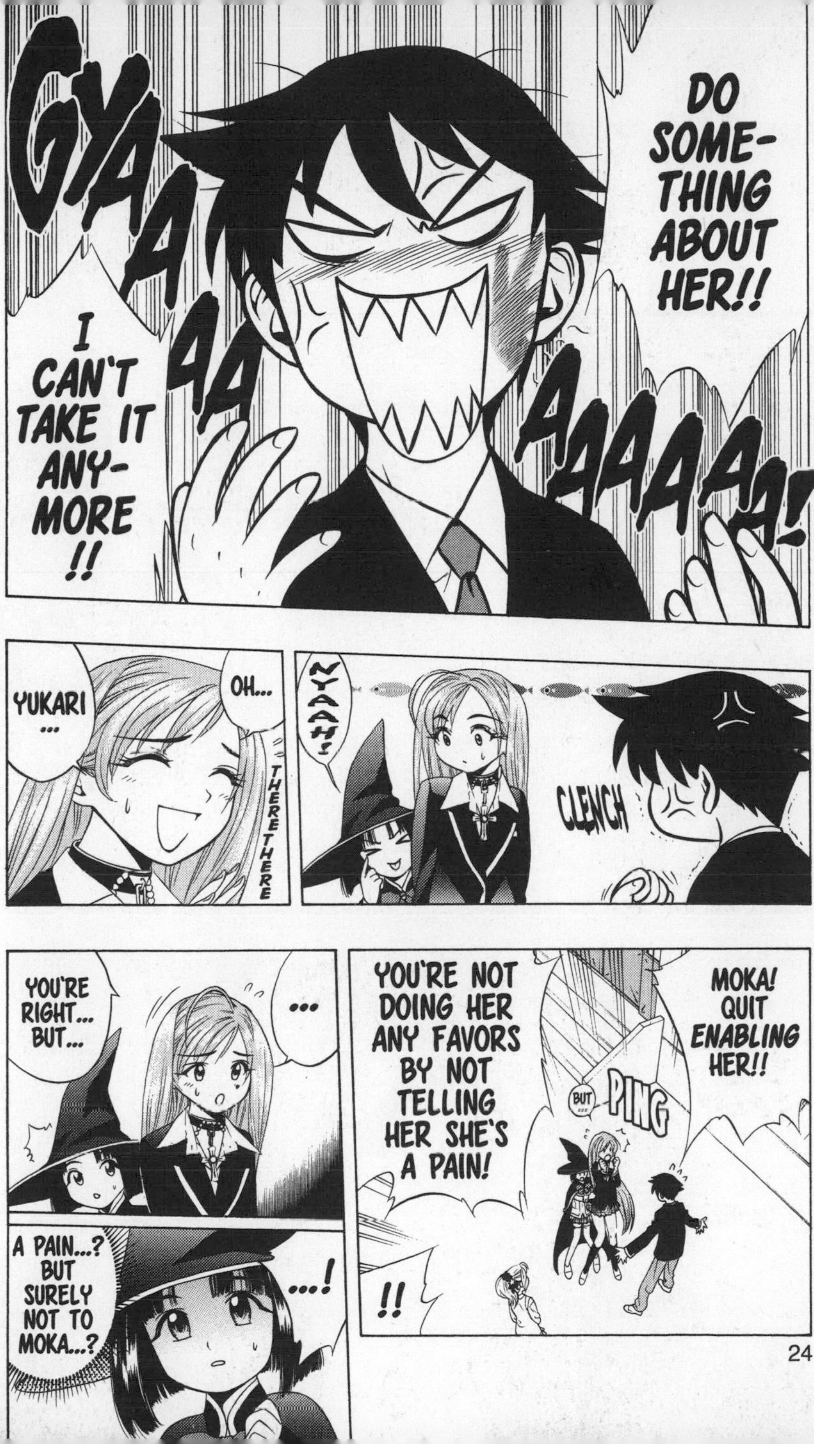
DO SOMETHING ABOUT HER!!
GYAAAAAAAAAA!
I CAN'T TAKE IT ANYMORE!!
NYAAH!
CLENCH
OH...
YUKARI...
THERE THERE
MOKA! QUIT ENABLING HER!!
YOU'RE NOT DOING HER ANY FAVORS BY NOT TELLING HER SHE'S A PAIN!
PING
BUT...
!!
...
YOU'RE RIGHT... BUT...
...!
A PAIN...? BUT SURELY NOT TO MOKA...?

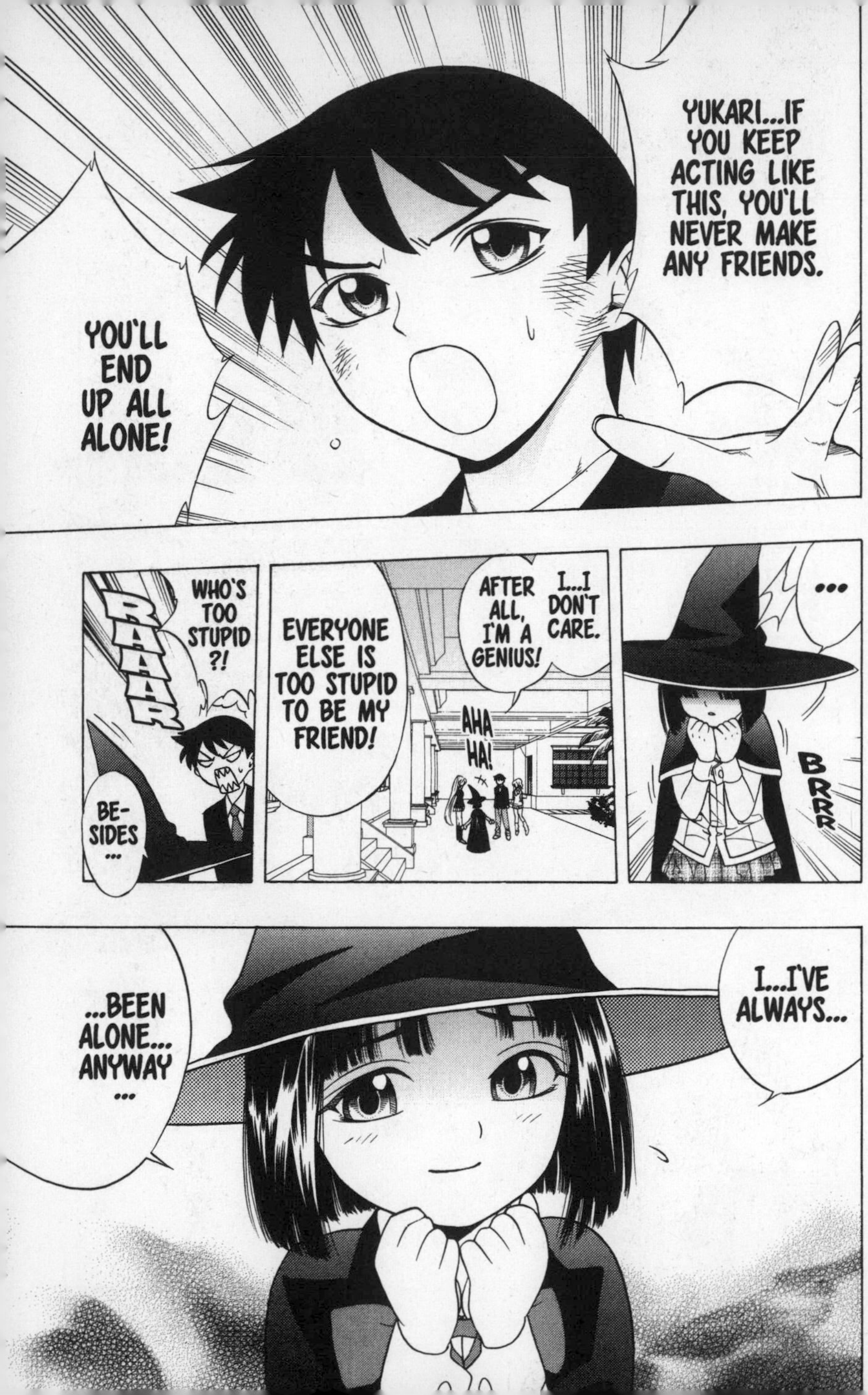
YUKARI...IF YOU KEEP ACTING LIKE THIS, YOU'LL NEVER MAKE ANY FRIENDS.
YOU'LL END UP ALL ALONE!
...
BRRR
I...I DON'T CARE.
AFTER ALL, I'M A GENIUS!
EVERYONE ELSE IS TOO STUPID TO BE MY FRIEND!
AHA HA!
WHO'S TOO STUPID ?!
RAAAAR
BE-SIDES ...
I...I'VE ALWAYS...
...BEEN ALONE... ANYWAY ...

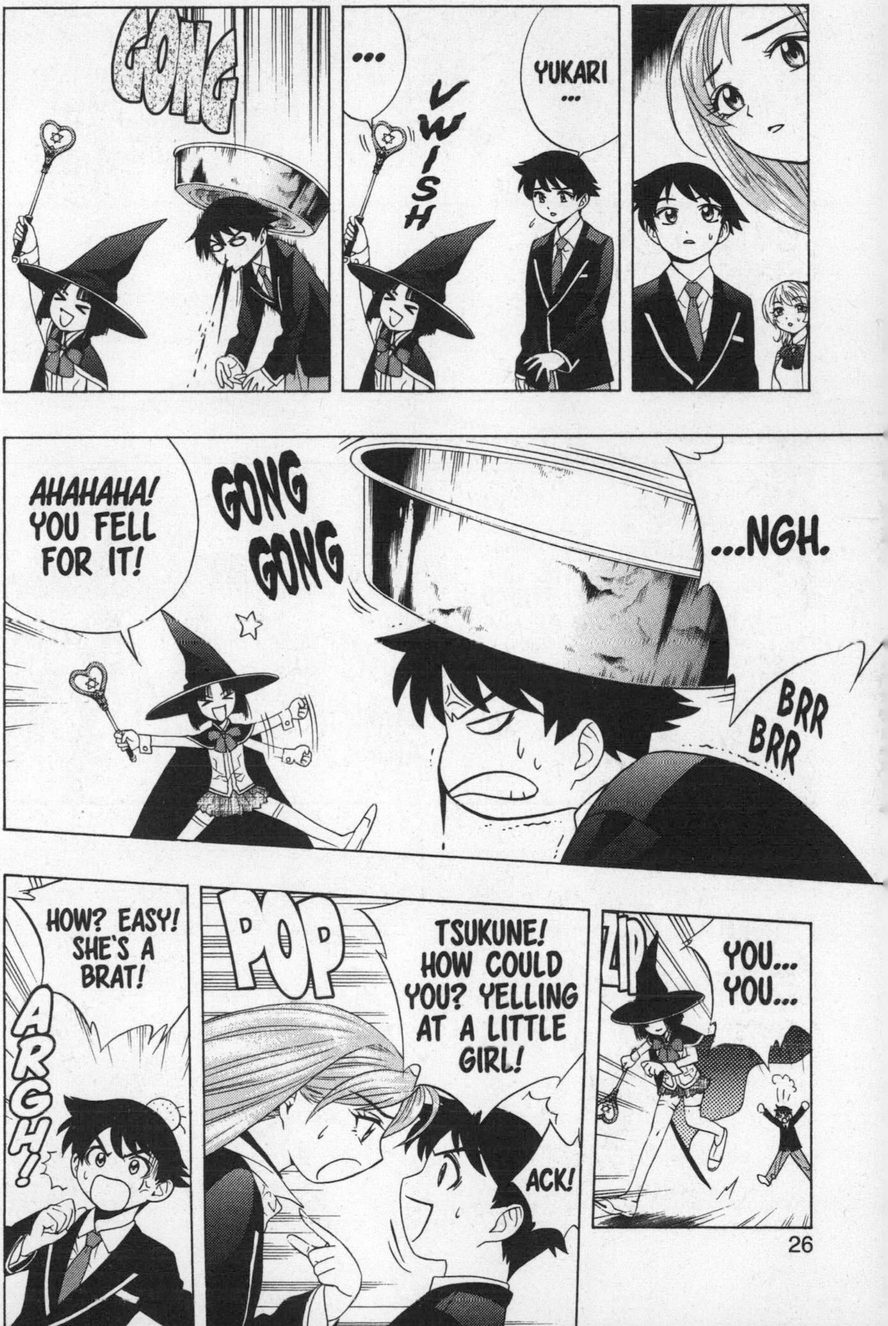

YUKARI ...
...
VWISH
GONG
...NGH.
BRR BRR
GONG GONG
AHAHAHA! YOU FELL FOR IT!
ZIP
YOU... YOU...
TSUKUNE! HOW COULD YOU? YELLING AT A LITTLE GIRL!
POP
ACK!
HOW? EASY! SHE'S A BRAT!
ARGH!

READ THIS WAY

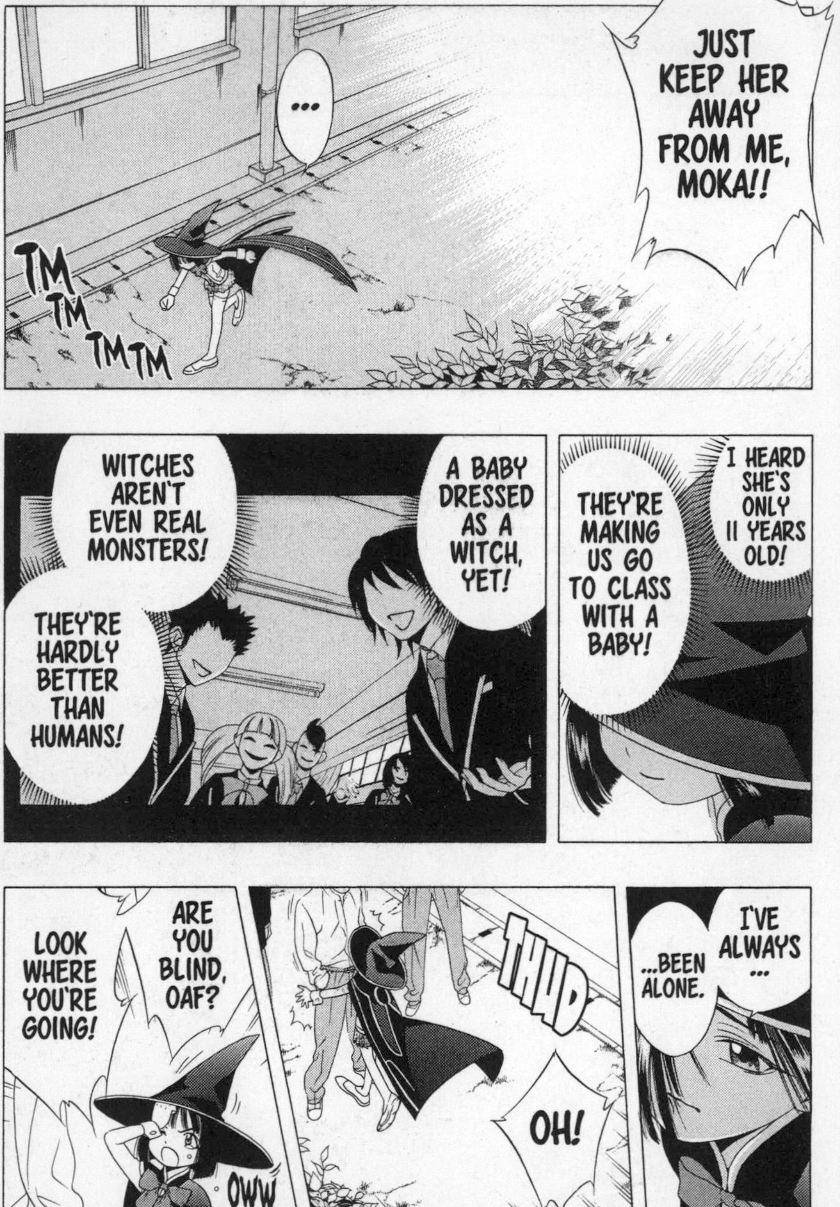

JUST KEEP HER AWAY FROM ME, MOKA!!
...
TM TM TM TM
I HEARD SHE'S ONLY 11 YEARS OLD!
THEY'RE MAKING US GO TO CLASS WITH A BABY!
A BABY DRESSED AS A WITCH, YET!
WITCHES AREN'T EVEN REAL MONSTERS!
THEY'RE HARDLY BETTER THAN HUMANS!
I'VE ALWAYS ...
...BEEN ALONE.
THUD
OH!
ARE YOU BLIND, OAF?
LOOK WHERE YOU'RE GOING!
OWW

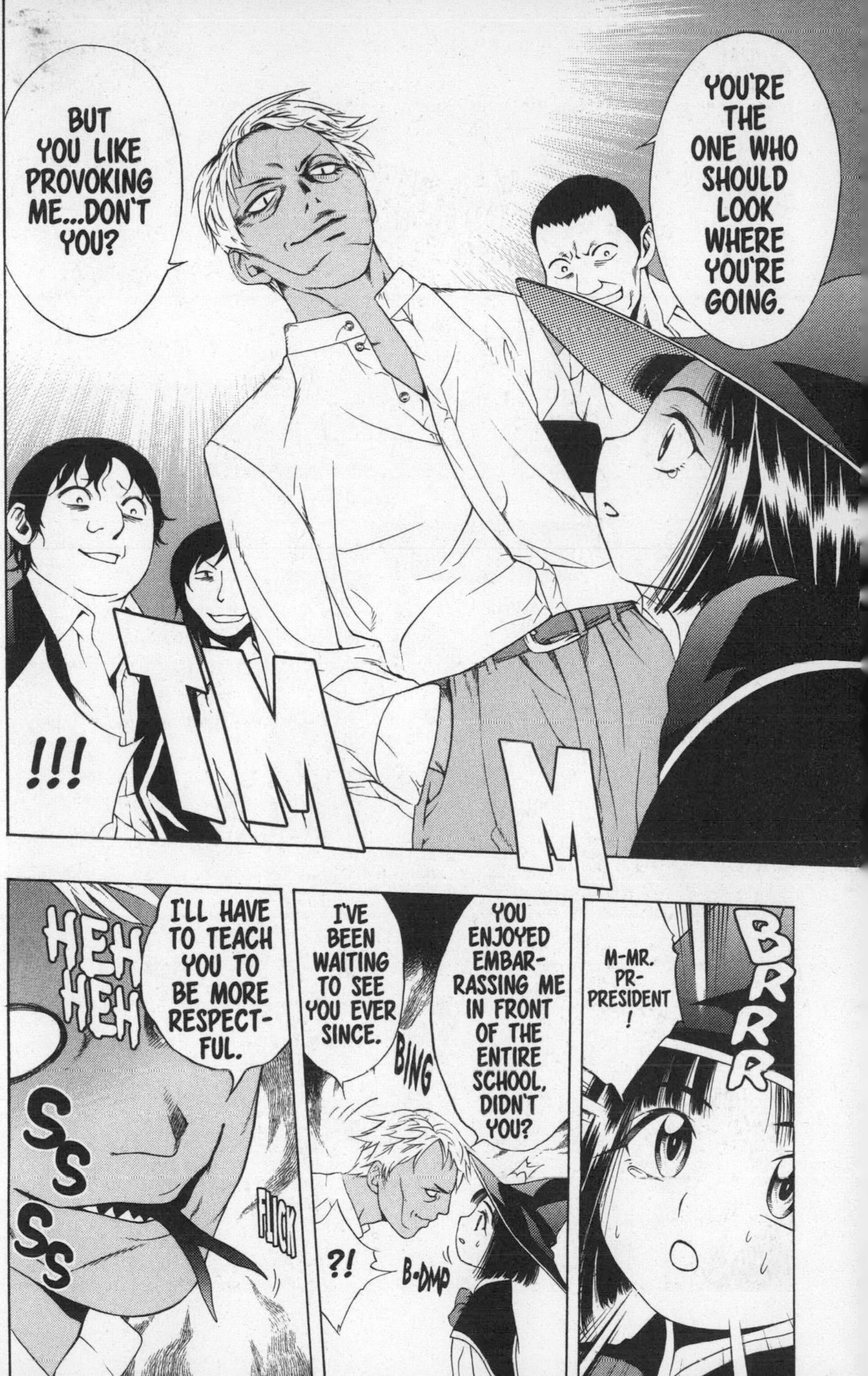
YOU'RE THE ONE WHO SHOULD LOOK WHERE YOU'RE GOING.
BUT YOU LIKE PROVOKING ME...DON'T YOU?
TIMM
!!!
BRRR
M-MR. PR-PRESIDENT!
YOU ENJOYED EMBARRASSING ME IN FRONT OF THE ENTIRE SCHOOL, DIDN'T YOU?
I'VE BEEN WAITING TO SEE YOU EVER SINCE.
BING
FLICK
B-DMP
?!
I'LL HAVE TO TEACH YOU TO BE MORE RESPECTFUL.
HEH HEH
SS SS

READ THIS WAY

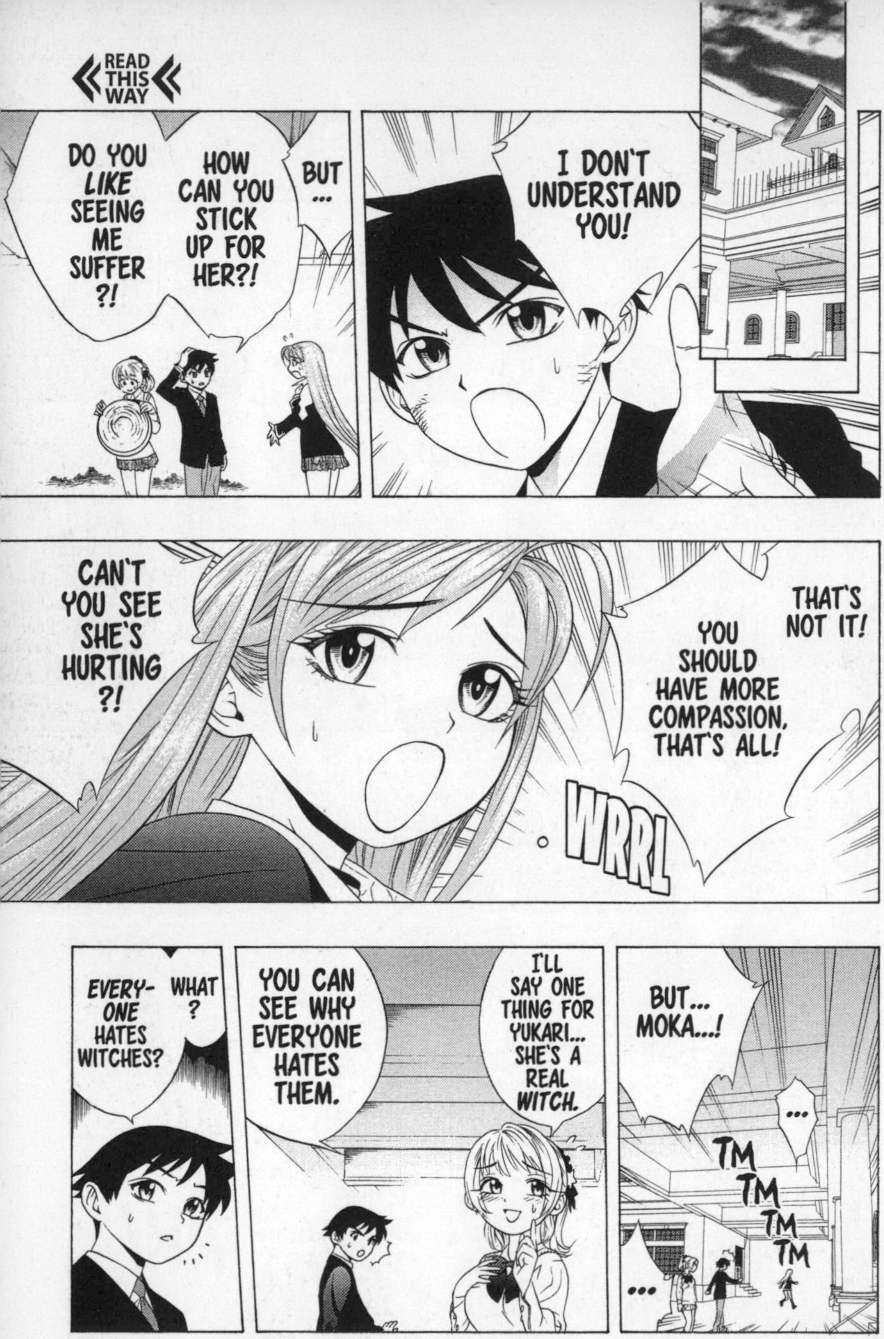
I DON'T UNDERSTAND YOU!
BUT ...
HOW CAN YOU STICK UP FOR HER?!
DO YOU LIKE SEEING ME SUFFER?!
THAT'S NOT IT!
YOU SHOULD HAVE MORE COMPASSION, THAT'S ALL!
WRRL
CAN'T YOU SEE SHE'S HURTING?!
BUT... MOKA...!
...
TM TM TM TM
...
I'LL SAY ONE THING FOR YUKARI... SHE'S A REAL WITCH.
YOU CAN SEE WHY EVERYONE HATES THEM.
WHAT?
EVERY-ONE HATES WITCHES?

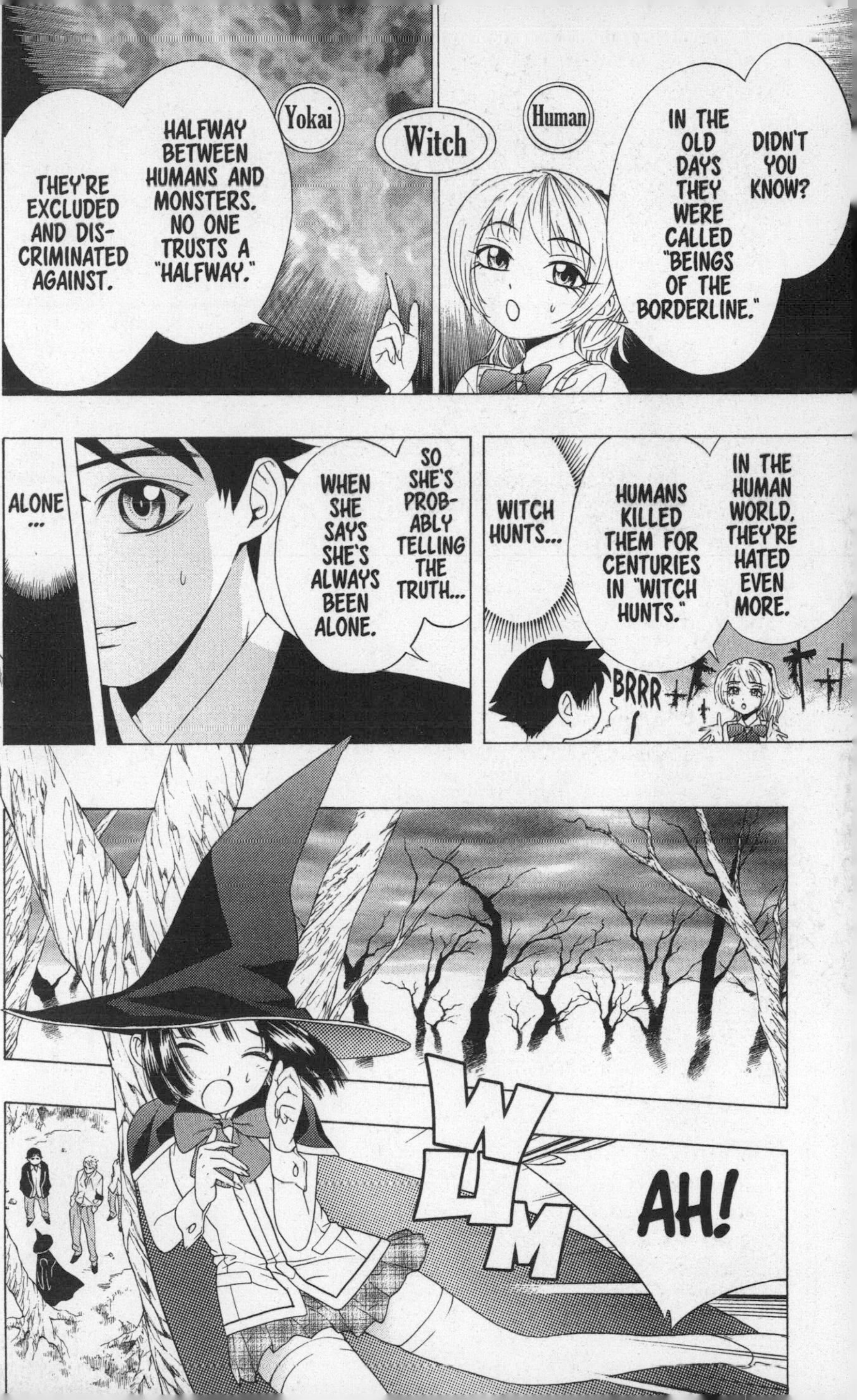
DIDN'T YOU KNOW?
IN THE OLD DAYS THEY WERE CALLED "BEINGS OF THE BORDERLINE."
Human
Witch
Yokai
HALFWAY BETWEEN HUMANS AND MONSTERS. NO ONE TRUSTS A "HALFWAY."
THEY'RE EXCLUDED AND DIS-CRIMINATED AGAINST.
IN THE HUMAN WORLD, THEY'RE HATED EVEN MORE.
HUMANS KILLED THEM FOR CENTURIES IN "WITCH HUNTS."
WITCH HUNTS...
BRRR
SO SHE'S PROBABLY TELLING THE TRUTH...
WHEN SHE SAYS SHE'S ALWAYS BEEN ALONE.
ALONE...
AH!
WUM

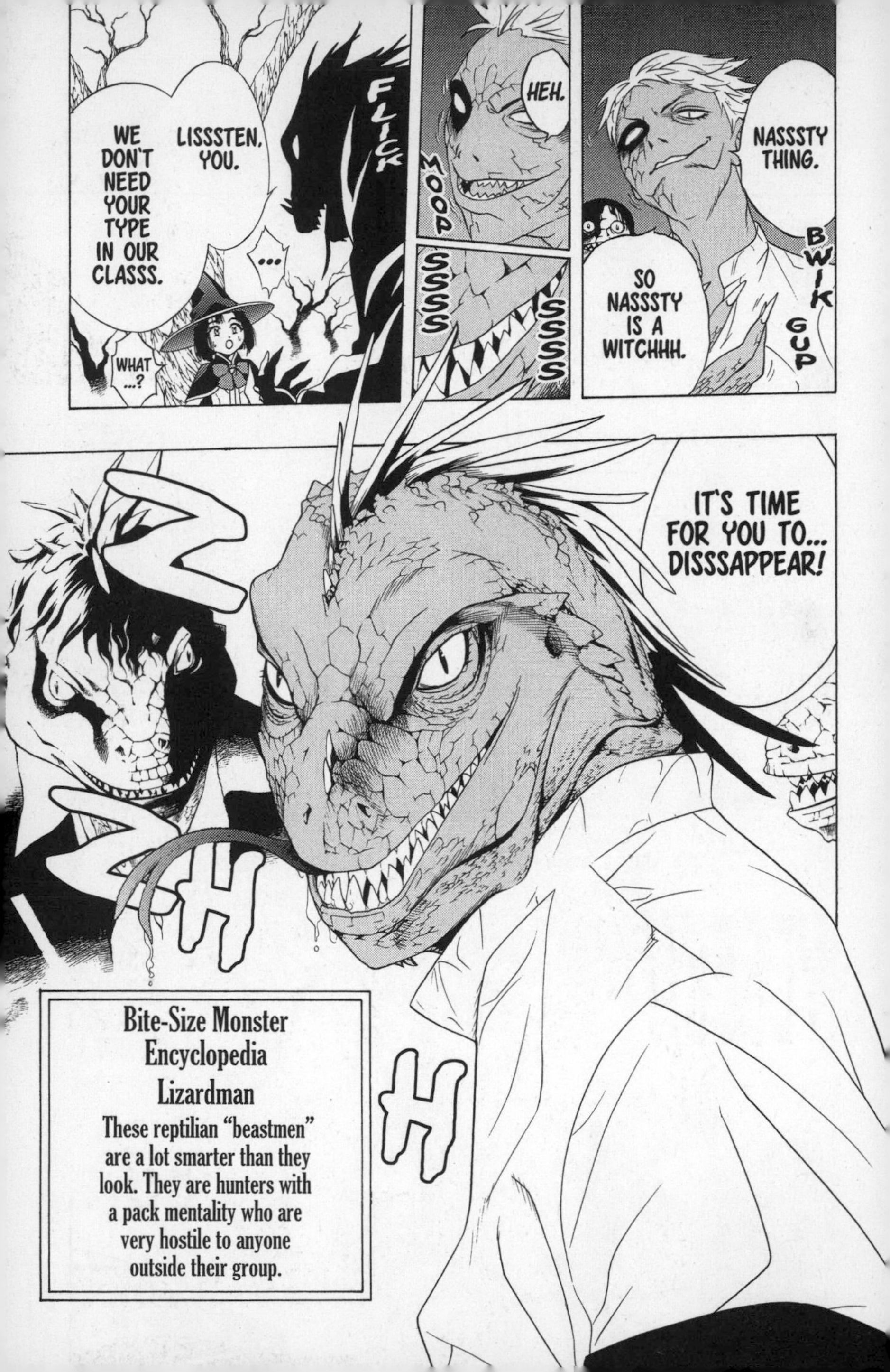
NASSSTY THING.
BWIK
GUP
SO NASSSTY IS A WITCHHH.
HEH.
MOOP
SSSS
SSSS
FLICK
LISSSTEN, YOU.
WE DON'T NEED YOUR TYPE IN OUR CLASSS.
...
WHAT ...?
IT'S TIME FOR YOU TO... DISSSAPPEAR!
Bite-Size Monster Encyclopedia
Lizardman
These reptilian "beastmen" are a lot smarter than they look. They are hunters with a pack mentality who are very hostile to anyone outside their group.

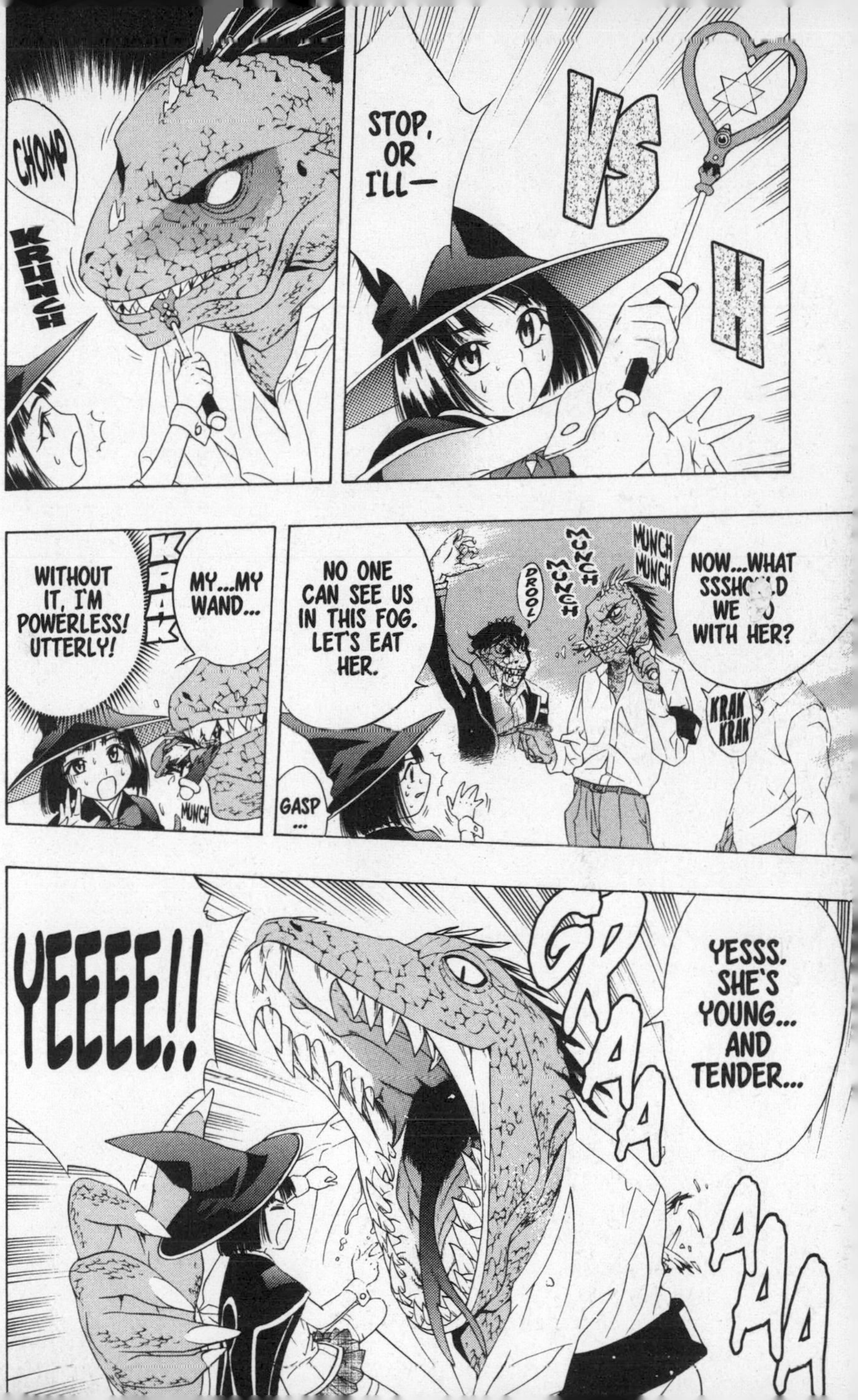
STOP, OR I'LL—
VS
H
CHOMP
KRUNCH
NOW...WHAT SSSHOULD WE DO WITH HER?
MUNCH MUNCH
KRAK KRAK
MUNCH MUNCH
DROOL
NO ONE CAN SEE US IN THIS FOG. LET'S EAT HER.
GASP...
MY...MY WAND...
KRAK
WITHOUT IT, I'M POWERLESS! UTTERLY!
MUNCH
YESSS. SHE'S YOUNG... AND TENDER...
GRAAA
AAAA
YEEEE!!

READ THIS WAY

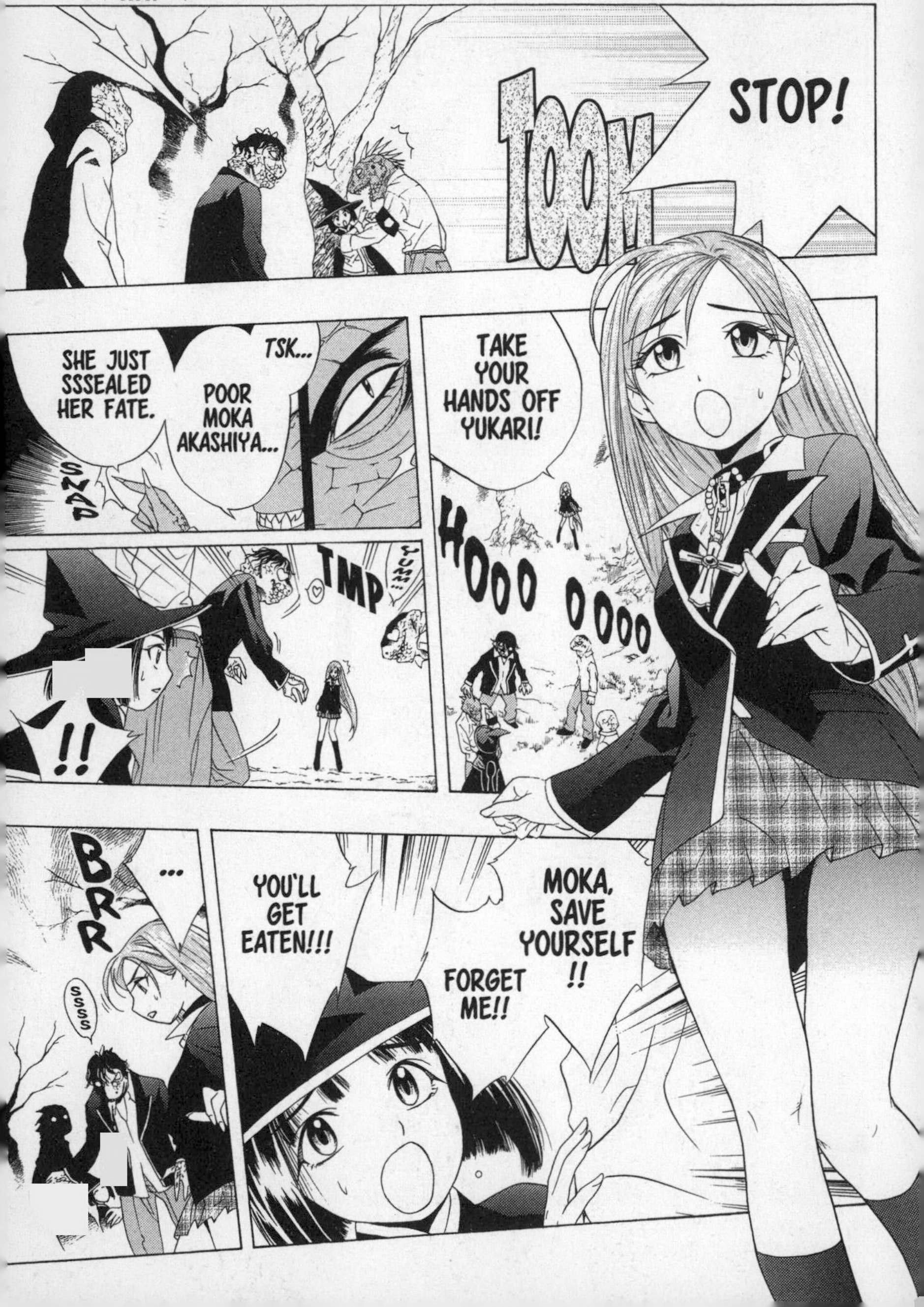
STOP!
TOOM
TAKE YOUR HANDS OFF YUKARI!
HOOO OOOO
TSK...
POOR MOKA AKASHIYA...
SHE JUST SSSEALED HER FATE.
SNAP
YUMM...
TMP
!!
MOKA, SAVE YOURSELF!!
FORGET ME!!
YOU'LL GET EATEN!!!
...
BRR
SSSS

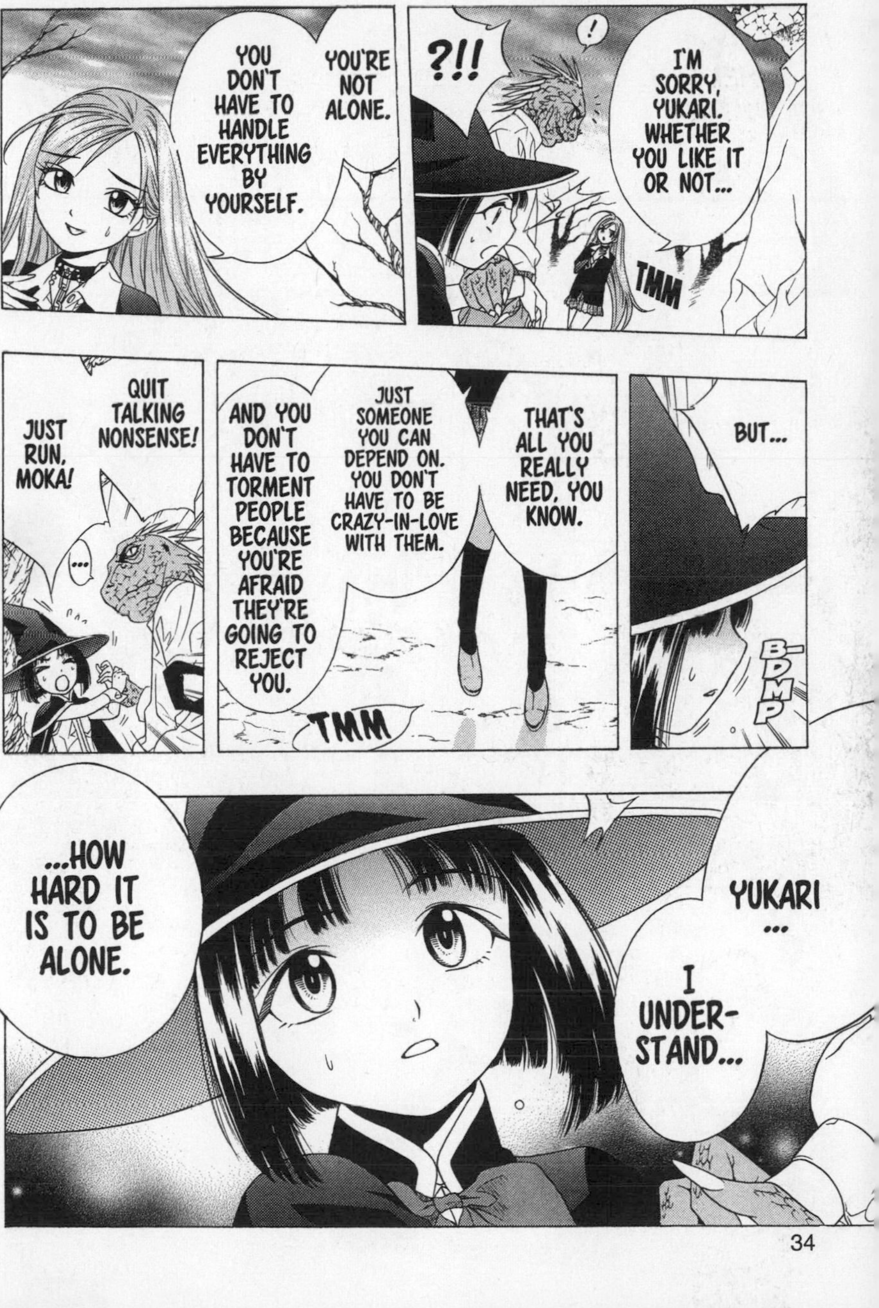

!
?!!
I'M SORRY, YUKARI. WHETHER YOU LIKE IT OR NOT...
TMM
YOU'RE NOT ALONE.
YOU DON'T HAVE TO HANDLE EVERYTHING BY YOURSELF.
BUT...
B-BDMP
THAT'S ALL YOU REALLY NEED, YOU KNOW.
JUST SOMEONE YOU CAN DEPEND ON. YOU DON'T HAVE TO BE CRAZY-IN-LOVE WITH THEM.
AND YOU DON'T HAVE TO TORMENT PEOPLE BECAUSE YOU'RE AFRAID THEY'RE GOING TO REJECT YOU.
TMM
QUIT TALKING NONSENSE!
JUST RUN, MOKA!
...
YUKARI...
I UNDERSTAND...
...HOW HARD IT IS TO BE ALONE.

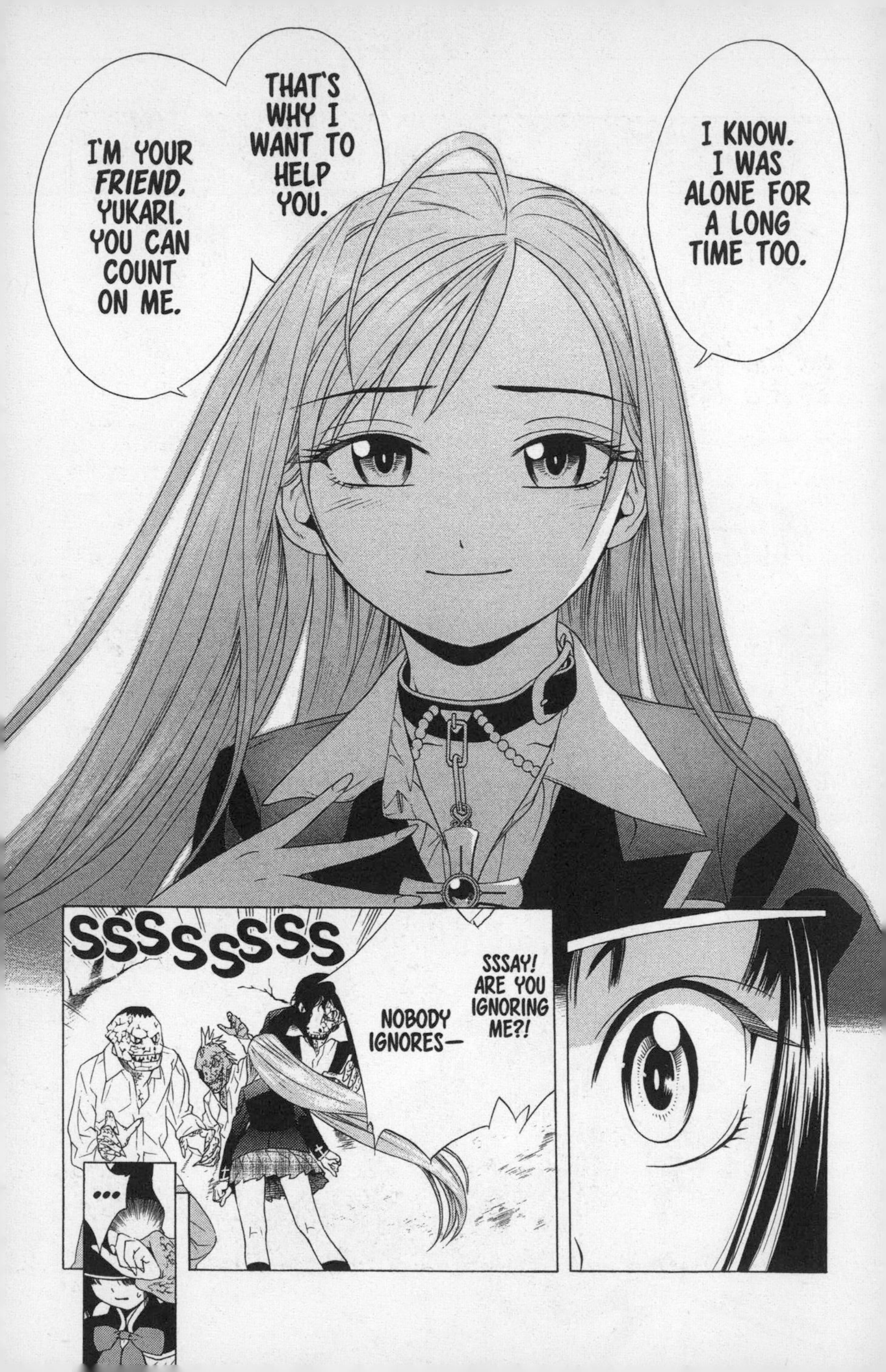
I KNOW. I WAS ALONE FOR A LONG TIME TOO.
THAT'S WHY I WANT TO HELP YOU.
I'M YOUR FRIEND, YUKARI. YOU CAN COUNT ON ME.
SSSAY! ARE YOU IGNORING ME?!
SSSSSSSS
NOBODY IGNORES—
...

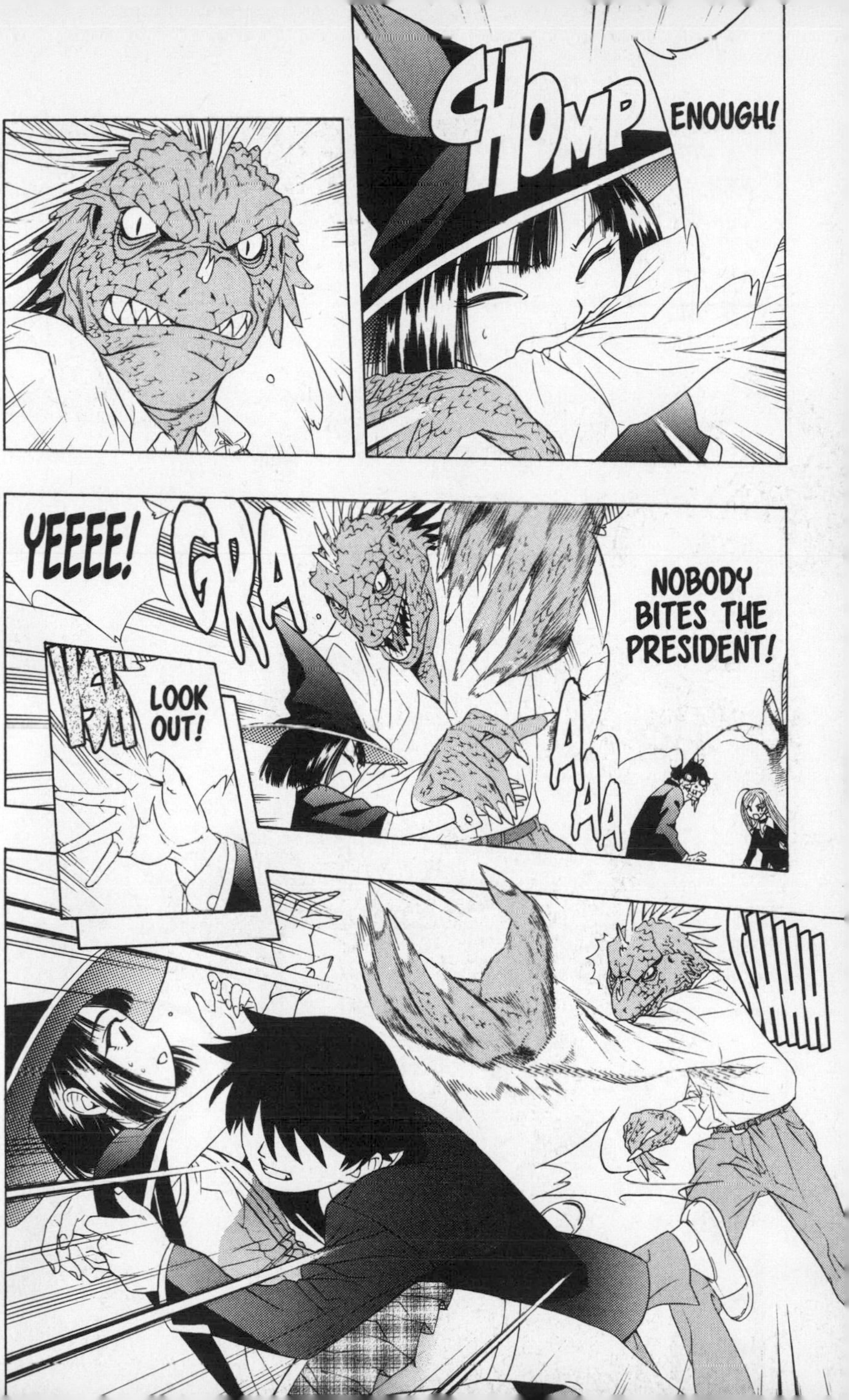
CHOMP
ENOUGH!
NOBODY BITES THE PRESIDENT!
GRA
YEEEE!
AAA
LOOK OUT!

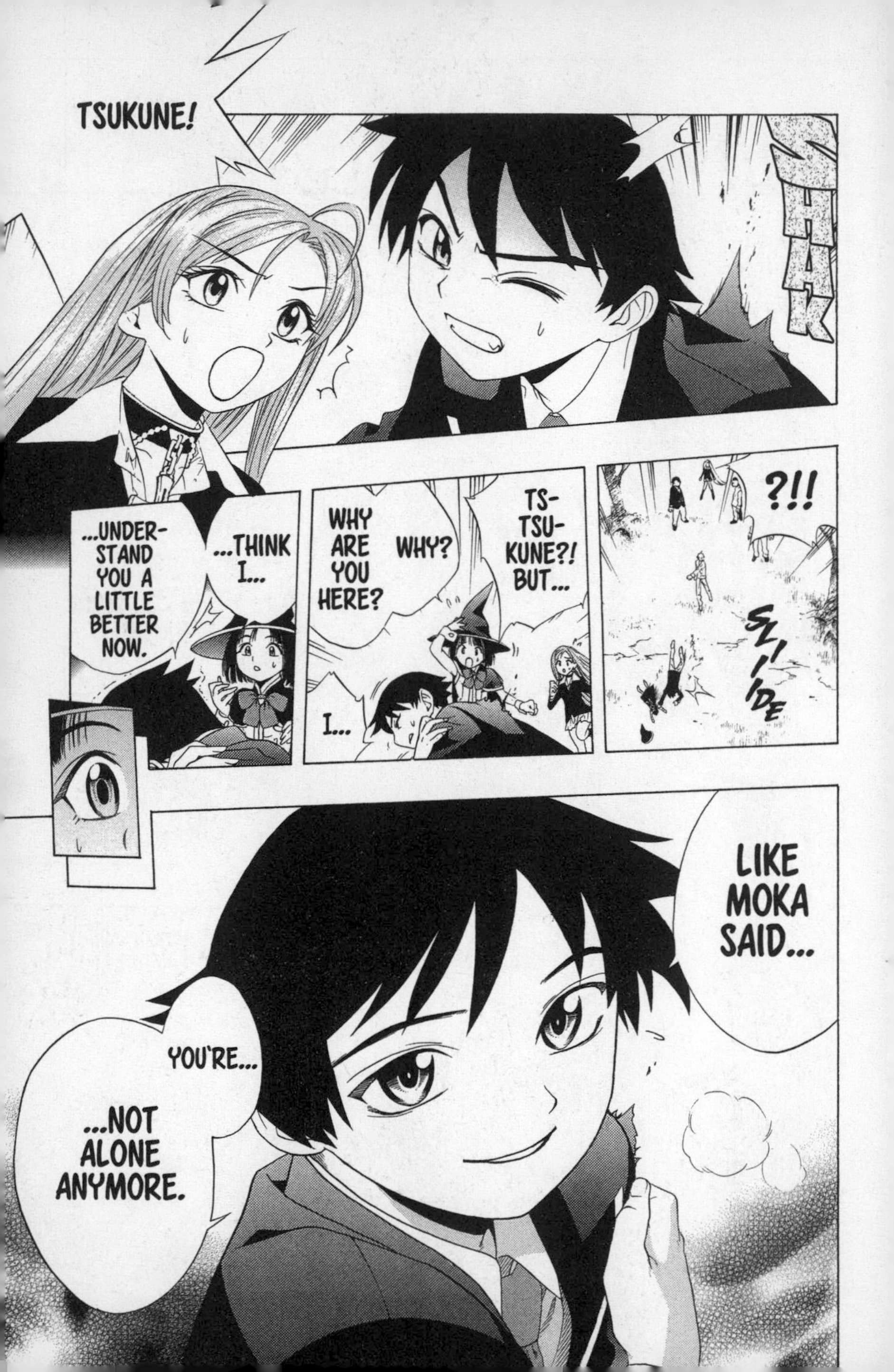
SHAK
TSUKUNE!
?!!
SLIIDE
TS-TSUKUNE?! BUT...
WHY?
WHY ARE YOU HERE?
I...
...THINK I...
...UNDERSTAND YOU A LITTLE BETTER NOW.
LIKE MOKA SAID...
YOU'RE...
...NOT ALONE ANYMORE.

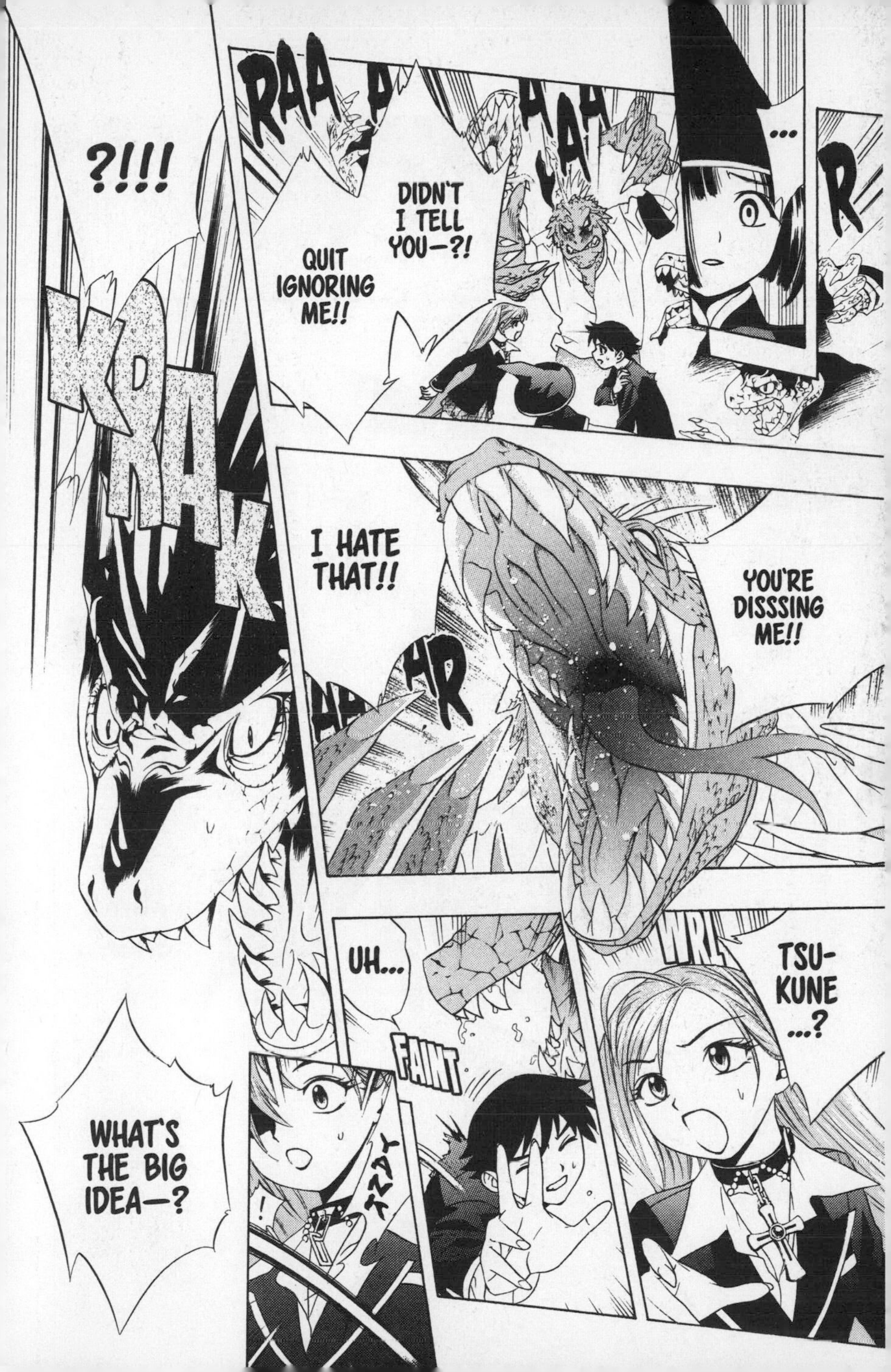
...
R
AAA
RAA
DIDN'T I TELL YOU-?!
QUIT IGNORING ME!!
YOU'RE DISSSING ME!!
I HATE THAT!!
HR
TSU-KUNE ...?
WRL
UH...
FAINT
YANK
!
?!!!
KRAK
WHAT'S THE BIG IDEA-?

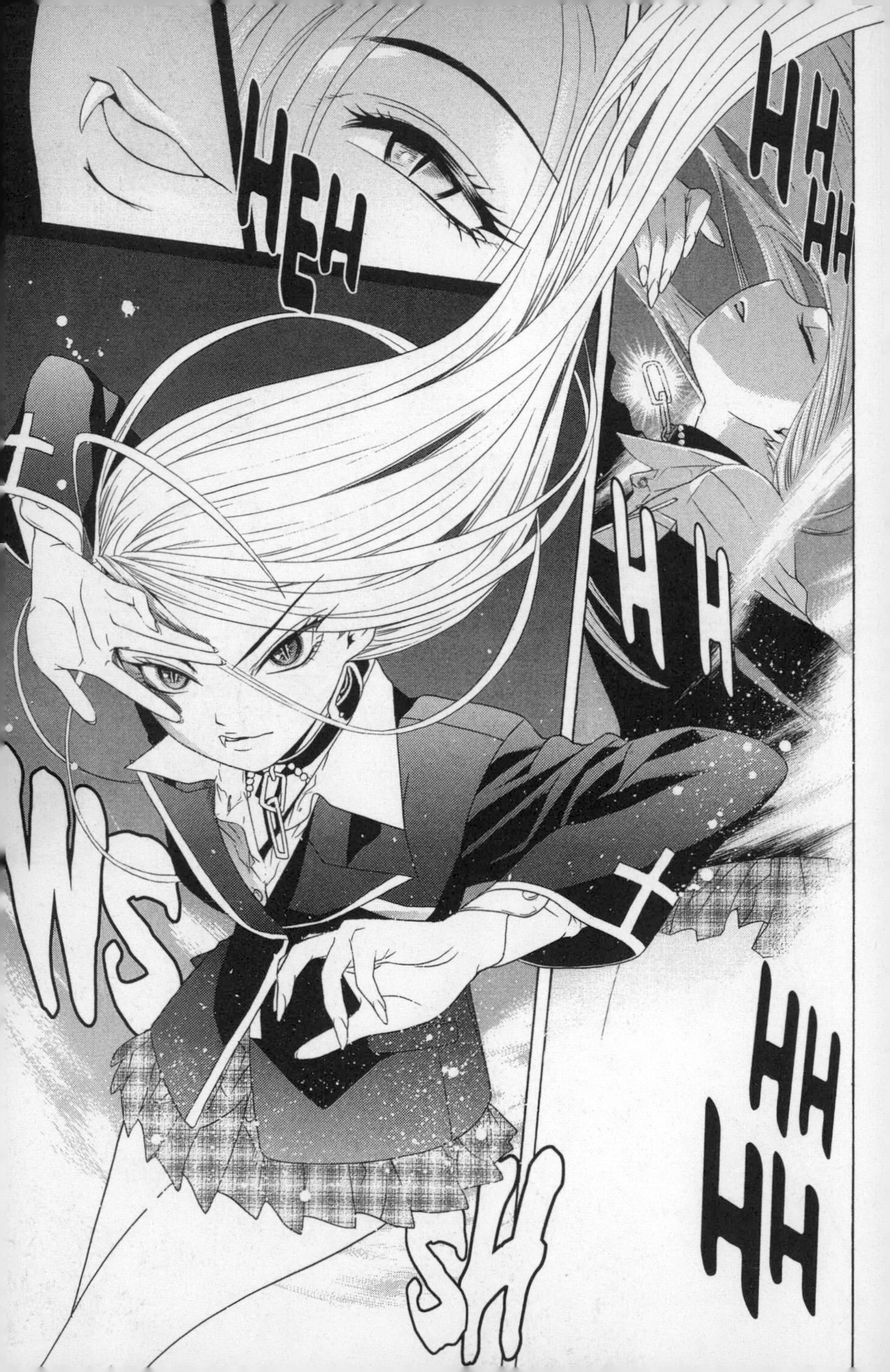
HEH HEH

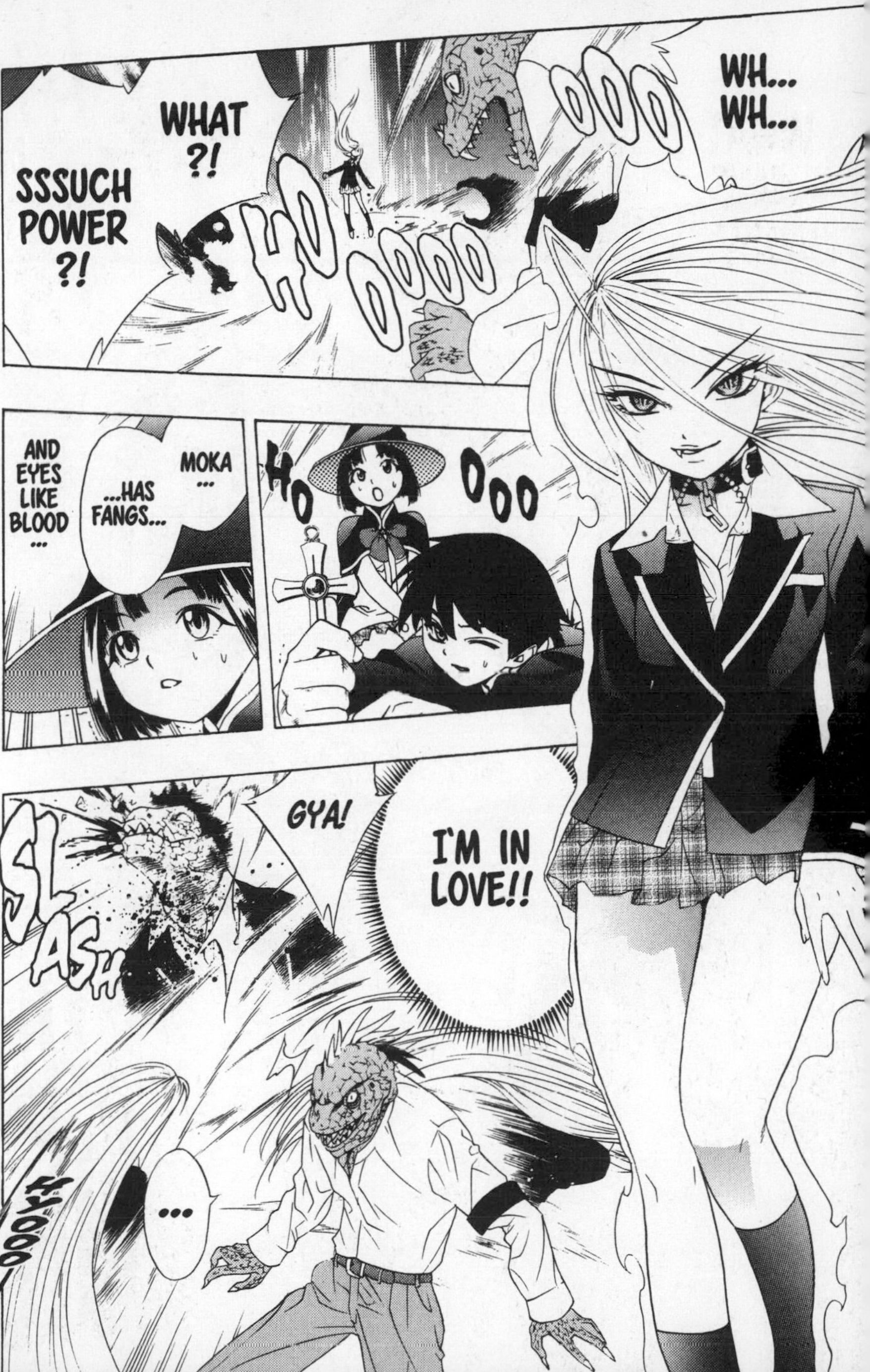
WH... WH...
HOOOOO OOO
WHAT ?!
SSSUCH POWER ?!
HO OOO
MOKA ...
...HAS FANGS...
AND EYES LIKE BLOOD ...
I'M IN LOVE!!
GYA!
SLASH
...
HYOOOO

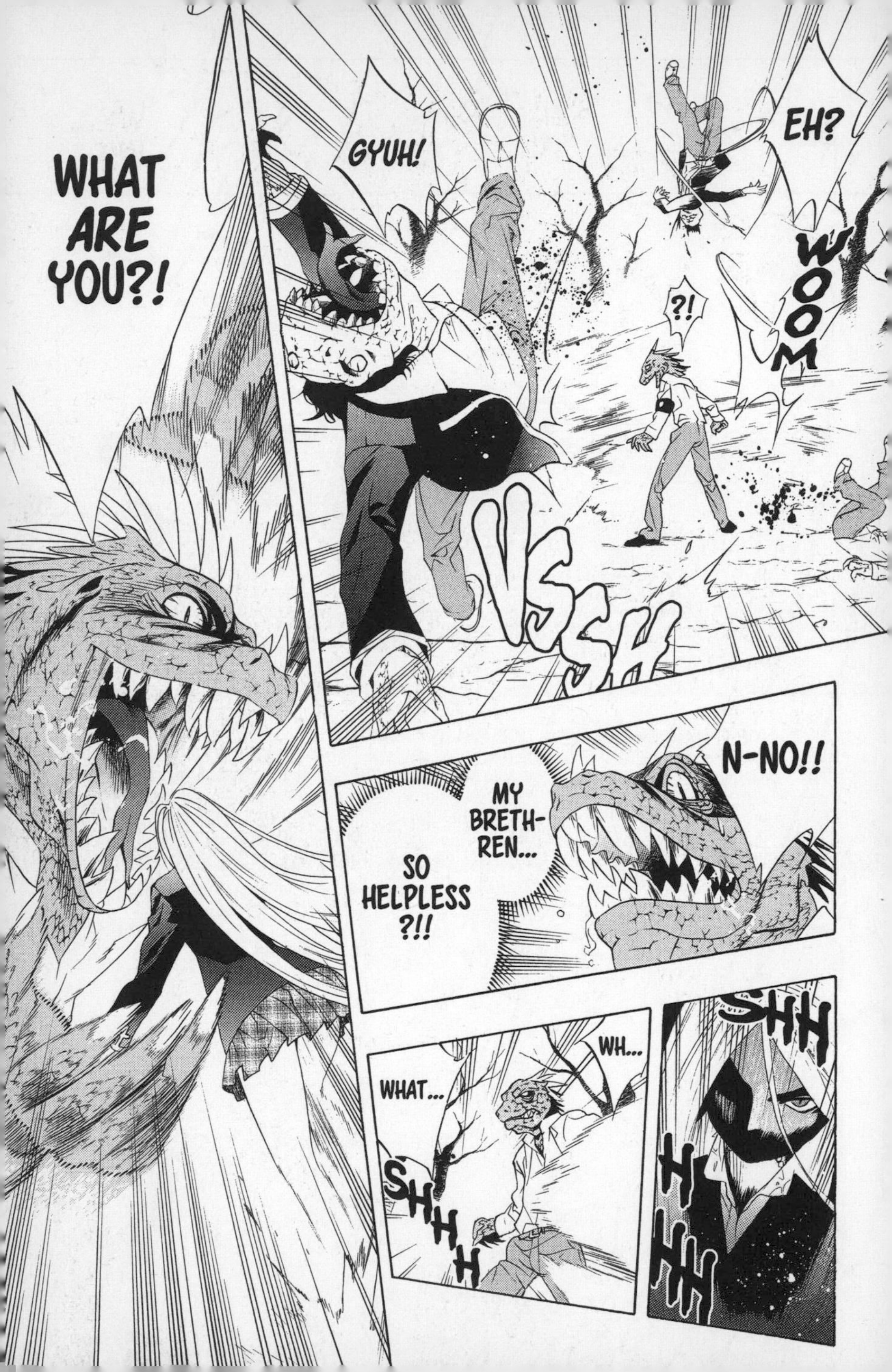
EH?
WOOM
GYUH!
?!
VSSH
N-NO!!
MY BRETH-REN...
SO HELPLESS?!!
SHHHHHHH
WH...
WHAT...
SHHHH
WHAT ARE YOU?!

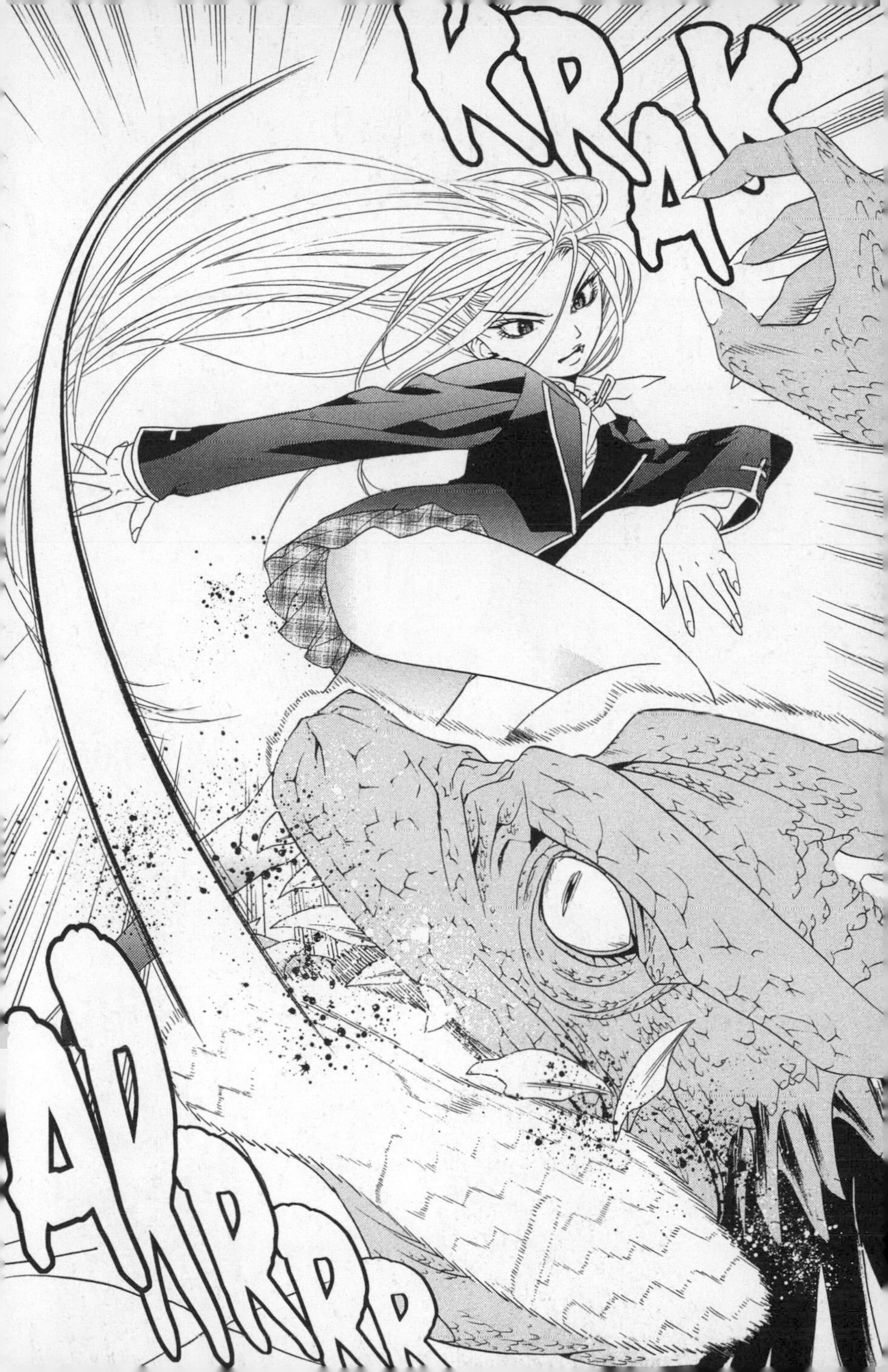
KRAK
AHRRRR

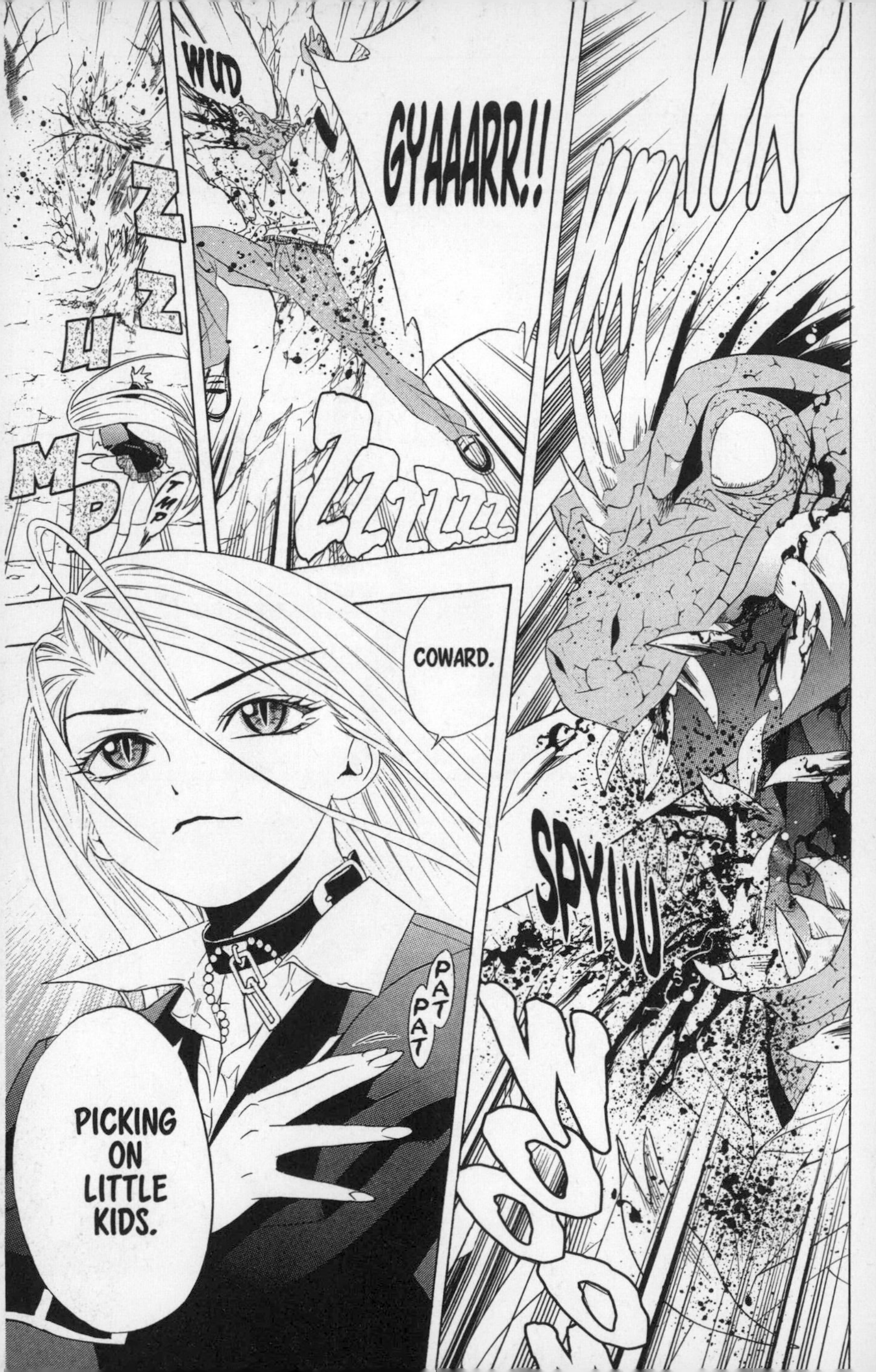

SPYUU
WUD
GYAARR!!
TMP
COWARD.
PAT PAT
PICKING ON LITTLE KIDS.

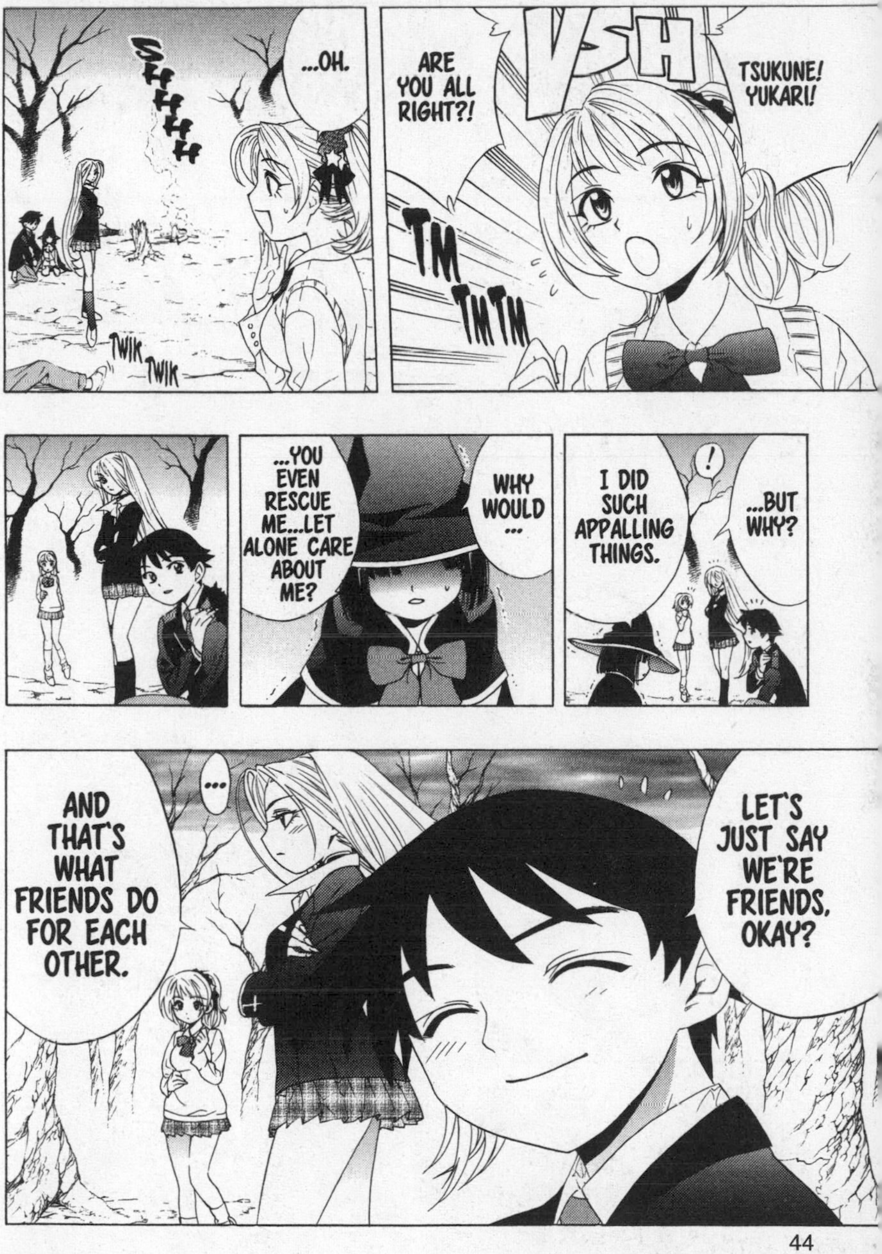
VSH
TSUKUNE! YUKARI!
ARE YOU ALL RIGHT?!
TM TMTM
...OH.
SHHHHH
TWIK TWIK
...BUT WHY?
!
I DID SUCH APPALLING THINGS.
WHY WOULD ...
...YOU EVEN RESCUE ME...LET ALONE CARE ABOUT ME?
LET'S JUST SAY WE'RE FRIENDS, OKAY?
...
AND THAT'S WHAT FRIENDS DO FOR EACH OTHER.

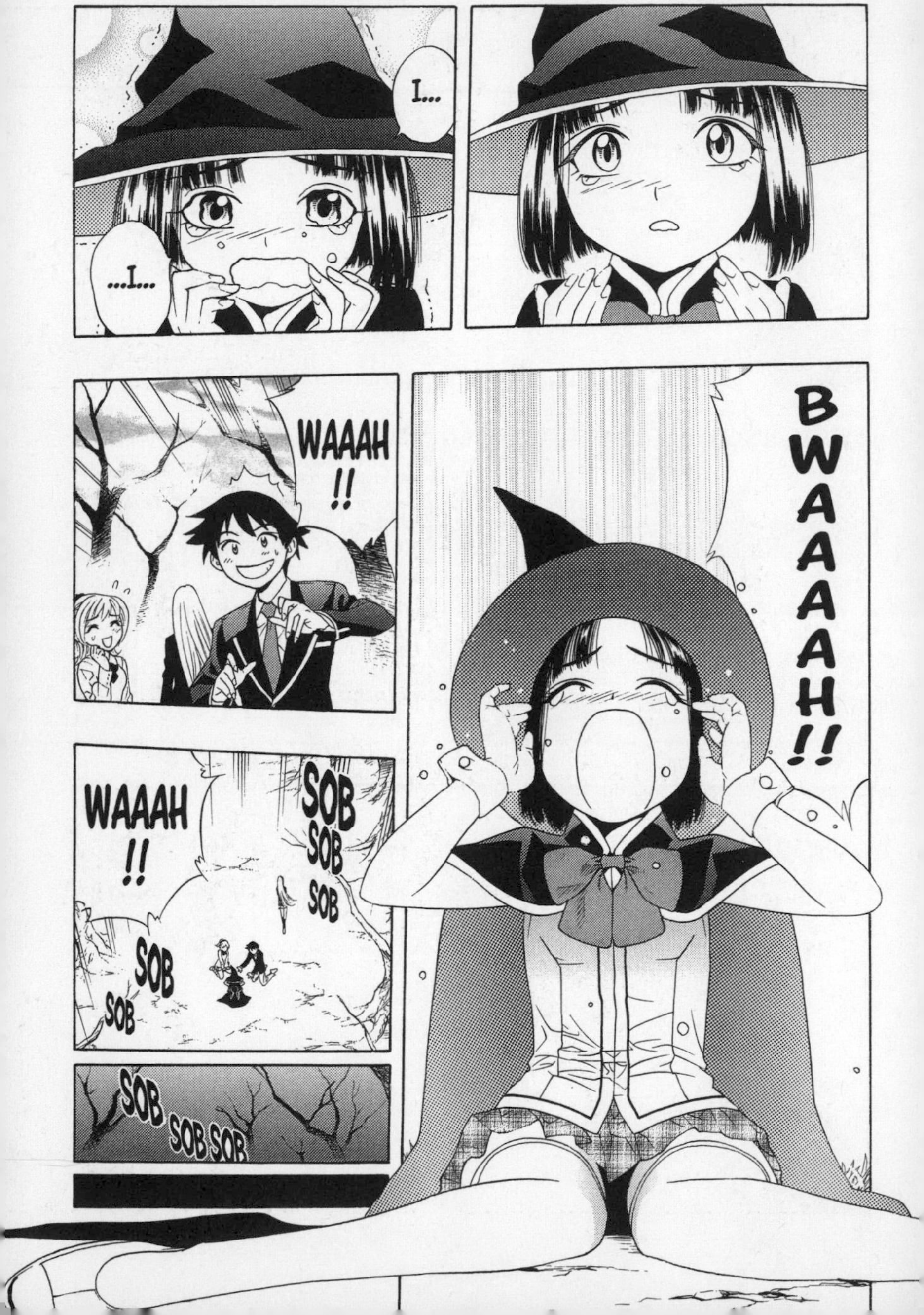
I...
...I...
BWAAAAH!!
WAAAH!!
WAAAH!!
SOB SOB SOB
SOB SOB
SOB SOB SOB

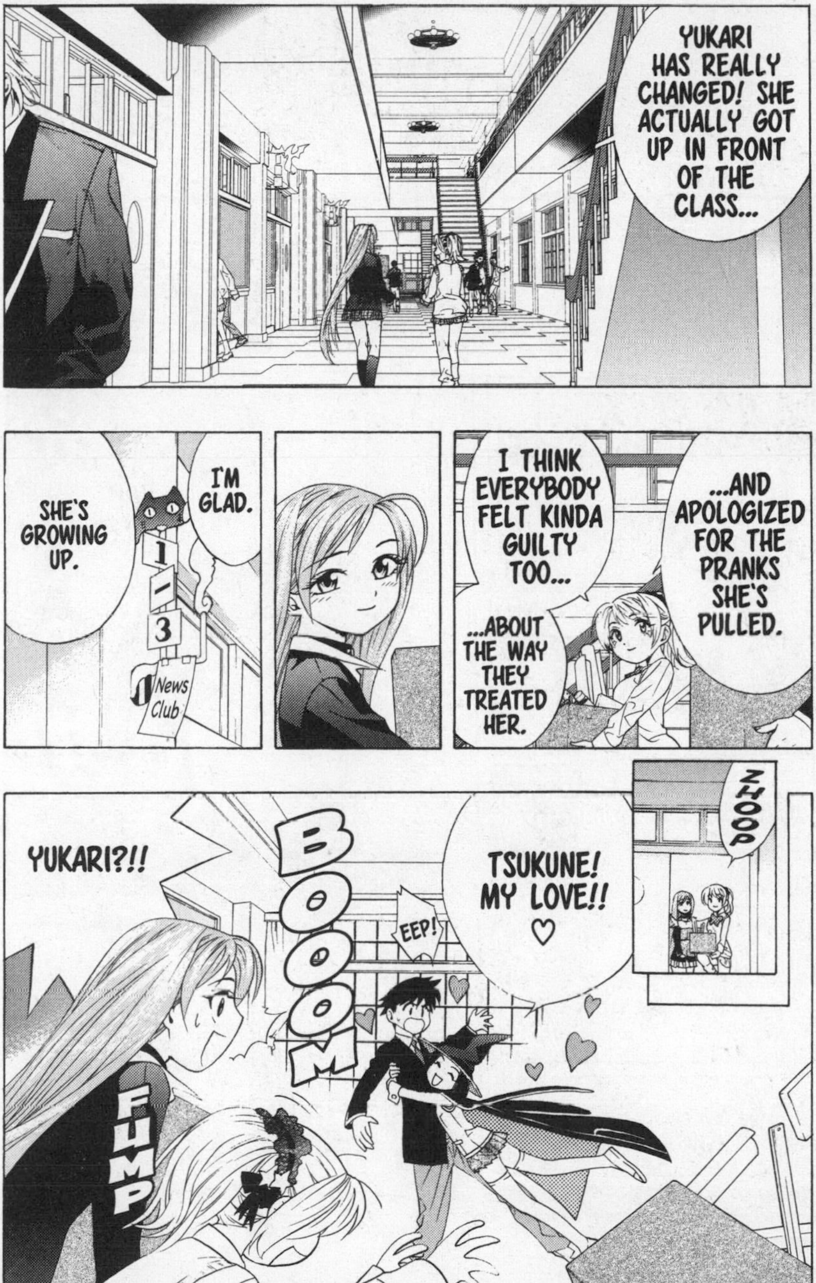
YUKARI HAS REALLY CHANGED! SHE ACTUALLY GOT UP IN FRONT OF THE CLASS...
...AND APOLOGIZED FOR THE PRANKS SHE'S PULLED.
I THINK EVERYBODY FELT KINDA GUILTY TOO...
...ABOUT THE WAY THEY TREATED HER.
I'M GLAD.
1-3
News Club
SHE'S GROWING UP.
ZHOOP
TSUKUNE! MY LOVE!! ♡
EEP!
BOOOOM
YUKARI?!!
FUMP

READ THIS WAY

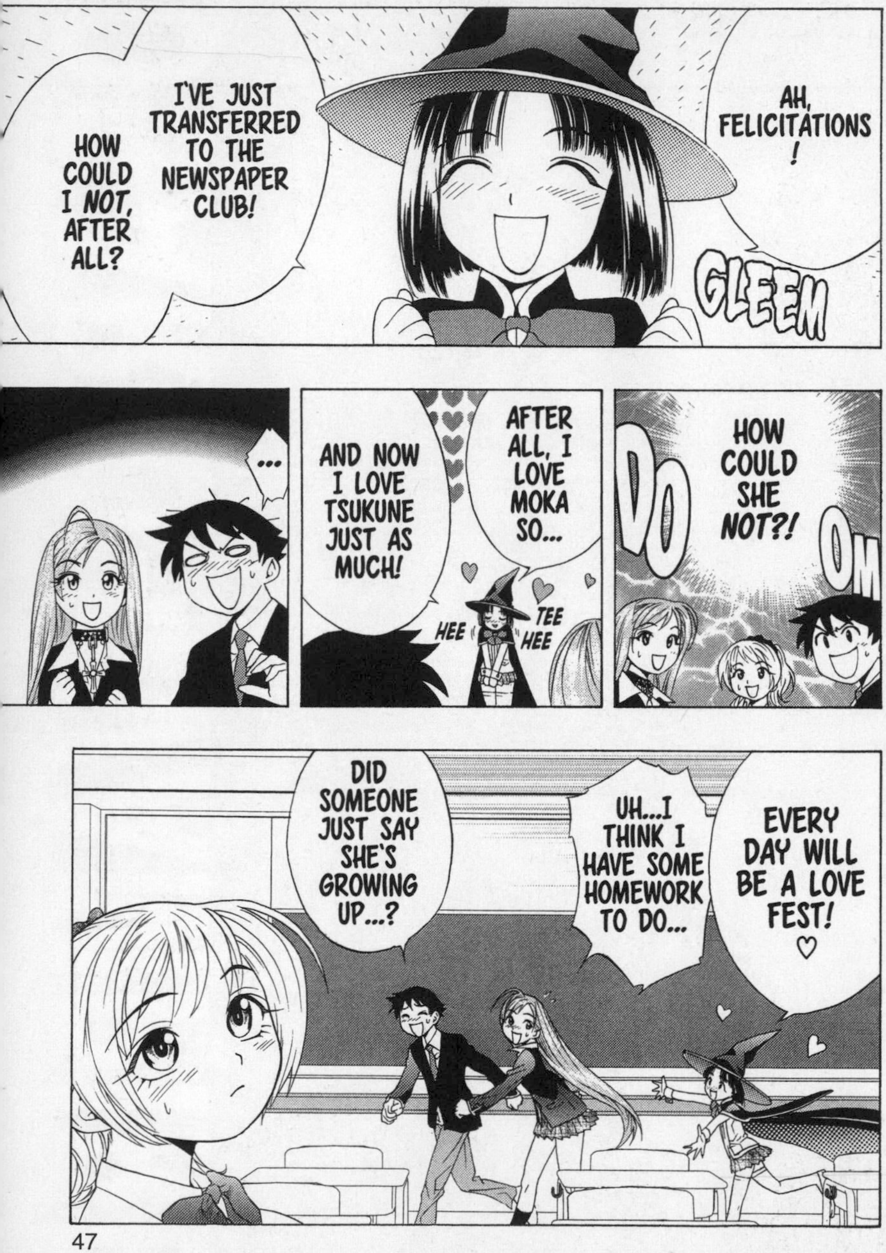
AH, FELICITATIONS!
GLEEM
I'VE JUST TRANSFERRED TO THE NEWSPAPER CLUB!
HOW COULD I *NOT*, AFTER ALL?
HOW COULD SHE *NOT*?!
DO OM
AFTER ALL, I LOVE MOKA SO...
AND NOW I LOVE TSUKUNE JUST AS MUCH!
TEE HEE
HEE
...
EVERY DAY WILL BE A LOVE FEST! ♡
UH...I THINK I HAVE SOME HOMEWORK TO DO...
DID SOMEONE JUST SAY SHE'S GROWING UP...?

ROSARIO+VAMPIRE

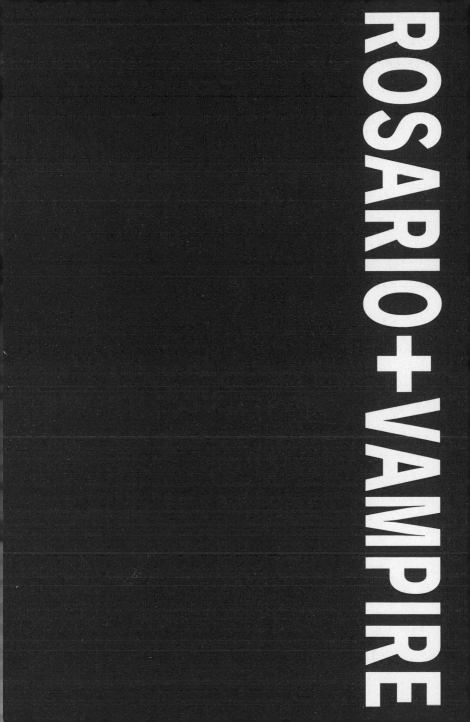

6: The Art of the Birthday

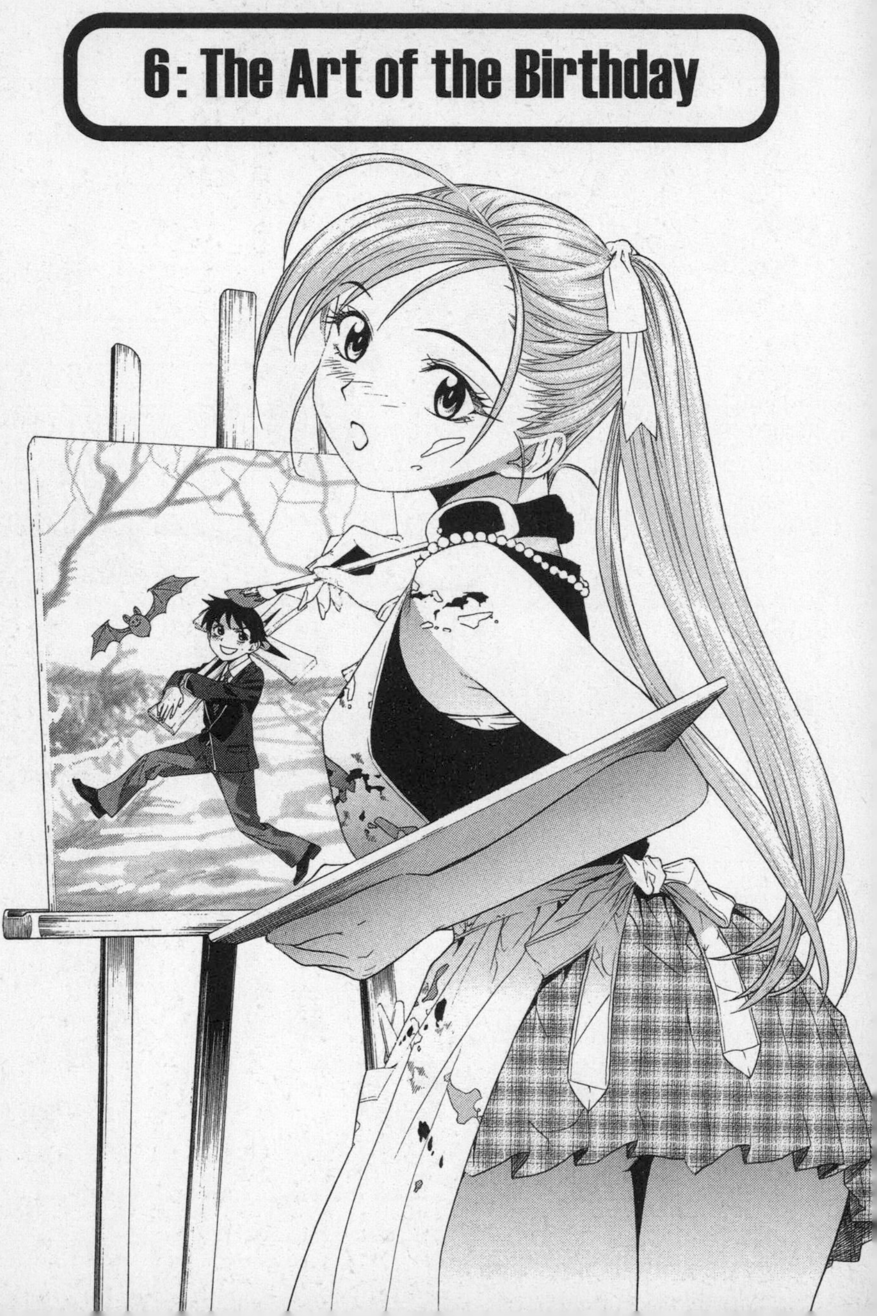

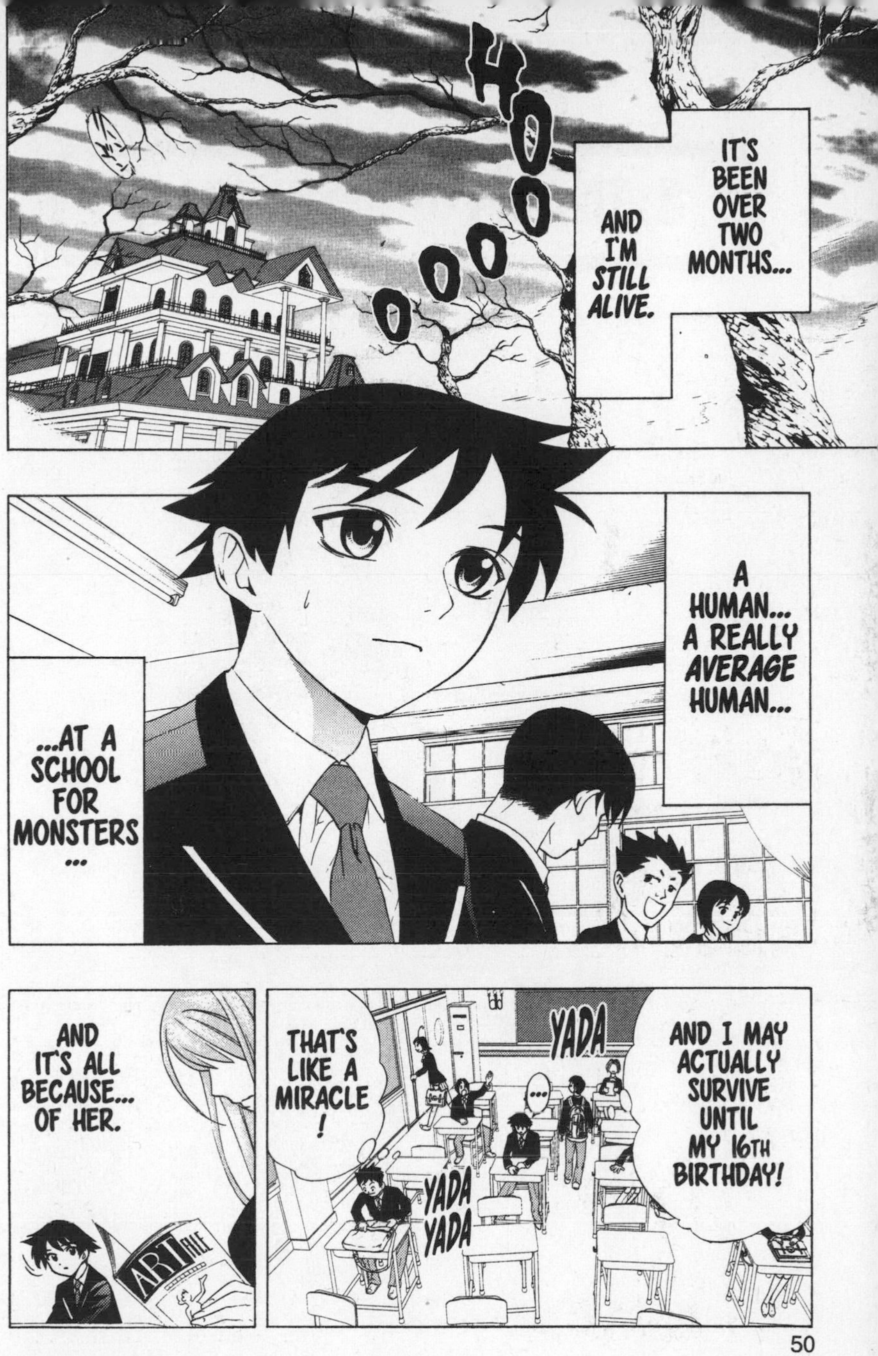
HOOOOO
IT'S BEEN OVER TWO MONTHS...
AND I'M STILL ALIVE.
A HUMAN... A REALLY AVERAGE HUMAN...
...AT A SCHOOL FOR MONSTERS...
AND I MAY ACTUALLY SURVIVE UNTIL MY 16TH BIRTHDAY!
YADA
...
THAT'S LIKE A MIRACLE!
YADA YADA
AND IT'S ALL BECAUSE... OF HER.
ART FILE

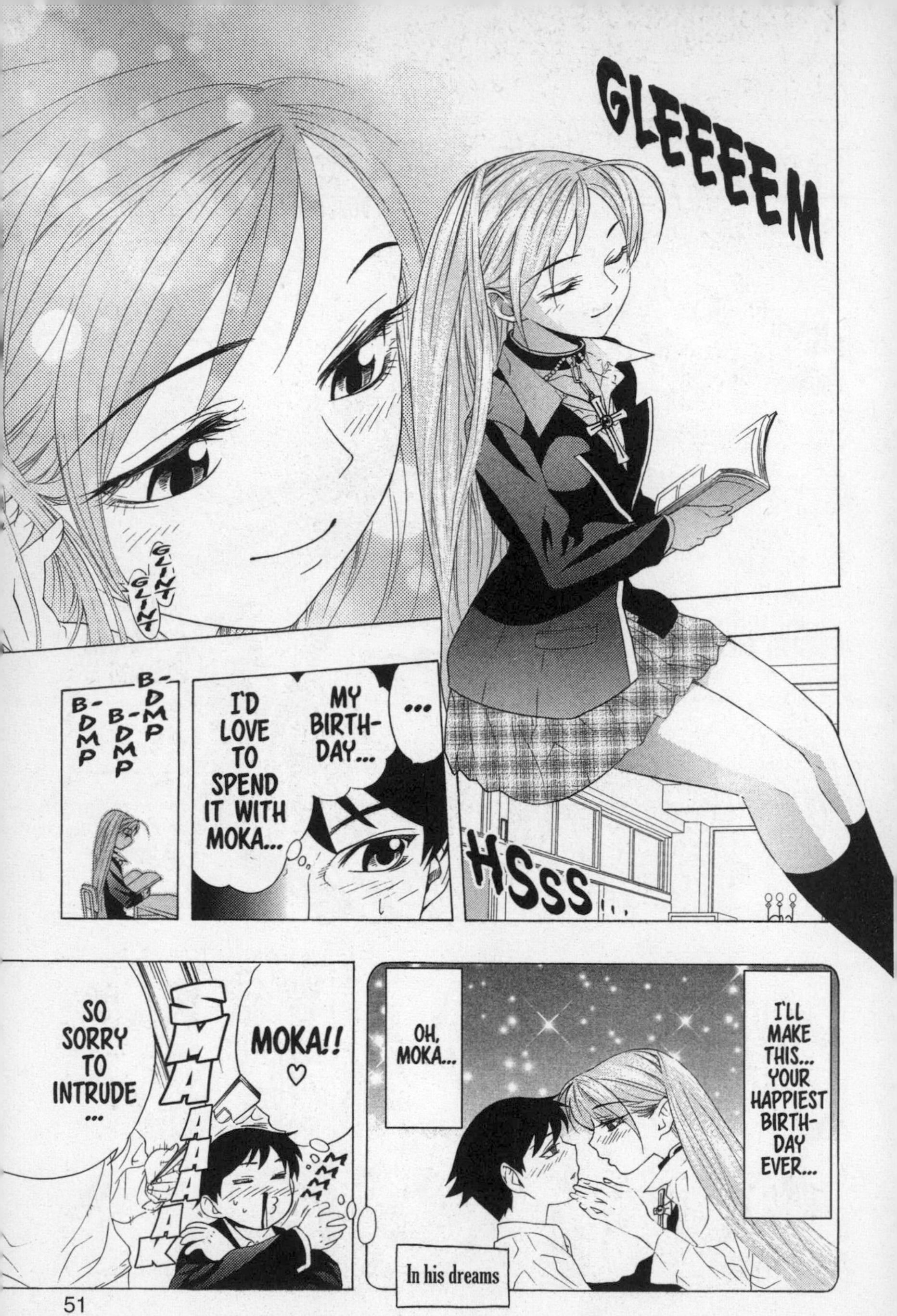
GLEEEEM
GLINT GLINT
HSSS...
...
MY BIRTH-DAY...
I'D LOVE TO SPEND IT WITH MOKA...
B-DMP B-DMP B-DMP
I'LL MAKE THIS... YOUR HAPPIEST BIRTH-DAY EVER...
OH, MOKA...
In his dreams
MOKA!! ♡
SMAAAAAAK
MMMM
SO SORRY TO INTRUDE ...

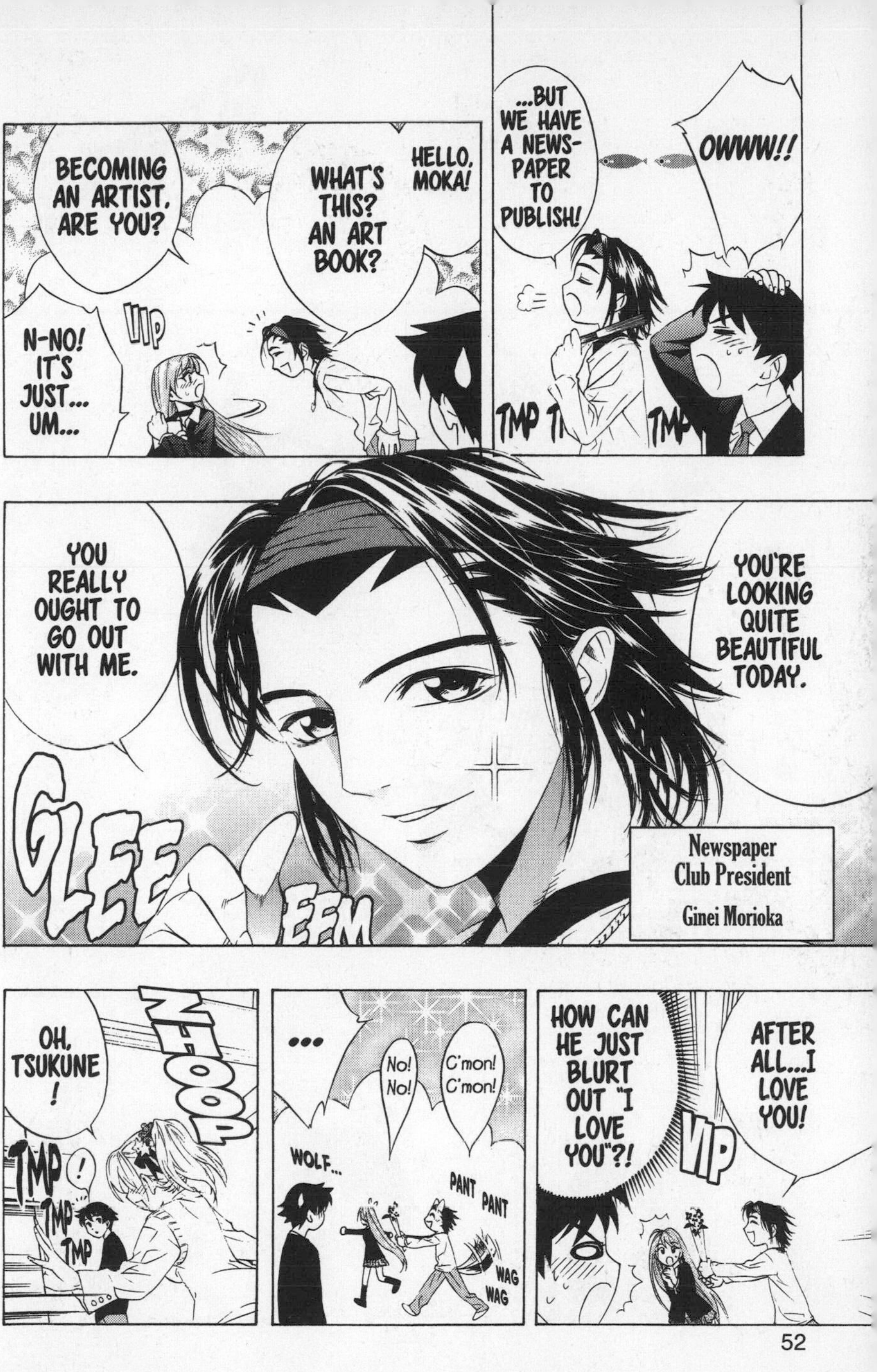

OWWW!!
...BUT WE HAVE A NEWSPAPER TO PUBLISH!
TMP TMP
HELLO, MOKA!
WHAT'S THIS? AN ART BOOK?
BECOMING AN ARTIST, ARE YOU?
VIP
N-NO! IT'S JUST... UM...
YOU'RE LOOKING QUITE BEAUTIFUL TODAY.
Newspaper Club President
Ginei Morioka
YOU REALLY OUGHT TO GO OUT WITH ME.
EEM
GLEE
AFTER ALL...I LOVE YOU!
VIP
HOW CAN HE JUST BLURT OUT "I LOVE YOU"?!
...
C'mon! C'mon!
No! No!
PANT PANT
WOLF...
WAG WAG
ZHOOP
OH, TSUKUNE!
!
TMP TMP TMP

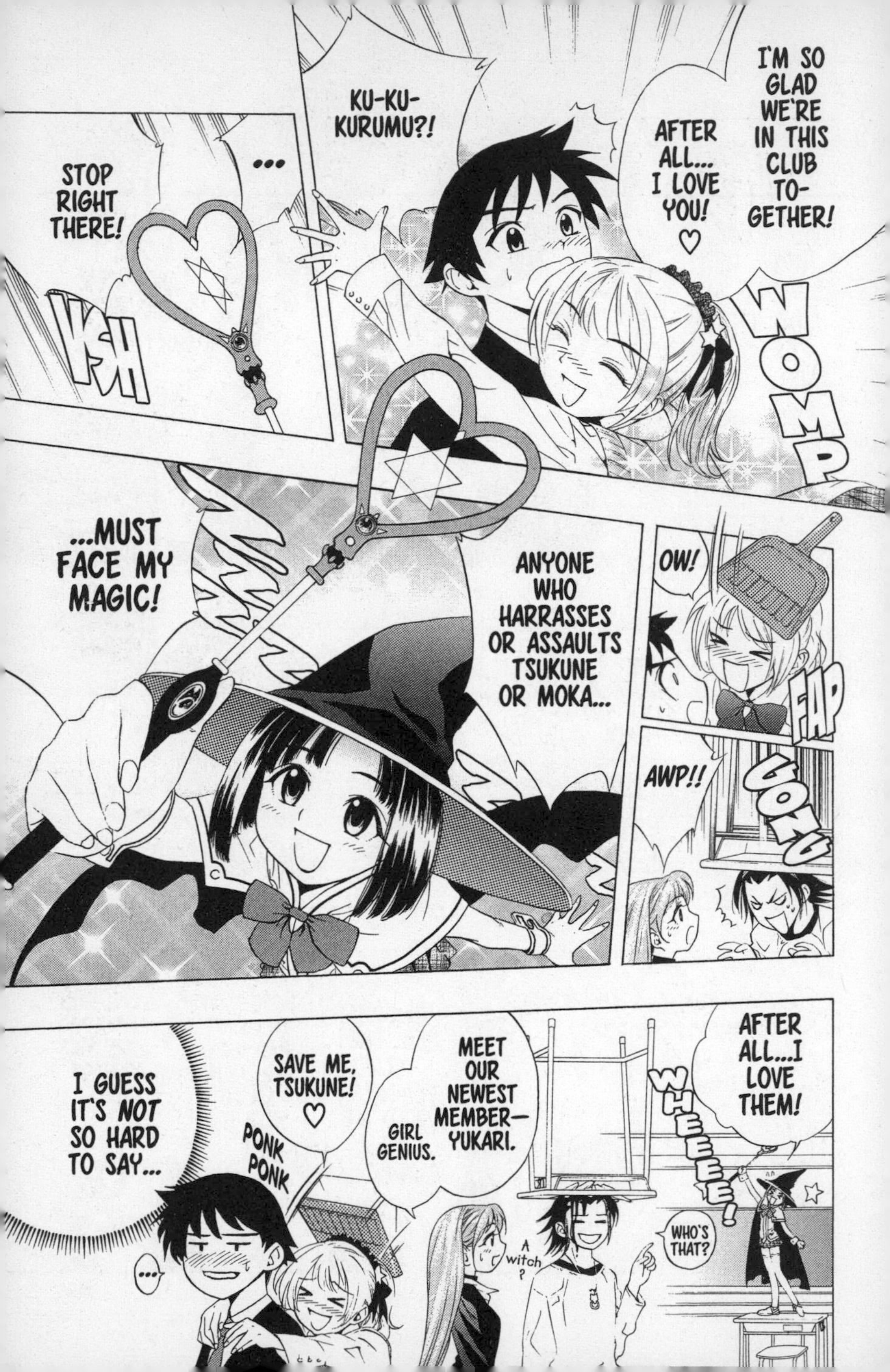
I'M SO GLAD WE'RE IN THIS CLUB TO-GETHER!
AFTER ALL... I LOVE YOU! ♡
WOMP
KU-KU-KURUMU?!
...
STOP RIGHT THERE!
VSH
OW!
FAP
AWP!!
GONG
ANYONE WHO HARRASSES OR ASSAULTS TSUKUNE OR MOKA...
...MUST FACE MY MAGIC!
AFTER ALL...I LOVE THEM!
WHEEEE!
WHO'S THAT?
A witch?
MEET OUR NEWEST MEMBER—YUKARI.
GIRL GENIUS.
SAVE ME, TSUKUNE! ♡
PONK PONK
I GUESS IT'S *NOT* SO HARD TO SAY...
...

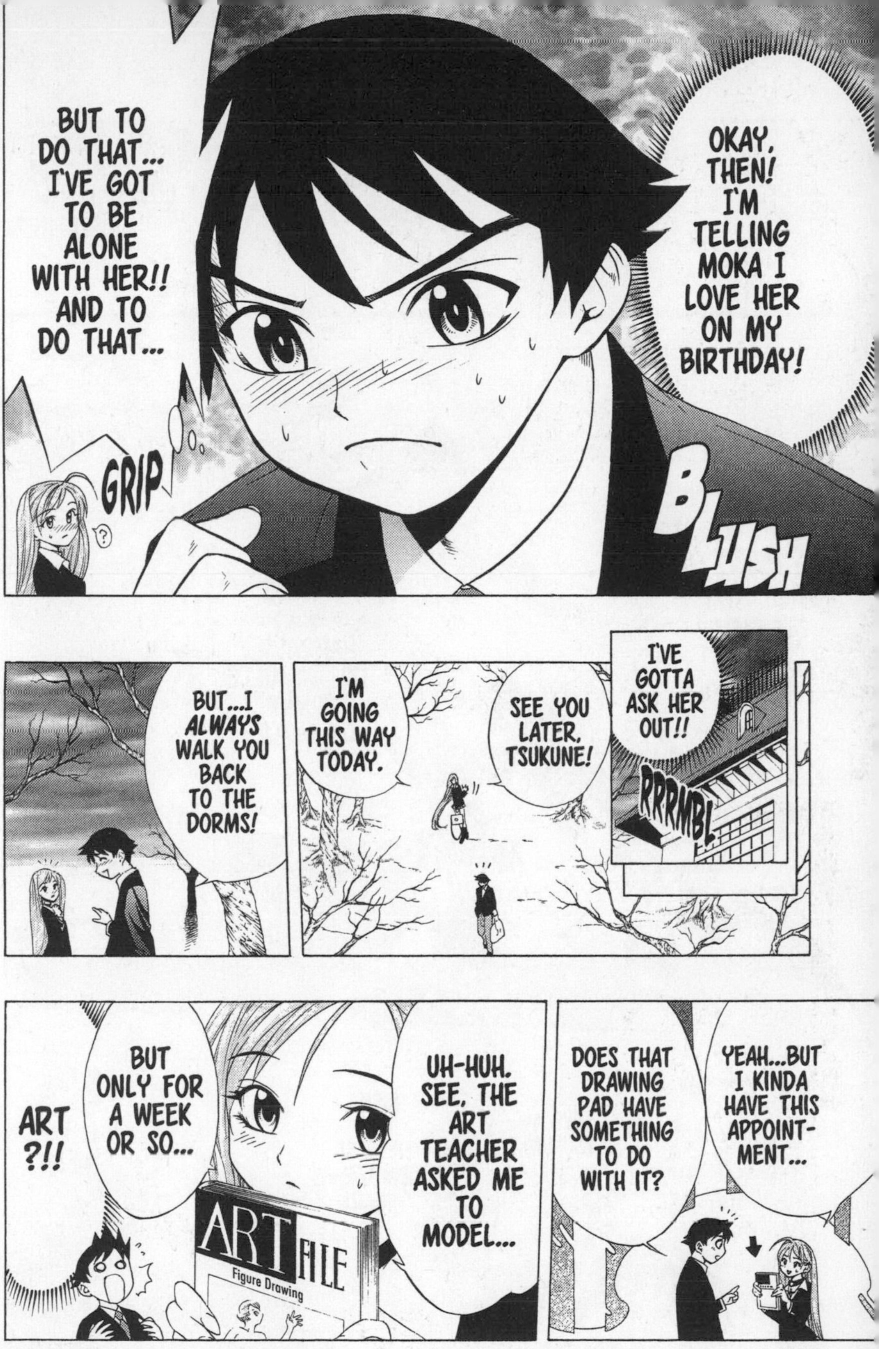
OKAY, THEN! I'M TELLING MOKA I LOVE HER ON MY BIRTHDAY!
BLUSH
BUT TO DO THAT... I'VE GOT TO BE ALONE WITH HER!! AND TO DO THAT...
GRIP
?
I'VE GOTTA ASK HER OUT!!
RRRMBL
SEE YOU LATER, TSUKUNE!
I'M GOING THIS WAY TODAY.
BUT...I ALWAYS WALK YOU BACK TO THE DORMS!
YEAH...BUT I KINDA HAVE THIS APPOINT-MENT...
DOES THAT DRAWING PAD HAVE SOMETHING TO DO WITH IT?
UH-HUH. SEE, THE ART TEACHER ASKED ME TO MODEL...
BUT ONLY FOR A WEEK OR SO...
ART FILE
Figure Drawing
ART ?!!

READ THIS WAY

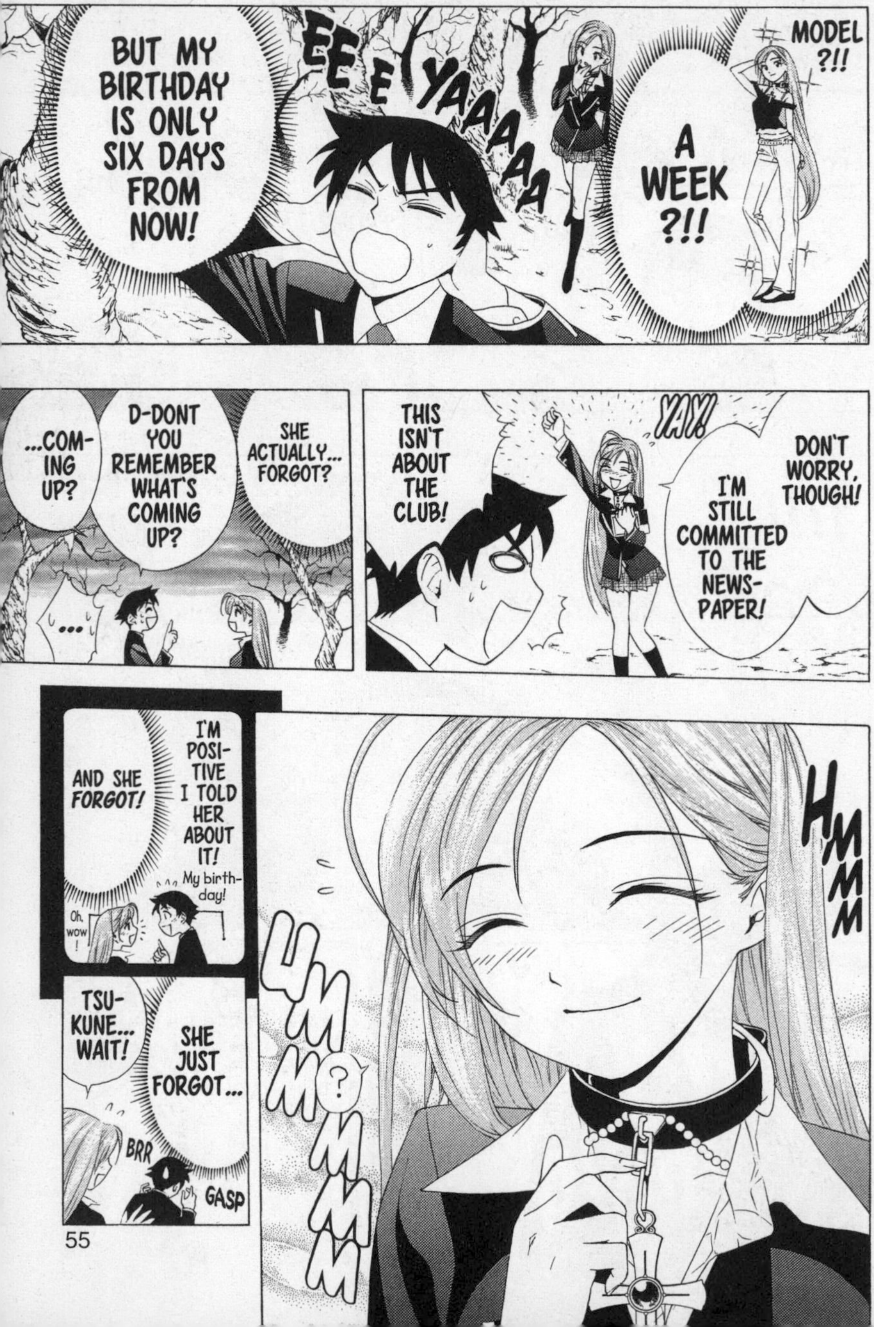
MODEL?!!
A WEEK?!!
EEEYAAAAAA
BUT MY BIRTHDAY IS ONLY SIX DAYS FROM NOW!
YAY!
DON'T WORRY, THOUGH!
I'M STILL COMMITTED TO THE NEWSPAPER!
THIS ISN'T ABOUT THE CLUB!
SHE ACTUALLY... FORGOT?
D-DONT YOU REMEMBER WHAT'S COMING UP?
...COMING UP?
...
HMMMM
UMMMMMMMM
?
I'M POSITIVE I TOLD HER ABOUT IT!
AND SHE FORGOT!
My birthday!
Oh, wow!
SHE JUST FORGOT...
TSUKUNE... WAIT!
BRR
GASP

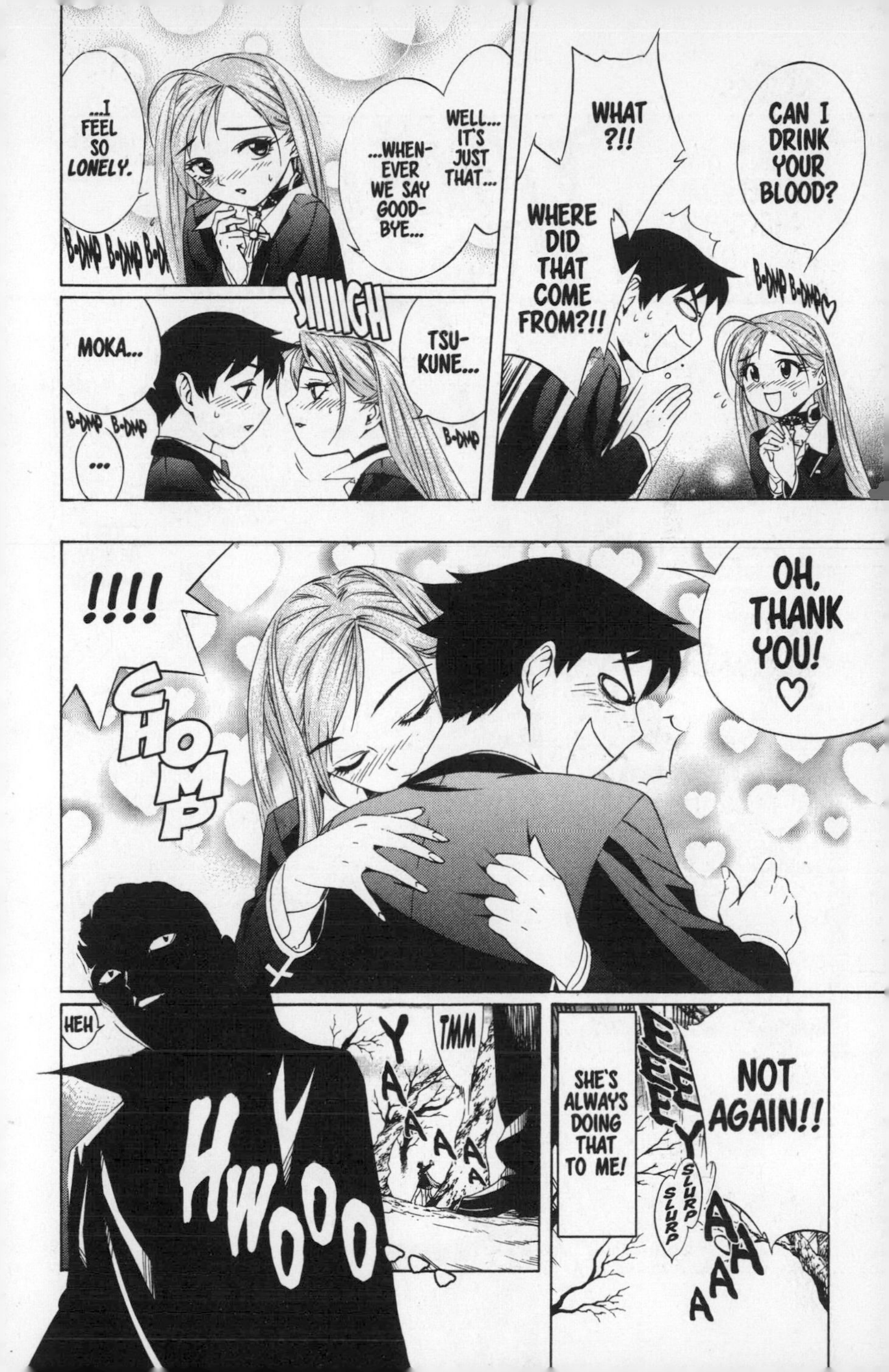
CAN I DRINK YOUR BLOOD?
B-DMP B-DMP♡
WHAT?!!
WHERE DID THAT COME FROM?!!
WELL... IT'S JUST THAT...
...WHEN-EVER WE SAY GOOD-BYE...
...I FEEL SO LONELY.
B-DMP B-DMP B-DI
SHIIIGH
TSU-KUNE...
B-DMP
MOKA...
B-DMP B-DMP
...
OH, THANK YOU! ♡
!!!!
CHOMP
NOT AGAIN!!
EEEEYAAAAA
SLURP SLURP
SHE'S ALWAYS DOING THAT TO ME!
TMM
YAAAAA
HEH
HWOOO

READ THIS WAY

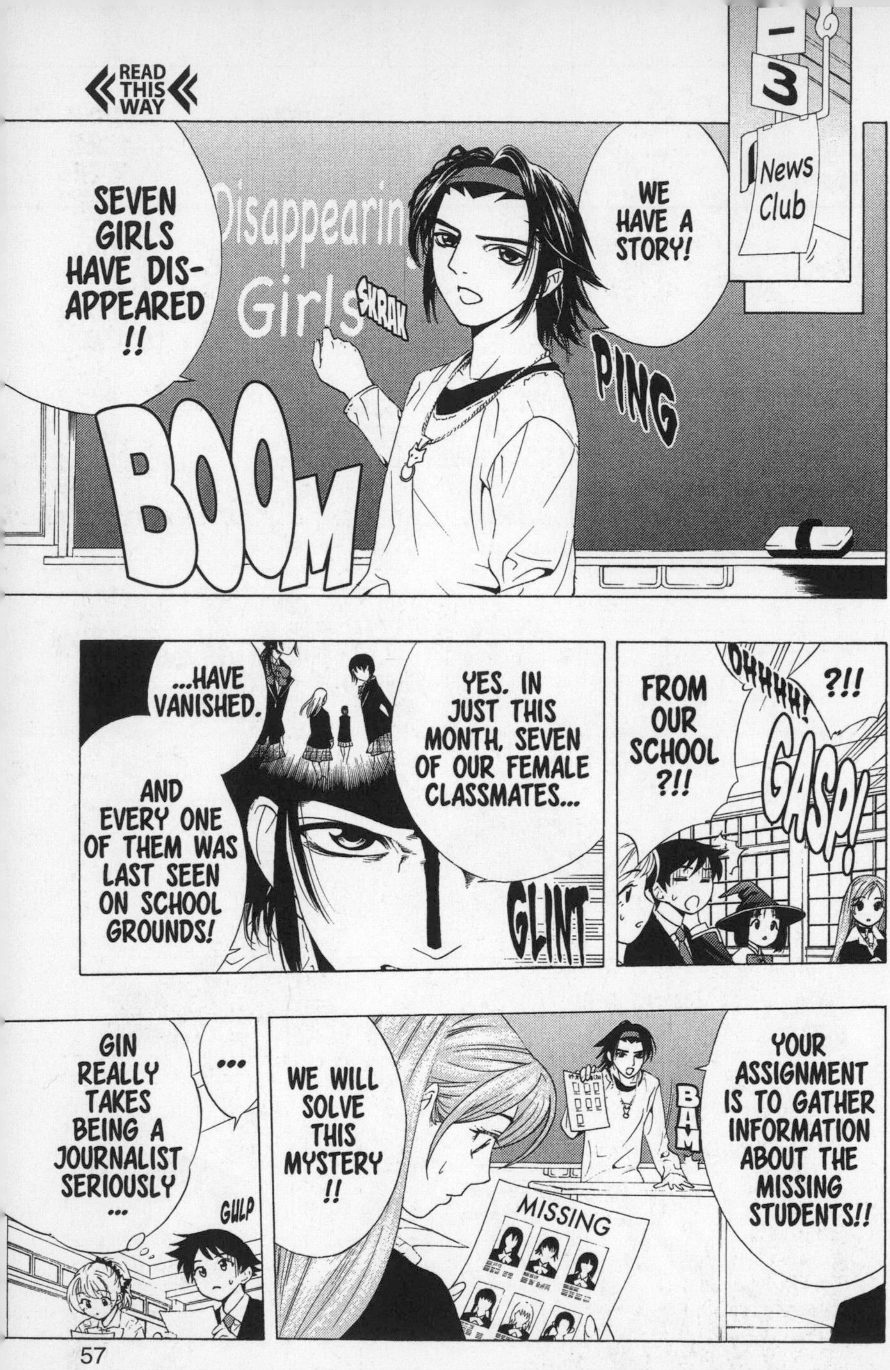

3
News Club
WE HAVE A STORY!
PING
Disappearing Girls
SKRAK
SEVEN GIRLS HAVE DIS-APPEARED!!
BOOM
?!!
OHHHH!
GASP!
FROM OUR SCHOOL?!!
YES. IN JUST THIS MONTH, SEVEN OF OUR FEMALE CLASSMATES...
...HAVE VANISHED.
AND EVERY ONE OF THEM WAS LAST SEEN ON SCHOOL GROUNDS!
GLINT
YOUR ASSIGNMENT IS TO GATHER INFORMATION ABOUT THE MISSING STUDENTS!!
BAM
WE WILL SOLVE THIS MYSTERY!!
MISSING
...
GIN REALLY TAKES BEING A JOURNALIST SERIOUSLY...
GULP

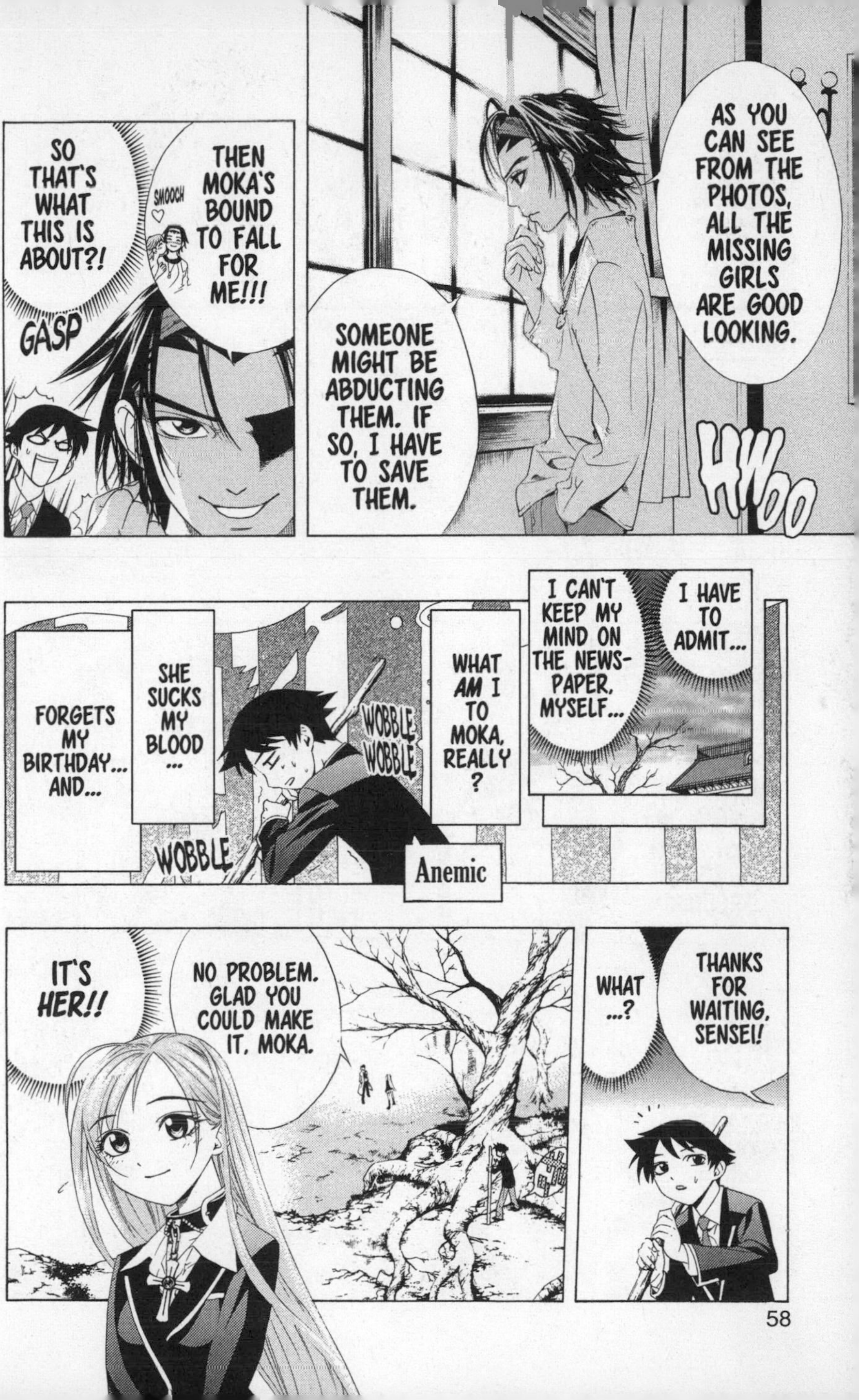
AS YOU CAN SEE FROM THE PHOTOS, ALL THE MISSING GIRLS ARE GOOD LOOKING.
HWOO
SOMEONE MIGHT BE ABDUCTING THEM. IF SO, I HAVE TO SAVE THEM.
THEN MOKA'S BOUND TO FALL FOR ME!!!
SMOOCH
SO THAT'S WHAT THIS IS ABOUT?!
GASP
I HAVE TO ADMIT...
I CAN'T KEEP MY MIND ON THE NEWSPAPER, MYSELF...
WHAT *AM* I TO MOKA, REALLY?
WOBBLE WOBBLE
SHE SUCKS MY BLOOD...
FORGETS MY BIRTHDAY... AND...
WOBBLE
Anemic
THANKS FOR WAITING, SENSEI!
WHAT...?
NO PROBLEM. GLAD YOU COULD MAKE IT, MOKA.
IT'S *HER!!*

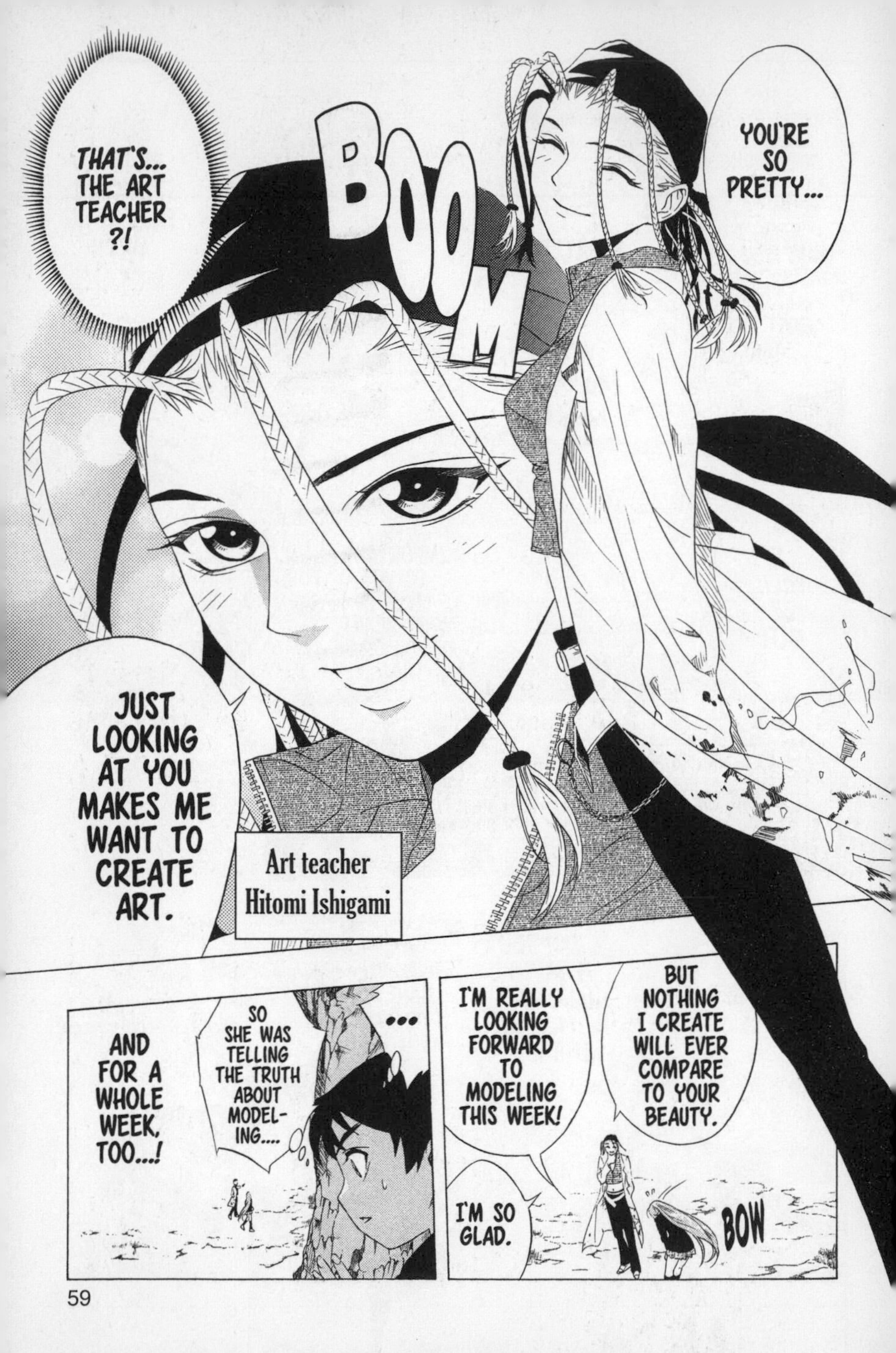
YOU'RE SO PRETTY...
BOOM
THAT'S... THE ART TEACHER ?!
JUST LOOKING AT YOU MAKES ME WANT TO CREATE ART.
Art teacher Hitomi Ishigami
BUT NOTHING I CREATE WILL EVER COMPARE TO YOUR BEAUTY.
I'M REALLY LOOKING FORWARD TO MODELING THIS WEEK!
BOW
I'M SO GLAD.
...
SO SHE WAS TELLING THE TRUTH ABOUT MODEL-ING....
AND FOR A WHOLE WEEK, TOO...!

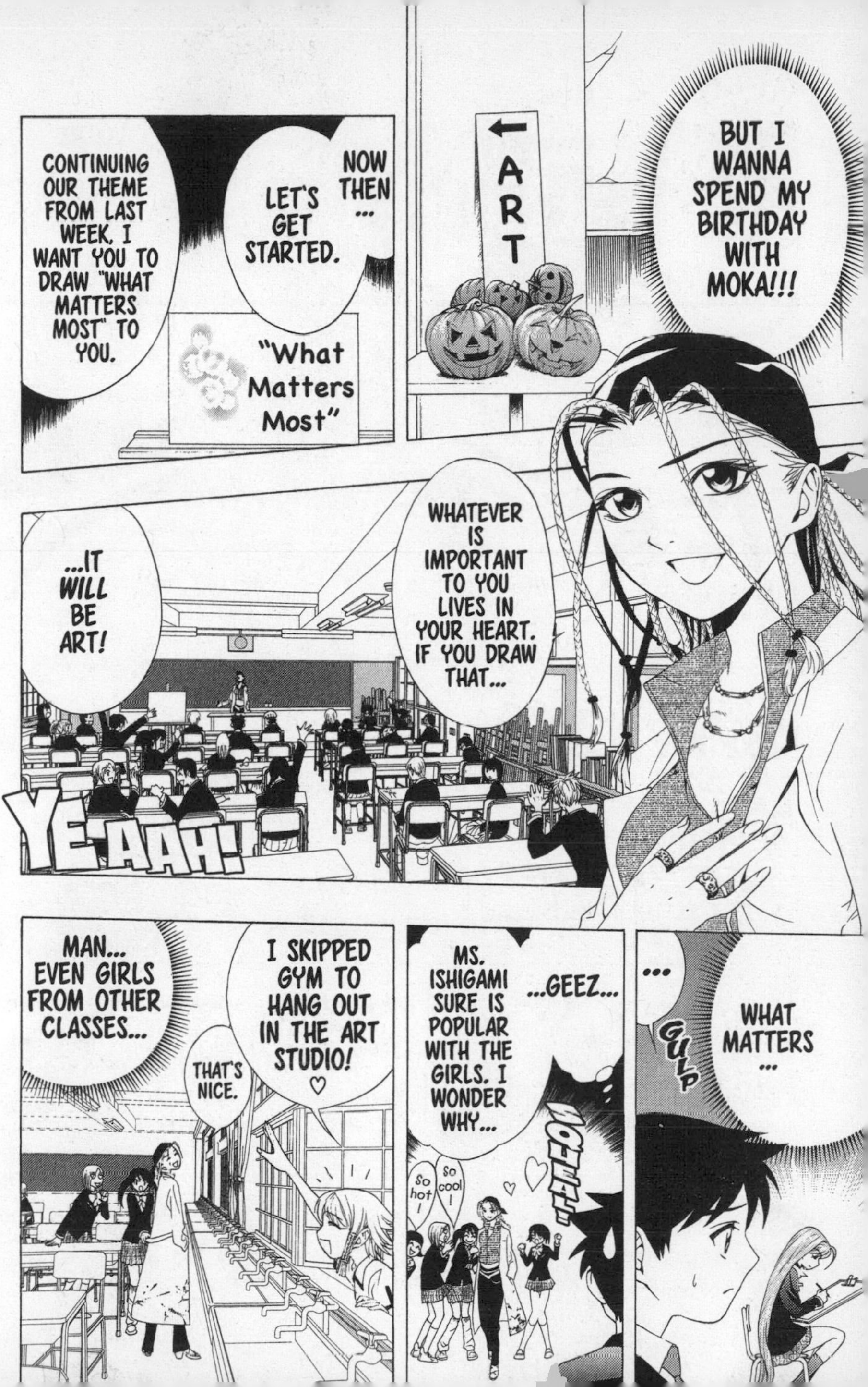
BUT I WANNA SPEND MY BIRTHDAY WITH MOKA!!!
ART
NOW THEN...
LET'S GET STARTED.
CONTINUING OUR THEME FROM LAST WEEK, I WANT YOU TO DRAW "WHAT MATTERS MOST" TO YOU.
"What Matters Most"
WHATEVER IS IMPORTANT TO YOU LIVES IN YOUR HEART. IF YOU DRAW THAT...
...IT WILL BE ART!
YEAAAH!
...
WHAT MATTERS...
GULP
...GEEZ...
MS. ISHIGAMI SURE IS POPULAR WITH THE GIRLS. I WONDER WHY...
SQUEAL!
So cool!
So hot!
I SKIPPED GYM TO HANG OUT IN THE ART STUDIO! ♡
MAN... EVEN GIRLS FROM OTHER CLASSES...
THAT'S NICE.

READ THIS WAY

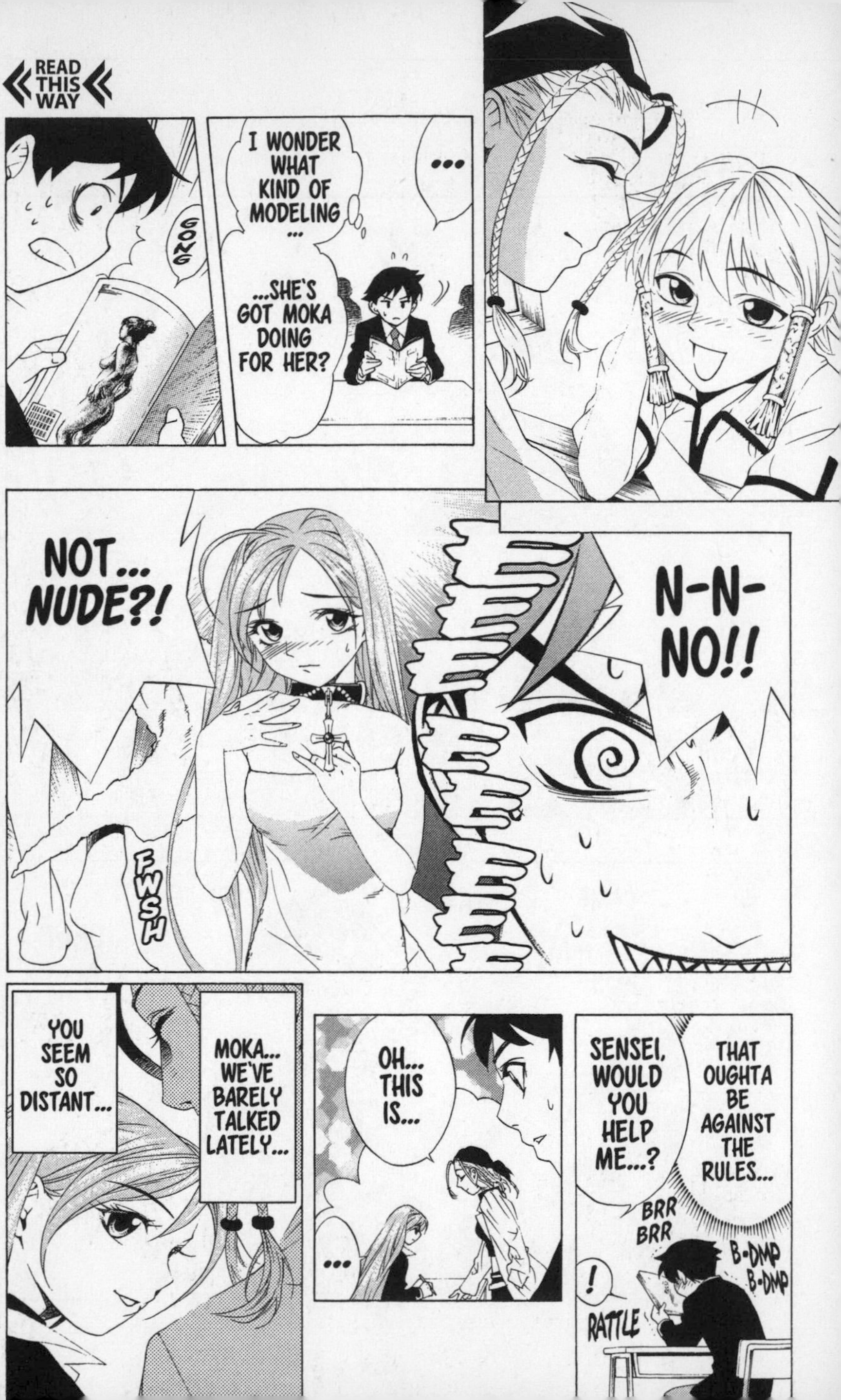
...
I WONDER WHAT KIND OF MODELING...
...SHE'S GOT MOKA DOING FOR HER?
GONG
N-N-NO!!
EEEEEEEE
NOT... NUDE?!
FWSH
THAT OUGHTA BE AGAINST THE RULES...
SENSEI, WOULD YOU HELP ME...?
BRR BRR
B-DMP B-DMP
!
RATTLE
OH... THIS IS...
...
MOKA... WE'VE BARELY TALKED LATELY...
YOU SEEM SO DISTANT...

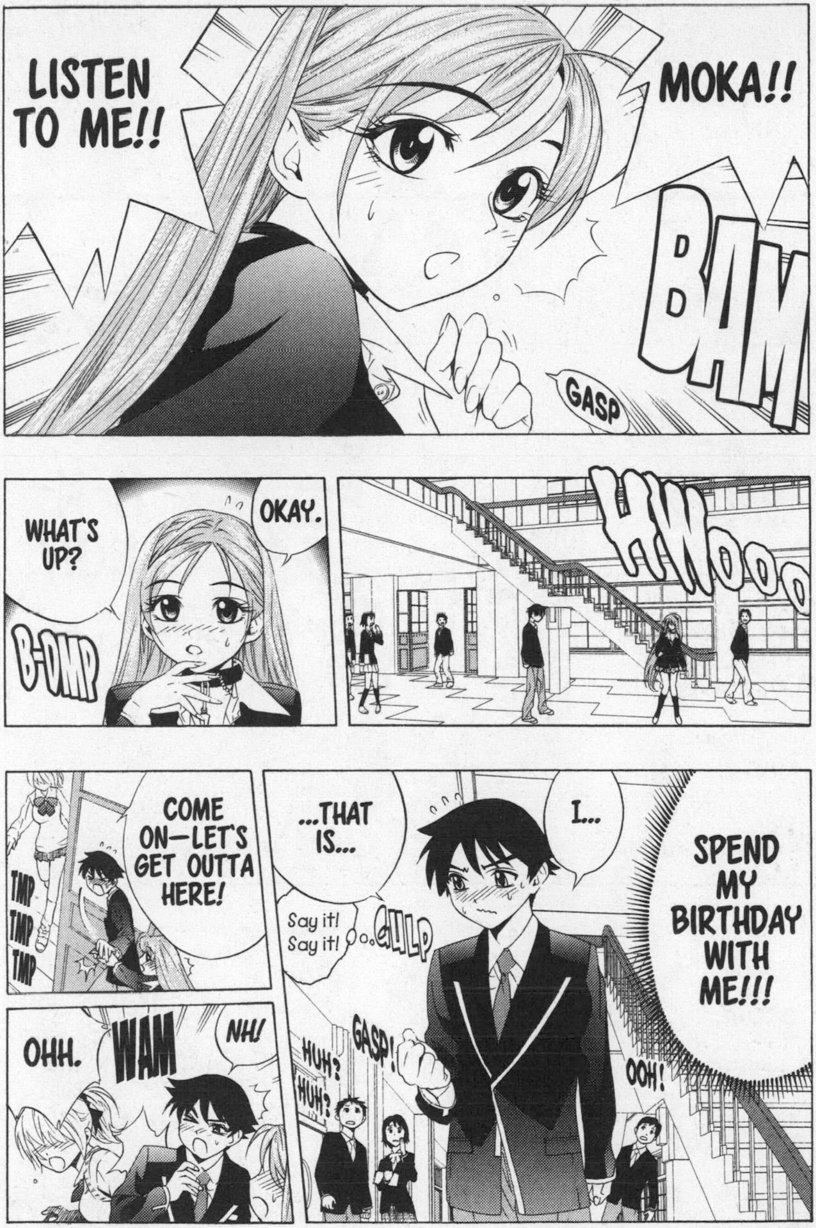

MOKA!!
LISTEN TO ME!!
BAM
GASP
HWNOOOO
OKAY.
WHAT'S UP?
B-DOMP
I...
SPEND MY BIRTHDAY WITH ME!!!
...THAT IS...
GULP
Say it! Say it!
GASP!
HUH? HUH?
OOH!
COME ON—LET'S GET OUTTA HERE!
TMP TMP TMP
NH!
WAM
OHH.

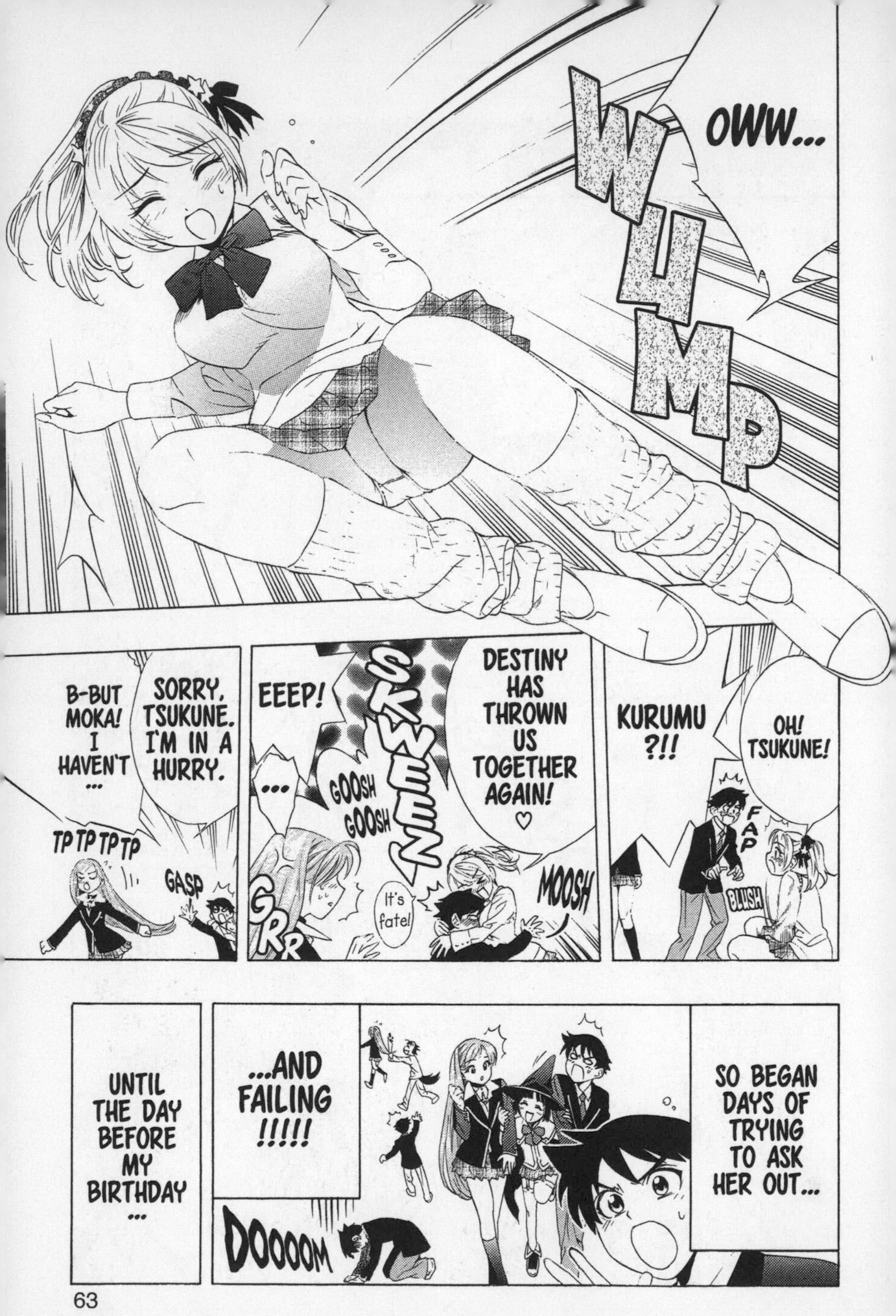
OWW...
WHUMP
OH! TSUKUNE!
KURUMU ?!!
FAP
BLUSH
DESTINY HAS THROWN US TOGETHER AGAIN! ♡
SKWEEZ
MOOSH
EEEP!
GOOSH GOOSH
...
It's fate!
GRR
SORRY, TSUKUNE. I'M IN A HURRY.
B-BUT MOKA! I HAVEN'T ...
TP TP TP TP
GASP
SO BEGAN DAYS OF TRYING TO ASK HER OUT...
...AND FAILING !!!!!
DOOOOM
UNTIL THE DAY BEFORE MY BIRTHDAY ...

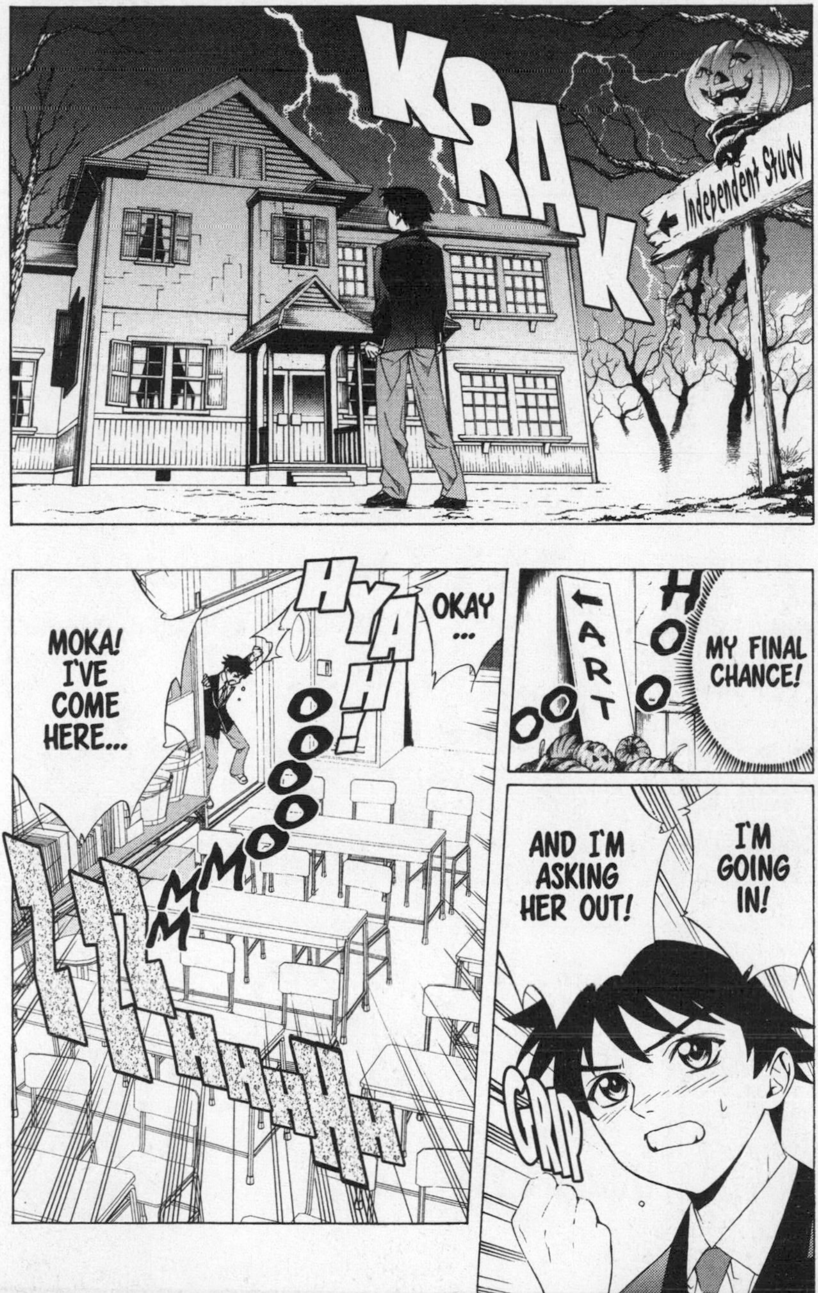
KRAK
Independent Study
ART
HOOOOO
MY FINAL CHANCE!
I'M GOING IN!
AND I'M ASKING HER OUT!
GRIP
OKAY...
MOKA! I'VE COME HERE...
HYAH!!
OOOOOO
MMMM

READ THIS WAY

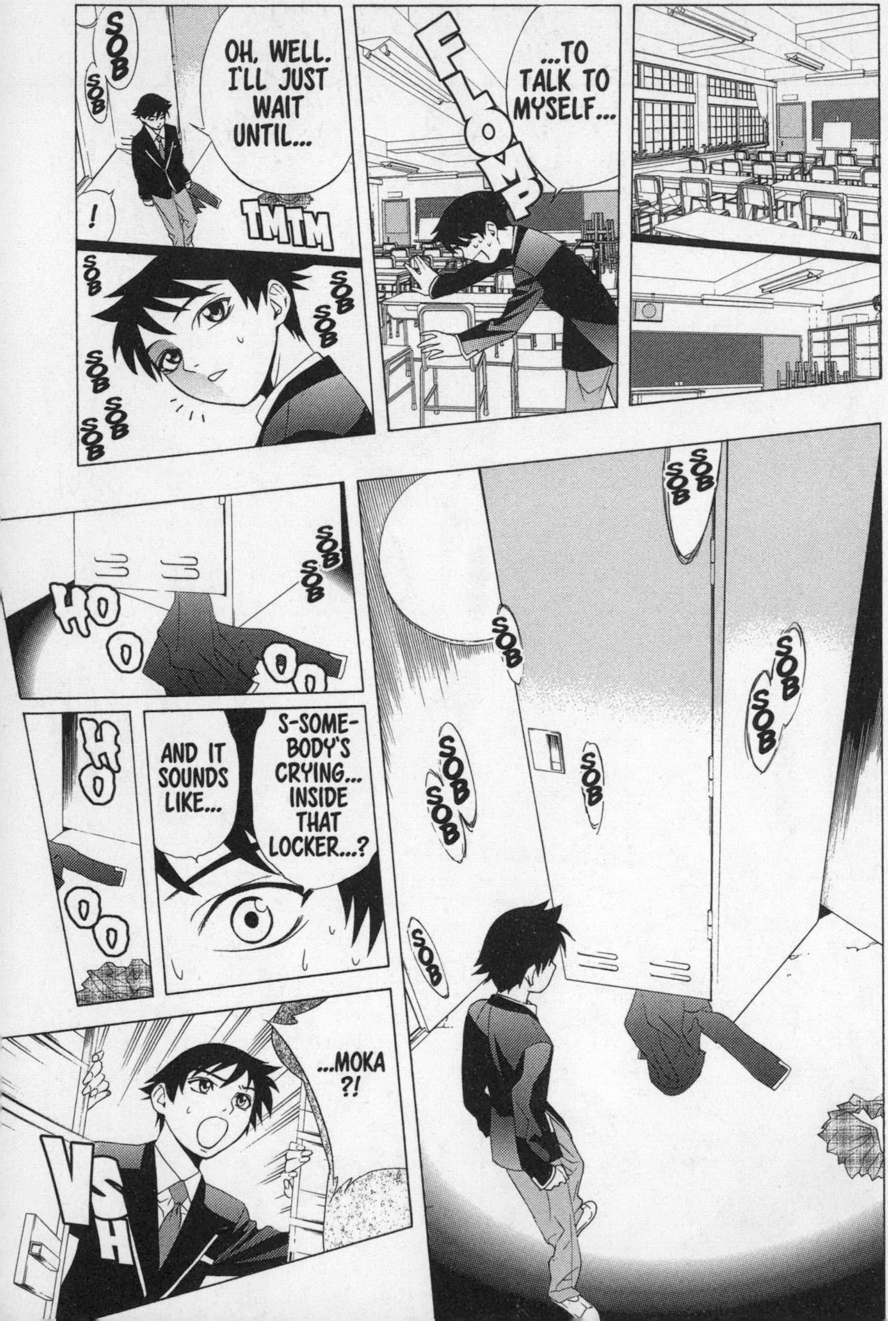

FLOMP
...TO TALK TO MYSELF...
SOB SOB
OH, WELL. I'LL JUST WAIT UNTIL...
!
TMTM
SOB SOB SOB SOB SOB SOB
SOB SOB
SOB
SOB SOB
SOB SOB
SOB
SOB
SOB SOB
HOOOO
S-SOME-BODY'S CRYING... INSIDE THAT LOCKER...?
AND IT SOUNDS LIKE...
HOOOO
...MOKA ?!
VSH

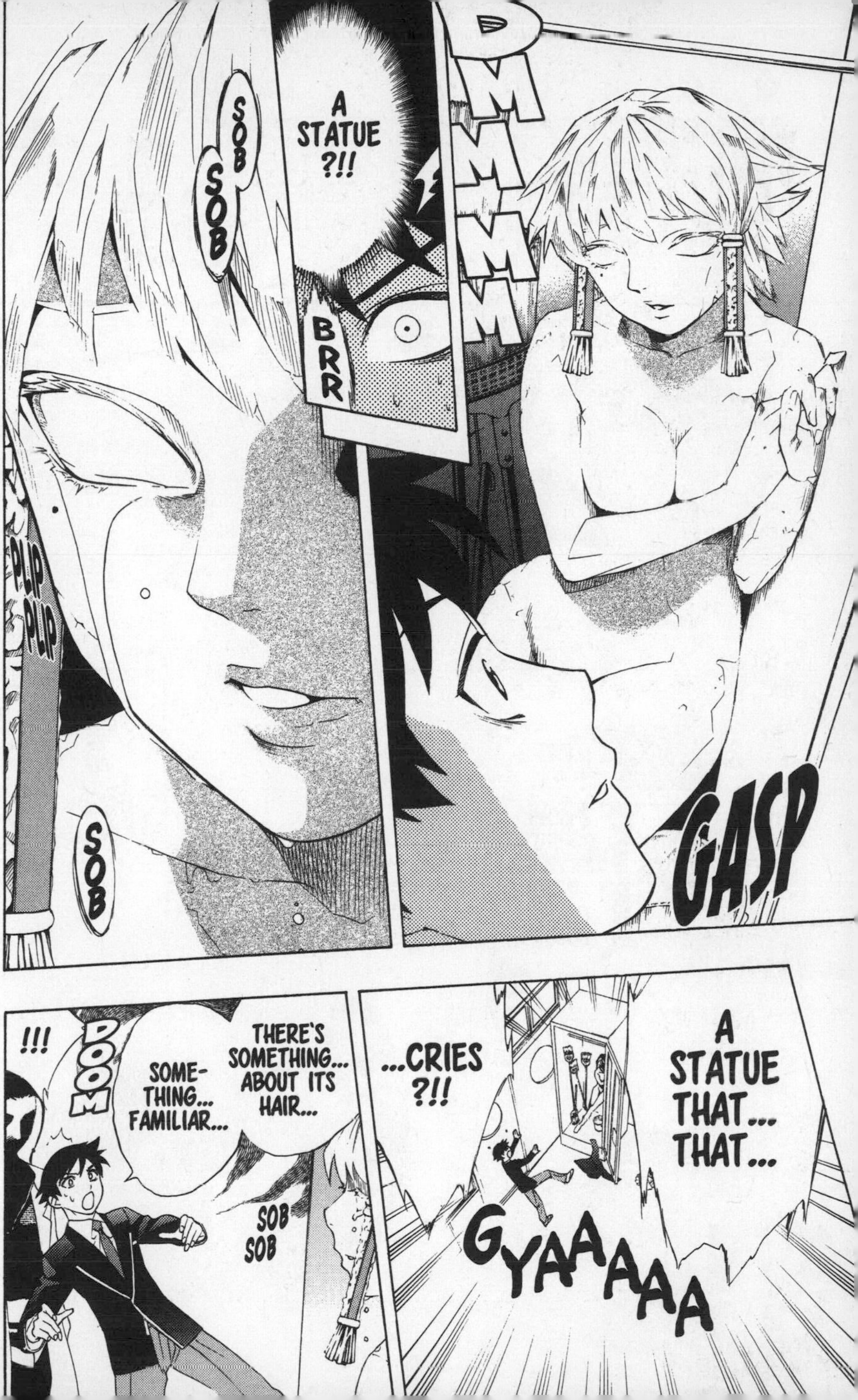
DMMMM
GASP
A STATUE ?!!
BRR
SOB SOB
PLIP PLIP
SOB
A STATUE THAT... THAT...
...CRIES ?!!
GYAAAAAA
THERE'S SOMETHING... ABOUT ITS HAIR...
SOME-THING... FAMILIAR...
DOOM
!!!
SOB SOB

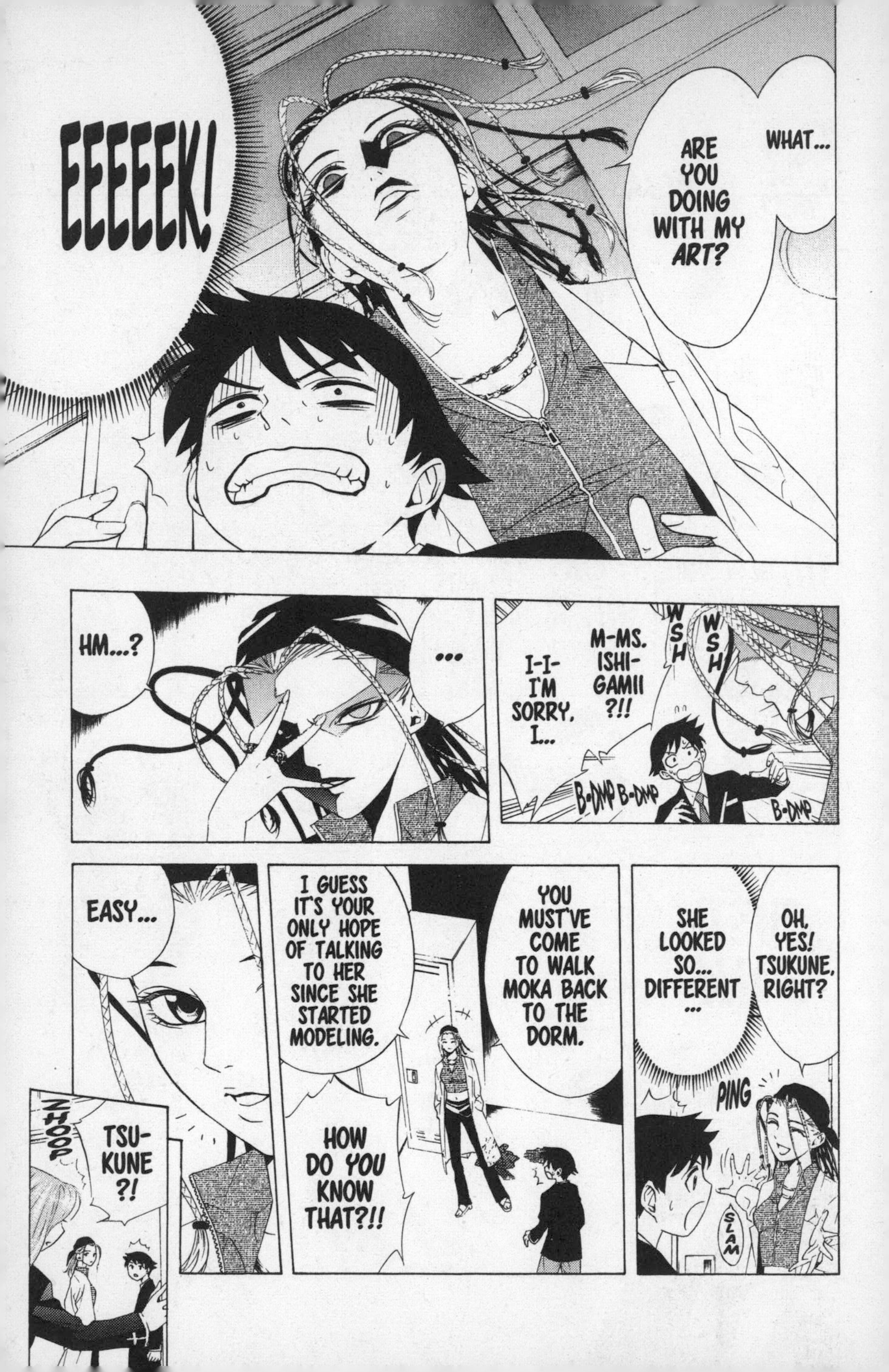
WHAT... ARE YOU DOING WITH MY ART?
EEEEEK!
WSH WSH
M-MS. ISHIGAMII?!!
I-I-I'M SORRY, I...
B-DMP B-DMP B-DMP
...
HM...?
OH, YES! TSUKUNE, RIGHT?
SHE LOOKED SO... DIFFERENT...
PING
SLAM
YOU MUST'VE COME TO WALK MOKA BACK TO THE DORM.
I GUESS IT'S YOUR ONLY HOPE OF TALKING TO HER SINCE SHE STARTED MODELING.
HOW DO YOU KNOW THAT?!!
EASY...
ZHOOP
TSU-KUNE?!

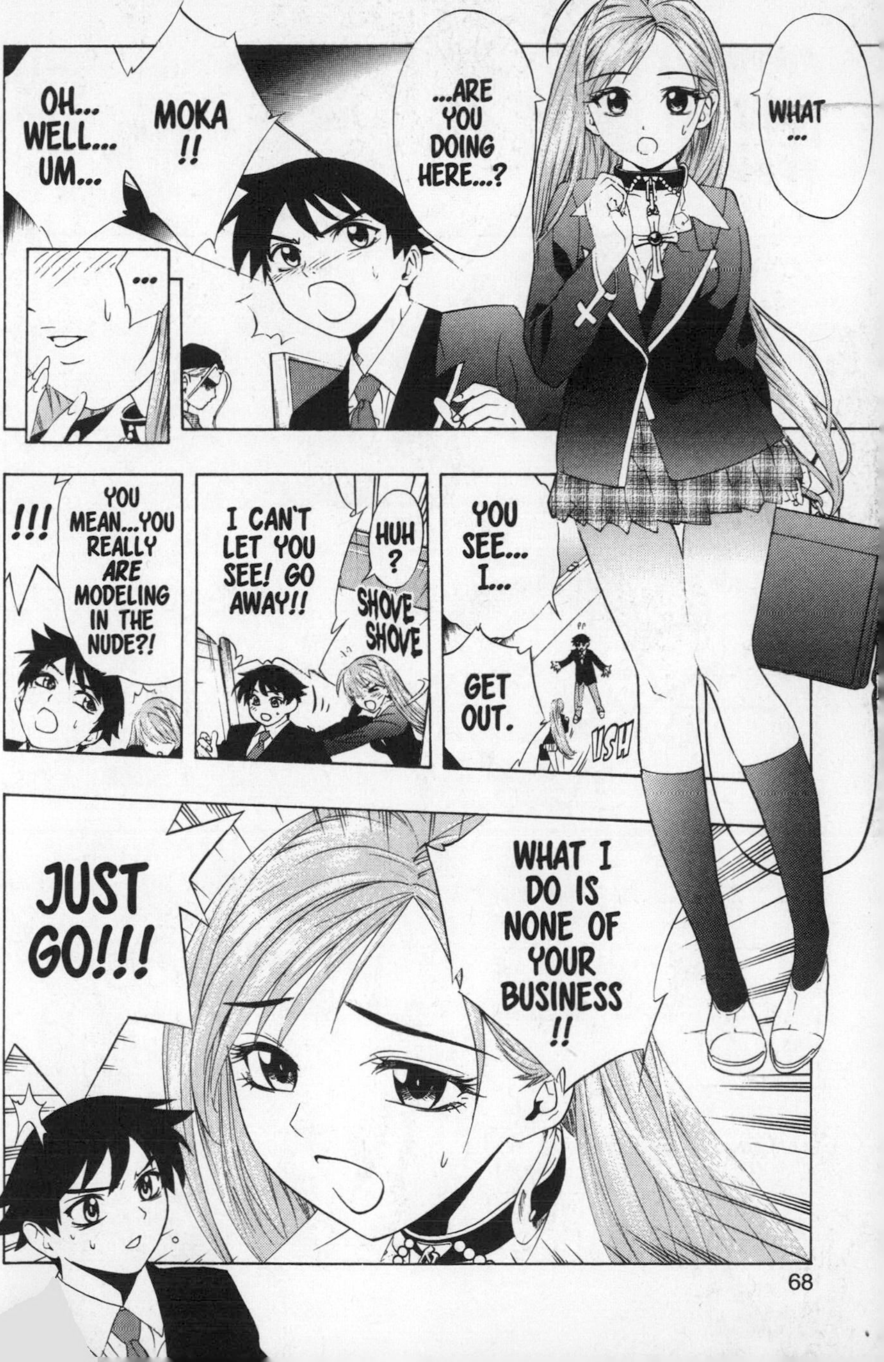
WHAT...
...ARE YOU DOING HERE...?
MOKA!!
OH... WELL... UM...
...
YOU SEE... I...
GET OUT.
USH
HUH?
SHOVE SHOVE
I CAN'T LET YOU SEE! GO AWAY!!
!!!
YOU MEAN...YOU REALLY ARE MODELING IN THE NUDE?!
WHAT I DO IS NONE OF YOUR BUSINESS!!
JUST GO!!!

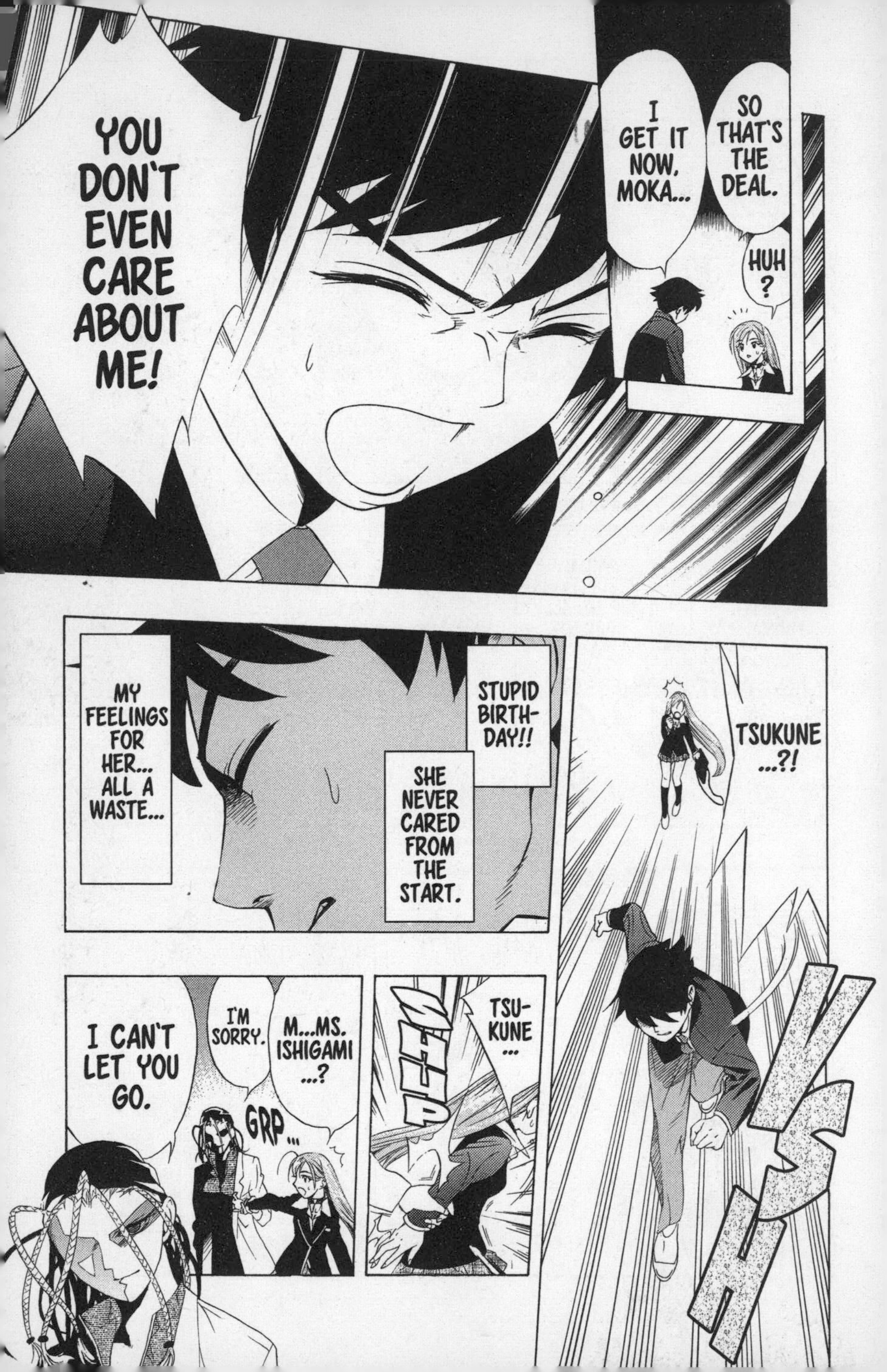
SO THAT'S THE DEAL.
I GET IT NOW, MOKA...
HUH?
YOU DON'T EVEN CARE ABOUT ME!
TSUKUNE ...?!
STUPID BIRTHDAY!!
SHE NEVER CARED FROM THE START.
MY FEELINGS FOR HER... ALL A WASTE...
TSU-KUNE ...
M...MS. ISHIGAMI ...?
I'M SORRY.
GRP...
I CAN'T LET YOU GO.

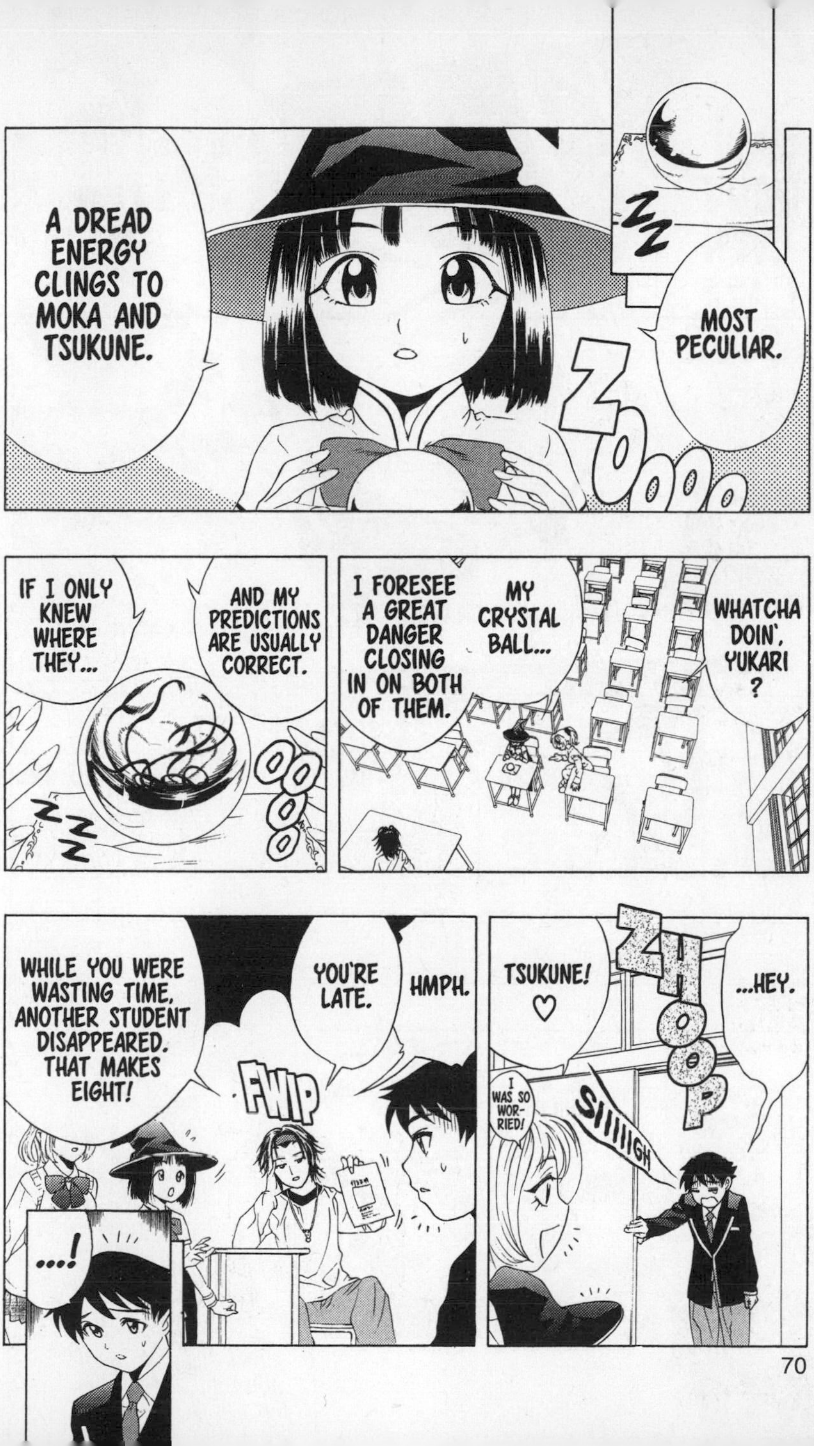
ZZ
MOST PECULIAR.
ZOOOO
A DREAD ENERGY CLINGS TO MOKA AND TSUKUNE.
WHATCHA DOIN', YUKARI ?
MY CRYSTAL BALL...
I FORESEE A GREAT DANGER CLOSING IN ON BOTH OF THEM.
AND MY PREDICTIONS ARE USUALLY CORRECT.
IF I ONLY KNEW WHERE THEY...
OOOO
ZZZ
...HEY.
ZHOOOP
TSUKUNE! ♡
SIIIIIGH
I WAS SO WOR-RIED!
HMPH.
YOU'RE LATE.
WHILE YOU WERE WASTING TIME, ANOTHER STUDENT DISAPPEARED. THAT MAKES EIGHT!
FWIP
...!

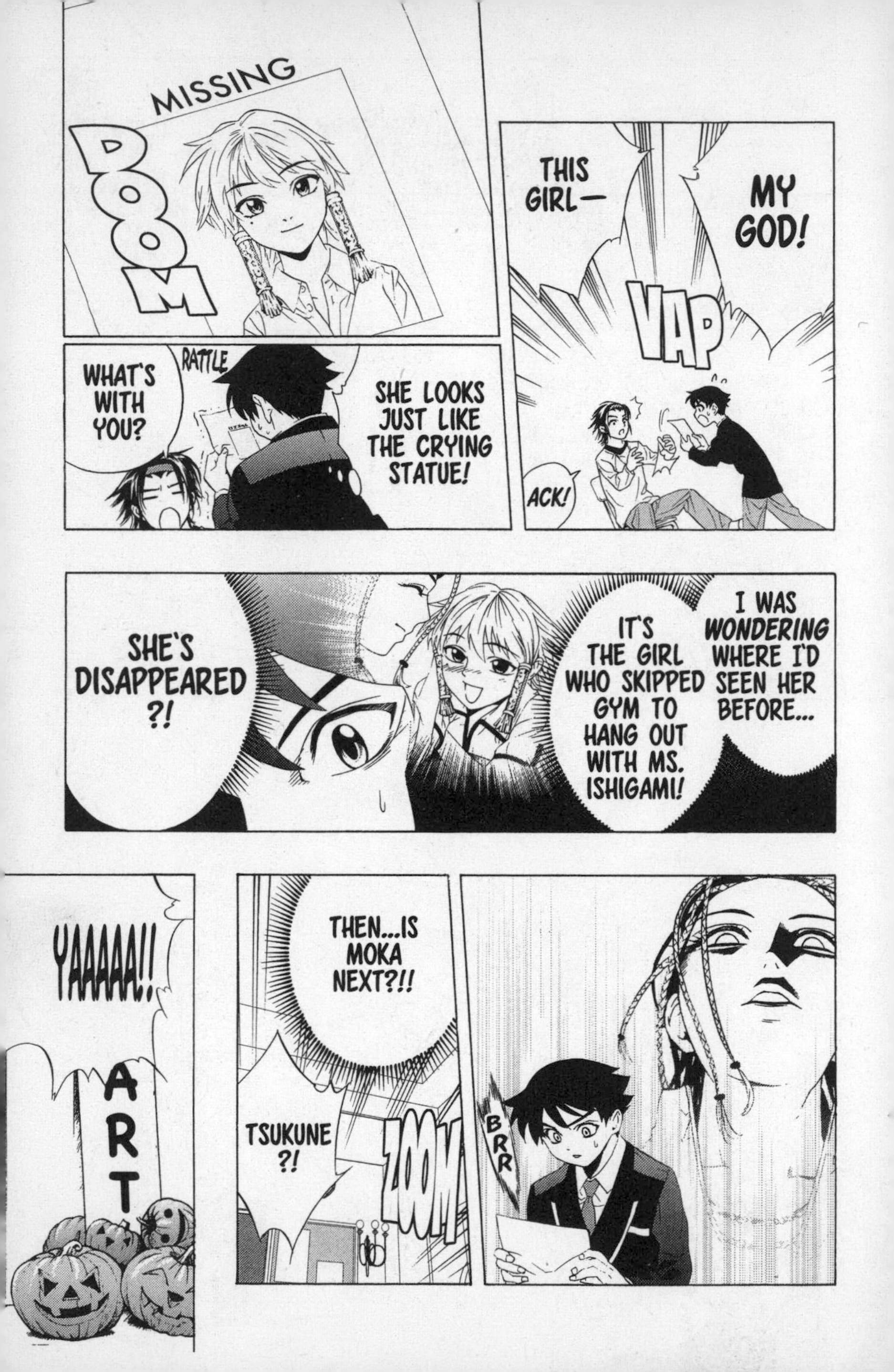
MY GOD!
THIS GIRL—
VAP
ACK!
MISSING
DOOM
SHE LOOKS JUST LIKE THE CRYING STATUE!
RATTLE
WHAT'S WITH YOU?
I WAS WONDERING WHERE I'D SEEN HER BEFORE...
IT'S THE GIRL WHO SKIPPED GYM TO HANG OUT WITH MS. ISHIGAMI!
SHE'S DISAPPEARED ?!
BRR
THEN...IS MOKA NEXT?!!
ZOOM
TSUKUNE ?!
YAAAAA!!
ART

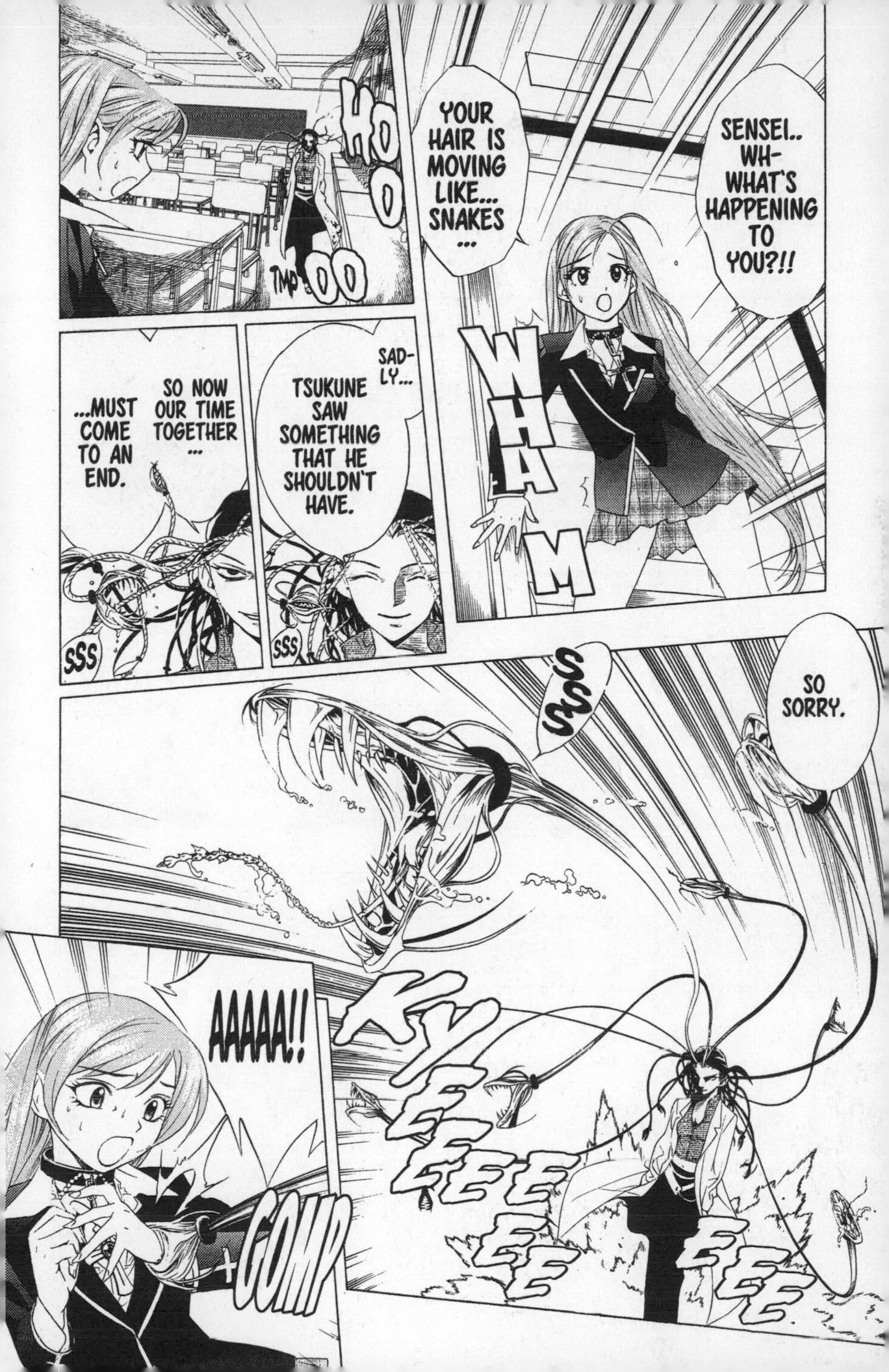

SENSEI.. WH- WHAT'S HAPPENING TO YOU?!!
YOUR HAIR IS MOVING LIKE... SNAKES ...
WHAM
HOOOOO
TMP
SAD-LY...
TSUKUNE SAW SOMETHING THAT HE SHOULDN'T HAVE.
SSS
SO NOW OUR TIME TOGETHER ...
...MUST COME TO AN END.
SSS
SO SORRY.
SSS
KYEEEEEEEEEEEE
AAAAA!!
GOMP

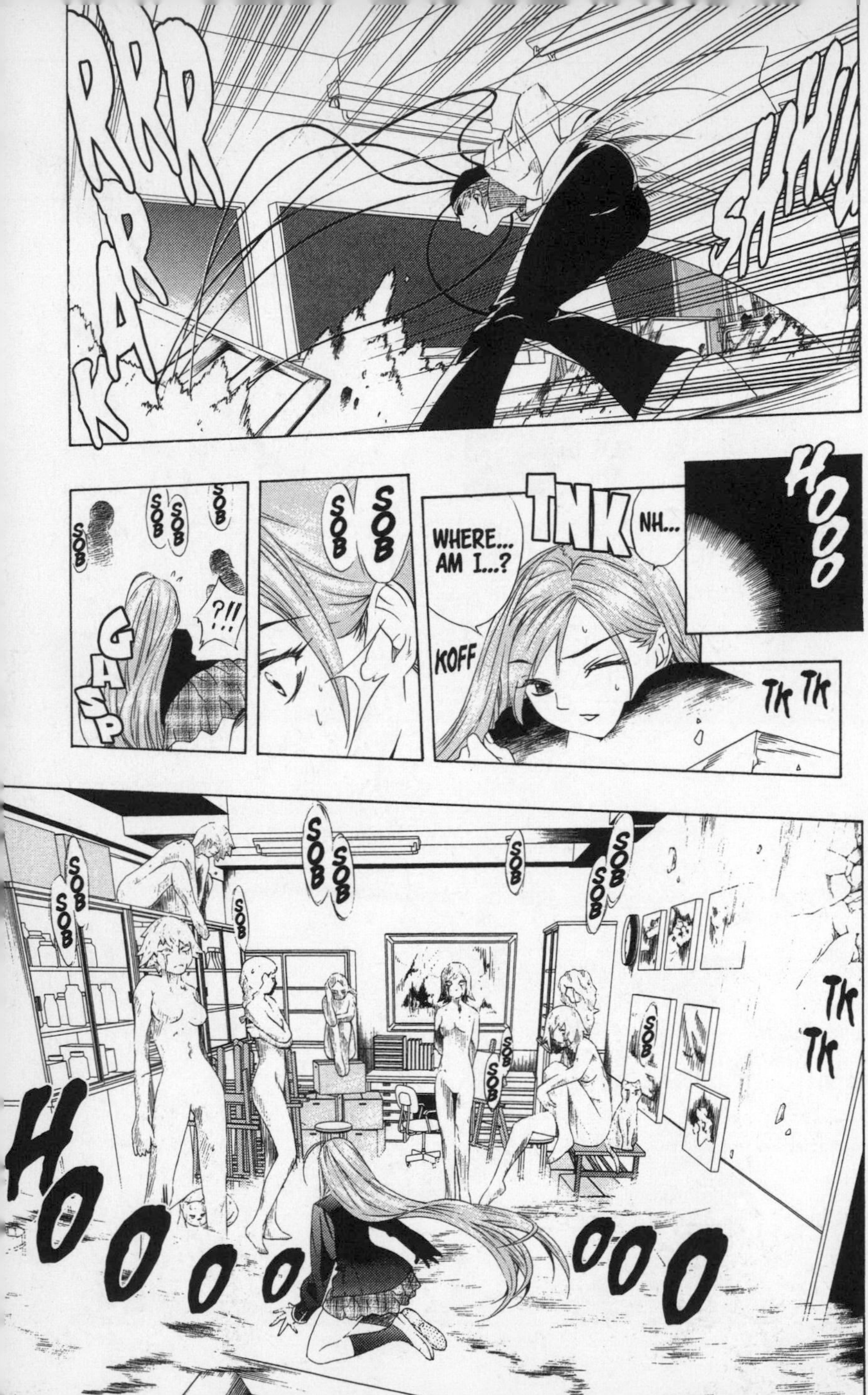
SHHU
RRRRAK
HOOO
TK TK
NH...
TNK
WHERE... AM I...?
KOFF
SOB SOB
SOB SOB SOB SOB
?!!
GASP
SOB SOB SOB SOB
SOB
SOB SOB
SOB SOB
SOB SOB
SOB
SOB SOB
SOB
TK TK
HOOOOOOOOO

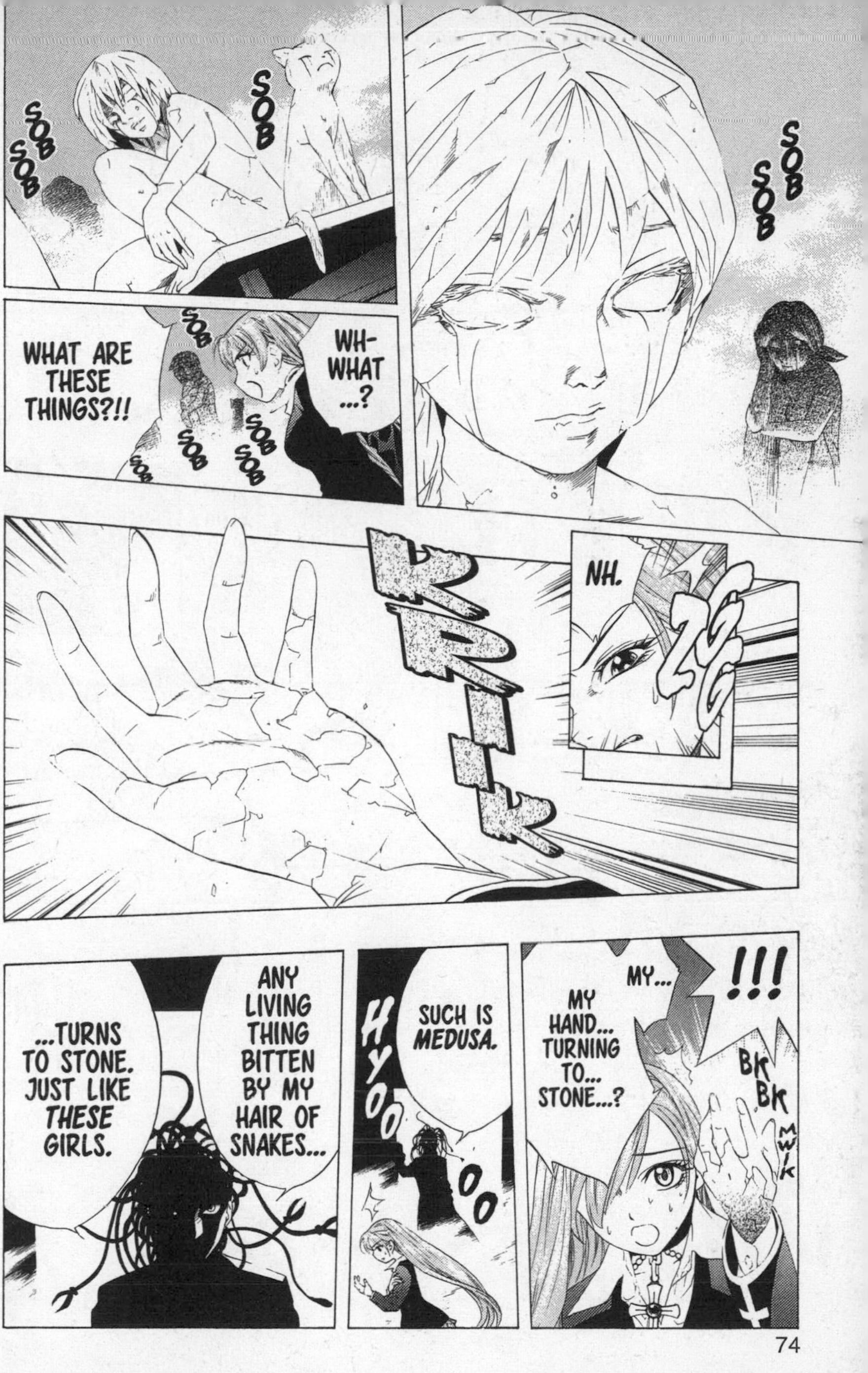
SOB SOB SOB
SOB SOB SOB
WH-WHAT...?
WHAT ARE THESE THINGS?!!
SOB SOB SOB SOB SOB
NH.
KRI-I-K
!!!
MY...
MY HAND... TURNING TO... STONE...?
BK BK
MWIK
SUCH IS *MEDUSA.*
HYOOOO
ANY LIVING THING BITTEN BY MY HAIR OF SNAKES...
...TURNS TO STONE. JUST LIKE *THESE* GIRLS.

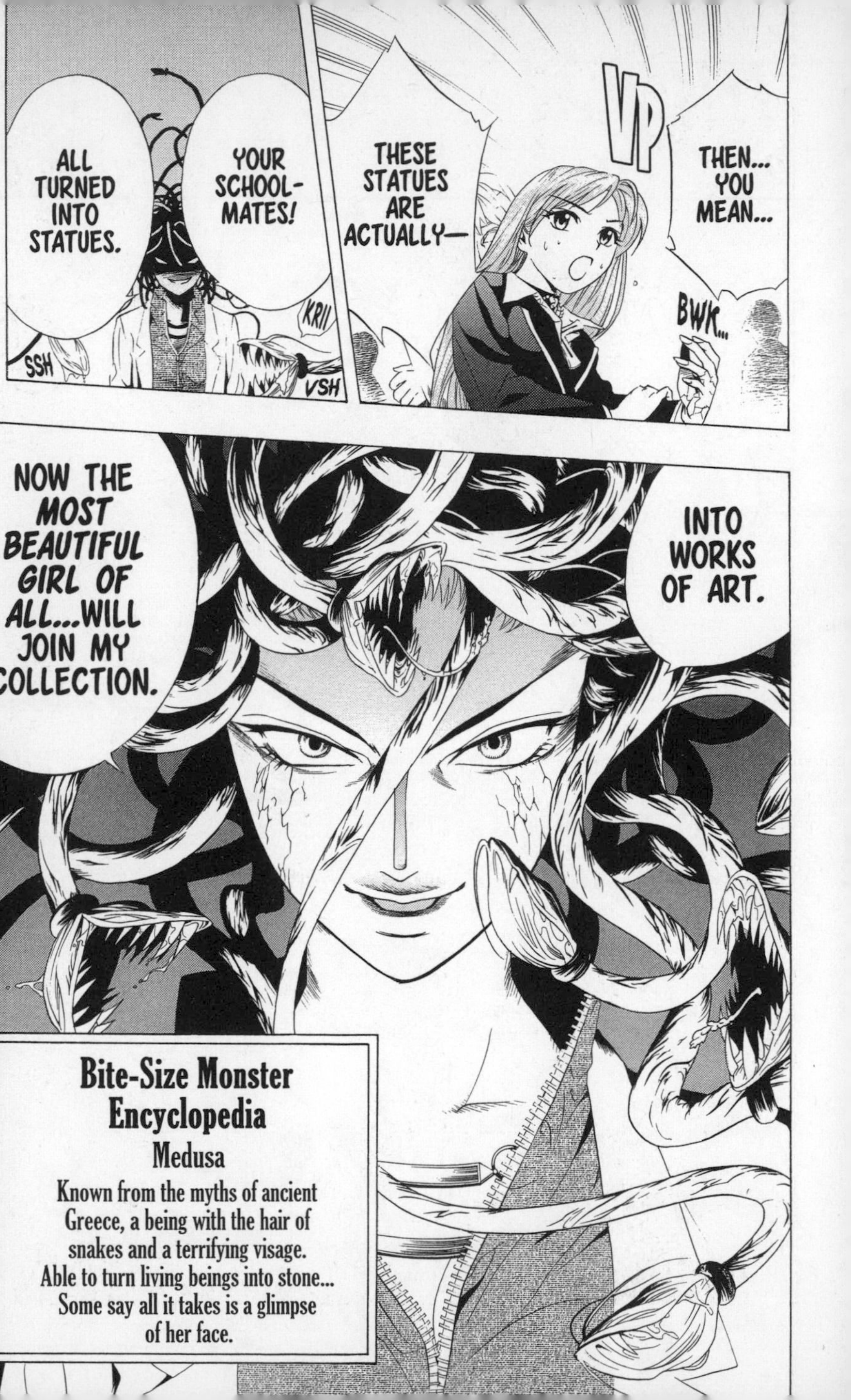
VP
THEN... YOU MEAN...
BWK...
THESE STATUES ARE ACTUALLY—
YOUR SCHOOL-MATES!
KRII
VSH
ALL TURNED INTO STATUES.
SSH
INTO WORKS OF ART.
NOW THE MOST BEAUTIFUL GIRL OF ALL...WILL JOIN MY COLLECTION.
Bite-Size Monster Encyclopedia
Medusa
Known from the myths of ancient Greece, a being with the hair of snakes and a terrifying visage. Able to turn living beings into stone... Some say all it takes is a glimpse of her face.

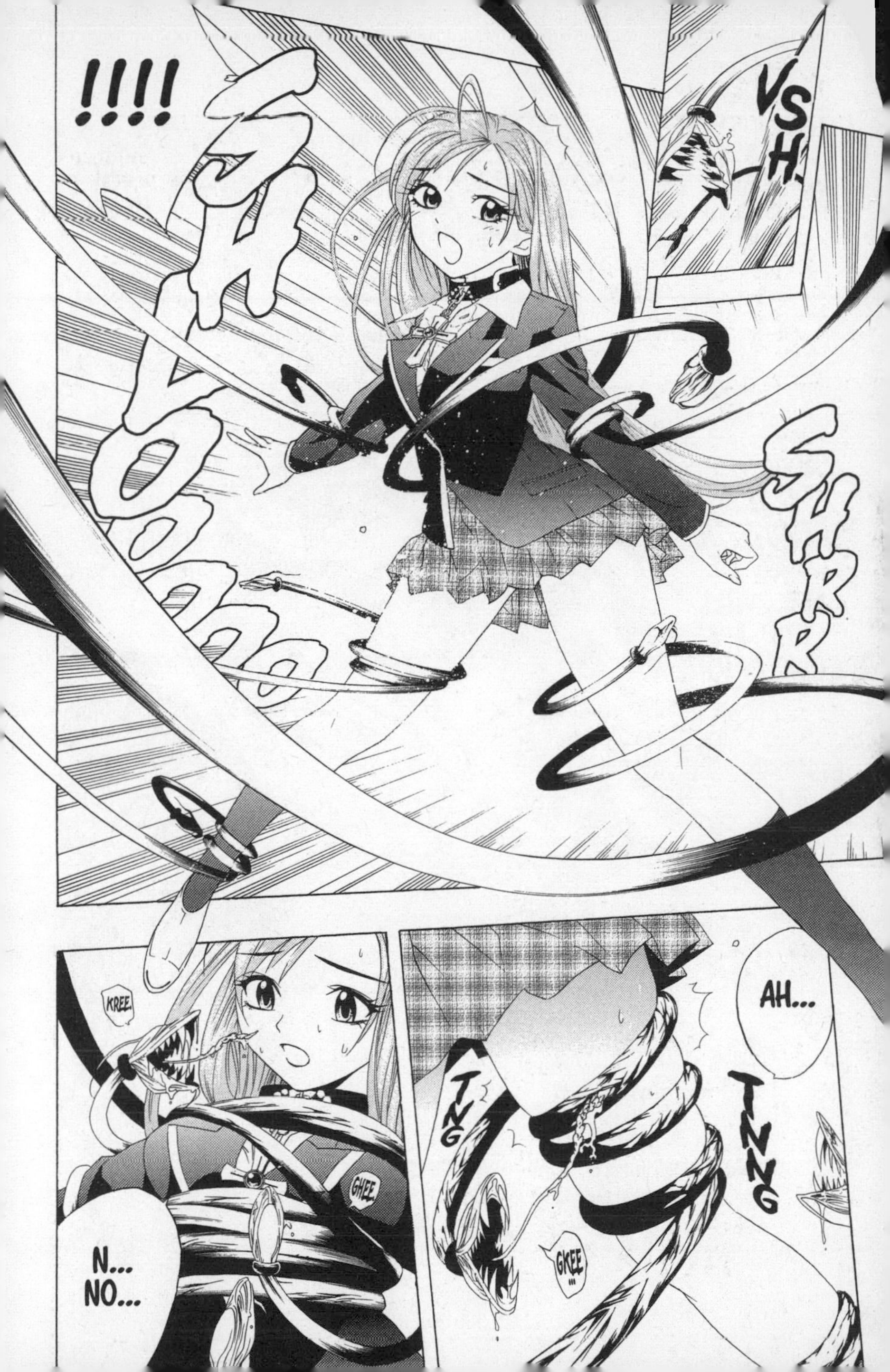
VSH
SHRR
!!!!
AH...
TNNG
TNG
GKEE...
KREE
GHEE
N... NO...

READ THIS WAY

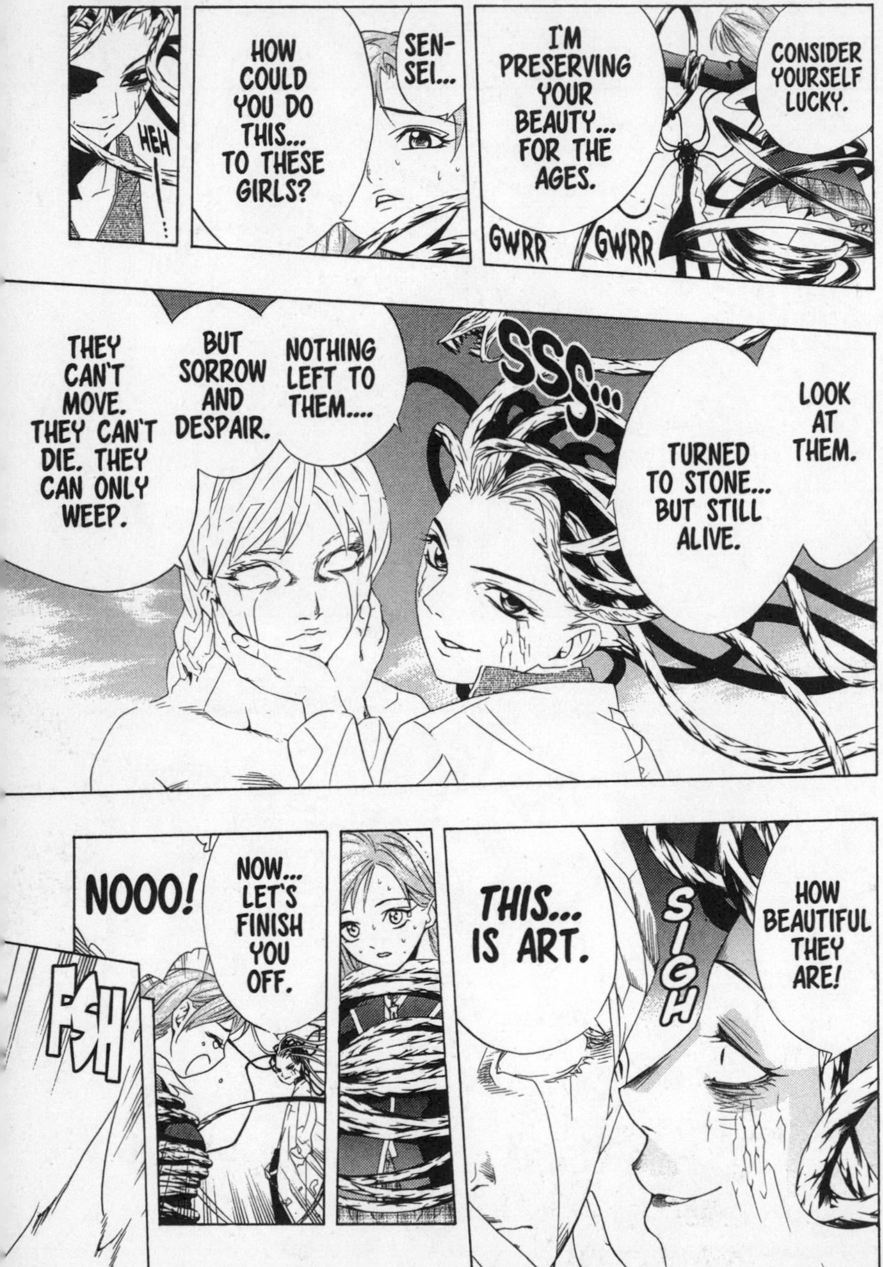

CONSIDER YOURSELF LUCKY.
I'M PRESERVING YOUR BEAUTY... FOR THE AGES.
GWRR
GWRR
SEN-SEI...
HOW COULD YOU DO THIS... TO THESE GIRLS?
HEH...
LOOK AT THEM.
TURNED TO STONE... BUT STILL ALIVE.
SSS...
NOTHING LEFT TO THEM....
BUT SORROW AND DESPAIR.
THEY CAN'T MOVE. THEY CAN'T DIE. THEY CAN ONLY WEEP.
HOW BEAUTIFUL THEY ARE!
SIGH
THIS... IS ART.
NOW... LET'S FINISH YOU OFF.
NOOO!
FSH

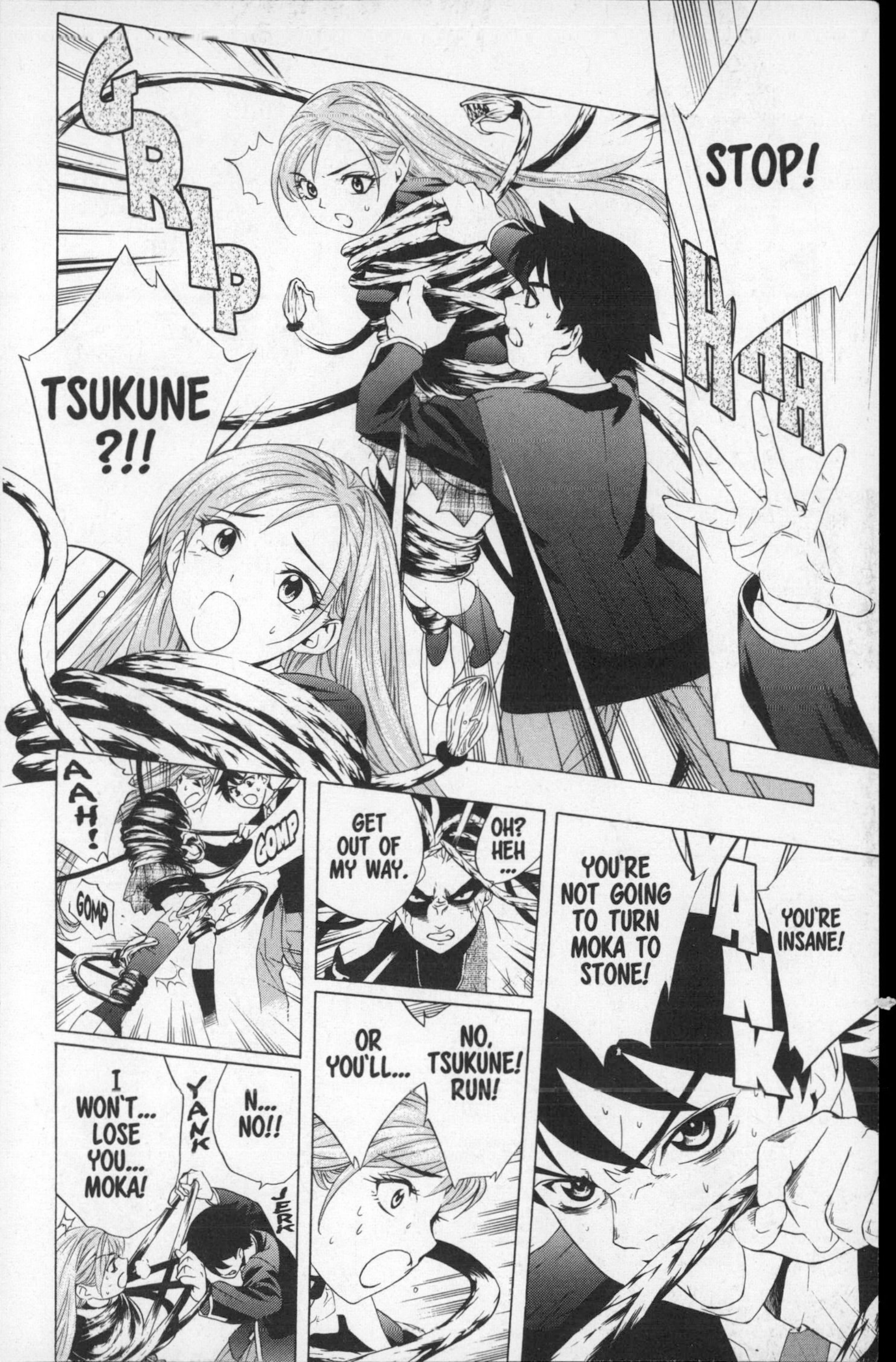
STOP!
GRIP
TSUKUNE ?!!
YANK
YOU'RE INSANE!
YOU'RE NOT GOING TO TURN MOKA TO STONE!
OH? HEH ...
GET OUT OF MY WAY.
AAH!
GOMP
GOMP
NO, TSUKUNE! RUN!
OR YOU'LL...
N... NO!!
YANK
I WON'T... LOSE YOU... MOKA!
JERK

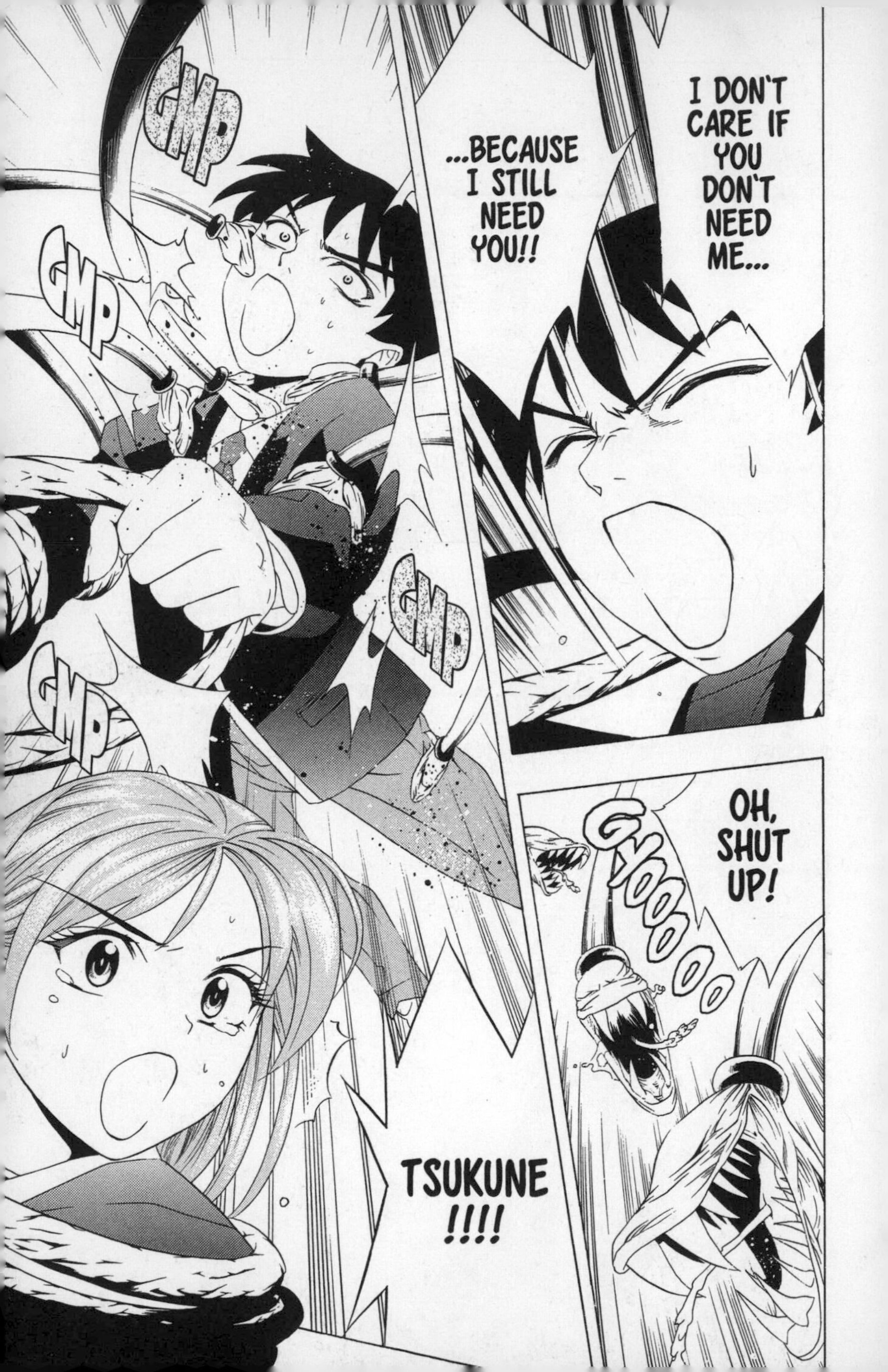
I DON'T CARE IF YOU DON'T NEED ME...
...BECAUSE I STILL NEED YOU!!
OH, SHUT UP!
GYOOOOO
GMP
GMP
GMP
GMP
TSUKUNE !!!!

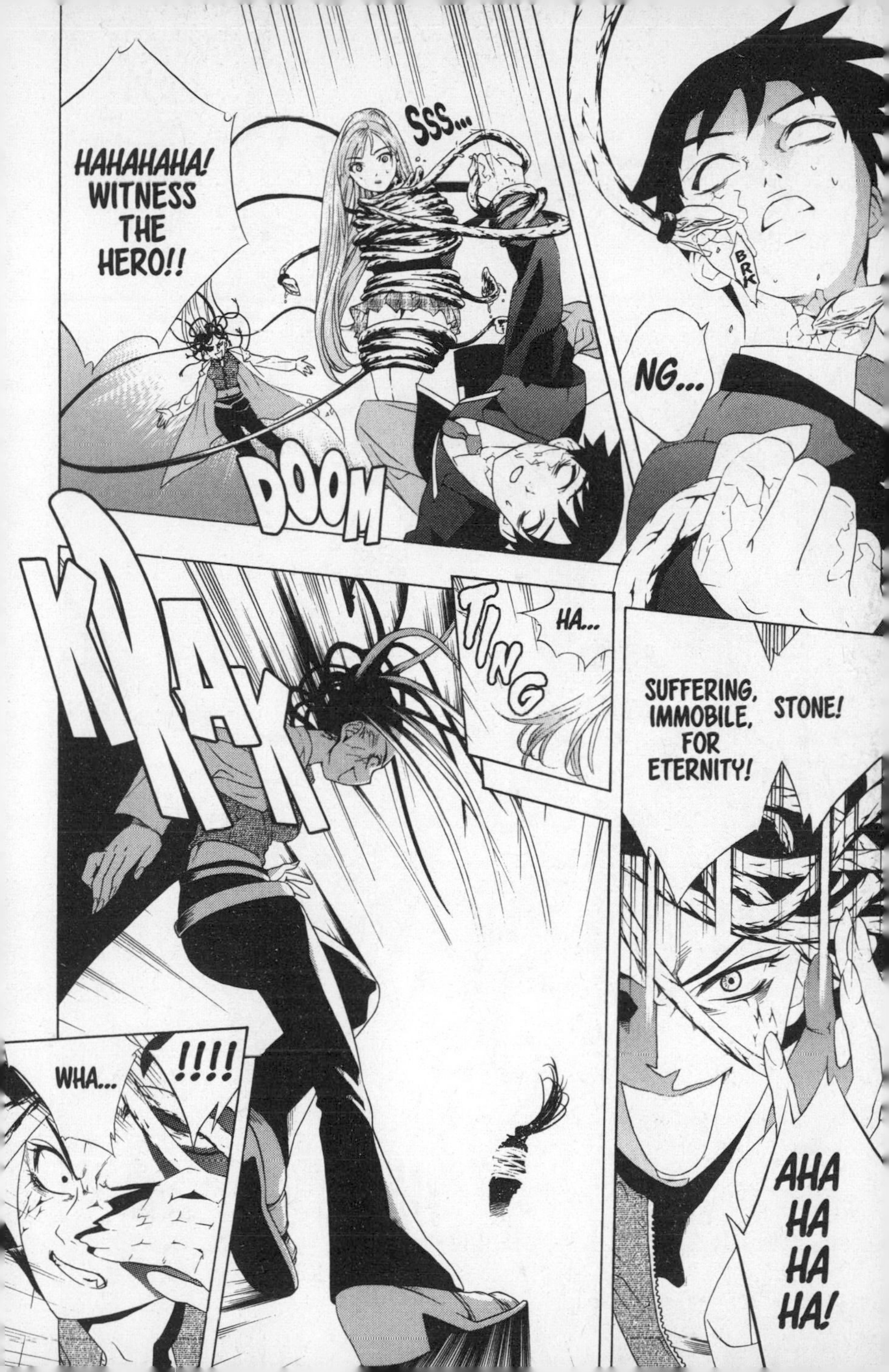
BRK
NG...
HAHAHAHA! WITNESS THE HERO!!
SSS...
DOOM
STONE!
SUFFERING, IMMOBILE, FOR ETERNITY!
AHA HA HA HA HA!
HA...
TING
KWAM
!!!!
WHA...

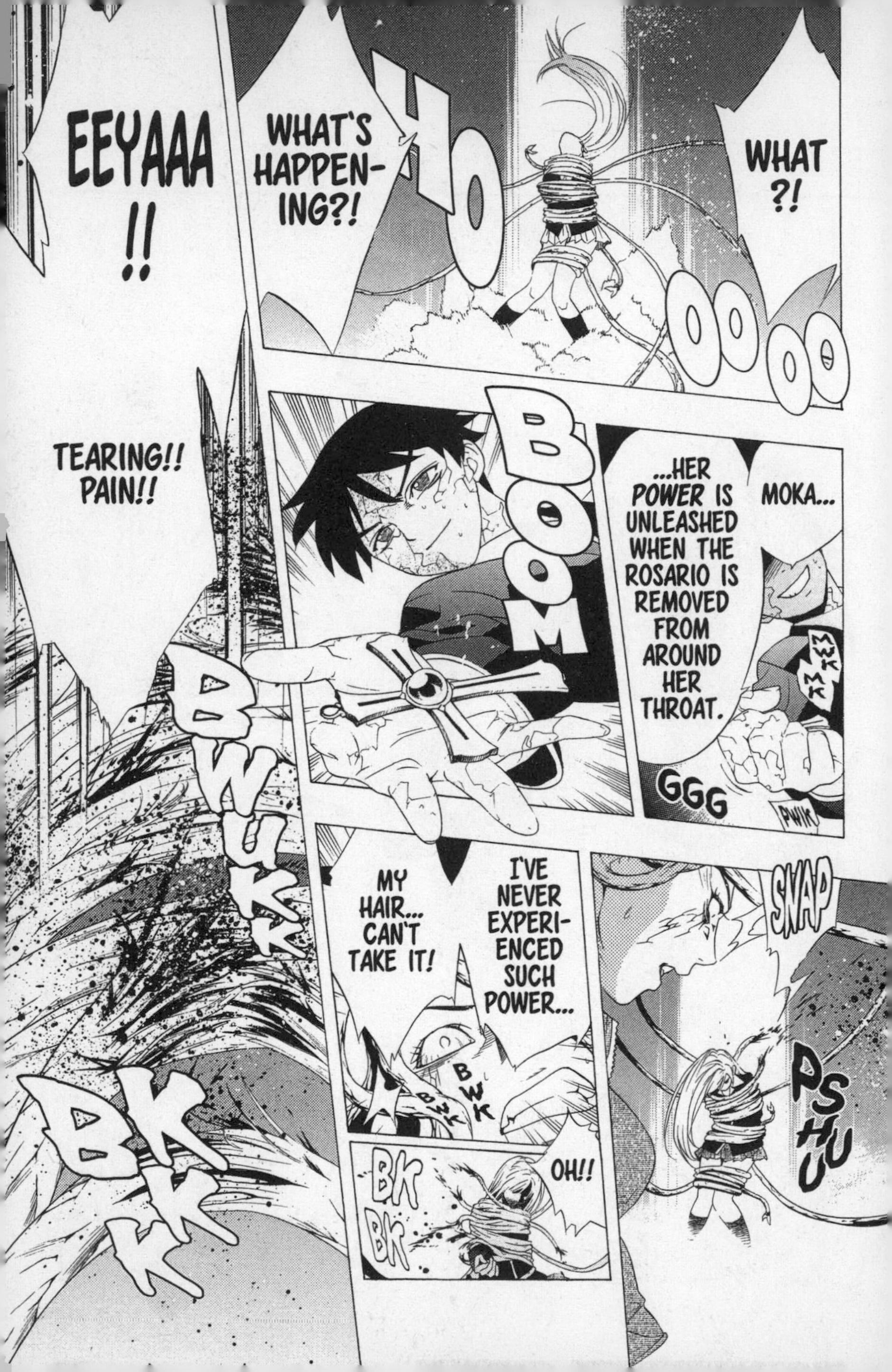
WHAT ?!
HOOOOOO
WHAT'S HAPPEN-ING?!
MOKA...
...HER POWER IS UNLEASHED WHEN THE ROSARIO IS REMOVED FROM AROUND HER THROAT.
MWK MK
GGG
PWIK
BOOM
SNAP
PSHUU
I'VE NEVER EXPERI-ENCED SUCH POWER...
MY HAIR... CAN'T TAKE IT!
BWK BWK
OH!!
BK BK
EEYAAA !!
TEARING!! PAIN!!
BWKK
BKKK

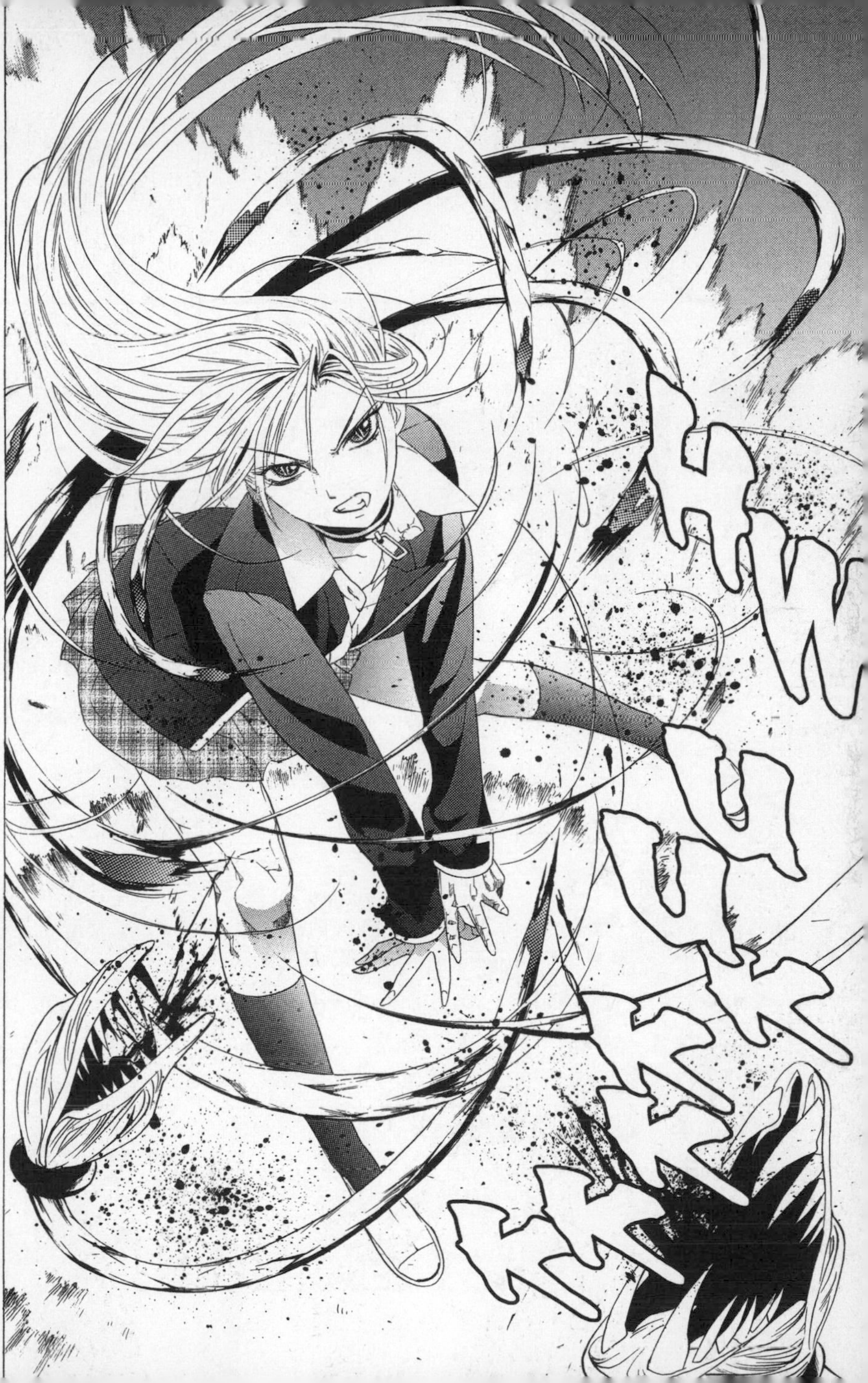
HWUUKKKK

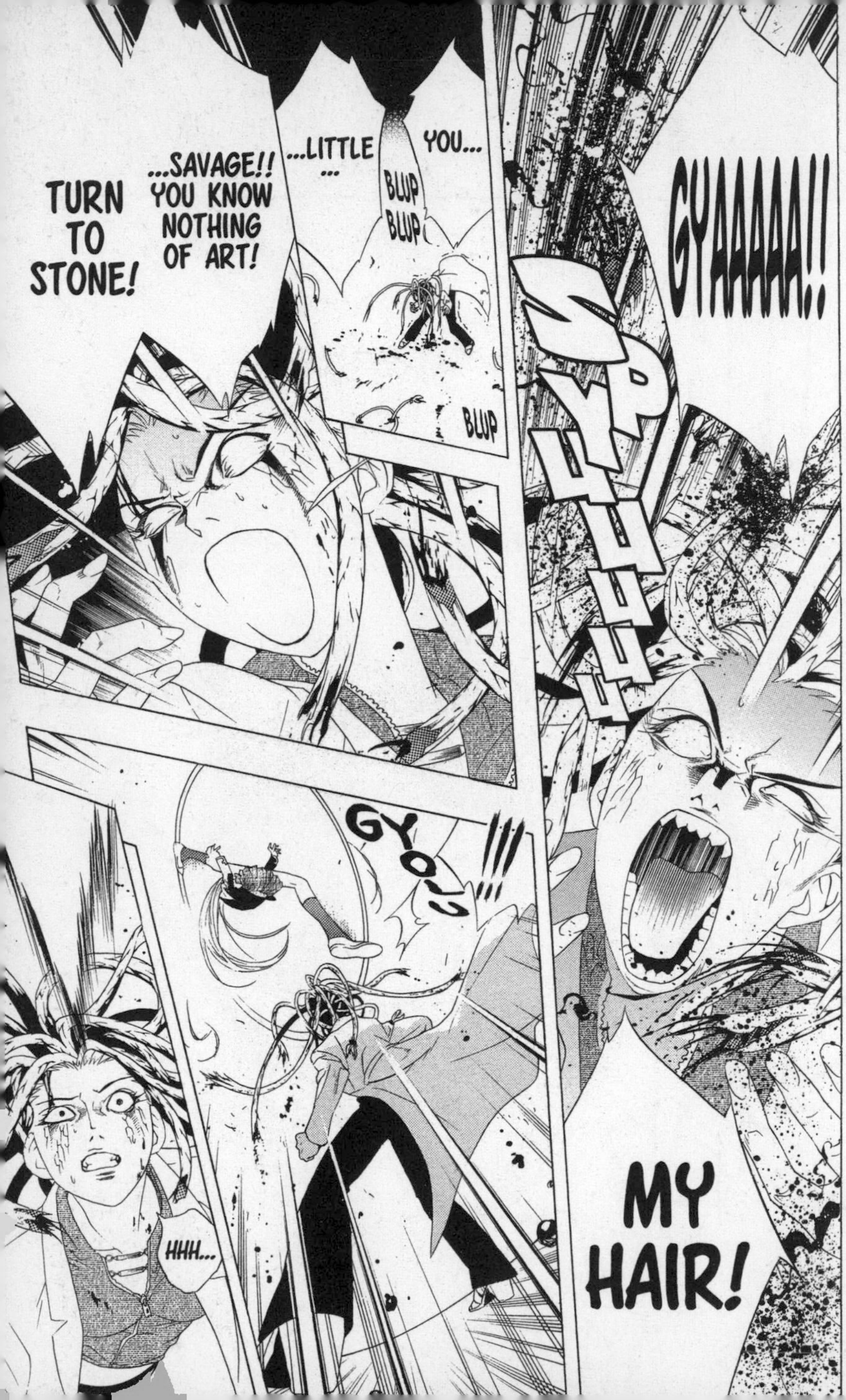
GYAAAAA!!
SPUUUUU
MY HAIR!
YOU...
...LITTLE ...
BLUP BLUP
BLUP
...SAVAGE!! YOU KNOW NOTHING OF ART!
TURN TO STONE!
GYO!!!
HHH...

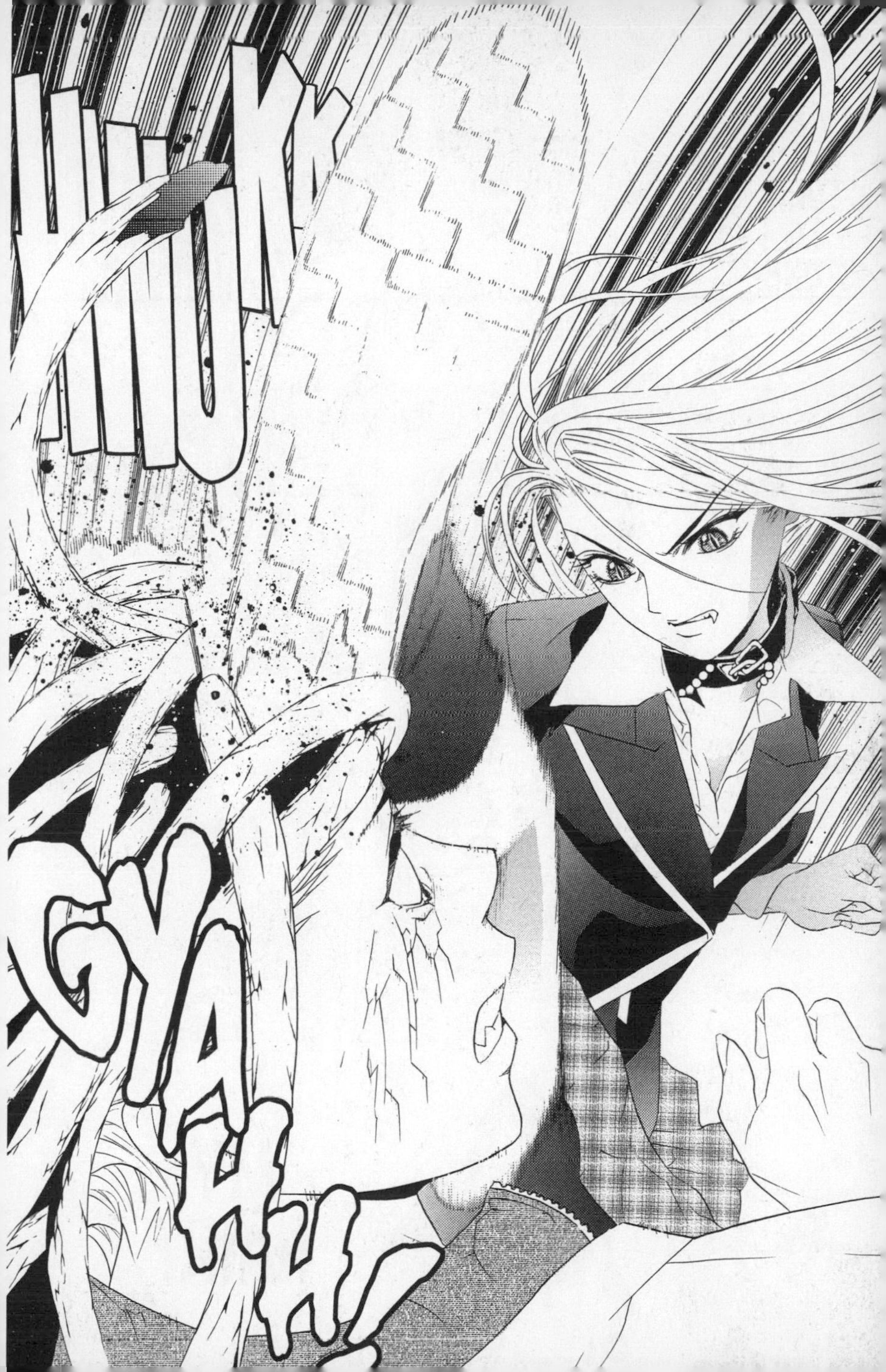
WHUKK
GYAAH!

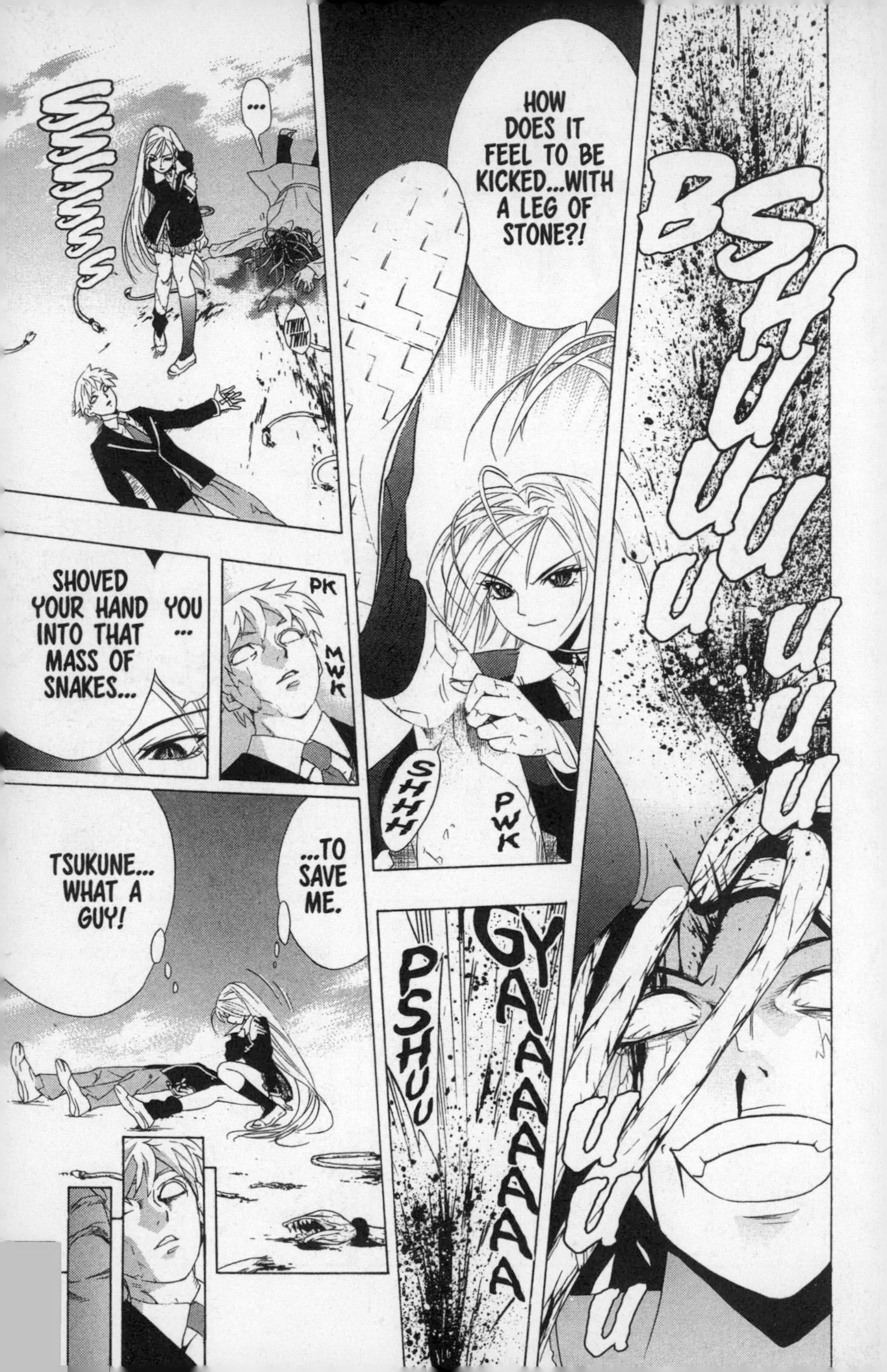
BSHUUUUUUUUUU
HOW DOES IT FEEL TO BE KICKED...WITH A LEG OF STONE?!
SHHH
PWK
...
SSSSSSS
TWIK TWIK
SHOVED YOUR HAND INTO THAT MASS OF SNAKES...
YOU ...
PK
MWK
GYAAAAAAAAA
PSHUU
...TO SAVE ME.
TSUKUNE... WHAT A GUY!

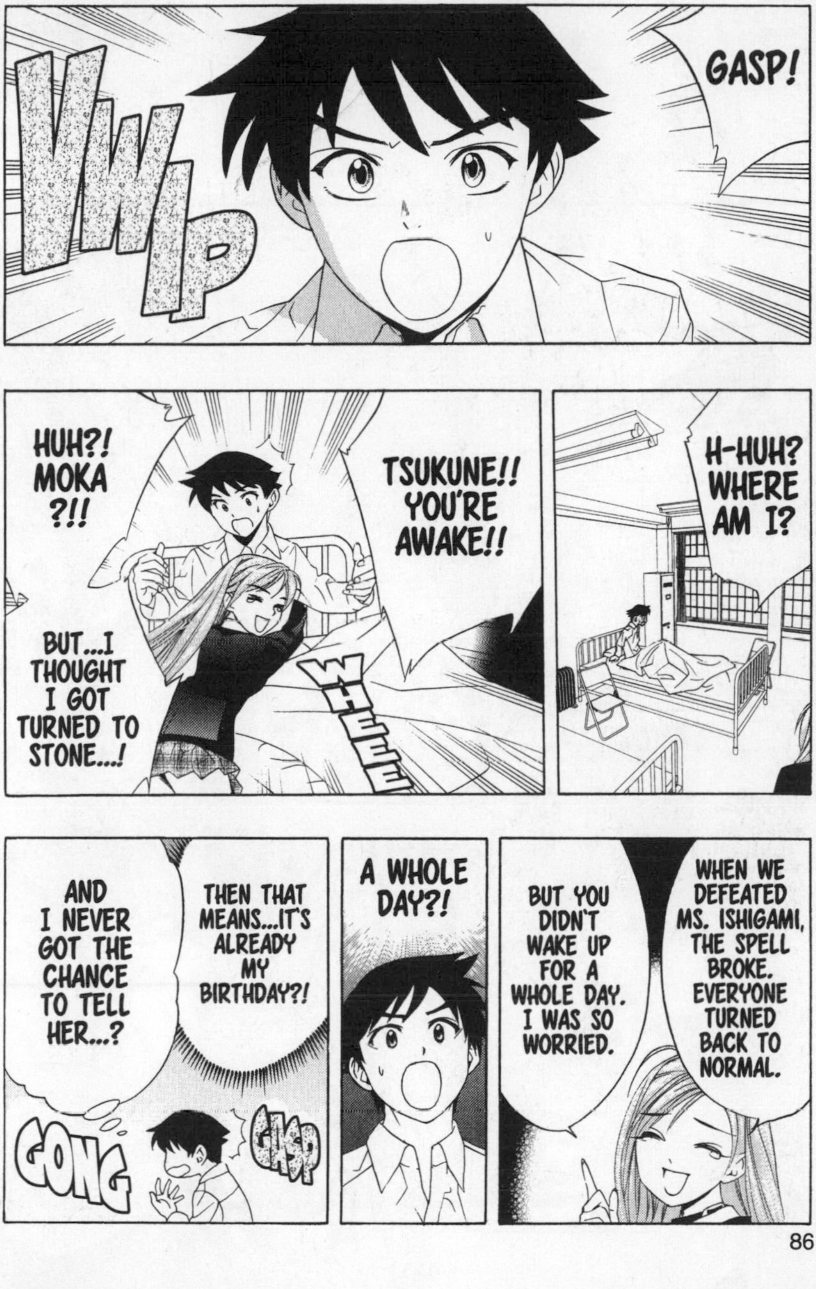
GASP!
VWIP
H-HUH? WHERE AM I?
TSUKUNE!! YOU'RE AWAKE!!
HUH?! MOKA ?!!
WHEEE
BUT...I THOUGHT I GOT TURNED TO STONE...!
WHEN WE DEFEATED MS. ISHIGAMI, THE SPELL BROKE. EVERYONE TURNED BACK TO NORMAL.
BUT YOU DIDN'T WAKE UP FOR A WHOLE DAY. I WAS SO WORRIED.
A WHOLE DAY?!
THEN THAT MEANS...IT'S ALREADY MY BIRTHDAY?!
AND I NEVER GOT THE CHANCE TO TELL HER...?
GONG

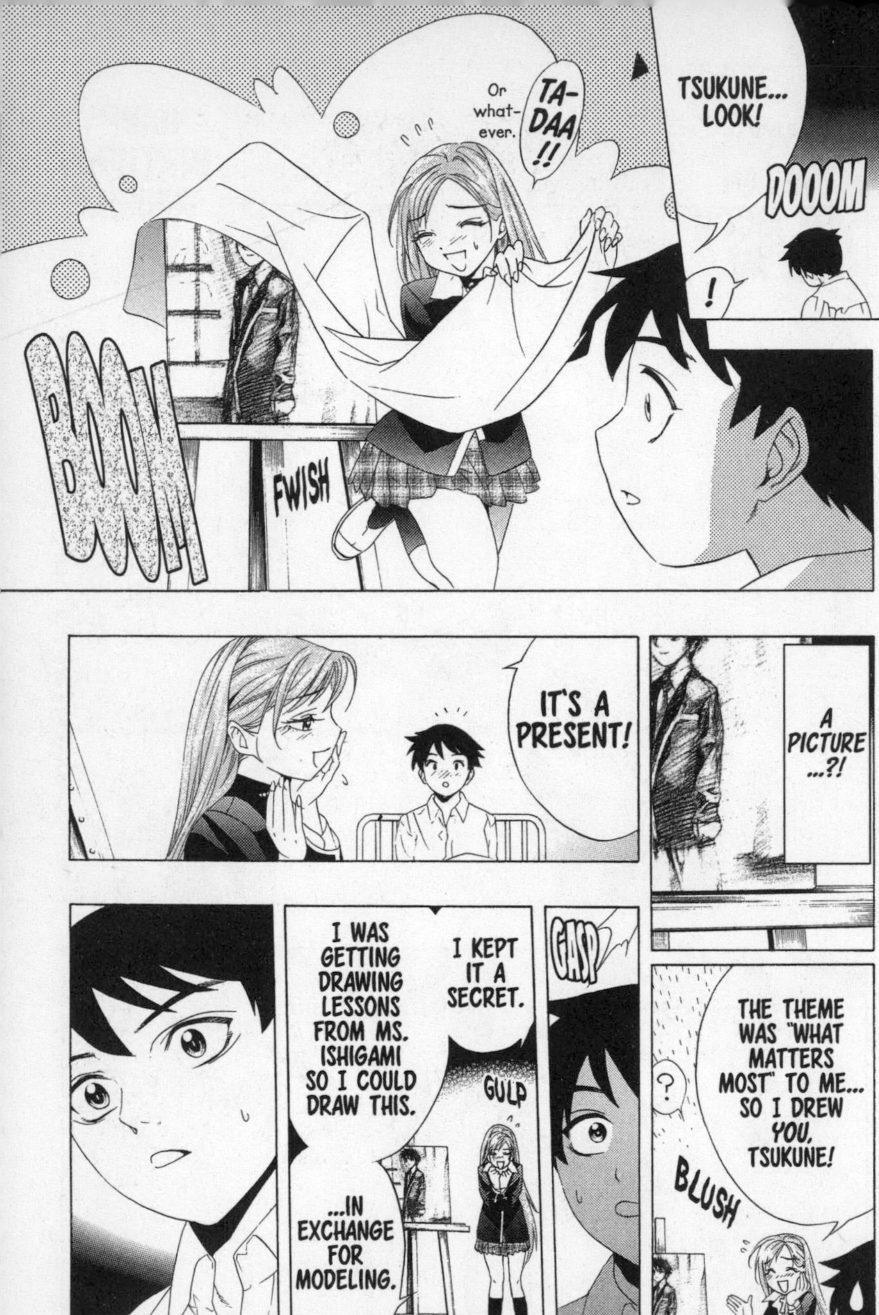
TSUKUNE... LOOK!
DOOOM
!
TA-DAA!!
Or whatever.
BOOM
FWISH
A PICTURE ...?!
IT'S A PRESENT!
THE THEME WAS "WHAT MATTERS MOST" TO ME... SO I DREW *YOU*, TSUKUNE!
?
BLUSH
GASP
I KEPT IT A SECRET.
I WAS GETTING DRAWING LESSONS FROM MS. ISHIGAMI SO I COULD DRAW THIS.
GULP
...IN EXCHANGE FOR MODELING.

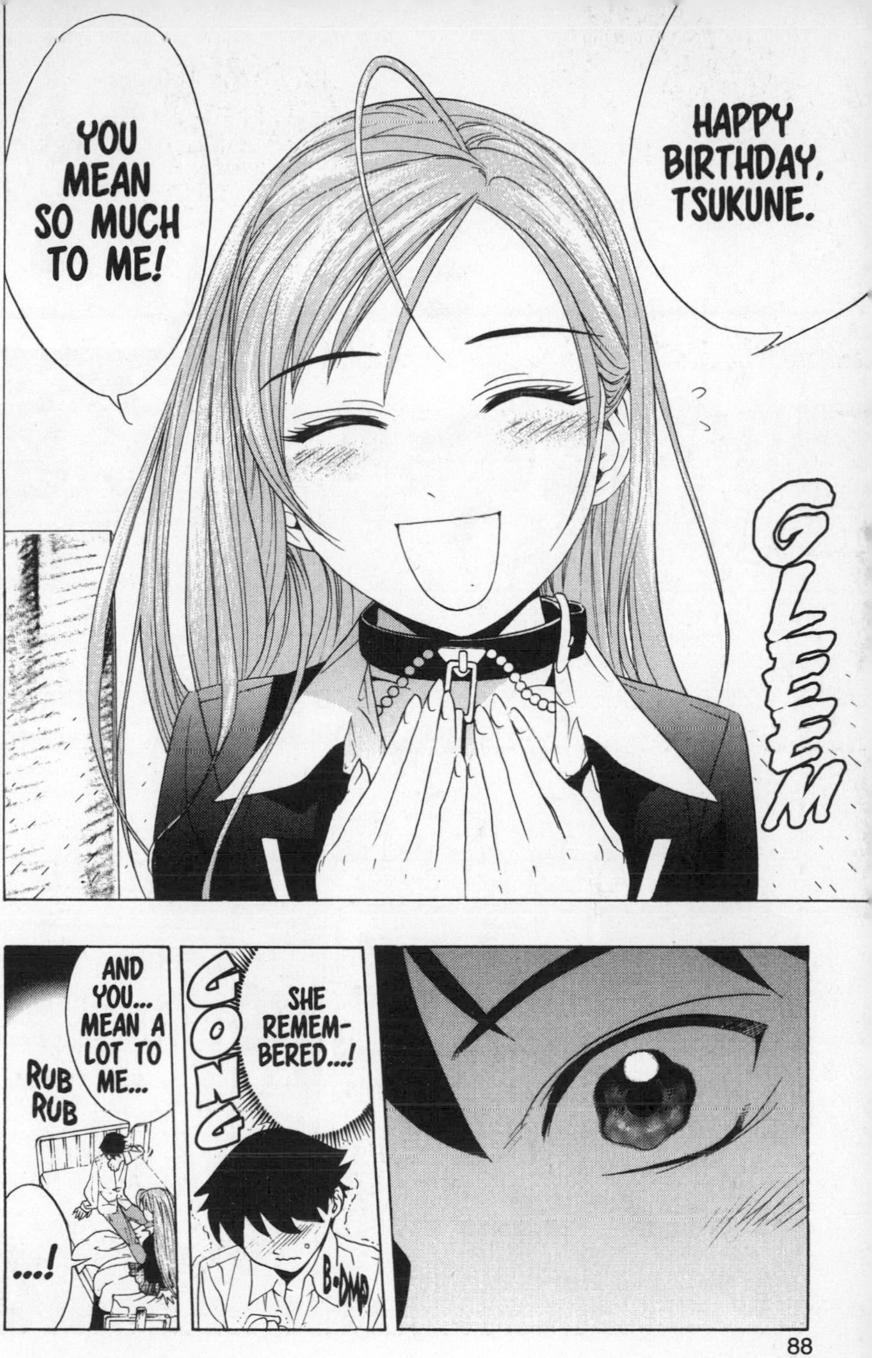
HAPPY BIRTHDAY, TSUKUNE.
GLEEM
YOU MEAN SO MUCH TO ME!
SHE REMEM-BERED...!
GONG
B-DMP
AND YOU... MEAN A LOT TO ME...
RUB RUB
...!

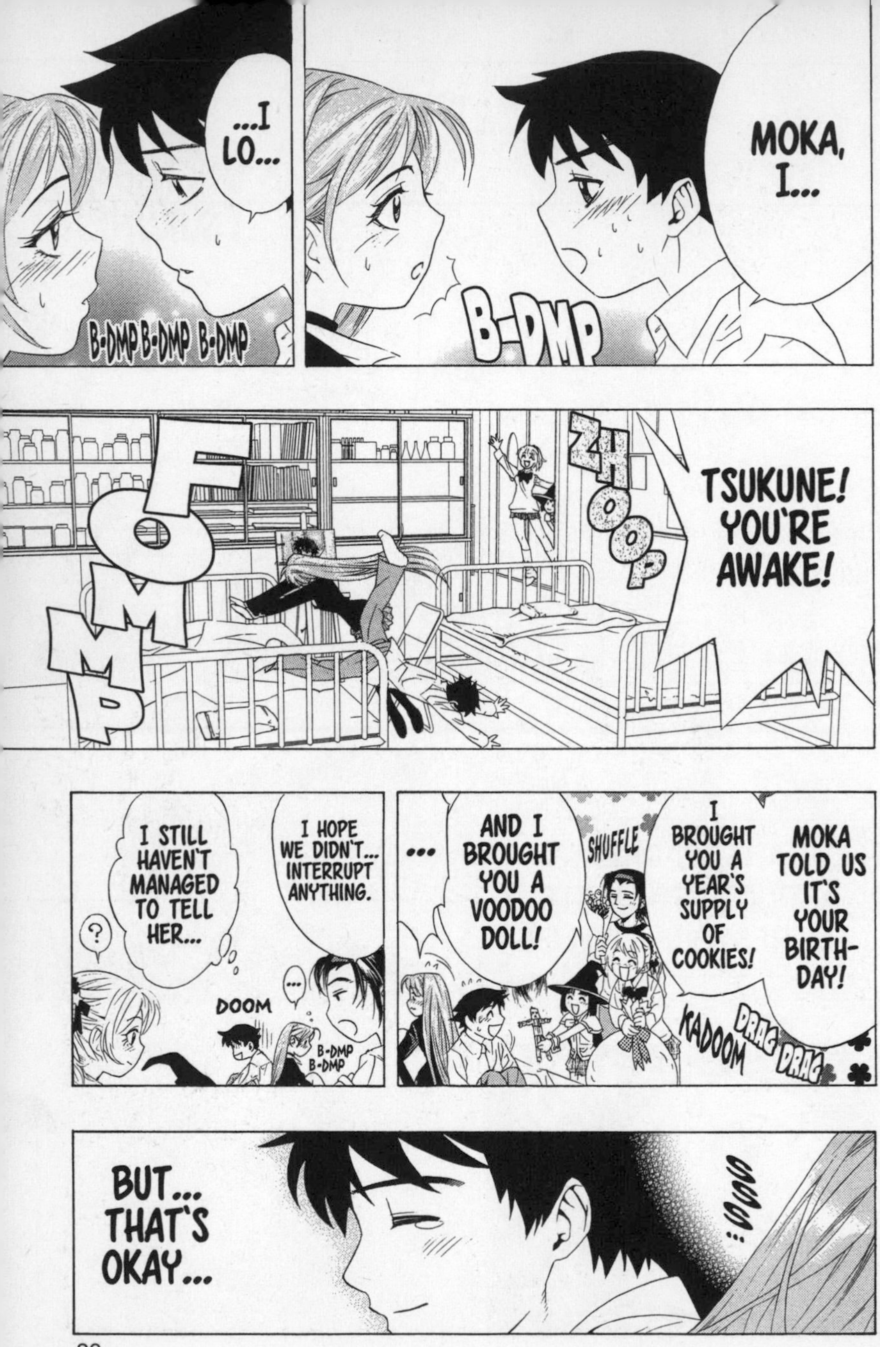

MOKA, I...
B-DMP
...I LO...
B-DMP B-DMP B-DMP
TSUKUNE! YOU'RE AWAKE!
ZHOOP
FOMMMP
MOKA TOLD US IT'S YOUR BIRTH-DAY!
I BROUGHT YOU A YEAR'S SUPPLY OF COOKIES!
SHUFFLE
AND I BROUGHT YOU A VOODOO DOLL!
...
DRAG DRAG
KADOOM
I HOPE WE DIDN'T... INTERRUPT ANYTHING.
...
B-DMP B-DMP
DOOM
I STILL HAVEN'T MANAGED TO TELL HER...
?
BUT... THAT'S OKAY...

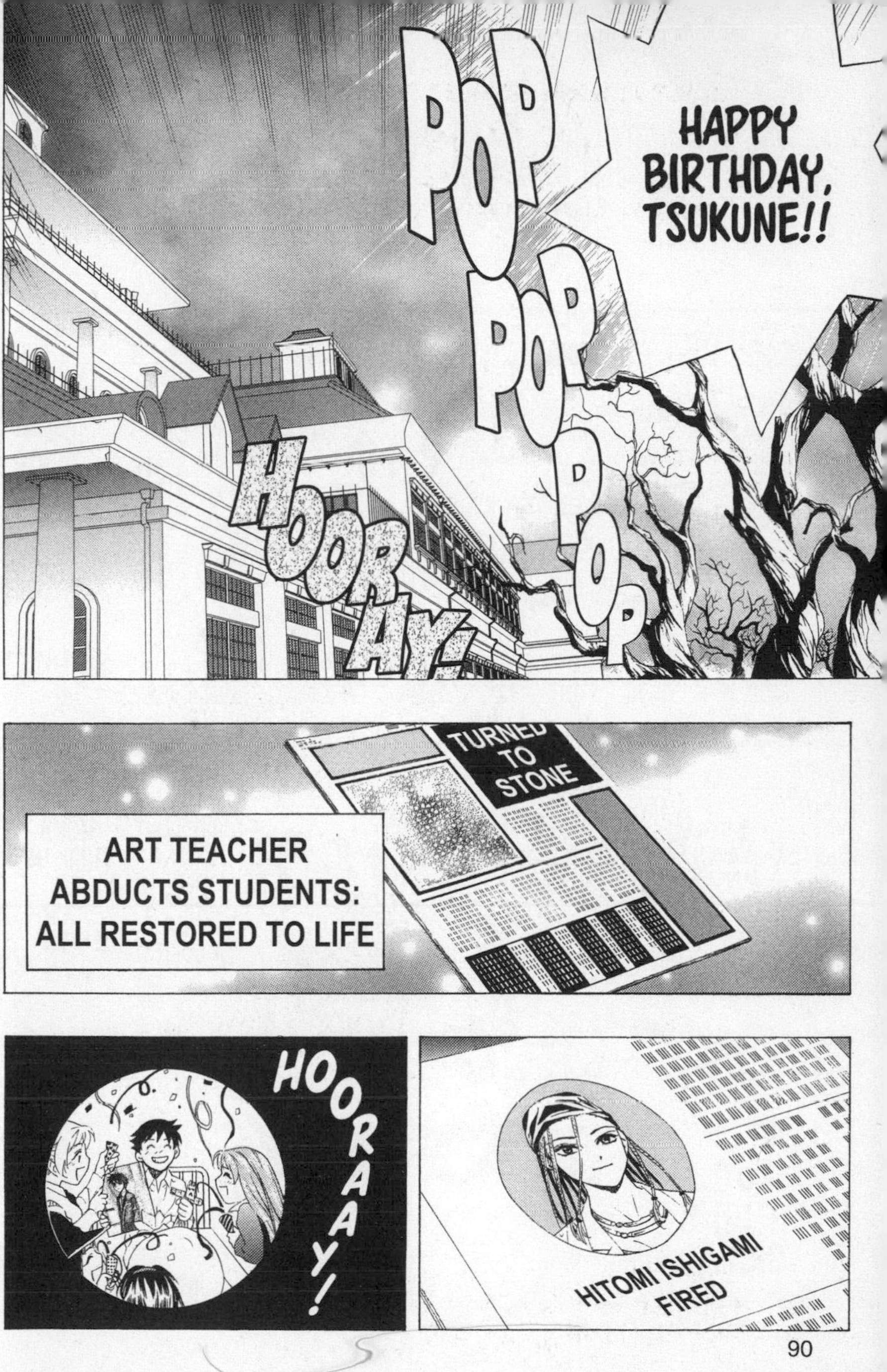
HAPPY BIRTHDAY, TSUKUNE!!
POP POP POP
HOORAY!
TURNED TO STONE
ART TEACHER ABDUCTS STUDENTS: ALL RESTORED TO LIFE
HITOMI ISHIGAMI FIRED
HOORAAAY!

7: Deadline!

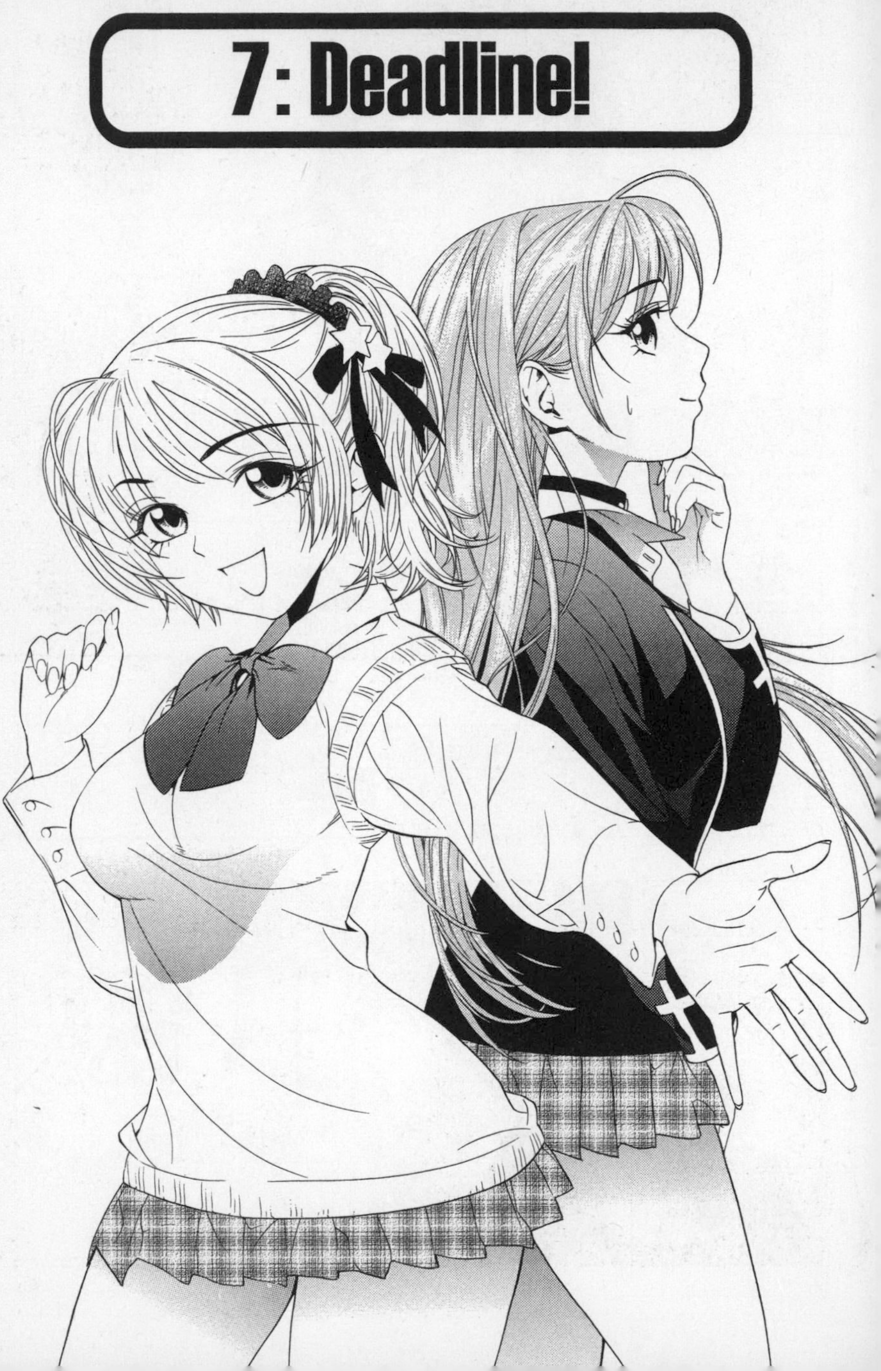

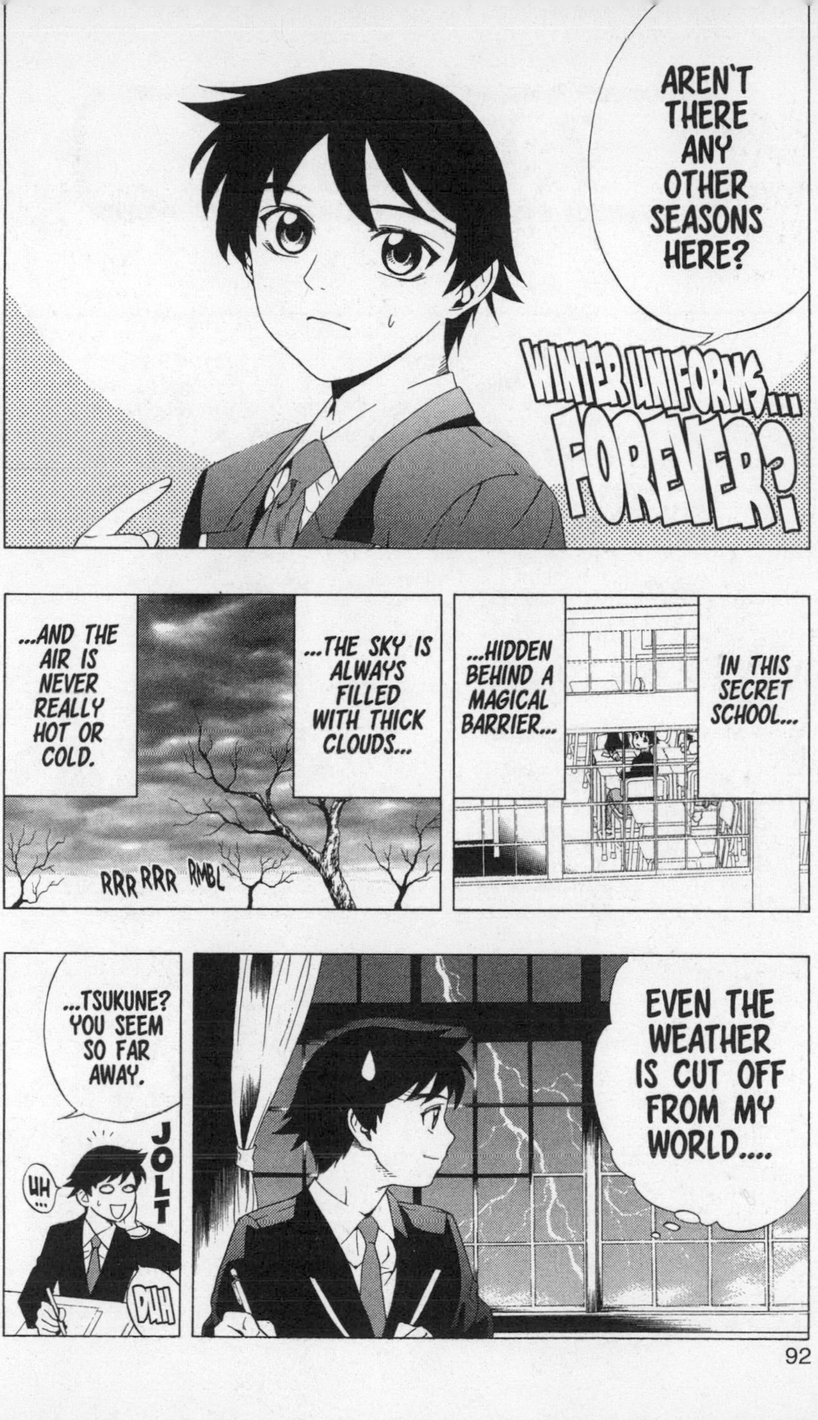
AREN'T THERE ANY OTHER SEASONS HERE?
WINTER UNIFORMS... FOREVER?
IN THIS SECRET SCHOOL...
...HIDDEN BEHIND A MAGICAL BARRIER...
...THE SKY IS ALWAYS FILLED WITH THICK CLOUDS...
...AND THE AIR IS NEVER REALLY HOT OR COLD.
RRR RRR RMBL
EVEN THE WEATHER IS CUT OFF FROM MY WORLD....
...TSUKUNE? YOU SEEM SO FAR AWAY.
JOLT
UH...
DUH

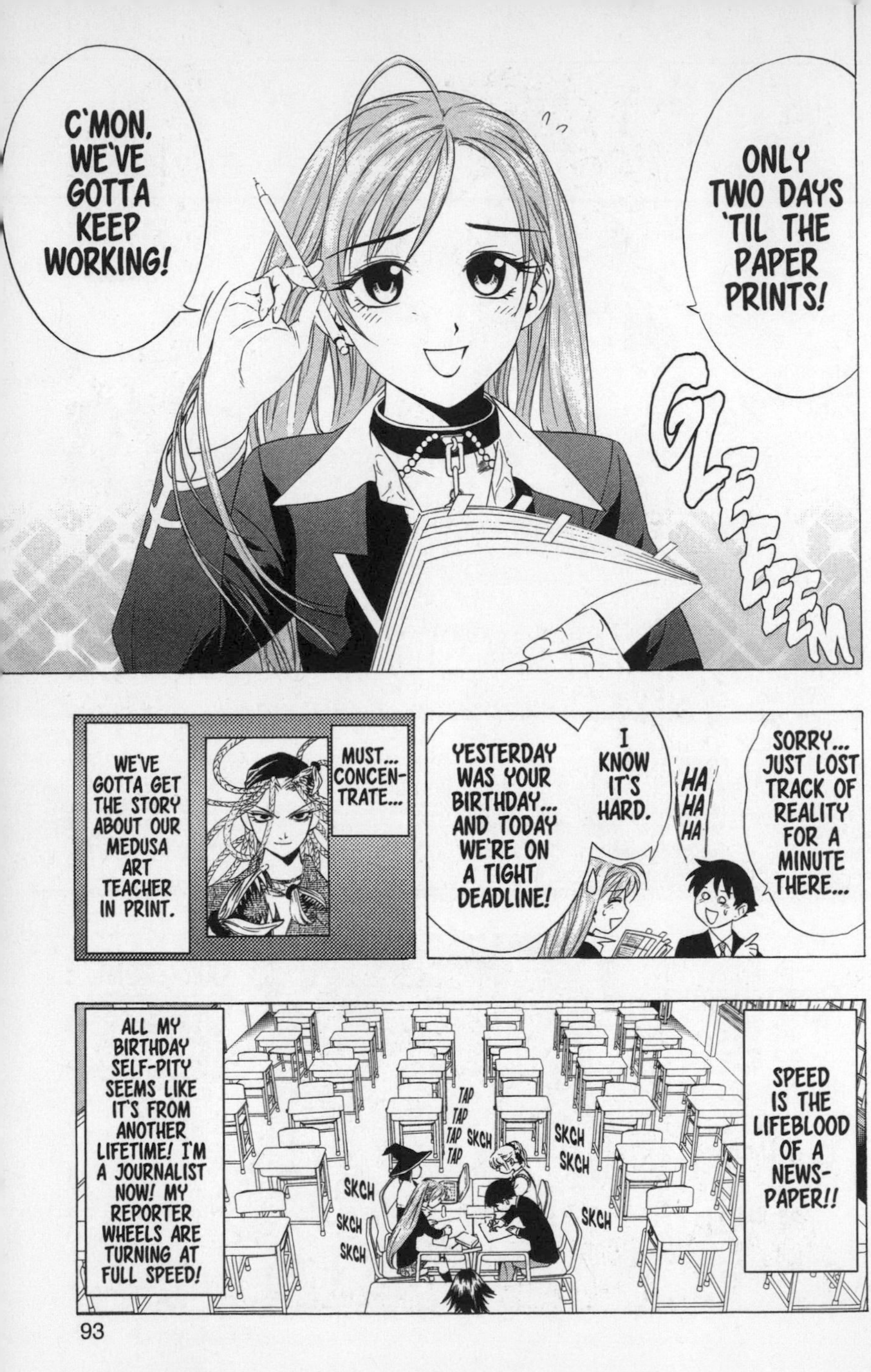
ONLY TWO DAYS 'TIL THE PAPER PRINTS!
C'MON, WE'VE GOTTA KEEP WORKING!
GLEEEEEM
SORRY... JUST LOST TRACK OF REALITY FOR A MINUTE THERE...
HA HA HA
I KNOW IT'S HARD.
YESTERDAY WAS YOUR BIRTHDAY... AND TODAY WE'RE ON A TIGHT DEADLINE!
MUST... CONCENTRATE...
WE'VE GOTTA GET THE STORY ABOUT OUR MEDUSA ART TEACHER IN PRINT.
SPEED IS THE LIFEBLOOD OF A NEWSPAPER!!
SKCH
SKCH SKCH
TAP TAP TAP TAP
SKCH
SKCH
SKCH SKCH
ALL MY BIRTHDAY SELF-PITY SEEMS LIKE IT'S FROM ANOTHER LIFETIME! I'M A JOURNALIST NOW! MY REPORTER WHEELS ARE TURNING AT FULL SPEED!

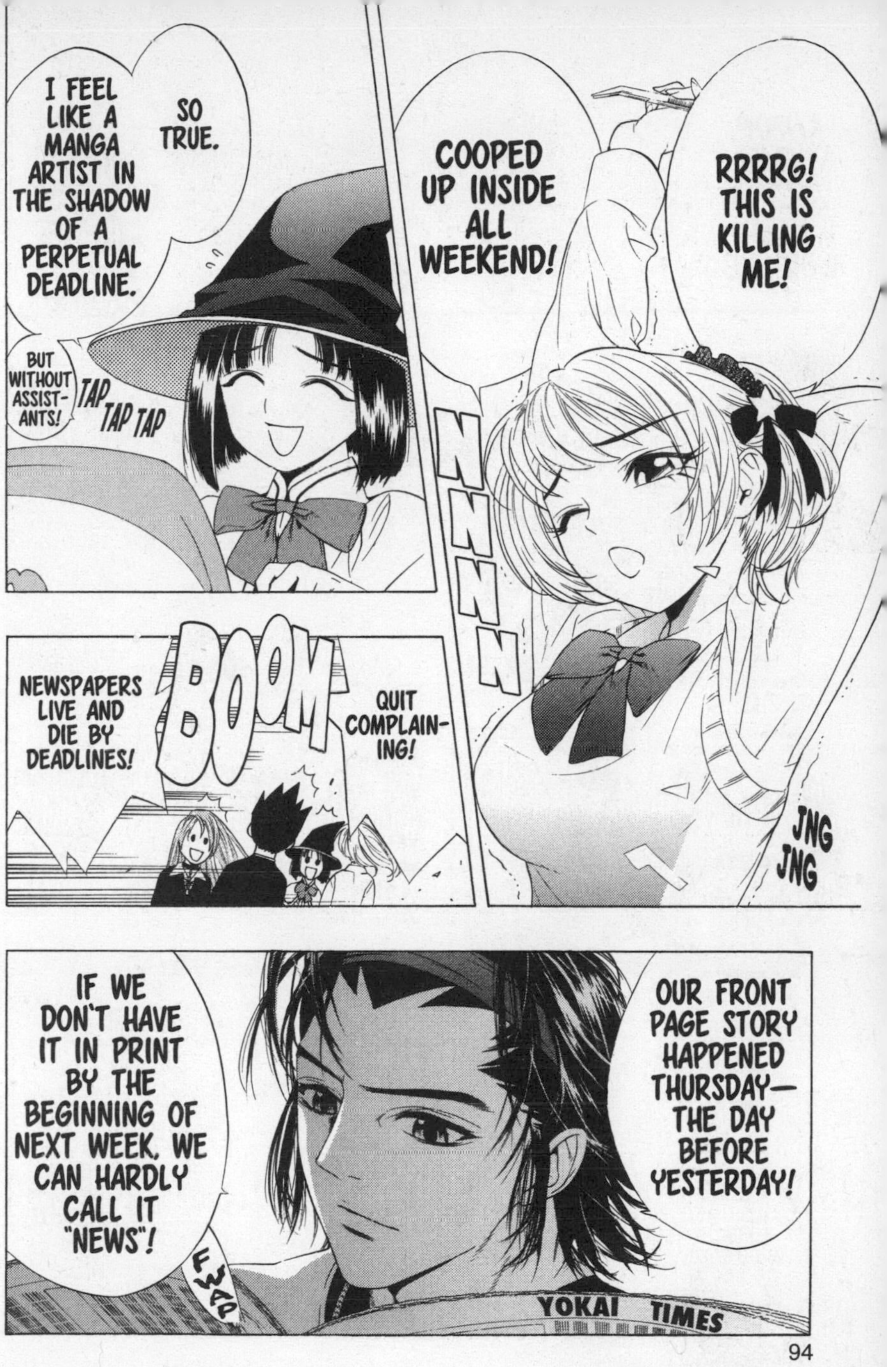
RRRRG! THIS IS KILLING ME!
COOPED UP INSIDE ALL WEEKEND!
NNNNN
JNG JNG
SO TRUE.
I FEEL LIKE A MANGA ARTIST IN THE SHADOW OF A PERPETUAL DEADLINE.
BUT WITHOUT ASSIST-ANTS!
TAP TAP TAP
QUIT COMPLAIN-ING!
BOOM
NEWSPAPERS LIVE AND DIE BY DEADLINES!
OUR FRONT PAGE STORY HAPPENED THURSDAY— THE DAY BEFORE YESTERDAY!
IF WE DON'T HAVE IT IN PRINT BY THE BEGINNING OF NEXT WEEK, WE CAN HARDLY CALL IT "NEWS"!
FWAP
YOKAI TIMES

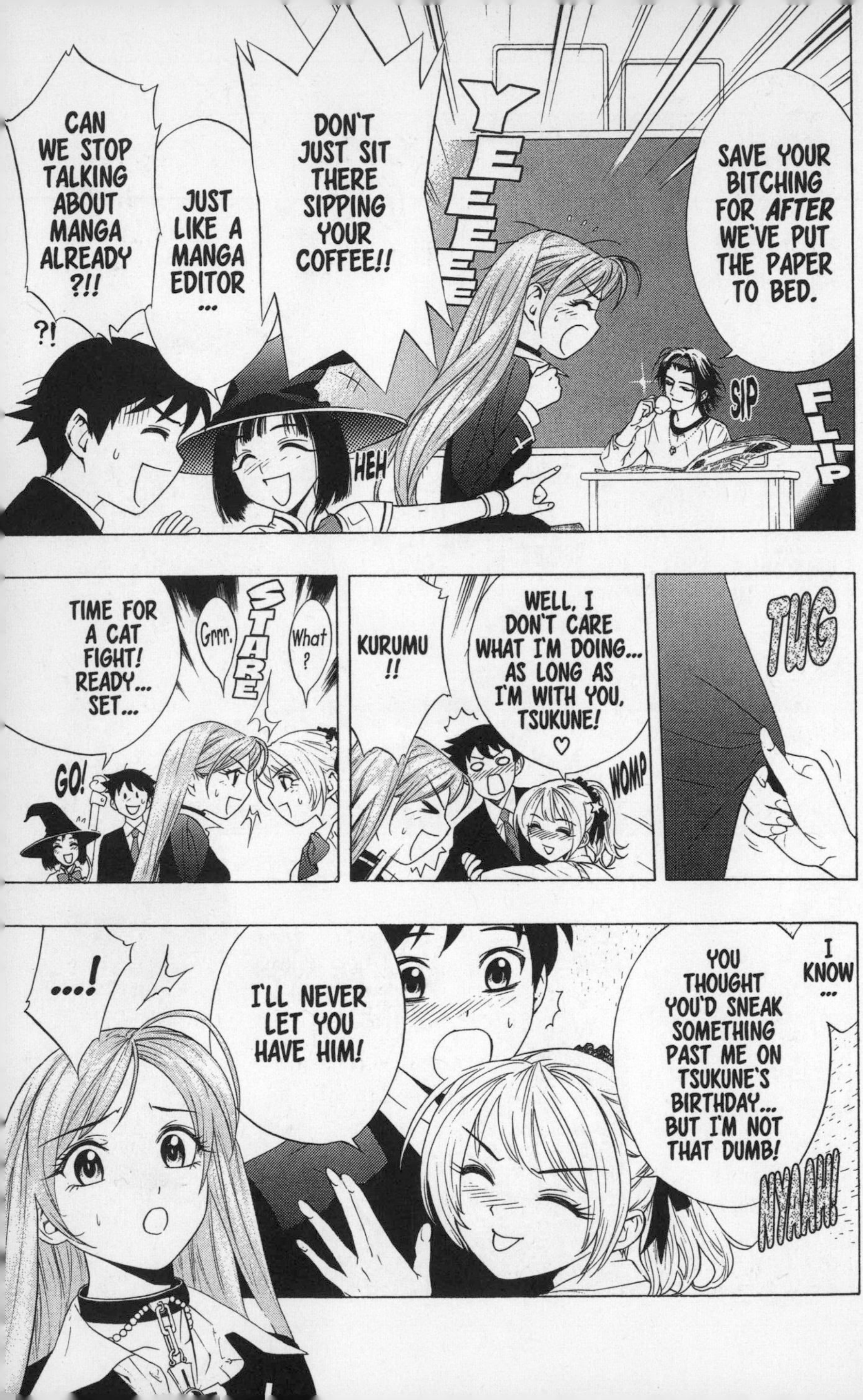
SAVE YOUR BITCHING FOR AFTER WE'VE PUT THE PAPER TO BED.
FLIP
SIP
YEEEEE
DON'T JUST SIT THERE SIPPING YOUR COFFEE!!
JUST LIKE A MANGA EDITOR ...
CAN WE STOP TALKING ABOUT MANGA ALREADY ?!!
HEH
?!
TUG
WELL, I DON'T CARE WHAT I'M DOING... AS LONG AS I'M WITH YOU, TSUKUNE! ♡
KURUMU !!
WOMP
What ?
STARE
Grrr.
TIME FOR A CAT FIGHT! READY... SET...
GO!
I KNOW ...
YOU THOUGHT YOU'D SNEAK SOMETHING PAST ME ON TSUKUNE'S BIRTHDAY... BUT I'M NOT THAT DUMB!
NYAAH!
I'LL NEVER LET YOU HAVE HIM!
...!

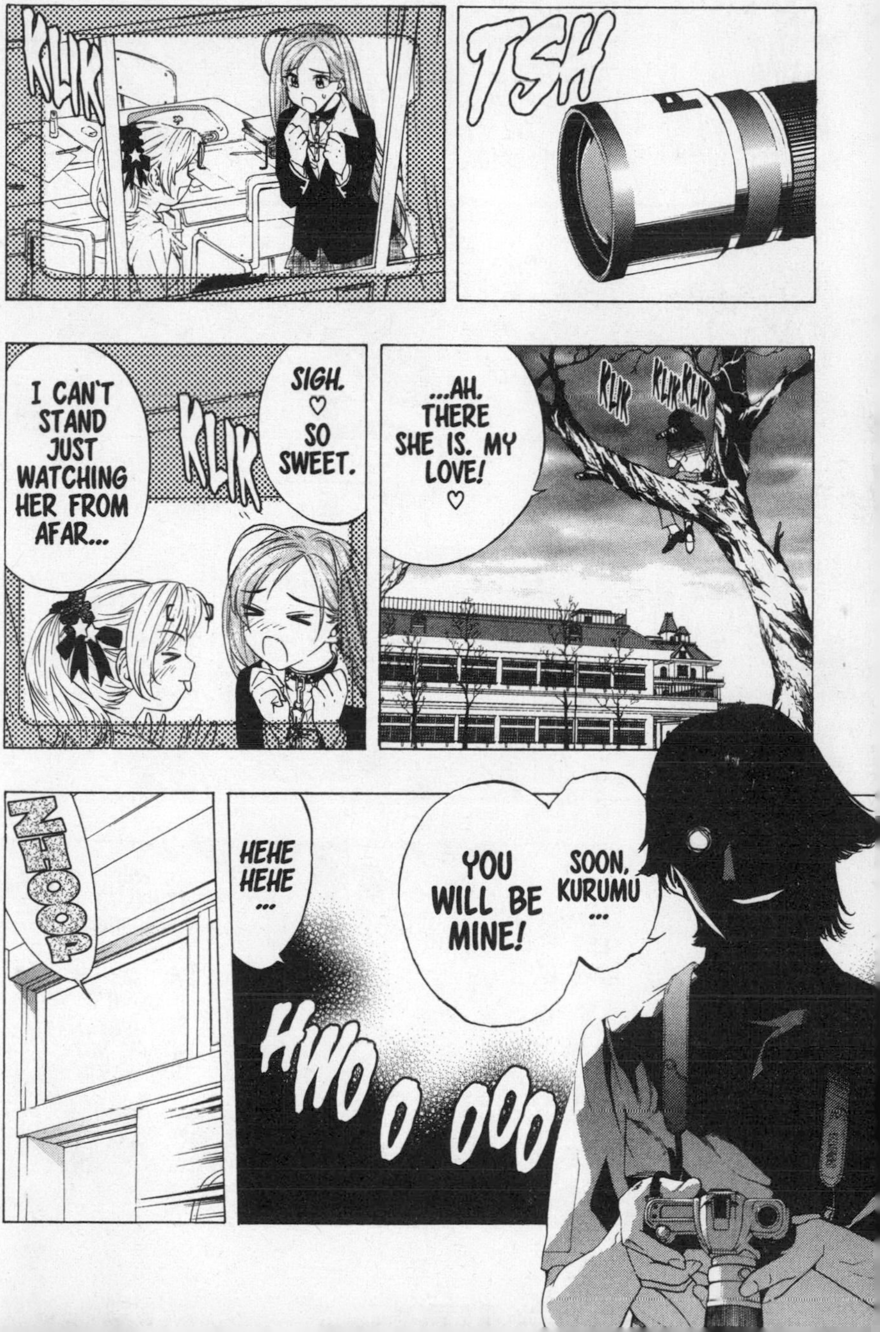
TSH
KLIK
KLIK KLIK KLIK
...AH. THERE SHE IS. MY LOVE! ♡
SIGH. ♡ SO SWEET.
KLIK
I CAN'T STAND JUST WATCHING HER FROM AFAR...
SOON, KURUMU ...
YOU WILL BE MINE!
HEHE HEHE ...
HWO O OOO
ZHOOP

READ THIS WAY

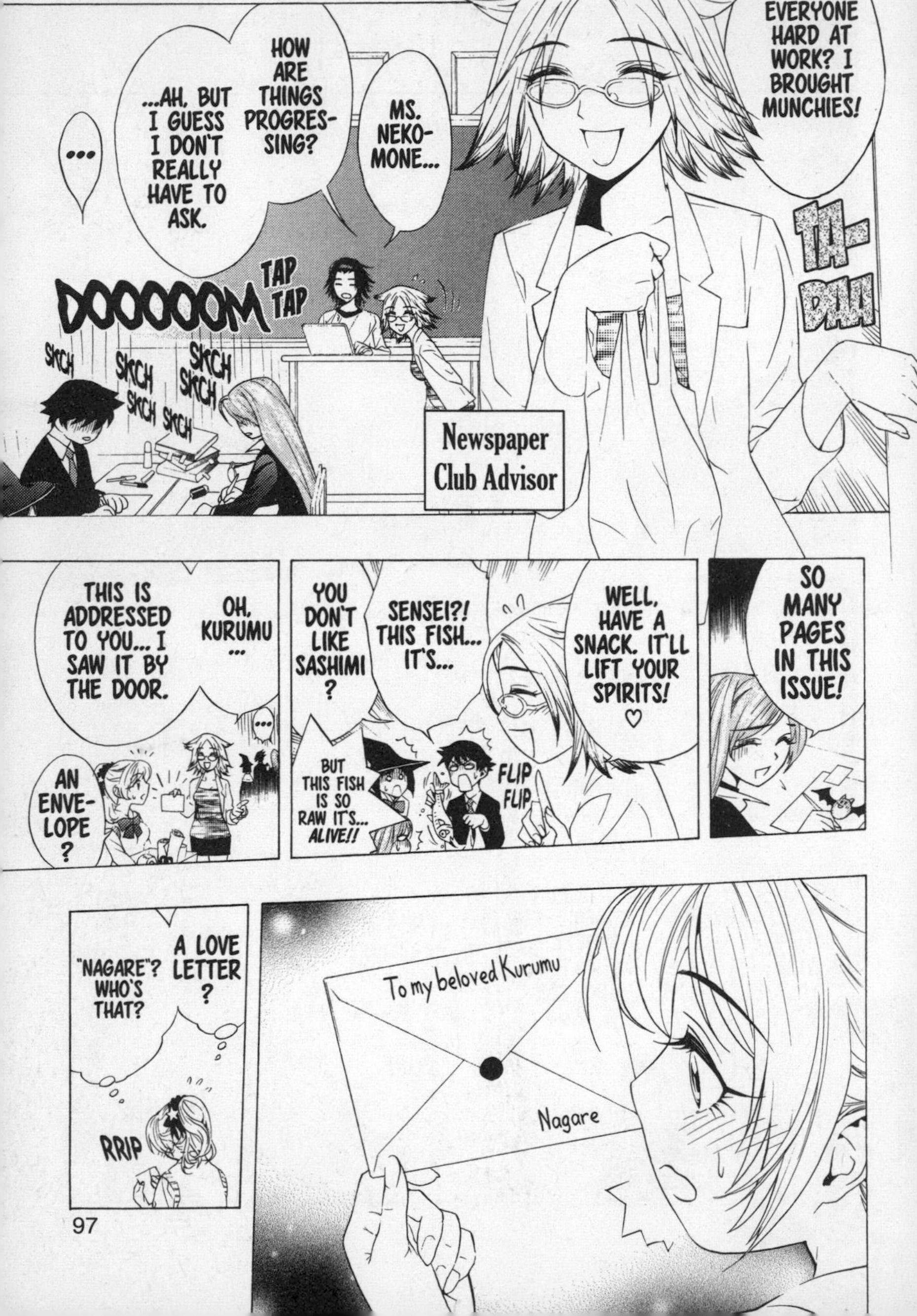

EVERYONE HARD AT WORK? I BROUGHT MUNCHIES!
TA-DAA
Newspaper Club Advisor
MS. NEKO-MONE...
HOW ARE THINGS PROGRES-SING?
...AH, BUT I GUESS I DON'T REALLY HAVE TO ASK.
...
TAP TAP
DOOOOOM
SKCH SKCH SKCH SKCH SKCH SKCH
SO MANY PAGES IN THIS ISSUE!
WELL, HAVE A SNACK. IT'LL LIFT YOUR SPIRITS! ♡
SENSEI?! THIS FISH... IT'S...
YOU DON'T LIKE SASHIMI?
FLIP FLIP
BUT THIS FISH IS SO RAW IT'S... ALIVE!!
OH, KURUMU...
THIS IS ADDRESSED TO YOU... I SAW IT BY THE DOOR.
...
AN ENVE-LOPE?
To my beloved Kurumu
Nagare
A LOVE LETTER?
"NAGARE"? WHO'S THAT?
RRIP

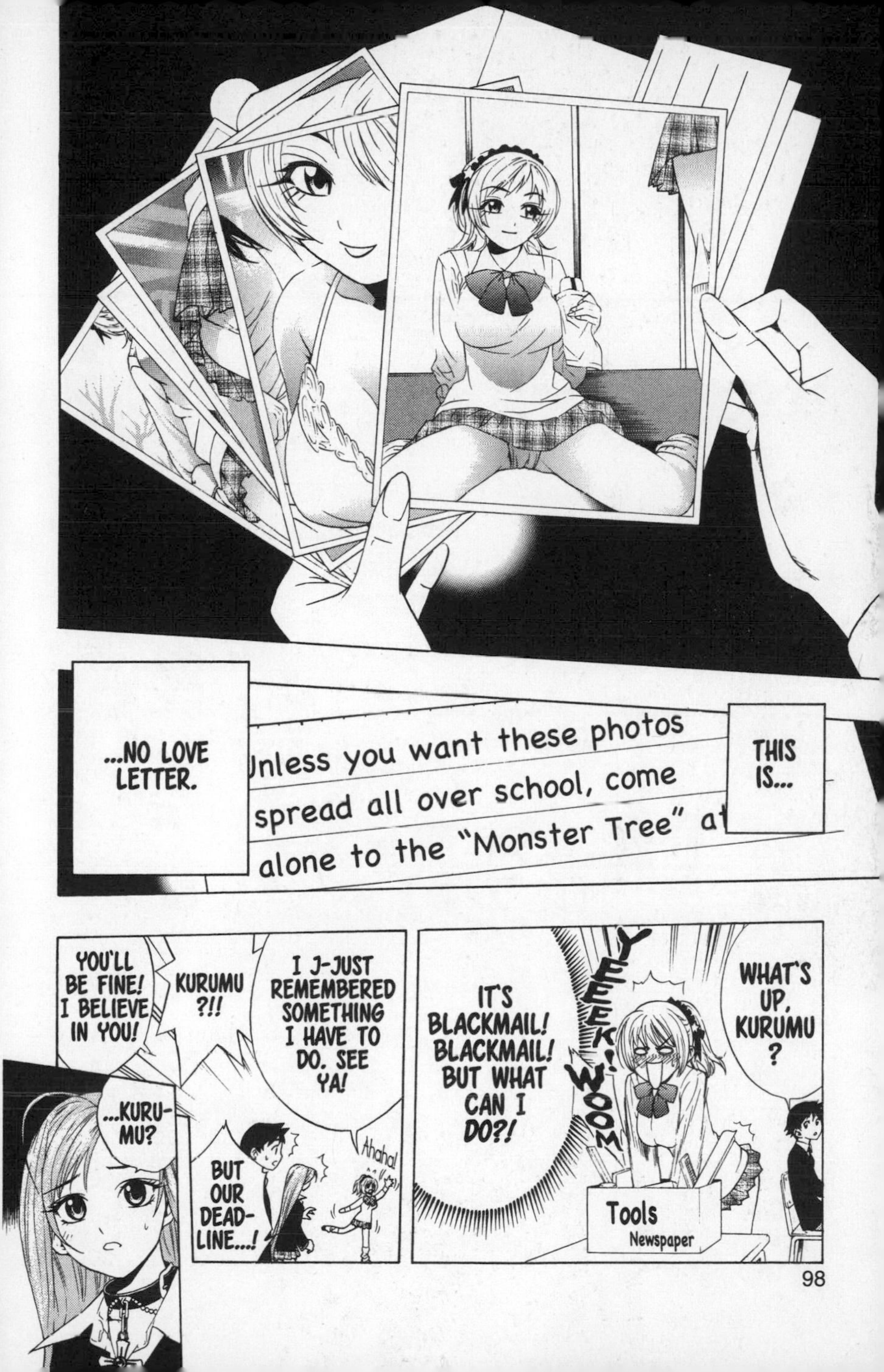
THIS IS...
Unless you want these photos spread all over school, come alone to the "Monster Tree" at
...NO LOVE LETTER.
WHAT'S UP, KURUMU?
YEEEK!
WOOM
IT'S BLACKMAIL! BLACKMAIL! BUT WHAT CAN I DO?!
Tools
Newspaper
I J-JUST REMEMBERED SOMETHING I HAVE TO DO. SEE YA!
KURUMU?!!
YOU'LL BE FINE! I BELIEVE IN YOU!
Ahaha!
BUT OUR DEADLINE...!
...KURUMU?

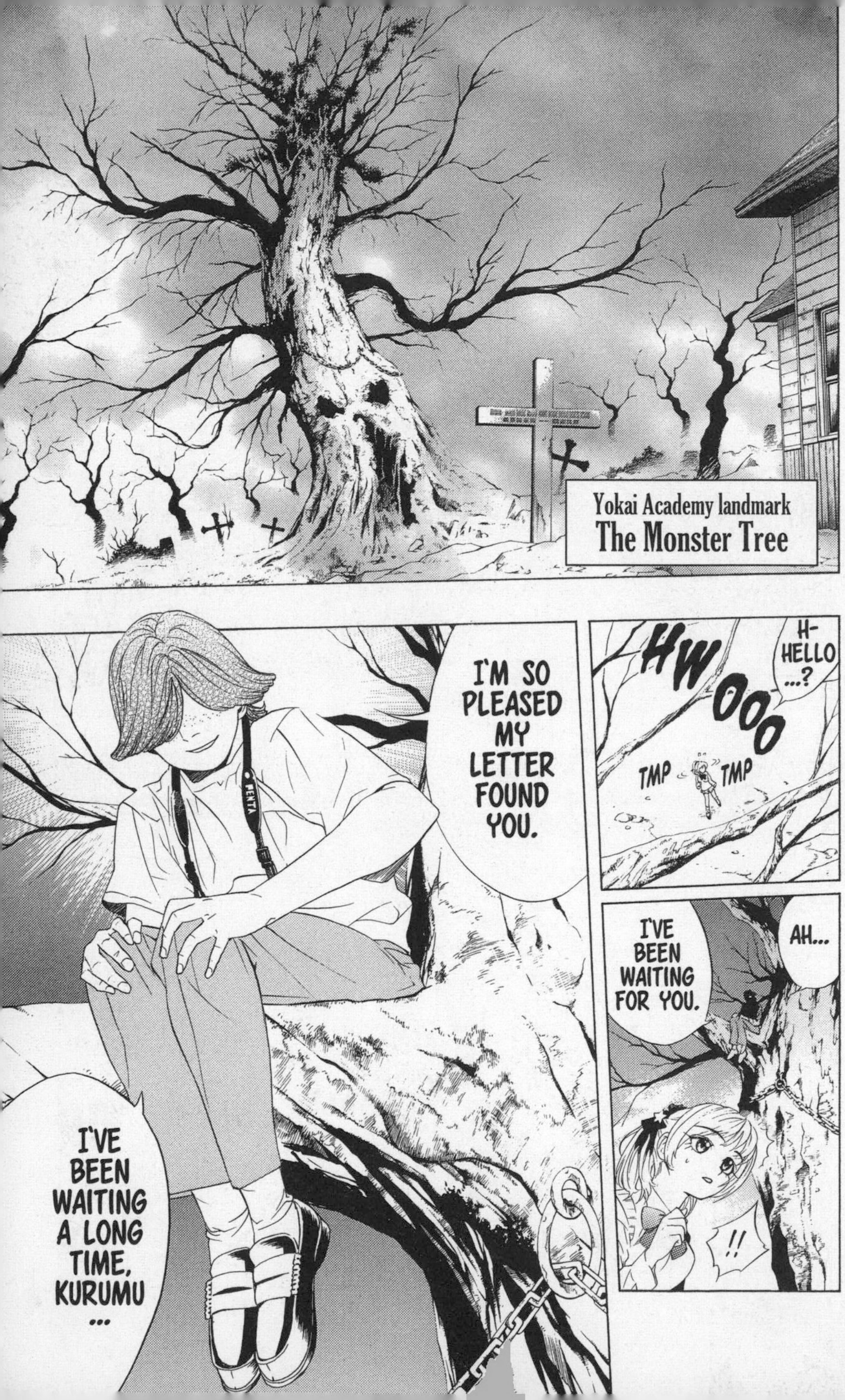
Yokai Academy landmark
The Monster Tree
H-HELLO ...?
HWOOO
TMP TMP
AH...
I'VE BEEN WAITING FOR YOU.
!!
I'M SO PLEASED MY LETTER FOUND YOU.
I'VE BEEN WAITING A LONG TIME, KURUMU ...

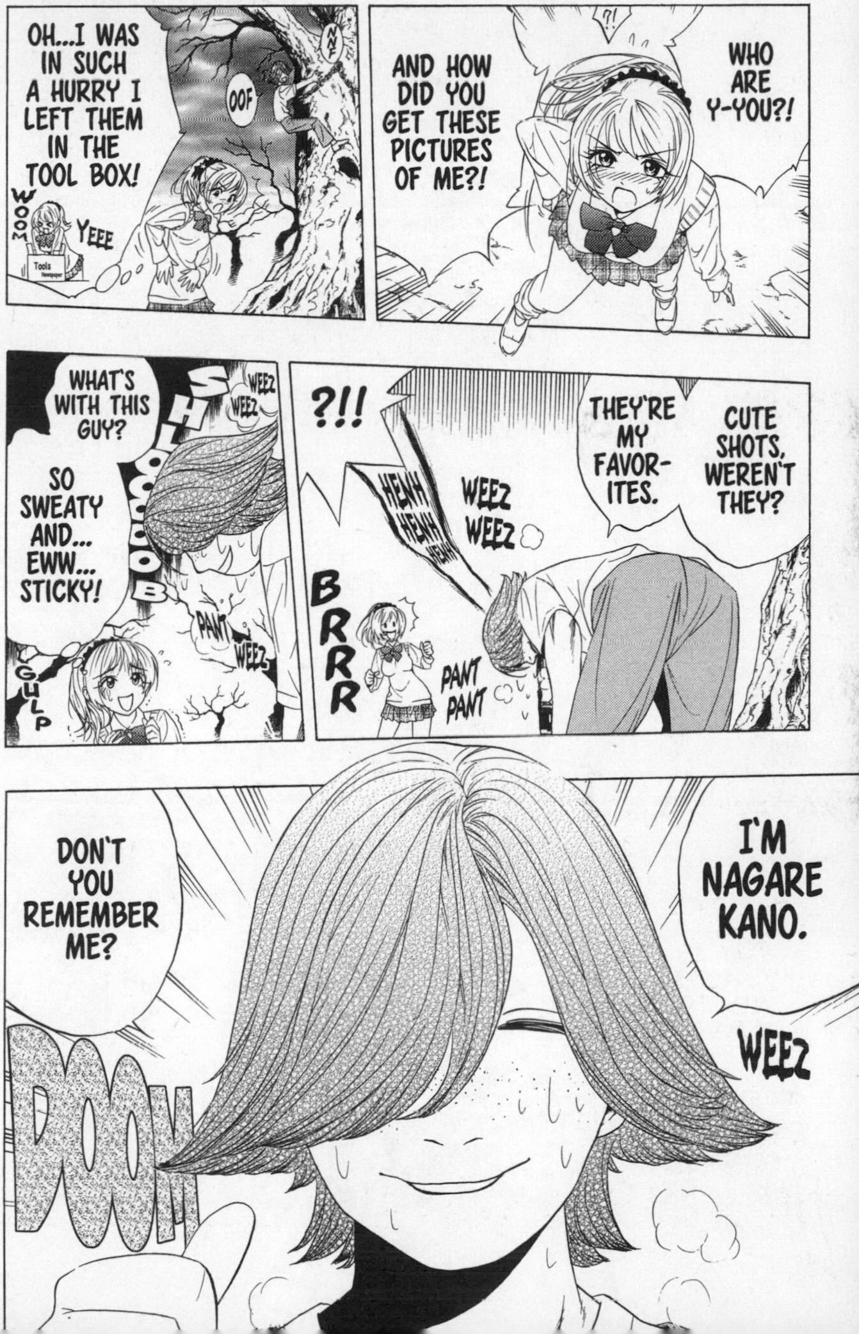
?!
WHO ARE Y-YOU?!
AND HOW DID YOU GET THESE PICTURES OF ME?!
NNF
OOF
OH...I WAS IN SUCH A HURRY I LEFT THEM IN THE TOOL BOX!
WOOM
YEEE
Tools
Newspaper
CUTE SHOTS, WEREN'T THEY?
THEY'RE MY FAVOR-ITES.
?!!
WEEZ WEEZ
HENH HENH HENH
BRRR
PANT PANT
WEEZ WEEZ
SHLOOOOOB
WHAT'S WITH THIS GUY?
SO SWEATY AND... EWW... STICKY!
PANT
WEEZ
GULP
I'M NAGARE KANO.
DON'T YOU REMEMBER ME?
WEEZ
DOOM

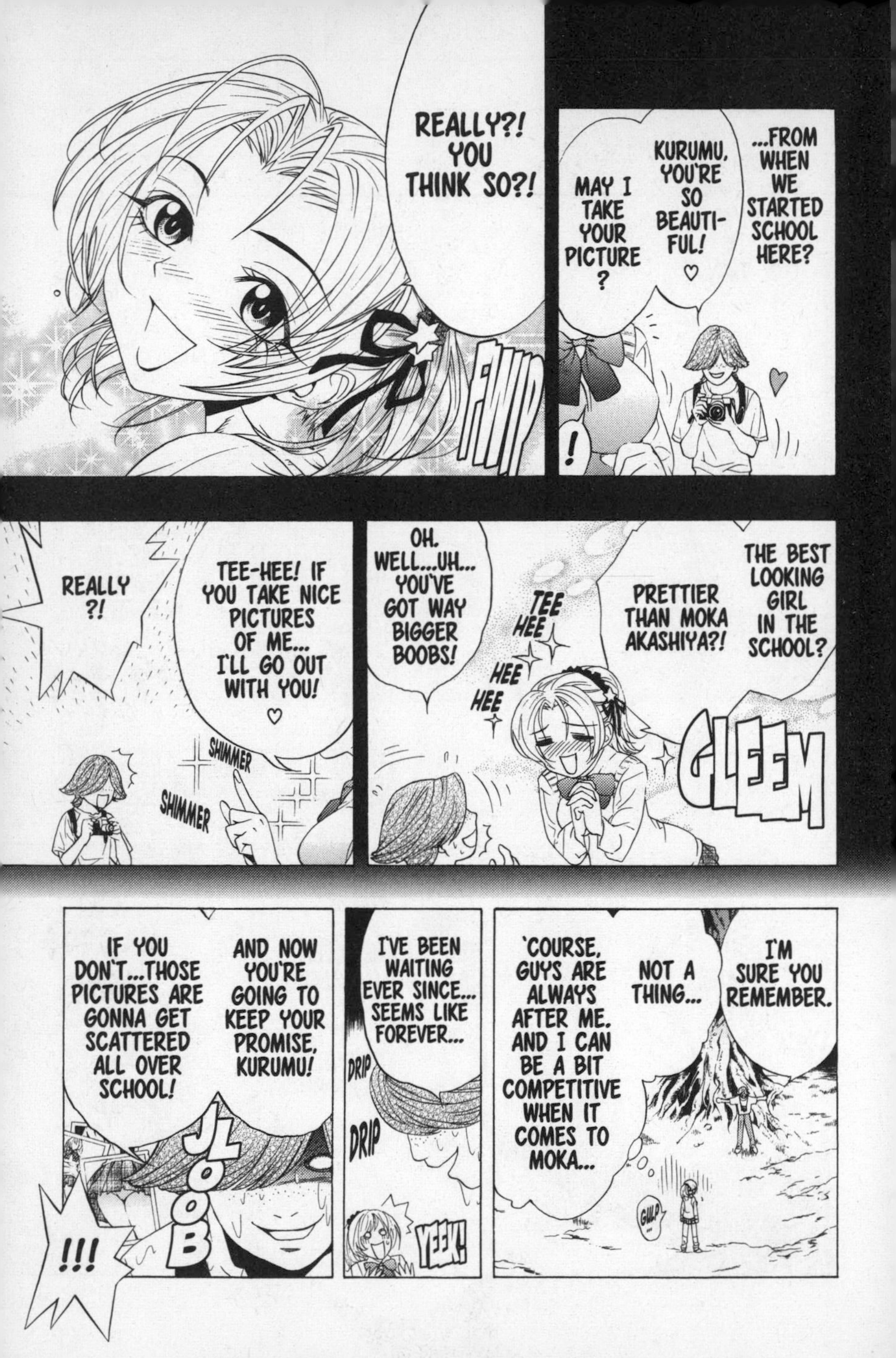
...FROM WHEN WE STARTED SCHOOL HERE?
KURUMU, YOU'RE SO BEAUTIFUL! ♡
MAY I TAKE YOUR PICTURE?
!
REALLY?! YOU THINK SO?!
FWIP
THE BEST LOOKING GIRL IN THE SCHOOL?
PRETTIER THAN MOKA AKASHIYA?!
GLEEM
TEE HEE
HEE HEE
OH. WELL...UH... YOU'VE GOT WAY BIGGER BOOBS!
TEE-HEE! IF YOU TAKE NICE PICTURES OF ME... I'LL GO OUT WITH YOU! ♡
REALLY ?!
SHIMMER
SHIMMER
I'M SURE YOU REMEMBER.
NOT A THING...
'COURSE, GUYS ARE ALWAYS AFTER ME. AND I CAN BE A BIT COMPETITIVE WHEN IT COMES TO MOKA...
GULP...
I'VE BEEN WAITING EVER SINCE... SEEMS LIKE FOREVER...
DRIP
DRIP
YEEK!
AND NOW YOU'RE GOING TO KEEP YOUR PROMISE, KURUMU!
IF YOU DON'T...THOSE PICTURES ARE GONNA GET SCATTERED ALL OVER SCHOOL!
JLOOB
!!!

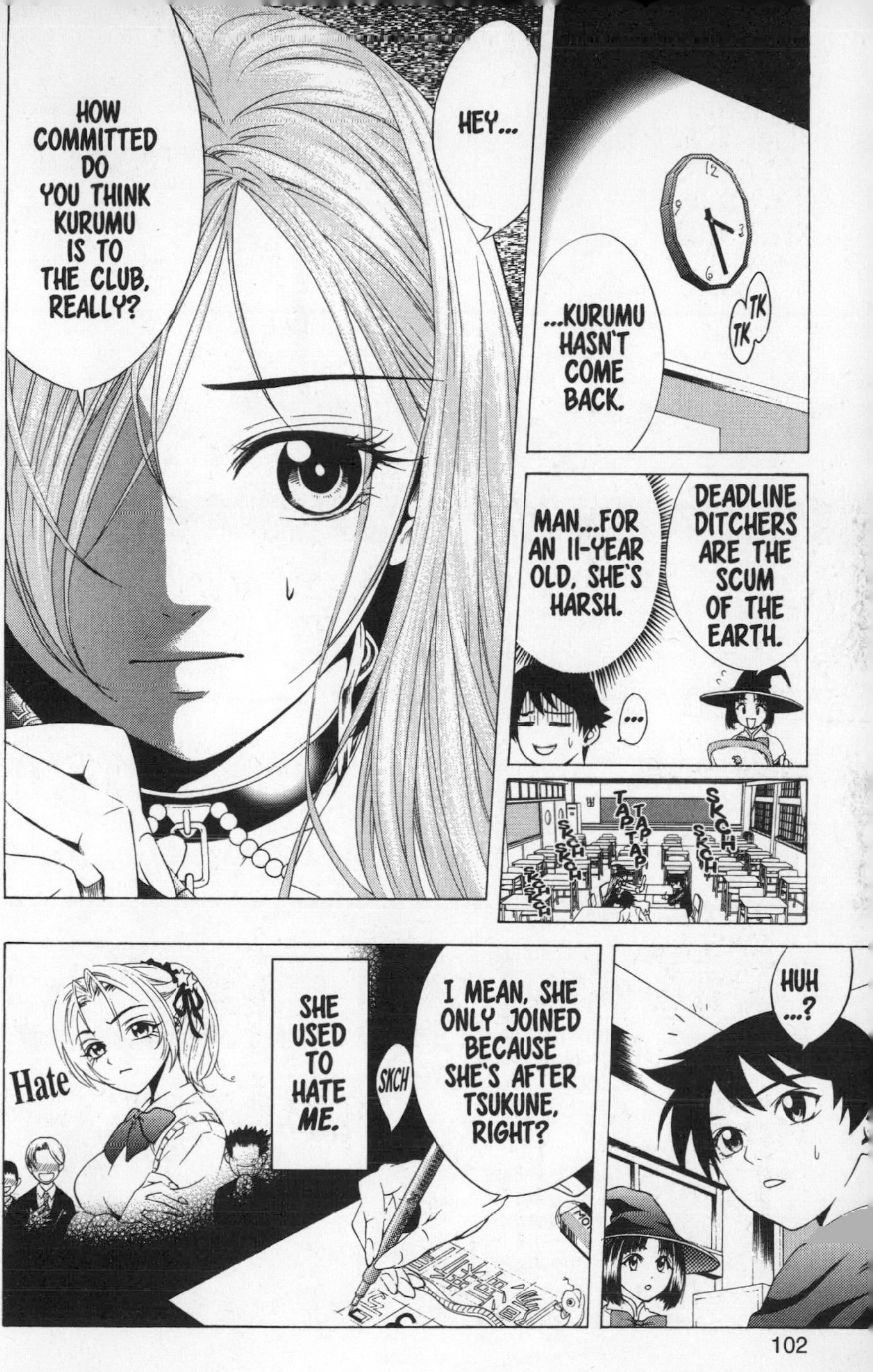
...KURUMU HASN'T COME BACK.
TK
TK
DEADLINE DITCHERS ARE THE SCUM OF THE EARTH.
MAN...FOR AN 11-YEAR OLD, SHE'S HARSH.
...
SKCH SKCH
TAP TAP
SKCH SKCH SKCH
SKCH SKCH
HEY...
HOW COMMITTED DO YOU THINK KURUMU IS TO THE CLUB, REALLY?
HUH ...?
I MEAN, SHE ONLY JOINED BECAUSE SHE'S AFTER TSUKUNE, RIGHT?
SKCH
SHE USED TO HATE *ME.*
Hate

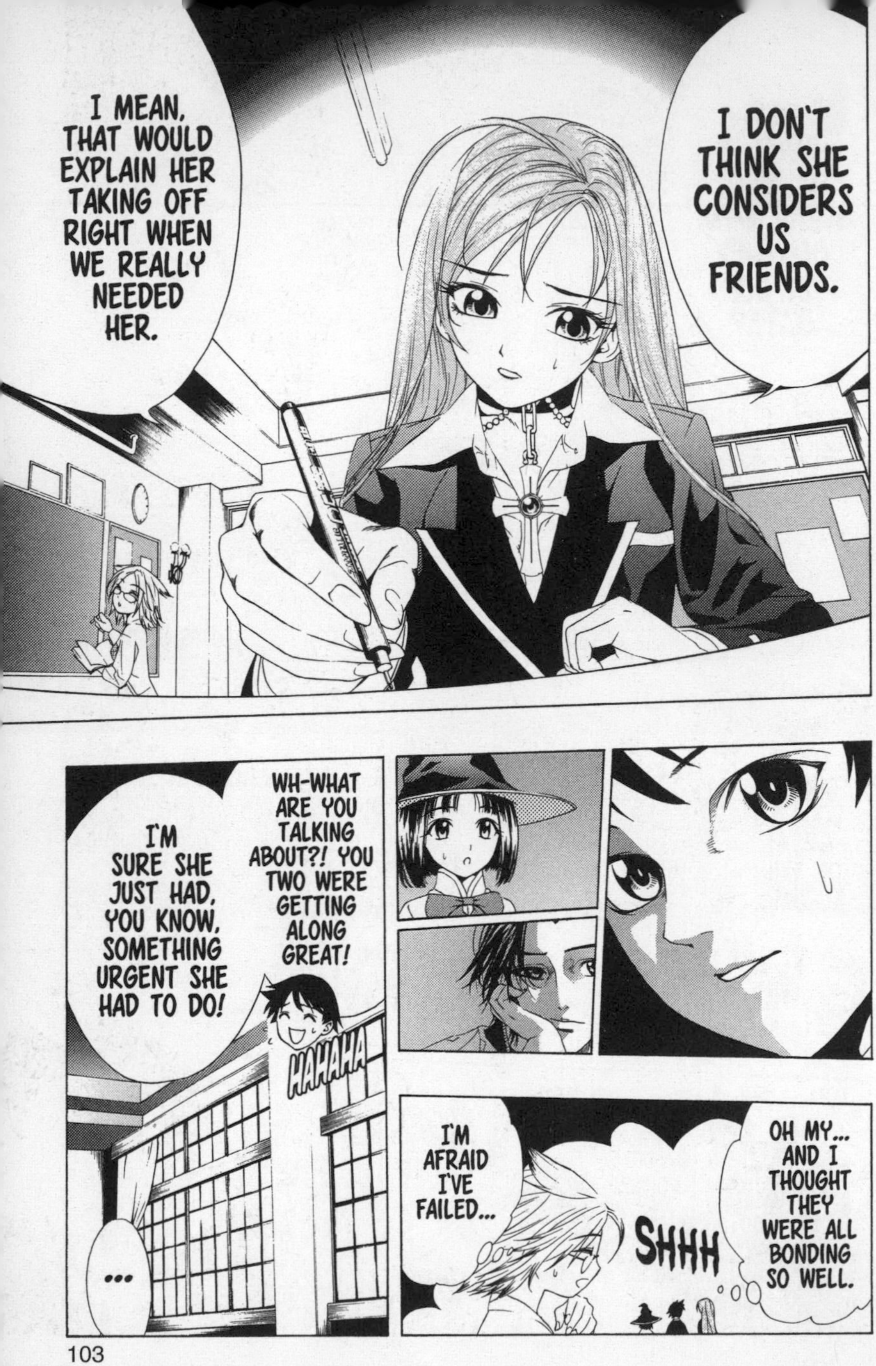
I DON'T THINK SHE CONSIDERS US FRIENDS.
I MEAN, THAT WOULD EXPLAIN HER TAKING OFF RIGHT WHEN WE REALLY NEEDED HER.
OH MY... AND I THOUGHT THEY WERE ALL BONDING SO WELL.
SHHH
I'M AFRAID I'VE FAILED...
WH-WHAT ARE YOU TALKING ABOUT?! YOU TWO WERE GETTING ALONG GREAT!
I'M SURE SHE JUST HAD, YOU KNOW, SOMETHING URGENT SHE HAD TO DO!
HAHAHA
...

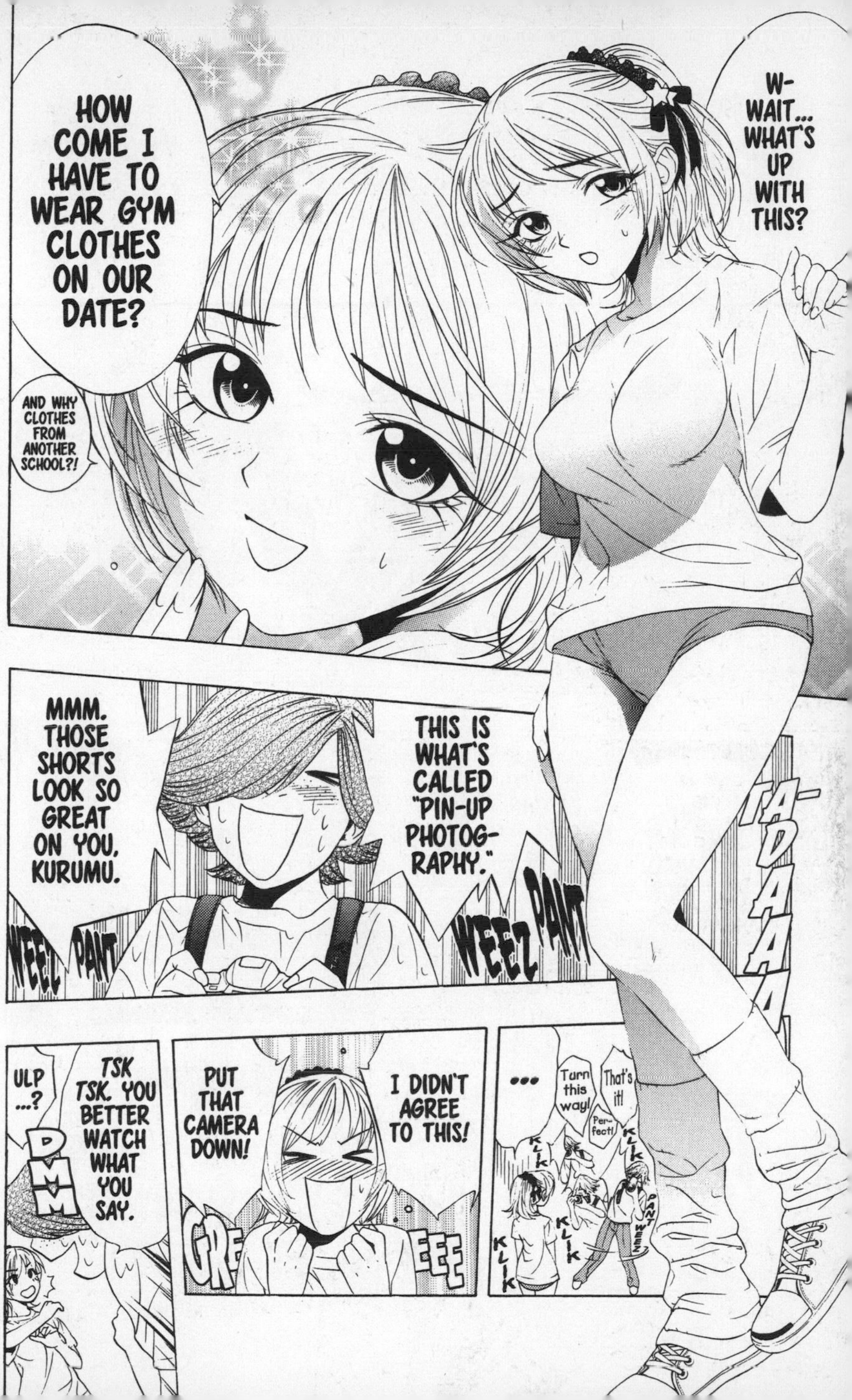
W-WAIT... WHAT'S UP WITH THIS?
HOW COME I HAVE TO WEAR GYM CLOTHES ON OUR DATE?
AND WHY CLOTHES FROM ANOTHER SCHOOL?!
TA-DAAAA
THIS IS WHAT'S CALLED "PIN-UP PHOTOGRAPHY."
WEEZ PANT
MMM. THOSE SHORTS LOOK SO GREAT ON YOU, KURUMU.
WEEZ PANT
...
That's it!
Turn this way!
Perfect!
KLIK
PANT WEEZ
KLIK
KLIK
KLIK
I DIDN'T AGREE TO THIS!
PUT THAT CAMERA DOWN!
GREEEE
TSK TSK. YOU BETTER WATCH WHAT YOU SAY.
ULP ...?
DMMM

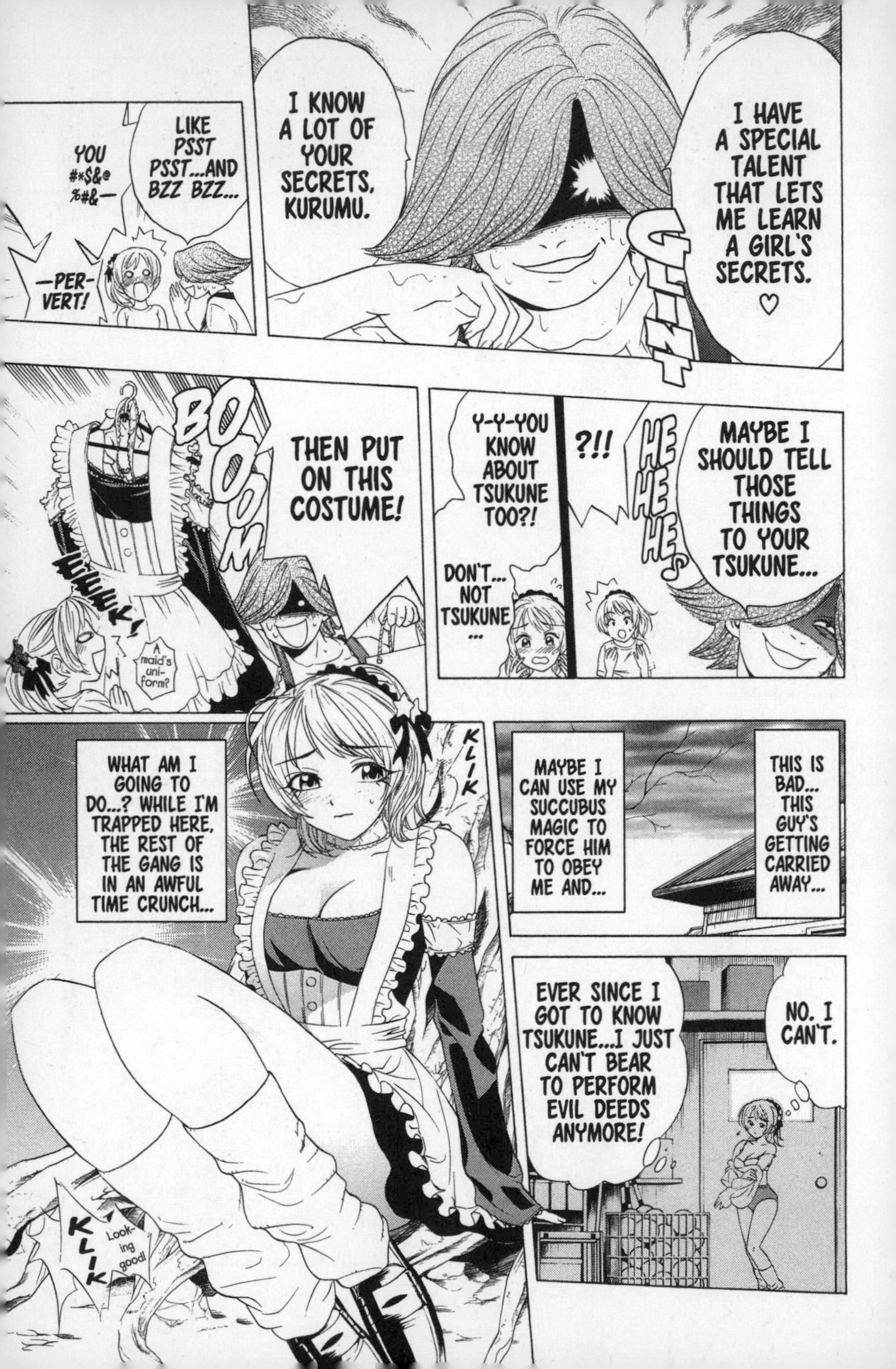
I HAVE A SPECIAL TALENT THAT LETS ME LEARN A GIRL'S SECRETS. ♡
GLINT
I KNOW A LOT OF YOUR SECRETS, KURUMU.
LIKE PSST PSST...AND BZZ BZZ...
YOU #*$&@%#&—
—PER-VERT!
MAYBE I SHOULD TELL THOSE THINGS TO YOUR TSUKUNE...
HE HE HE
?!!
Y-Y-YOU KNOW ABOUT TSUKUNE TOO?!
DON'T... NOT TSUKUNE ...
THEN PUT ON THIS COSTUME!
BOOOM
EEEEK!
A maid's uni-form?
THIS IS BAD... THIS GUY'S GETTING CARRIED AWAY...
MAYBE I CAN USE MY SUCCUBUS MAGIC TO FORCE HIM TO OBEY ME AND...
NO. I CAN'T.
EVER SINCE I GOT TO KNOW TSUKUNE...I JUST CAN'T BEAR TO PERFORM EVIL DEEDS ANYMORE!
KLIK
WHAT AM I GOING TO DO...? WHILE I'M TRAPPED HERE, THE REST OF THE GANG IS IN AN AWFUL TIME CRUNCH...
KLIK
Look-ing good!

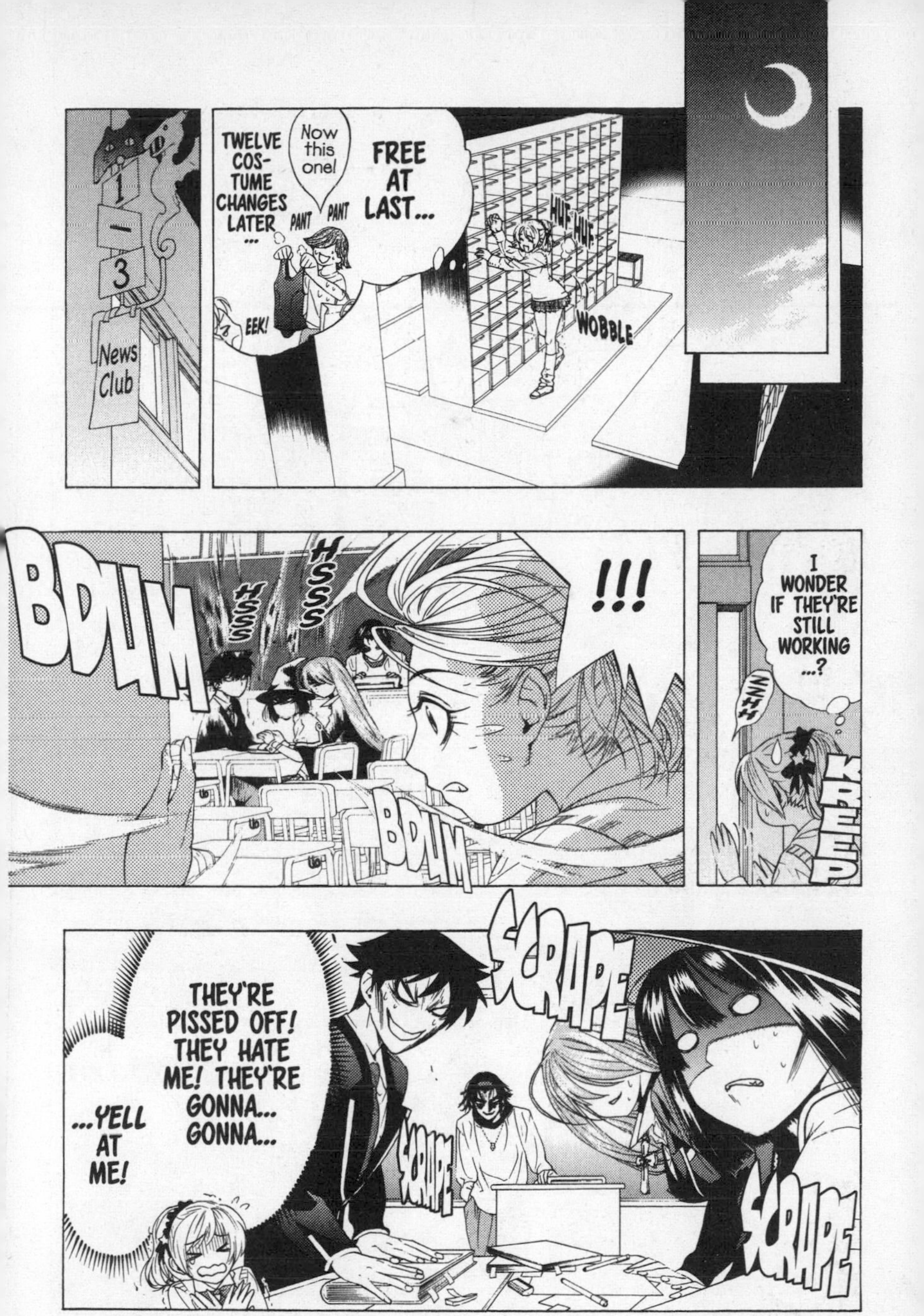
FREE AT LAST...
Now this one!
TWELVE COSTUME CHANGES LATER...
PANT PANT
HUF HUF
EEK!
WOBBLE
1-3
News Club
I WONDER IF THEY'RE STILL WORKING...?
KREEP
!!!
HSSS
HSSS
BDUM
BDUM
SCRAPE
THEY'RE PISSED OFF! THEY HATE ME! THEY'RE GONNA... GONNA...
...YELL AT ME!
SCRAPE
SCRAPE

READ THIS WAY

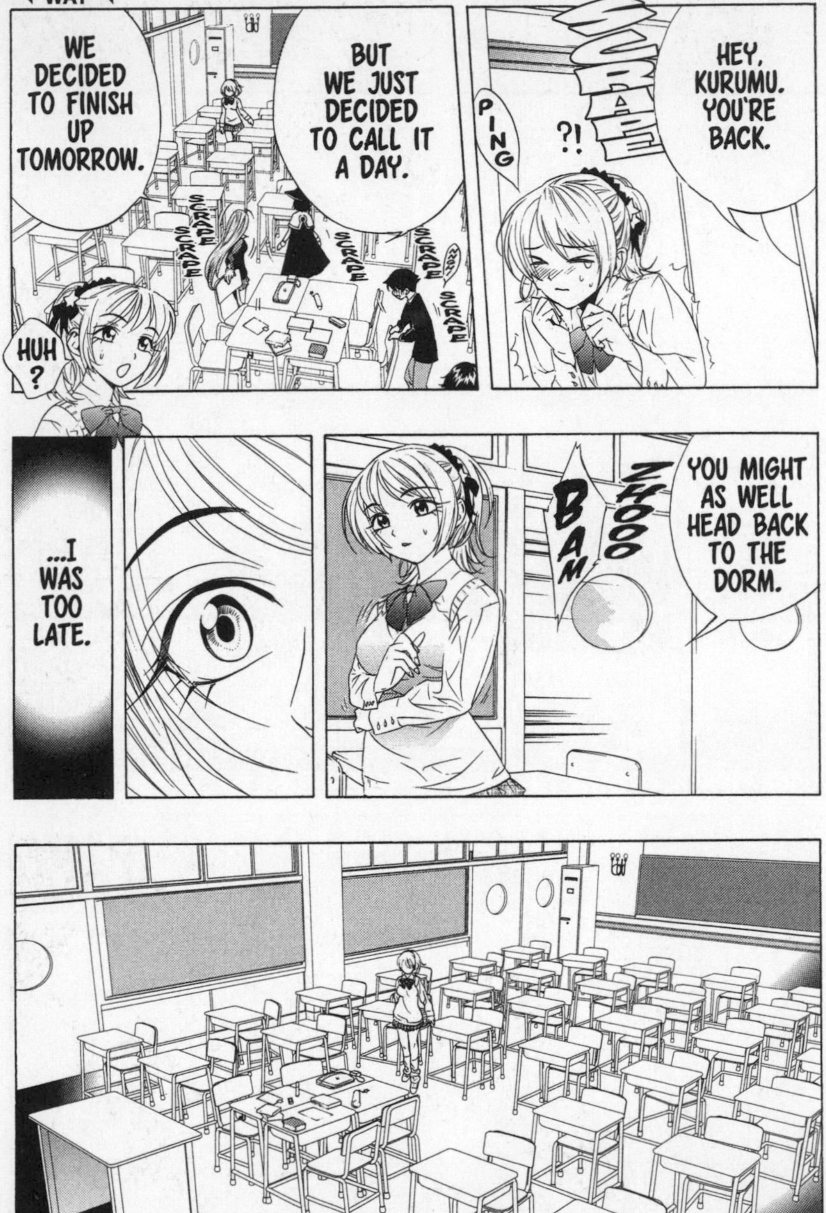
SCRAPE
PING
?!
HEY, KURUMU. YOU'RE BACK.
BUT WE JUST DECIDED TO CALL IT A DAY.
SCRAPE SCRAPE
SCRAPE SCRAPE
SCRAPE SCRAPE
WE DECIDED TO FINISH UP TOMORROW.
HUH?
YOU MIGHT AS WELL HEAD BACK TO THE DORM.
ZHOOOO
BAM
...I WAS TOO LATE.

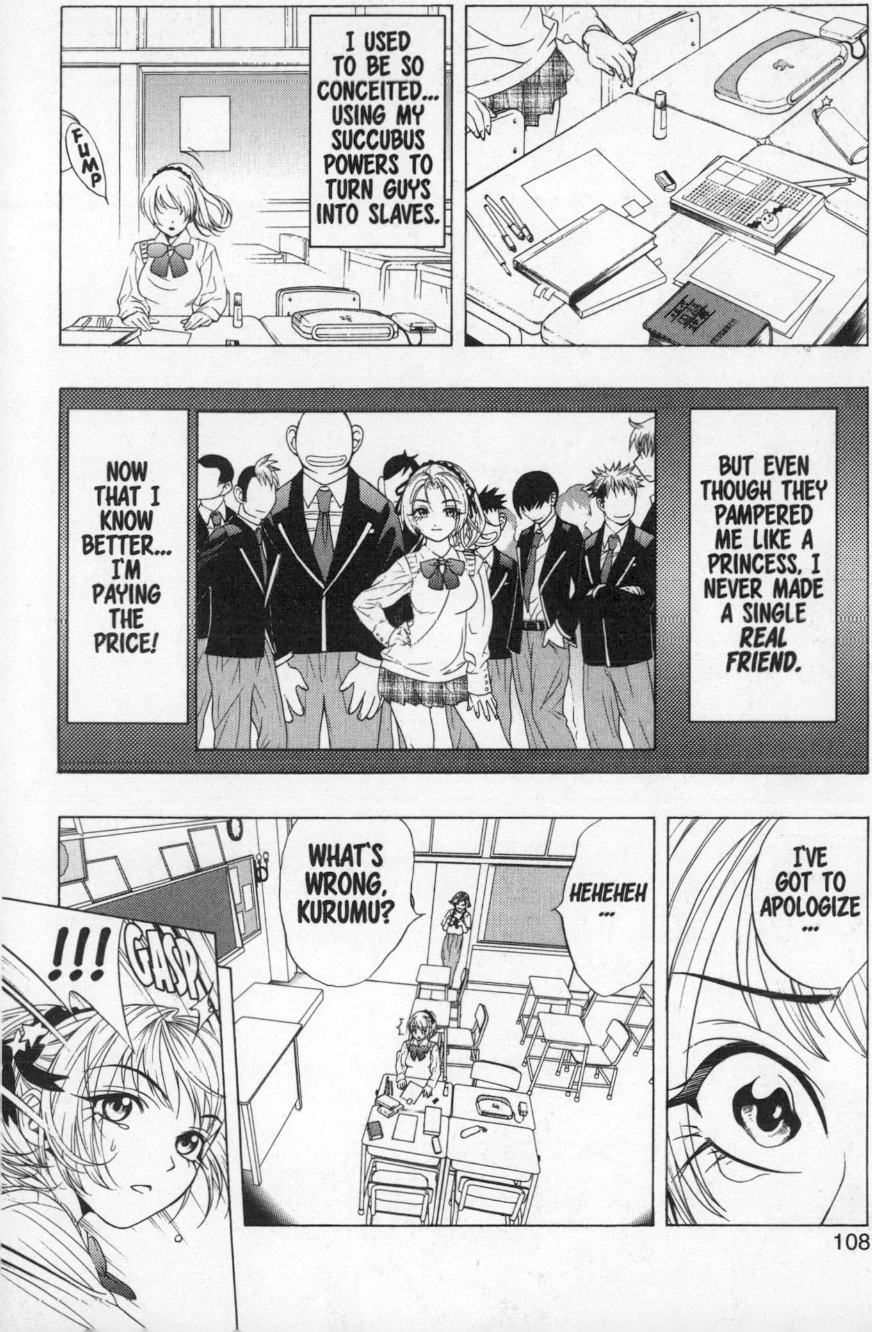
I USED TO BE SO CONCEITED... USING MY SUCCUBUS POWERS TO TURN GUYS INTO SLAVES.
FUMP
BUT EVEN THOUGH THEY PAMPERED ME LIKE A PRINCESS, I NEVER MADE A SINGLE REAL FRIEND.
NOW THAT I KNOW BETTER... I'M PAYING THE PRICE!
I'VE GOT TO APOLOGIZE...
HEHEHEH...
WHAT'S WRONG, KURUMU?
GASP
!!!

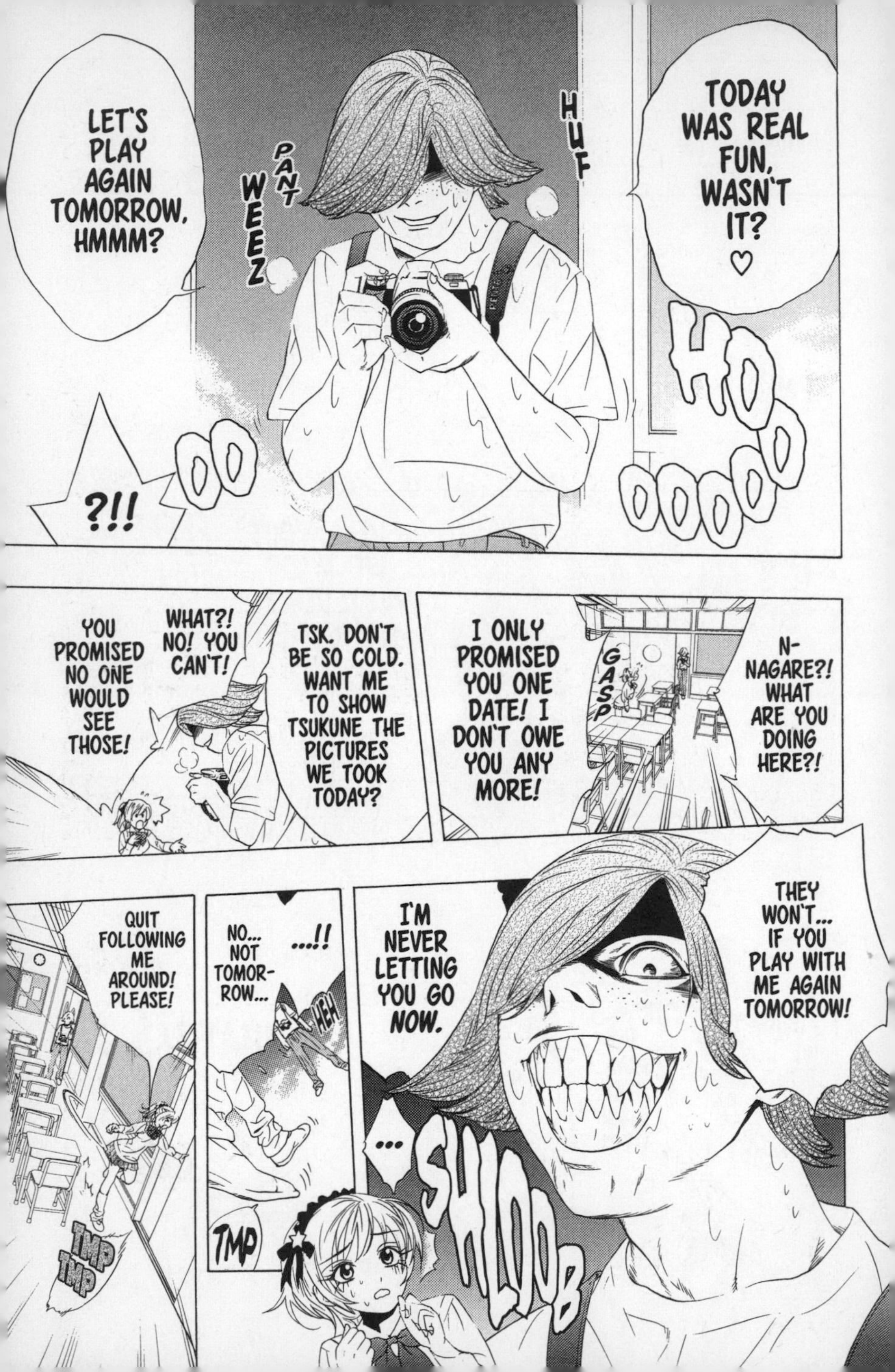
TODAY WAS REAL FUN, WASN'T IT? ♡
HUF
PANT
WEEZ
LET'S PLAY AGAIN TOMORROW, HMMM?
HOOOOOOO
OO
?!!
N-NAGARE?! WHAT ARE YOU DOING HERE?!
GASP
I ONLY PROMISED YOU ONE DATE! I DON'T OWE YOU ANY MORE!
TSK. DON'T BE SO COLD. WANT ME TO SHOW TSUKUNE THE PICTURES WE TOOK TODAY?
WHAT?! NO! YOU CAN'T!
YOU PROMISED NO ONE WOULD SEE THOSE!
THEY WON'T... IF YOU PLAY WITH ME AGAIN TOMORROW!
I'M NEVER LETTING YOU GO NOW.
SHLOOB
...
...!!
NO... NOT TOMORROW...
HEH
TMP
QUIT FOLLOWING ME AROUND! PLEASE!
TMP TMP

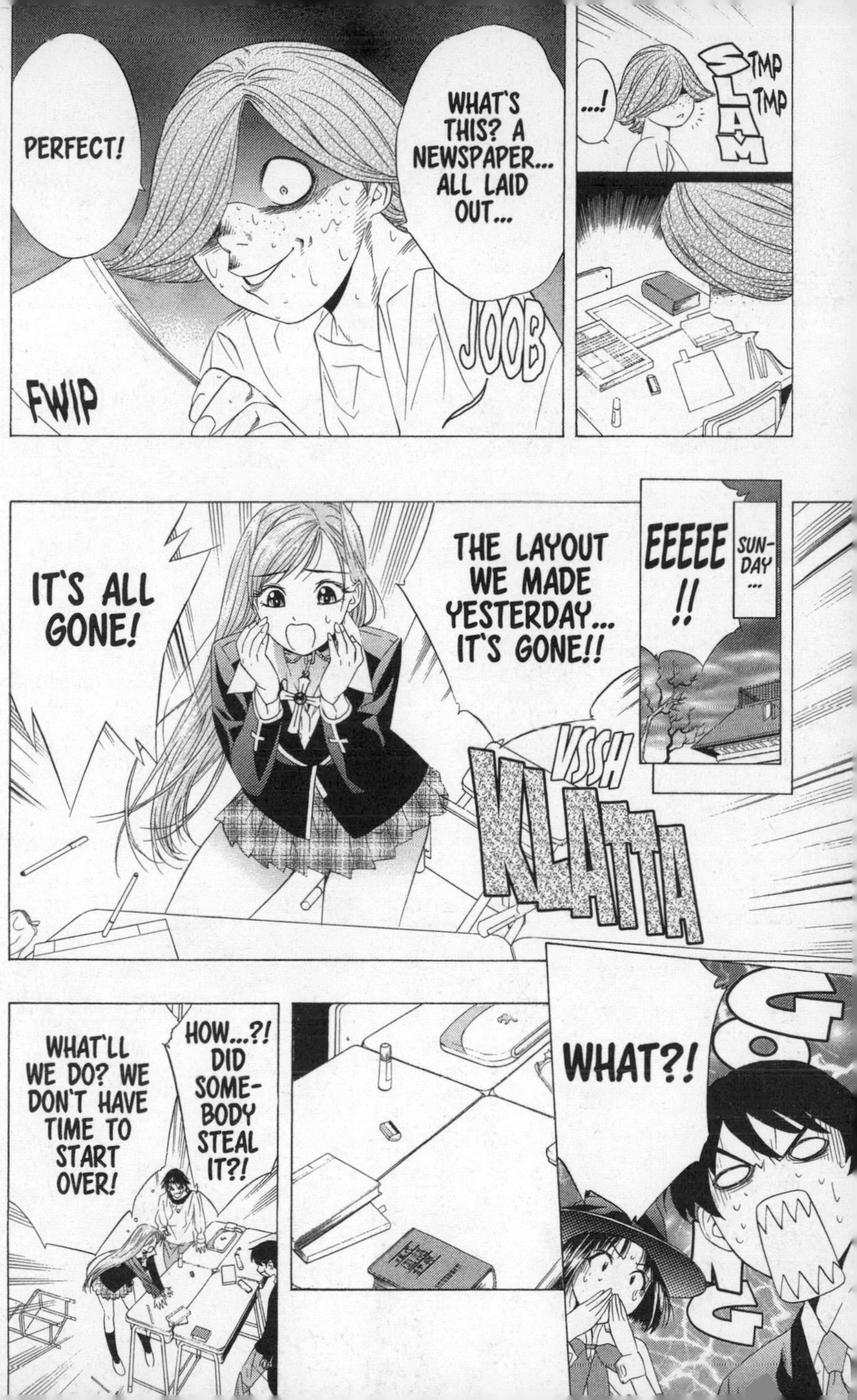
...!
SLAM
TMP TMP
WHAT'S THIS? A NEWSPAPER... ALL LAID OUT...
JOOB
PERFECT!
FWIP
SUN-DAY...
EEEEE !!
VSSH
KLATTA
THE LAYOUT WE MADE YESTERDAY... IT'S GONE!!
IT'S ALL GONE!
G
WHAT?!
HOW...?! DID SOME-BODY STEAL IT?!
WHAT'LL WE DO? WE DON'T HAVE TIME TO START OVER!

READ THIS WAY

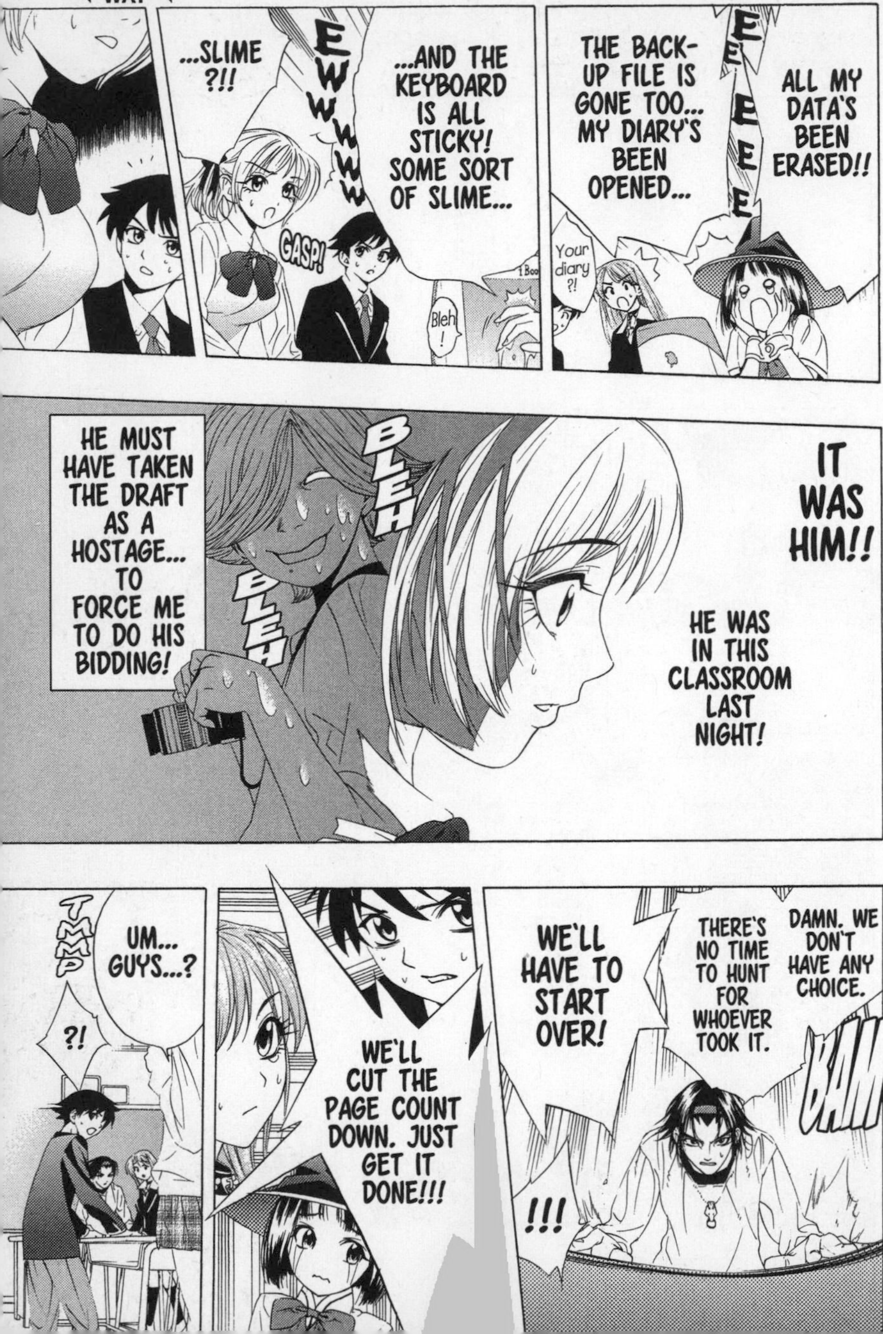

ALL MY DATA'S BEEN ERASED!!
EEEEEE
THE BACK-UP FILE IS GONE TOO... MY DIARY'S BEEN OPENED...
Your diary ?!
...AND THE KEYBOARD IS ALL STICKY! SOME SORT OF SLIME...
EWWWWWW
Bleh!
GASP!
...SLIME ?!!
IT WAS HIM!!
HE WAS IN THIS CLASSROOM LAST NIGHT!
BLEH
BLEH
HE MUST HAVE TAKEN THE DRAFT AS A HOSTAGE... TO FORCE ME TO DO HIS BIDDING!
DAMN. WE DON'T HAVE ANY CHOICE.
THERE'S NO TIME TO HUNT FOR WHOEVER TOOK IT.
WHAM
WE'LL HAVE TO START OVER!
!!!
WE'LL CUT THE PAGE COUNT DOWN. JUST GET IT DONE!!!
UM... GUYS...?
TMMP
?!

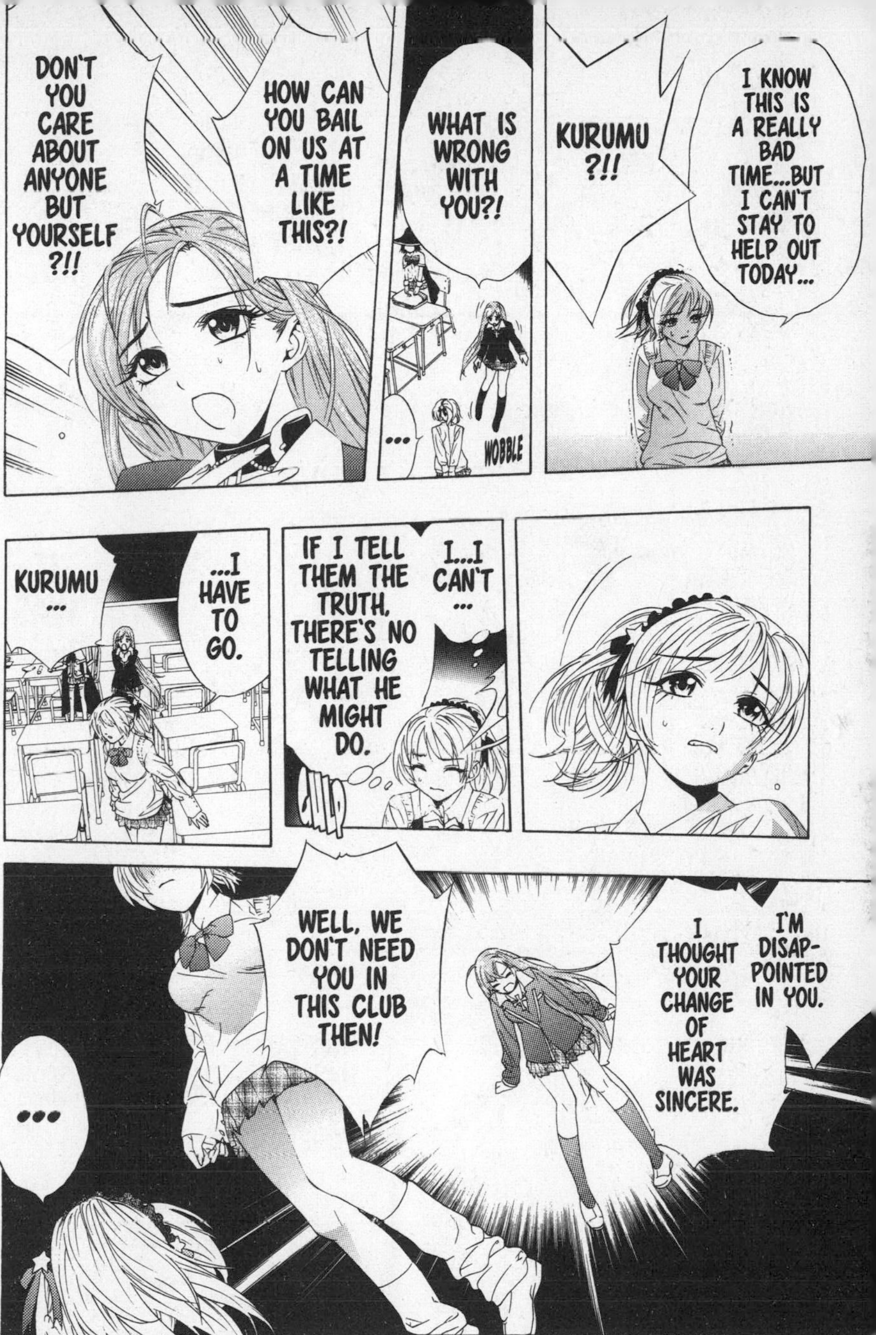
I KNOW THIS IS A REALLY BAD TIME...BUT I CAN'T STAY TO HELP OUT TODAY...
KURUMU ?!!
WHAT IS WRONG WITH YOU?!
...
WOBBLE
HOW CAN YOU BAIL ON US AT A TIME LIKE THIS?!
DON'T YOU CARE ABOUT ANYONE BUT YOURSELF ?!!
I...I CAN'T ...
IF I TELL THEM THE TRUTH, THERE'S NO TELLING WHAT HE MIGHT DO.
...I HAVE TO GO.
KURUMU ...
I'M DISAPPOINTED IN YOU.
I THOUGHT YOUR CHANGE OF HEART WAS SINCERE.
WELL, WE DON'T NEED YOU IN THIS CLUB THEN!
...

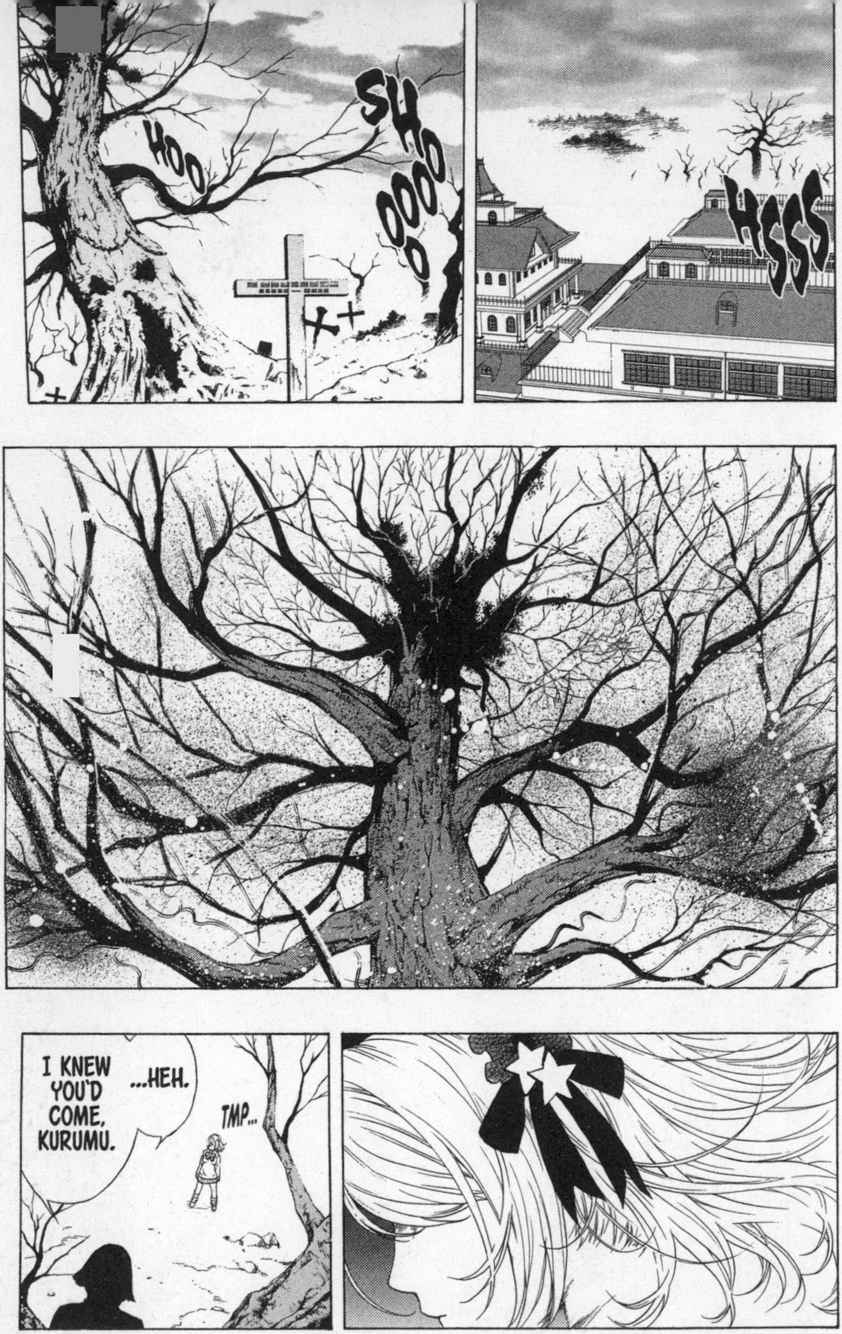
HSSS
SHOOOOO
HOO
...HEH.
I KNEW YOU'D COME, KURUMU.
TMP...

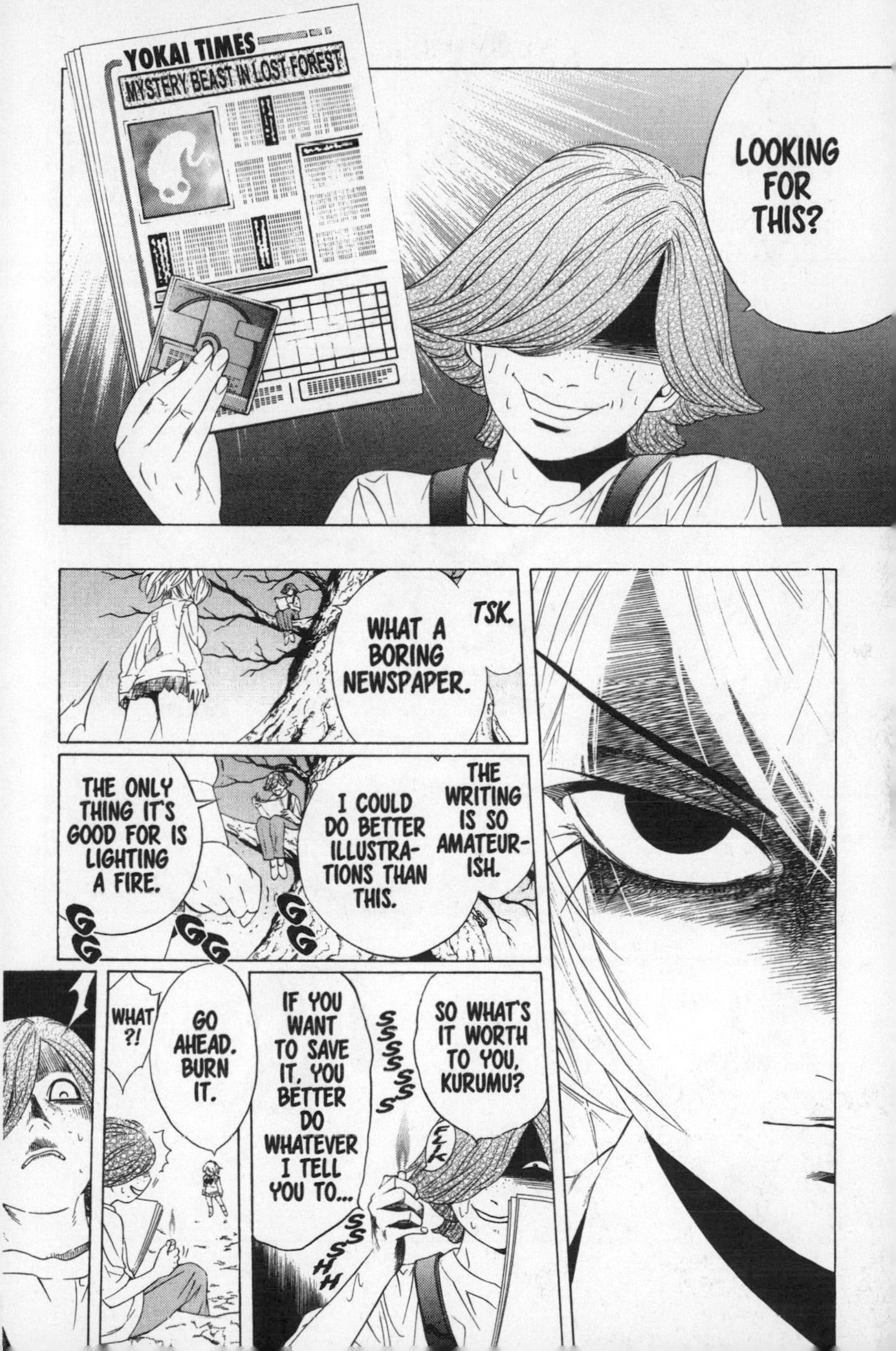
LOOKING FOR THIS?
YOKAI TIMES
MYSTERY BEAST IN LOST FOREST
TSK.
WHAT A BORING NEWSPAPER.
THE WRITING IS SO AMATEURISH.
I COULD DO BETTER ILLUSTRATIONS THAN THIS.
THE ONLY THING IT'S GOOD FOR IS LIGHTING A FIRE.
GG
GG
GG
SO WHAT'S IT WORTH TO YOU, KURUMU?
FLIK
SSSSSS
IF YOU WANT TO SAVE IT, YOU BETTER DO WHATEVER I TELL YOU TO...
SSSHH
GO AHEAD. BURN IT.
WHAT?!

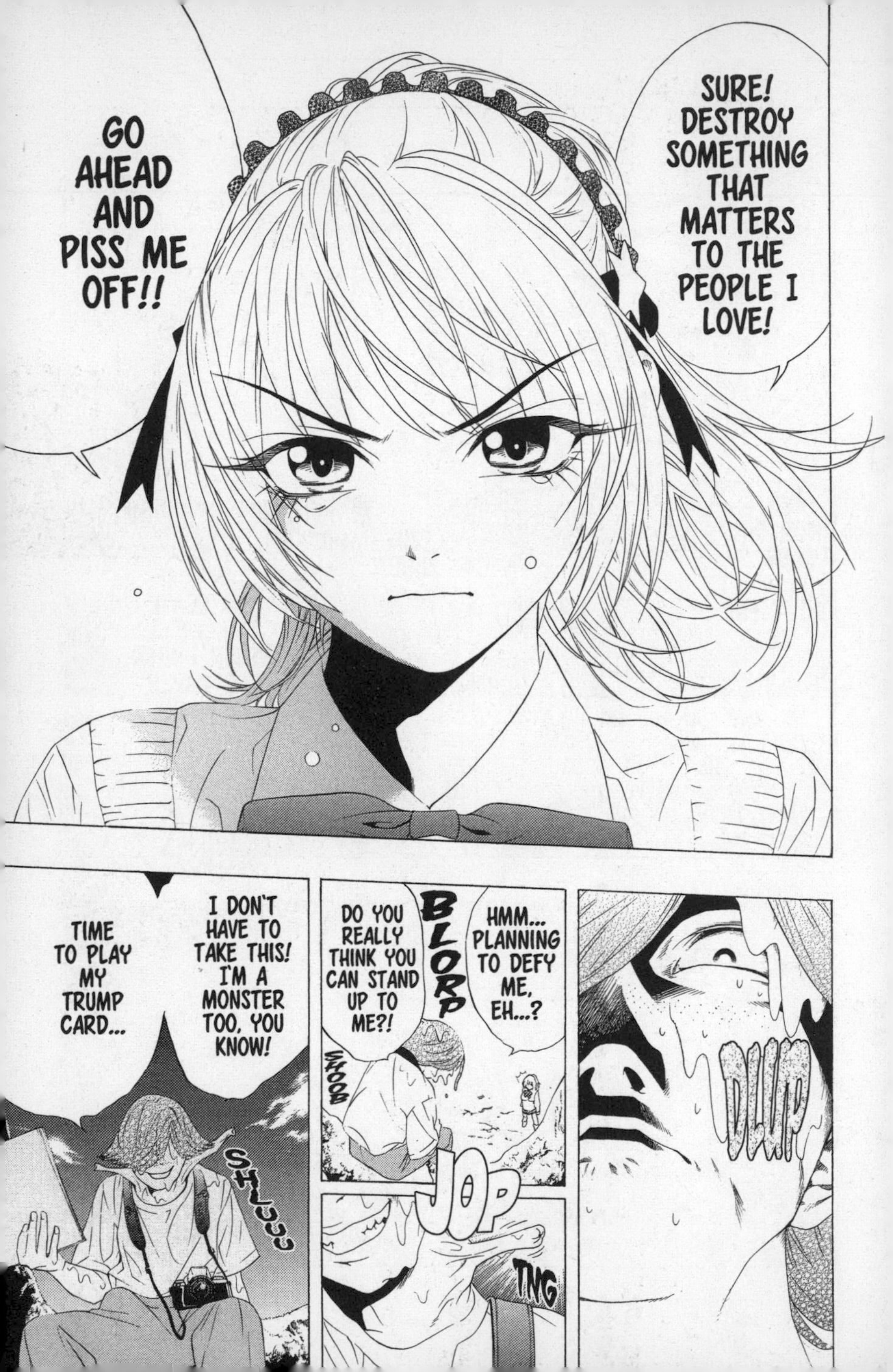
SURE! DESTROY SOMETHING THAT MATTERS TO THE PEOPLE I LOVE!
GO AHEAD AND PISS ME OFF!!
DLUP
HMM... PLANNING TO DEFY ME, EH...?
BLORP
DO YOU REALLY THINK YOU CAN STAND UP TO ME?!
SHOOB
JOP
TNG
I DON'T HAVE TO TAKE THIS! I'M A MONSTER TOO, YOU KNOW!
TIME TO PLAY MY TRUMP CARD...
SHLUUU

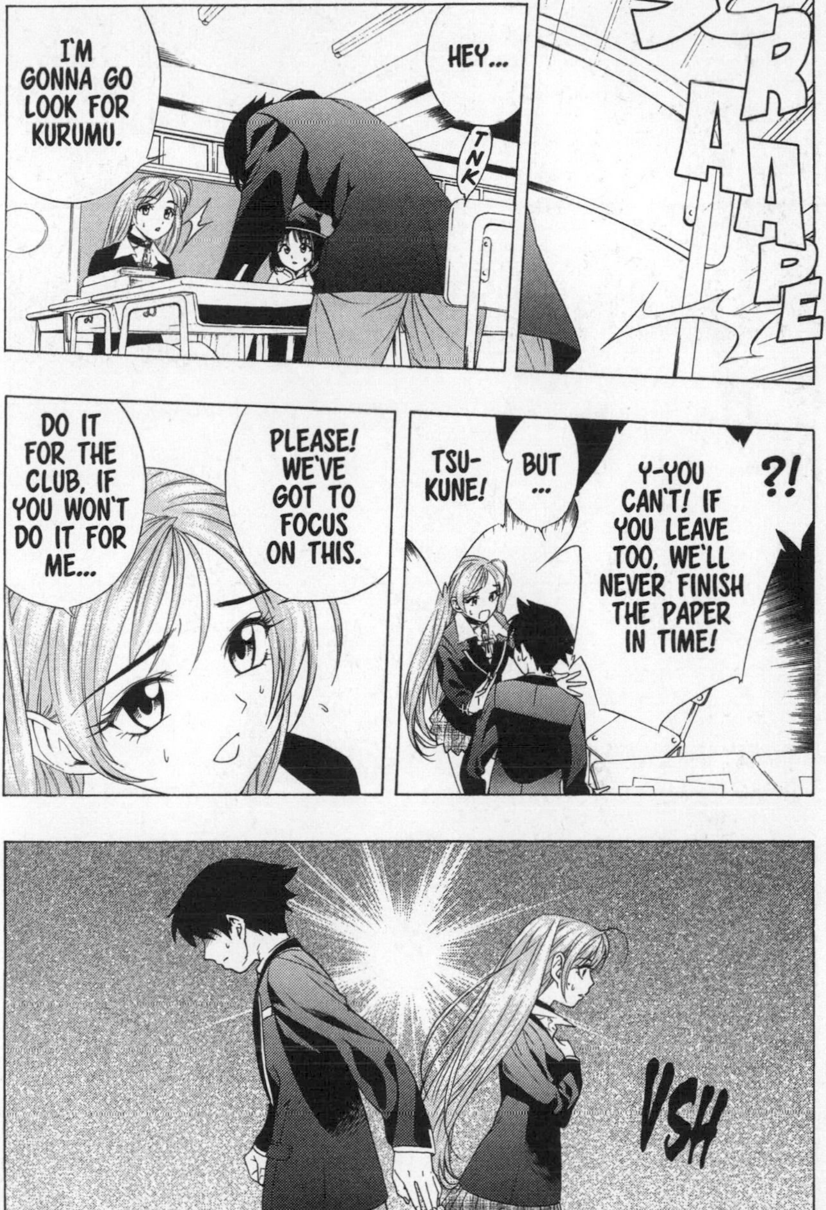
SCRAAPE
HEY...
TNK
I'M GONNA GO LOOK FOR KURUMU.
?!
Y-YOU CAN'T! IF YOU LEAVE TOO, WE'LL NEVER FINISH THE PAPER IN TIME!
BUT ...
TSU-KUNE!
PLEASE! WE'VE GOT TO FOCUS ON THIS.
DO IT FOR THE CLUB, IF YOU WON'T DO IT FOR ME...
VSH

READ THIS WAY

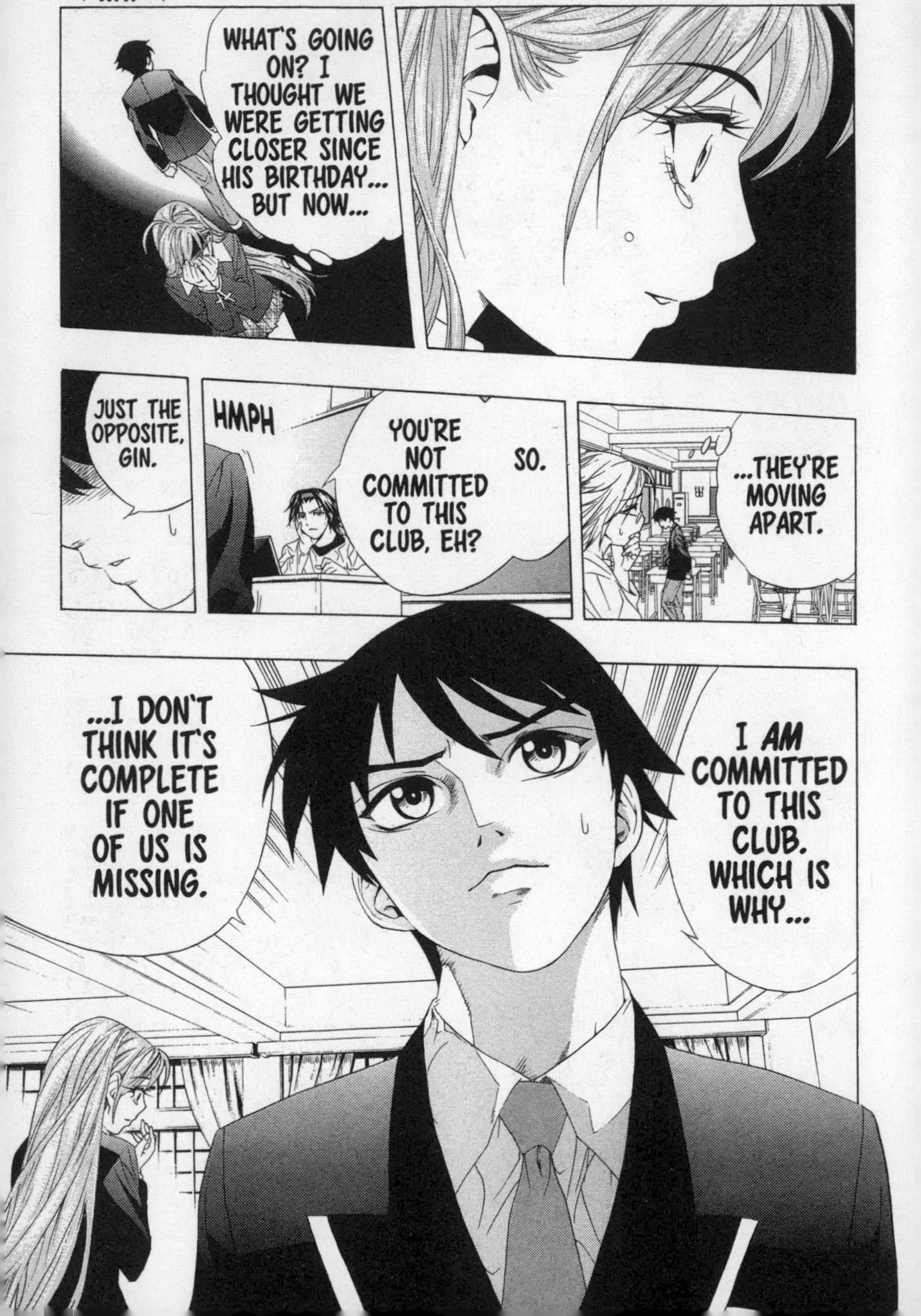

WHAT'S GOING ON? I THOUGHT WE WERE GETTING CLOSER SINCE HIS BIRTHDAY... BUT NOW...
...THEY'RE MOVING APART.
SO.
YOU'RE NOT COMMITTED TO THIS CLUB, EH?
HMPH
JUST THE OPPOSITE, GIN.
I *AM* COMMITTED TO THIS CLUB. WHICH IS WHY...
...I DON'T THINK IT'S COMPLETE IF ONE OF US IS MISSING.

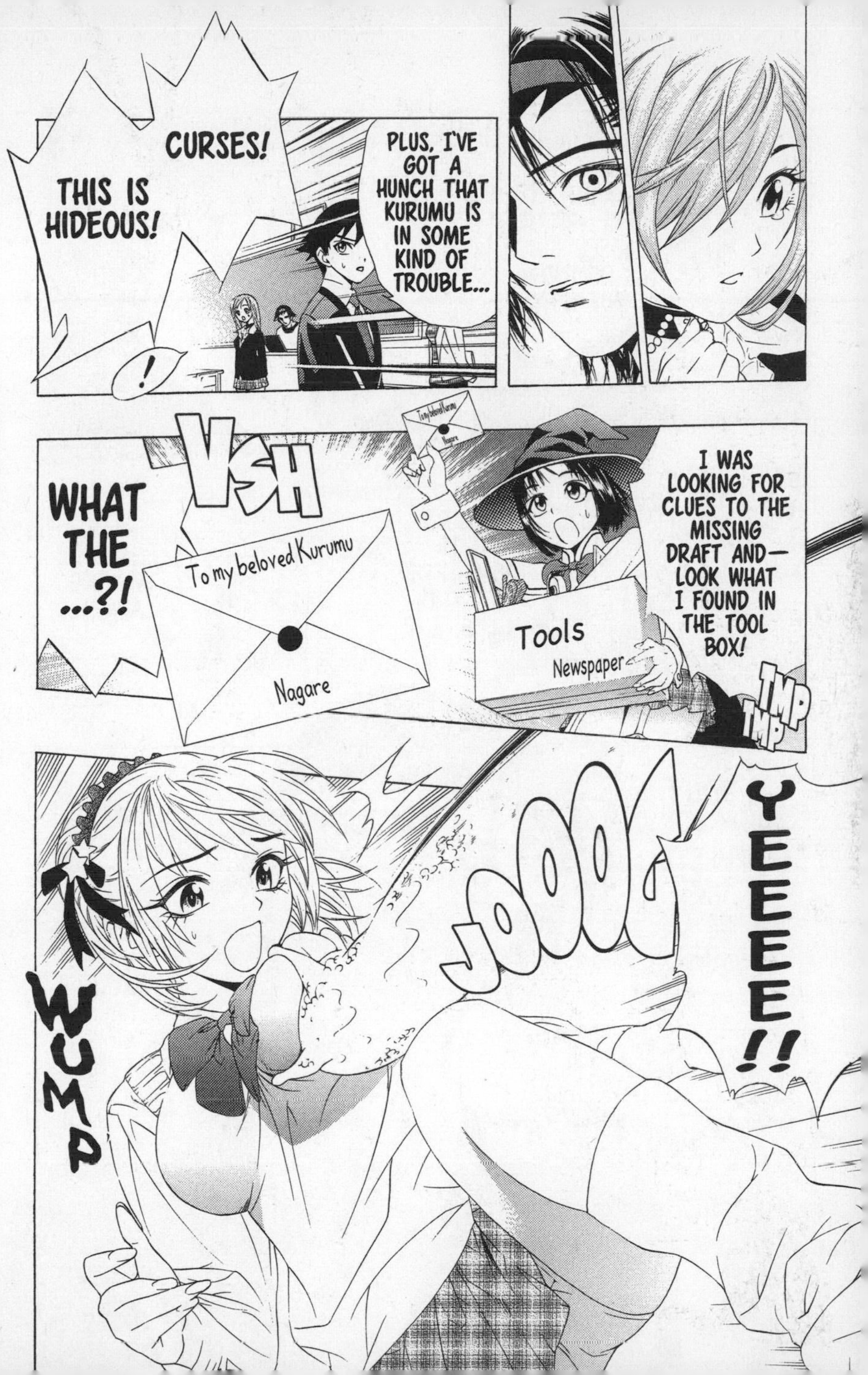

PLUS, I'VE GOT A HUNCH THAT KURUMU IS IN SOME KIND OF TROUBLE...
CURSES!
THIS IS HIDEOUS!
!
I WAS LOOKING FOR CLUES TO THE MISSING DRAFT AND— LOOK WHAT I FOUND IN THE TOOL BOX!
Tools
Newspaper
TMP TMP
VSH
To my beloved Kurumu
Nagare
WHAT THE ...?!
YEEEE!!
JOOOG
WUMP

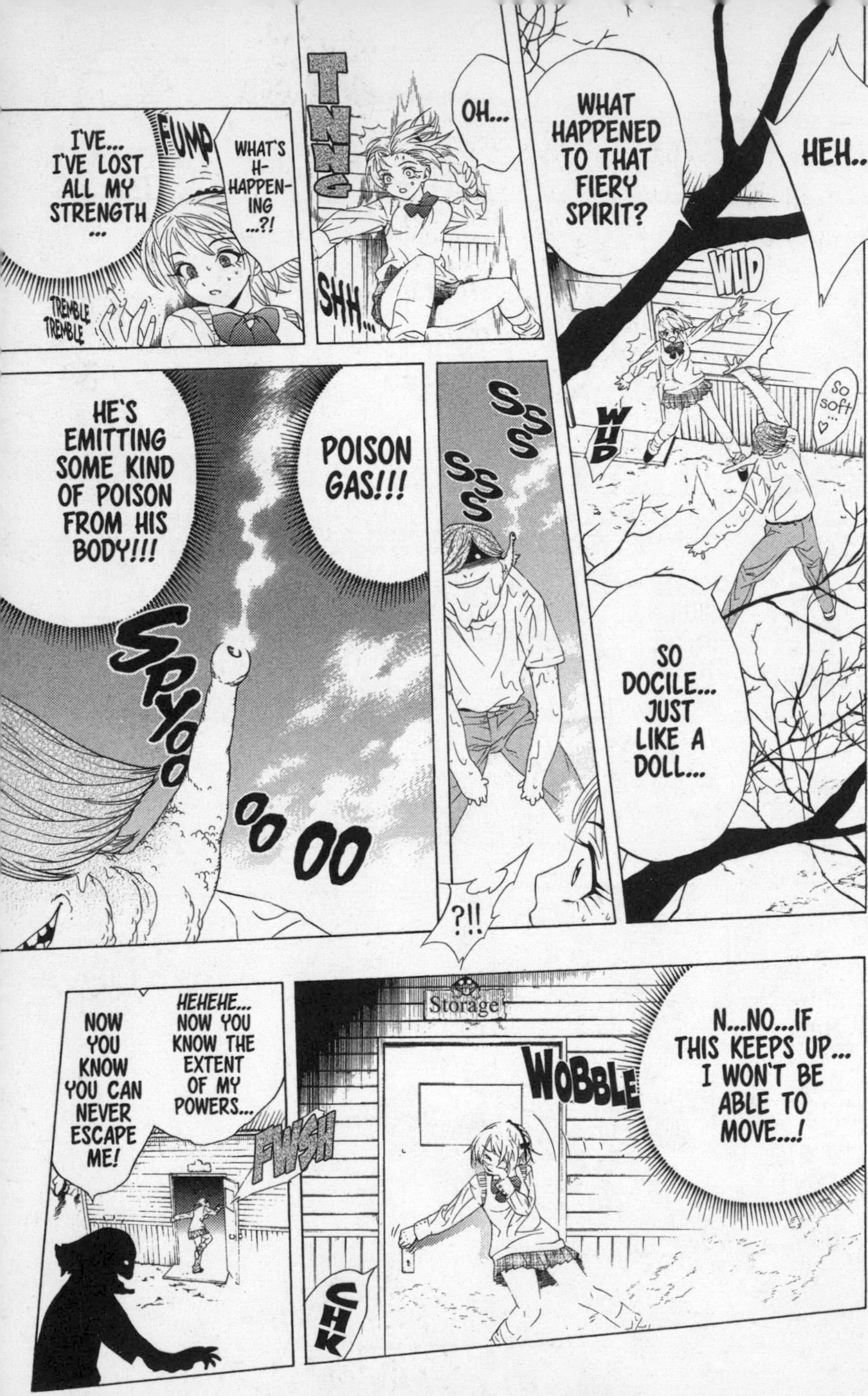
HEH...
WHAT HAPPENED TO THAT FIERY SPIRIT?
WUD
WUD
So soft... ♡
SO DOCILE... JUST LIKE A DOLL...
OH...
TNNG
WHAT'S H-HAPPENING...?!
SHH...
FUMP
I'VE... I'VE LOST ALL MY STRENGTH...
TREMBLE TREMBLE
SSS
SSS
?!!
POISON GAS!!!
HE'S EMITTING SOME KIND OF POISON FROM HIS BODY!!!
SPYOOOOOOOO
N...NO...IF THIS KEEPS UP... I WON'T BE ABLE TO MOVE...!
Storage
WOBBLE
CHK
HEHEHE... NOW YOU KNOW THE EXTENT OF MY POWERS...
NOW YOU KNOW YOU CAN NEVER ESCAPE ME!
FWSH

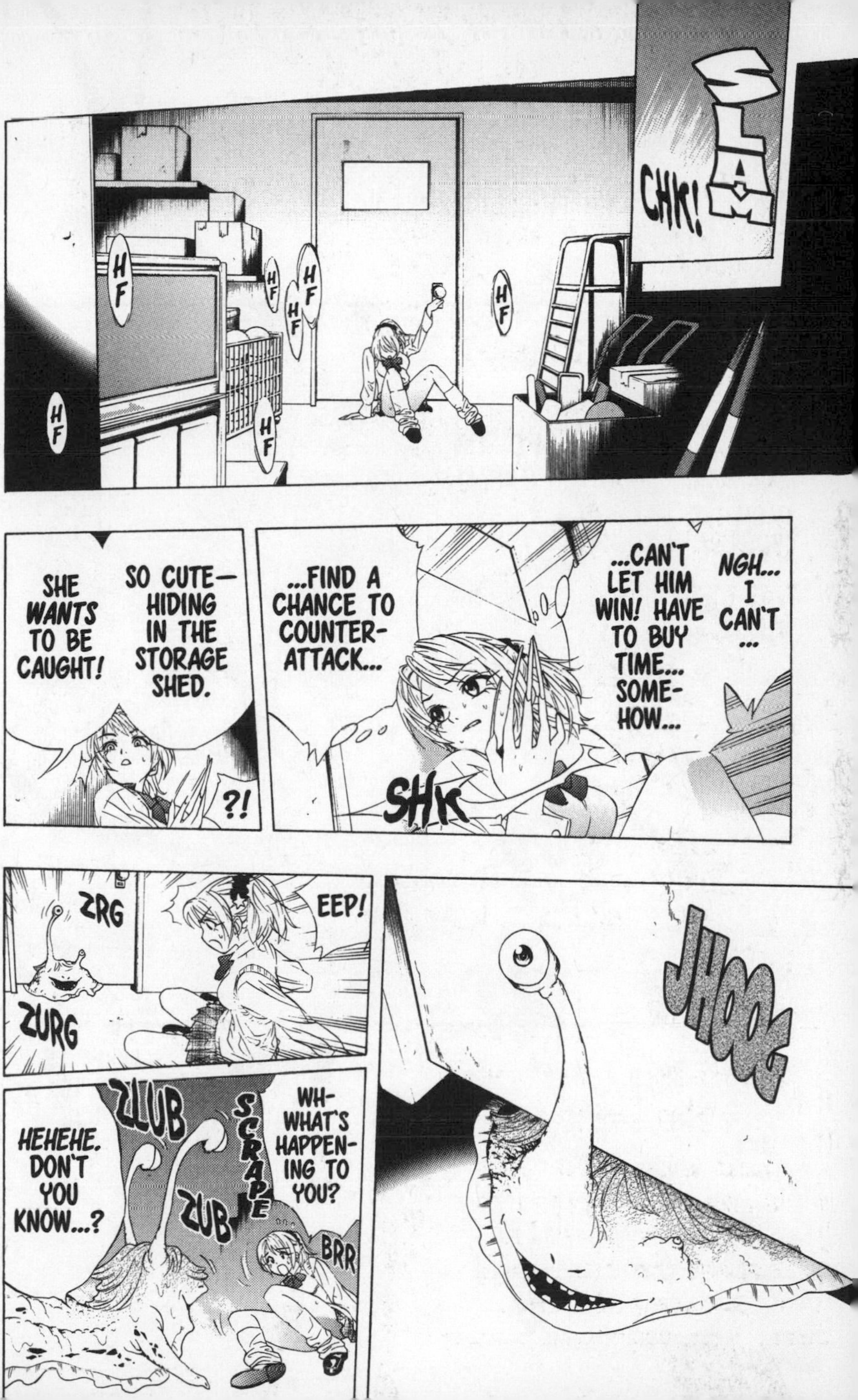
SLAM
CHK!
HF
HF
HF
HF
HF
HF
HF
NGH... I CAN'T ...
...CAN'T LET HIM WIN! HAVE TO BUY TIME... SOMEHOW...
...FIND A CHANCE TO COUNTER-ATTACK...
SHK
SO CUTE— HIDING IN THE STORAGE SHED.
SHE WANTS TO BE CAUGHT!
?!
JHOOG
EEP!
ZRG
ZURG
WH- WHAT'S HAPPENING TO YOU?
SCRAPE
ZLUB
HEHEHE. DON'T YOU KNOW...?
ZUB
BRR

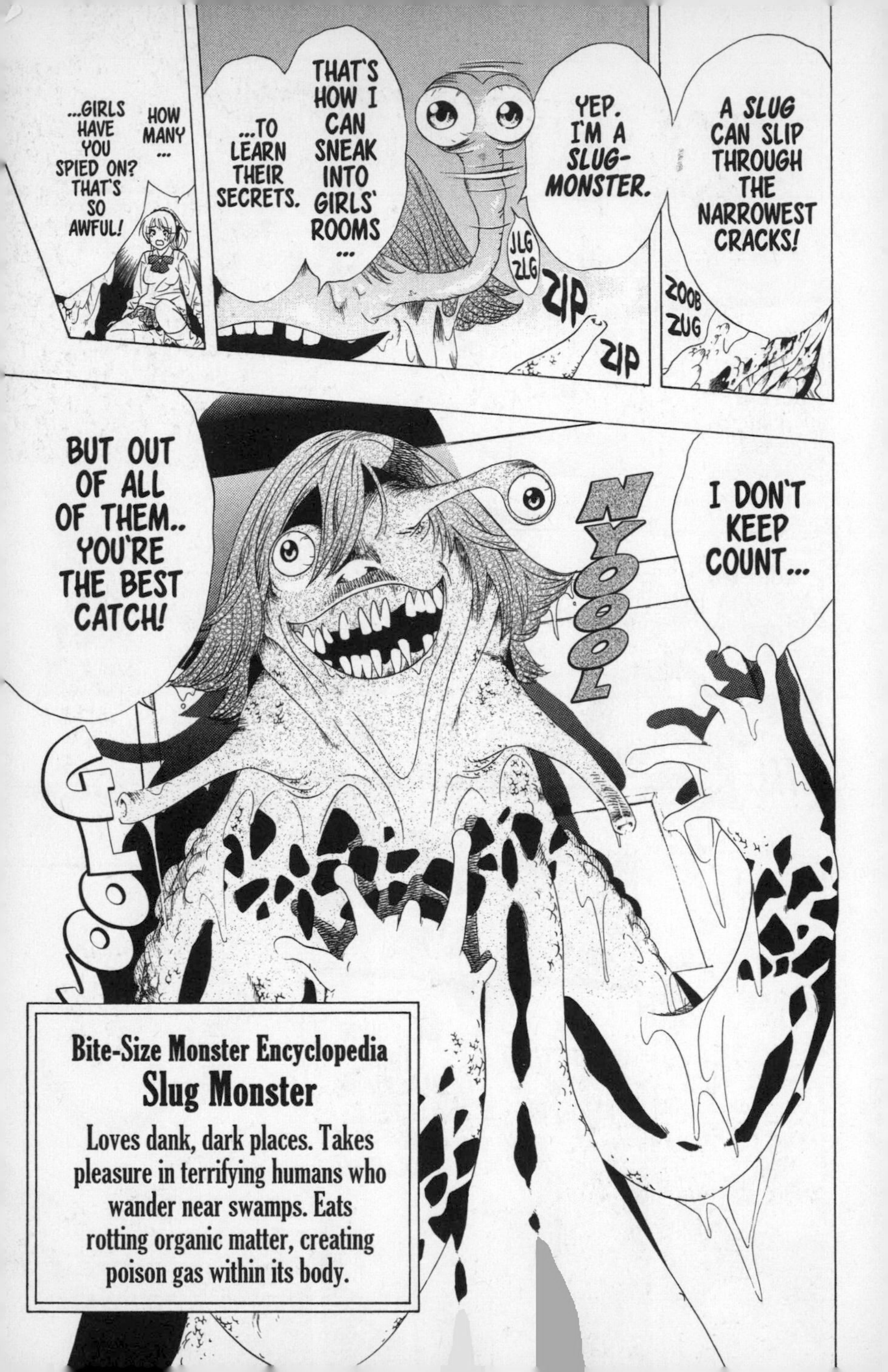
A SLUG CAN SLIP THROUGH THE NARROWEST CRACKS!
ZOOB ZUG
YEP. I'M A SLUG-MONSTER.
JLG ZLG
ZIP
ZIP
THAT'S HOW I CAN SNEAK INTO GIRLS' ROOMS...
...TO LEARN THEIR SECRETS.
HOW MANY...
...GIRLS HAVE YOU SPIED ON? THAT'S SO AWFUL!
I DON'T KEEP COUNT...
NYOOOOL
BUT OUT OF ALL OF THEM.. YOU'RE THE BEST CATCH!
Bite-Size Monster Encyclopedia
Slug Monster
Loves dank, dark places. Takes pleasure in terrifying humans who wander near swamps. Eats rotting organic matter, creating poison gas within its body.

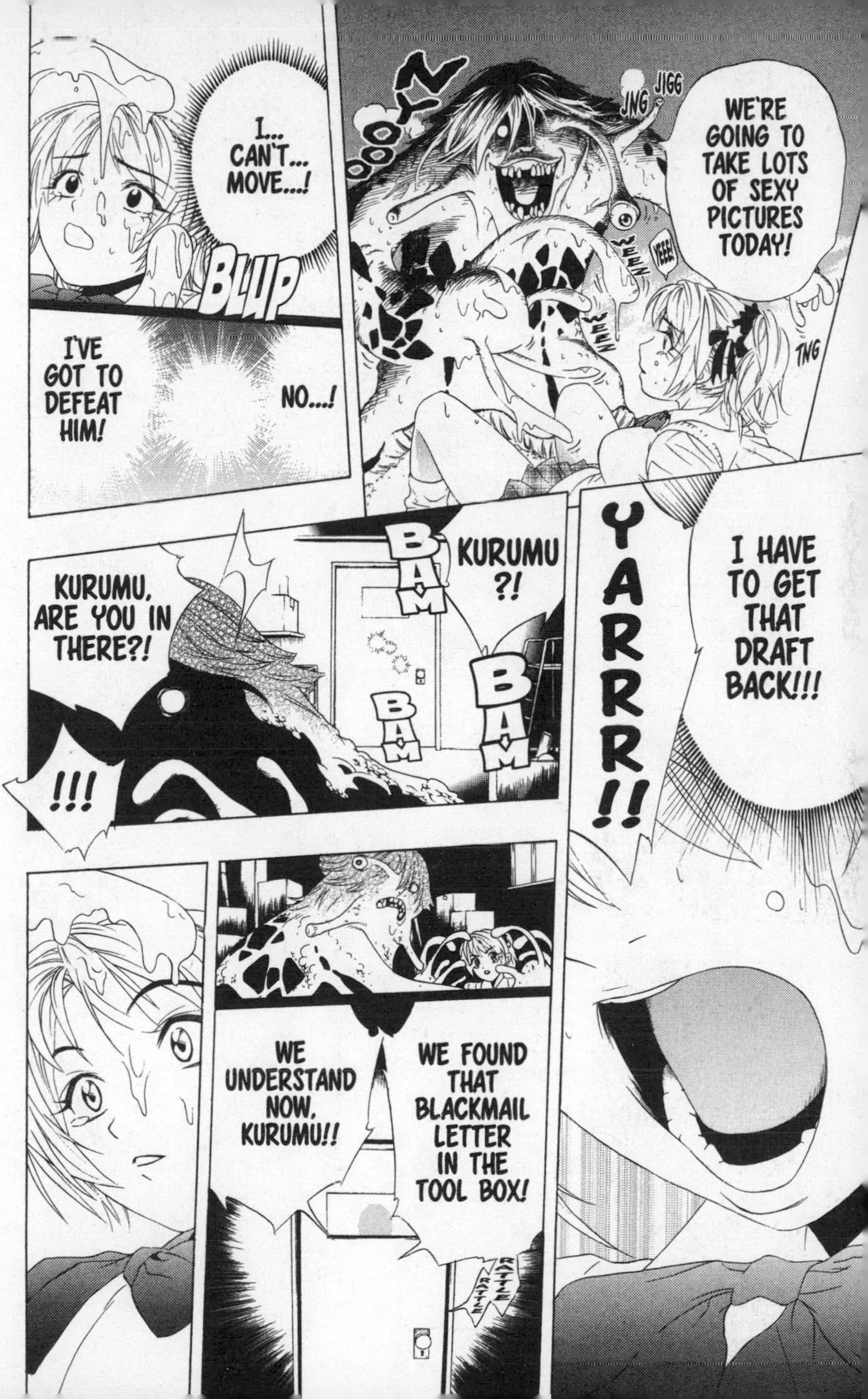
BOOOOYN
JNG JIGG
WE'RE GOING TO TAKE LOTS OF SEXY PICTURES TODAY!
WEEN
YEEE!
WEEN
TNG
I... CAN'T... MOVE...!
BLUP
NO...!
I'VE GOT TO DEFEAT HIM!
YARRR!!
I HAVE TO GET THAT DRAFT BACK!!!
BAM
KURUMU ?!
BAM
BAM
KURUMU, ARE YOU IN THERE?!
!!!
WE FOUND THAT BLACKMAIL LETTER IN THE TOOL BOX!
WE UNDERSTAND NOW, KURUMU!!
RATTLE
RATTLE

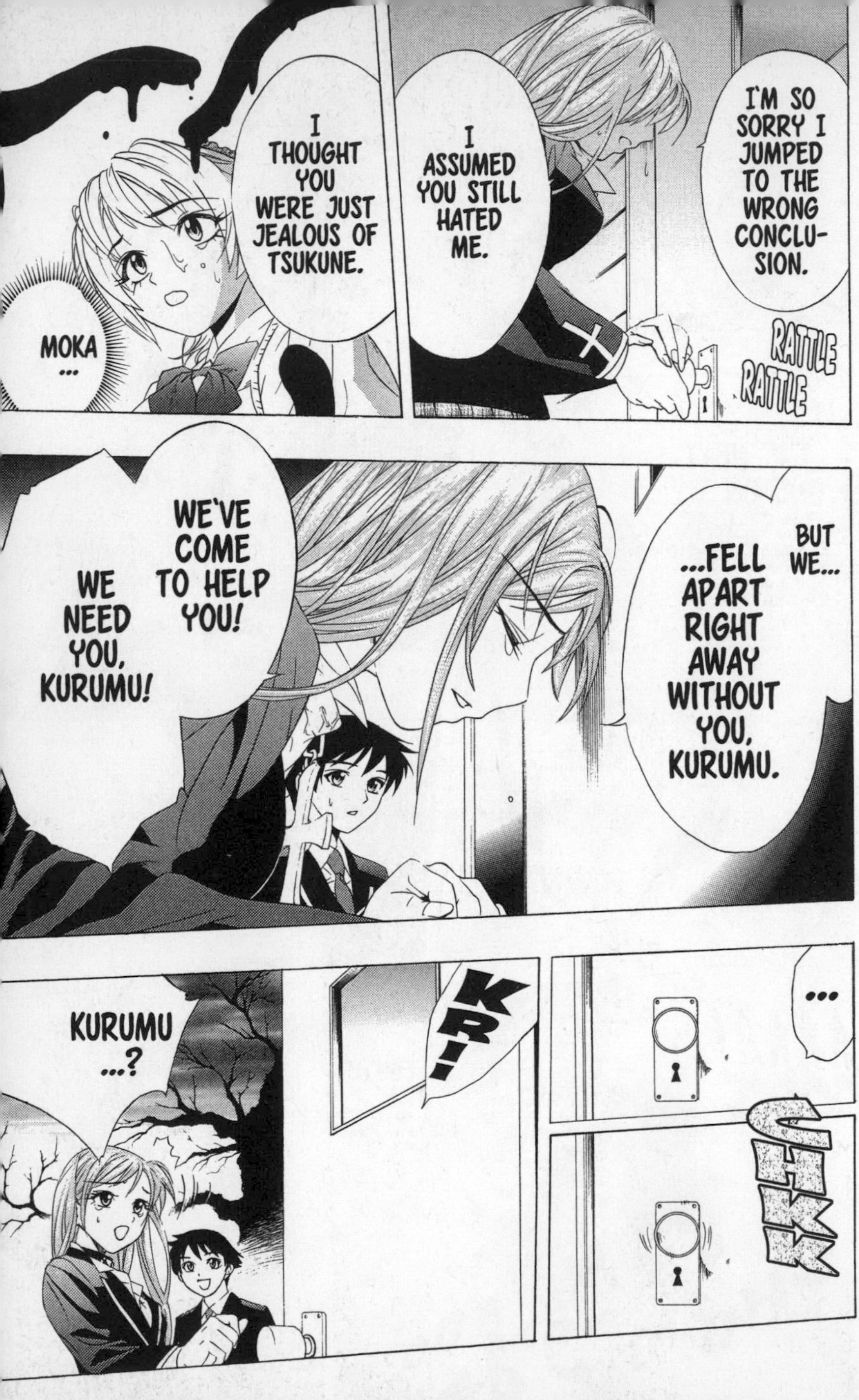
I'M SO SORRY I JUMPED TO THE WRONG CONCLUSION.
RATTLE RATTLE
I ASSUMED YOU STILL HATED ME.
I THOUGHT YOU WERE JUST JEALOUS OF TSUKUNE.
MOKA...
BUT WE...
...FELL APART RIGHT AWAY WITHOUT YOU, KURUMU.
WE'VE COME TO HELP YOU!
WE NEED YOU, KURUMU!
...
CHKK
KRI!
KURUMU ...?

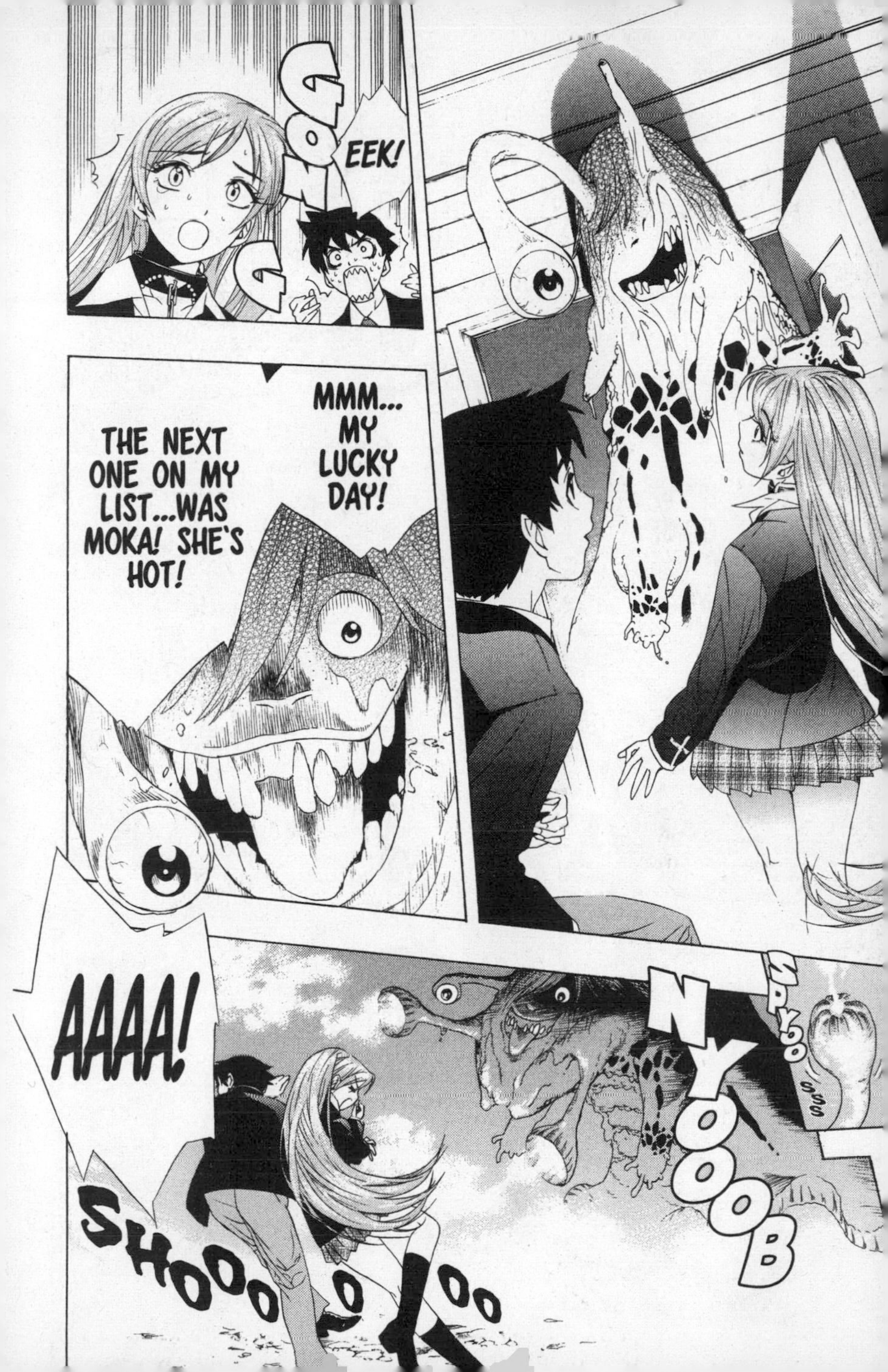
GONG
EEK!
MMM... MY LUCKY DAY!
THE NEXT ONE ON MY LIST...WAS MOKA! SHE'S HOT!
SPYOOSSS
NYOOOOB
AAAA!
SHOOOOOOO

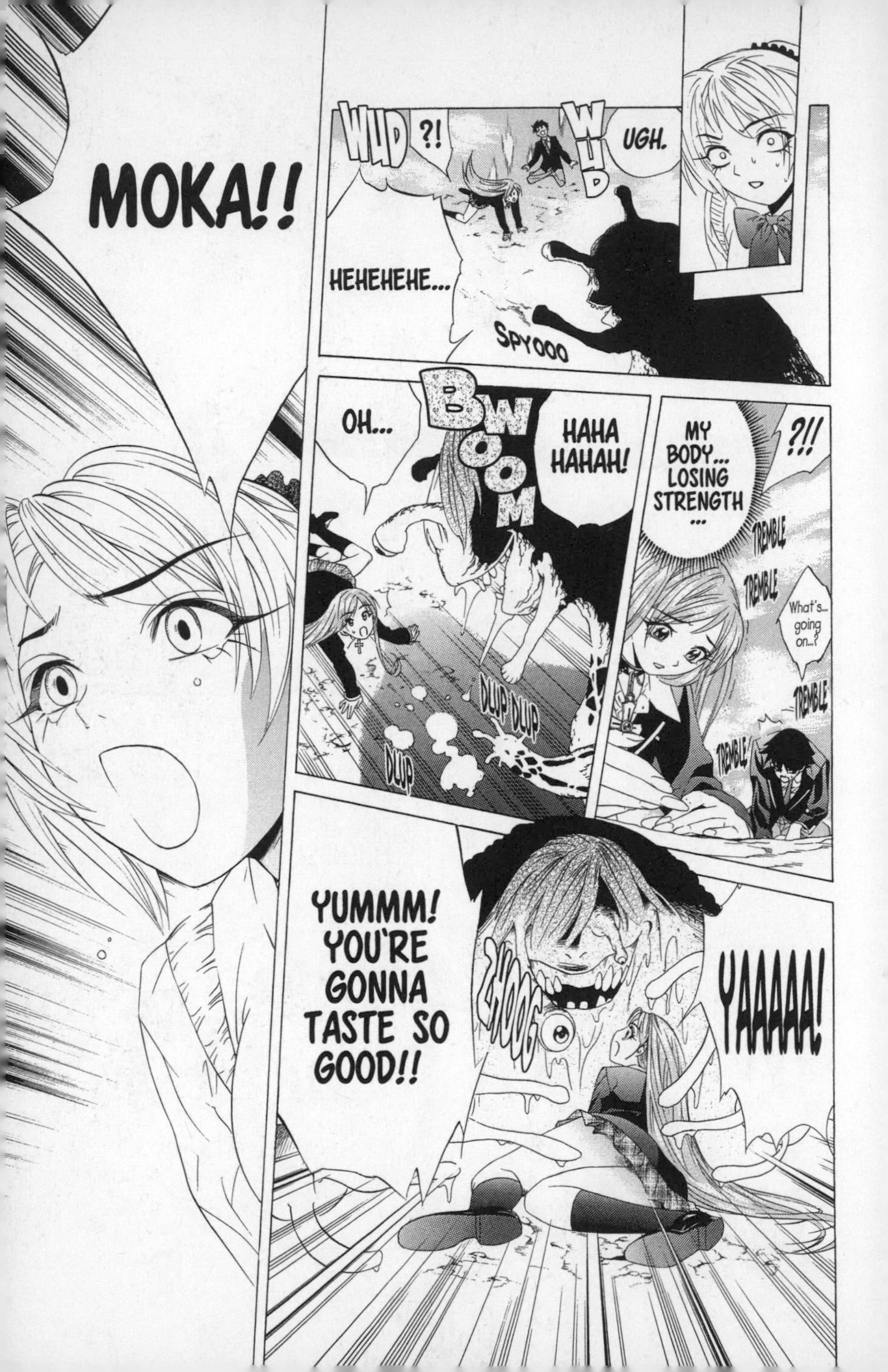
UGH.
WUD
?!
WUD
HEHEHEHE...
SPYOOO
?!!
MY BODY... LOSING STRENGTH ...
TREMBLE
TREMBLE
What's... going on...?
TREMBLE
TREMBLE
HAHA HAHAH!
BWOOM
OH...
DLUP DLUP
DLUP
YAAAAA!
ZHOOG
YUMMM! YOU'RE GONNA TASTE SO GOOD!!
MOKA!!

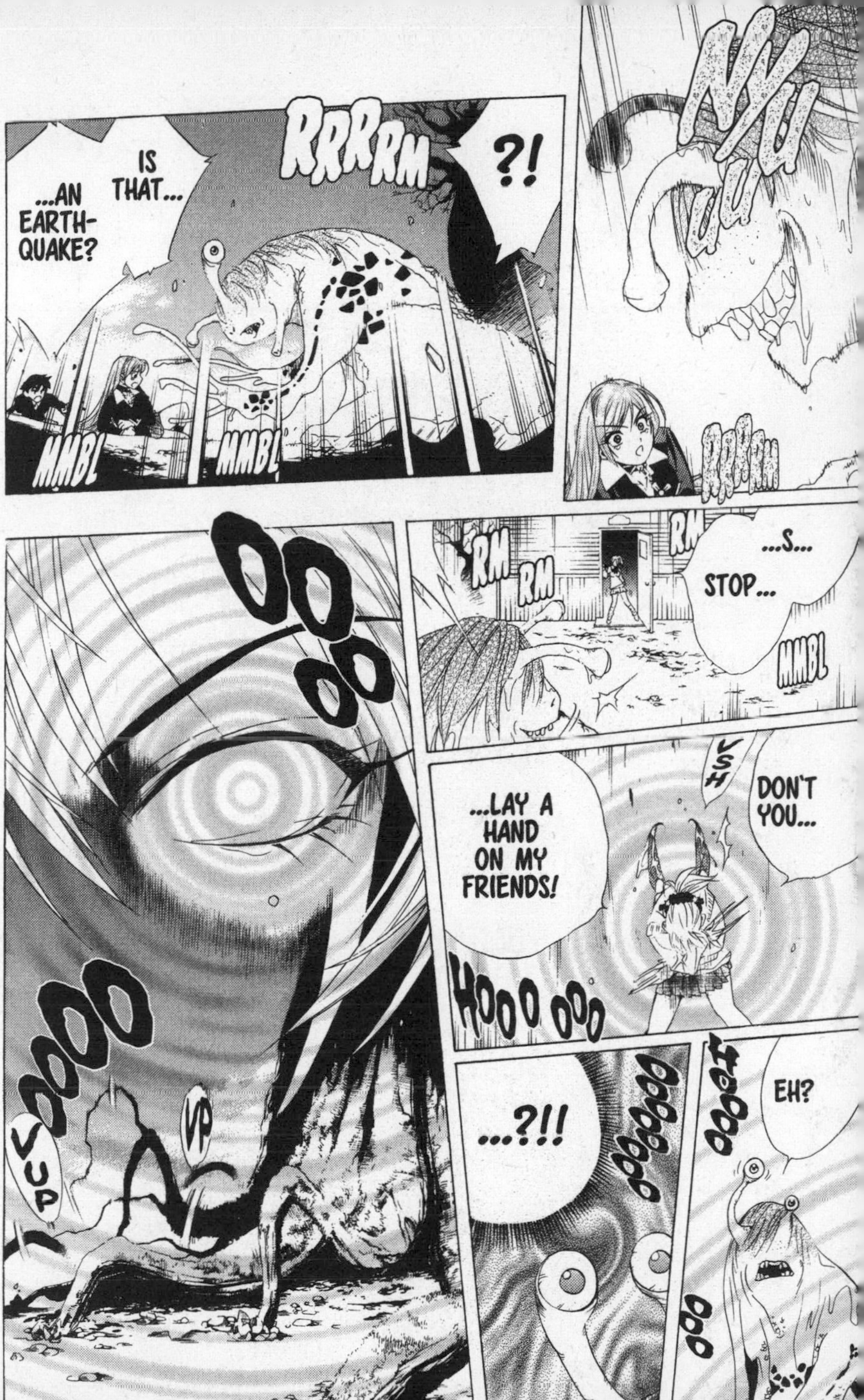

?!
RRRRM
IS THAT...
...AN EARTH-QUAKE?
MMBL
MMBL
RM
RM
RM
...S... STOP...
MMBL
VSH
DON'T YOU...
...LAY A HAND ON MY FRIENDS!
HOOO OOO
EH?
...?!!
VUP
VP

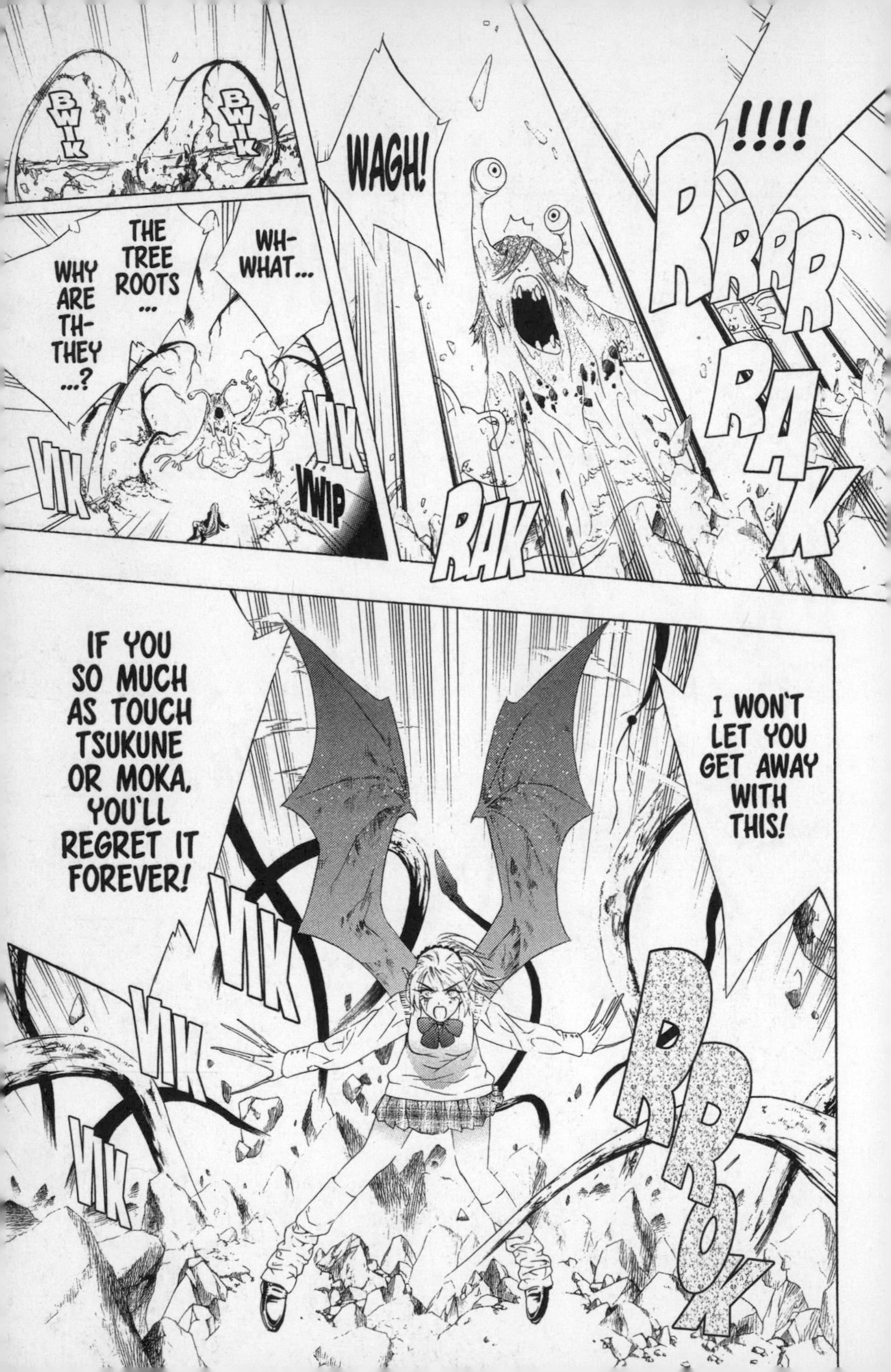
!!!!
RRRR
RAK
WAGH!
RAK
BWIK
BWIK
WH-WHAT...
THE TREE ROOTS...
WHY ARE TH-THEY...?
VIIK
VIIK
VWIP
I WON'T LET YOU GET AWAY WITH THIS!
IF YOU SO MUCH AS TOUCH TSUKUNE OR MOKA, YOU'LL REGRET IT FOREVER!
RRROK
VIIK
VIIK
VIIK

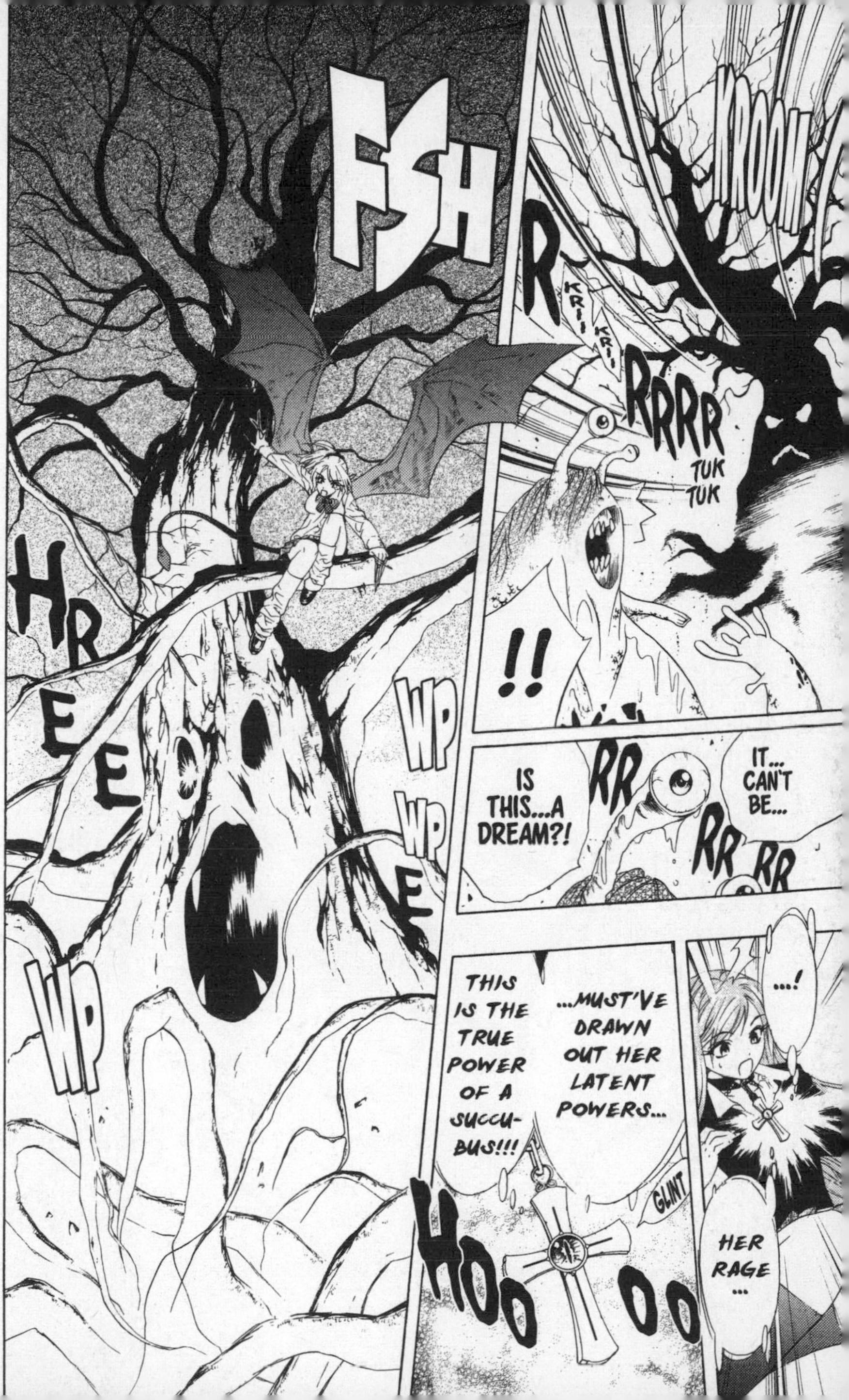

KROOM
KRII KRII
RRRR
TUK TUK
!!
IT... CAN'T BE...
RR RR RR RR
IS THIS...A DREAM?!
...!
HER RAGE...
...MUST'VE DRAWN OUT HER LATENT POWERS...
THIS IS THE TRUE POWER OF A SUCCUBUS!!!
GLINT
HOOOOO
FSH
HREEEE
WP WP
WP

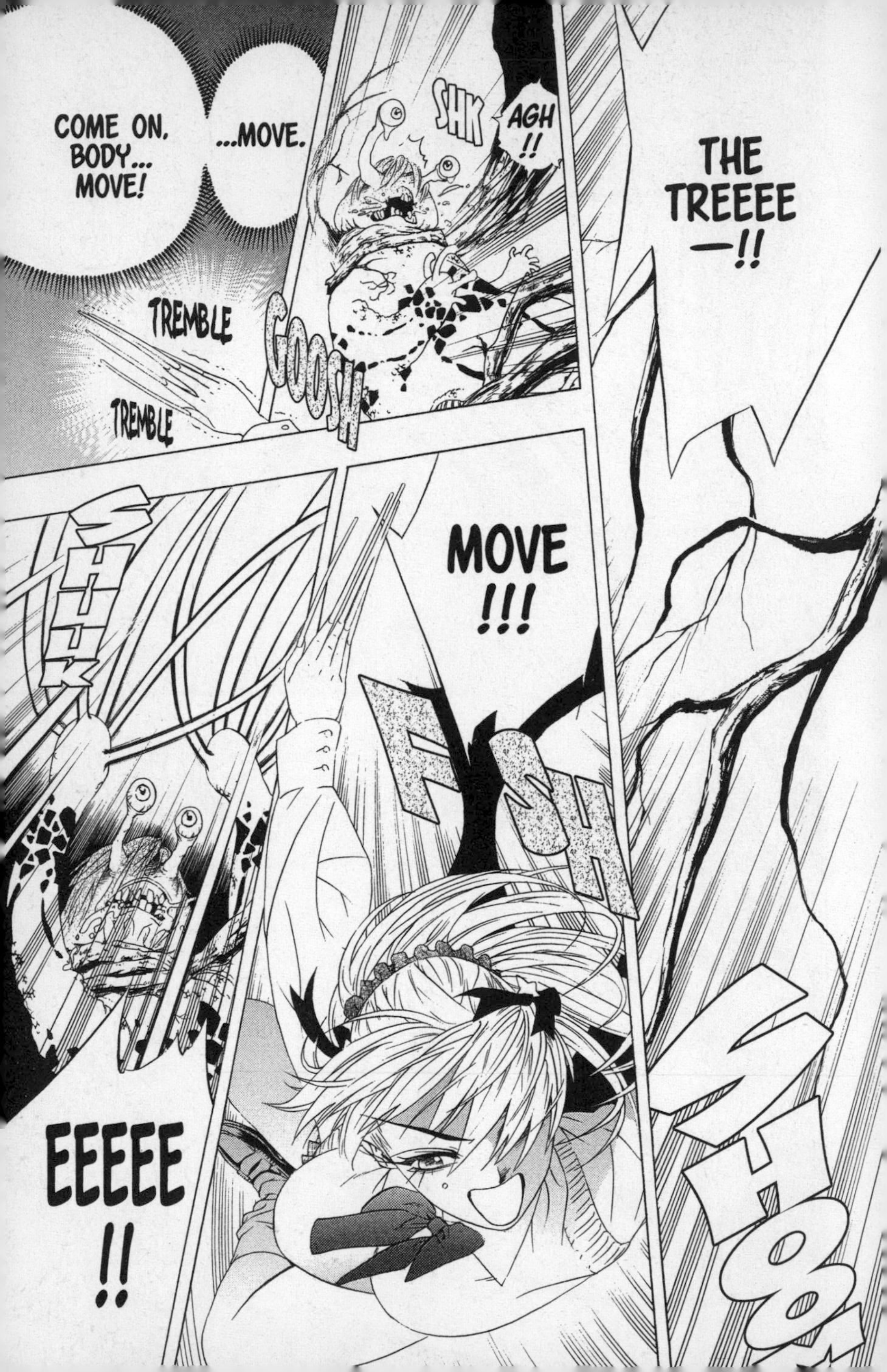
THE TREEEE—!!
SHOO
AGH!!
SHK
GOOSH
...MOVE.
COME ON, BODY... MOVE!
TREMBLE
TREMBLE
MOVE!!!
FWSH
SHUUK
EEEEE!!

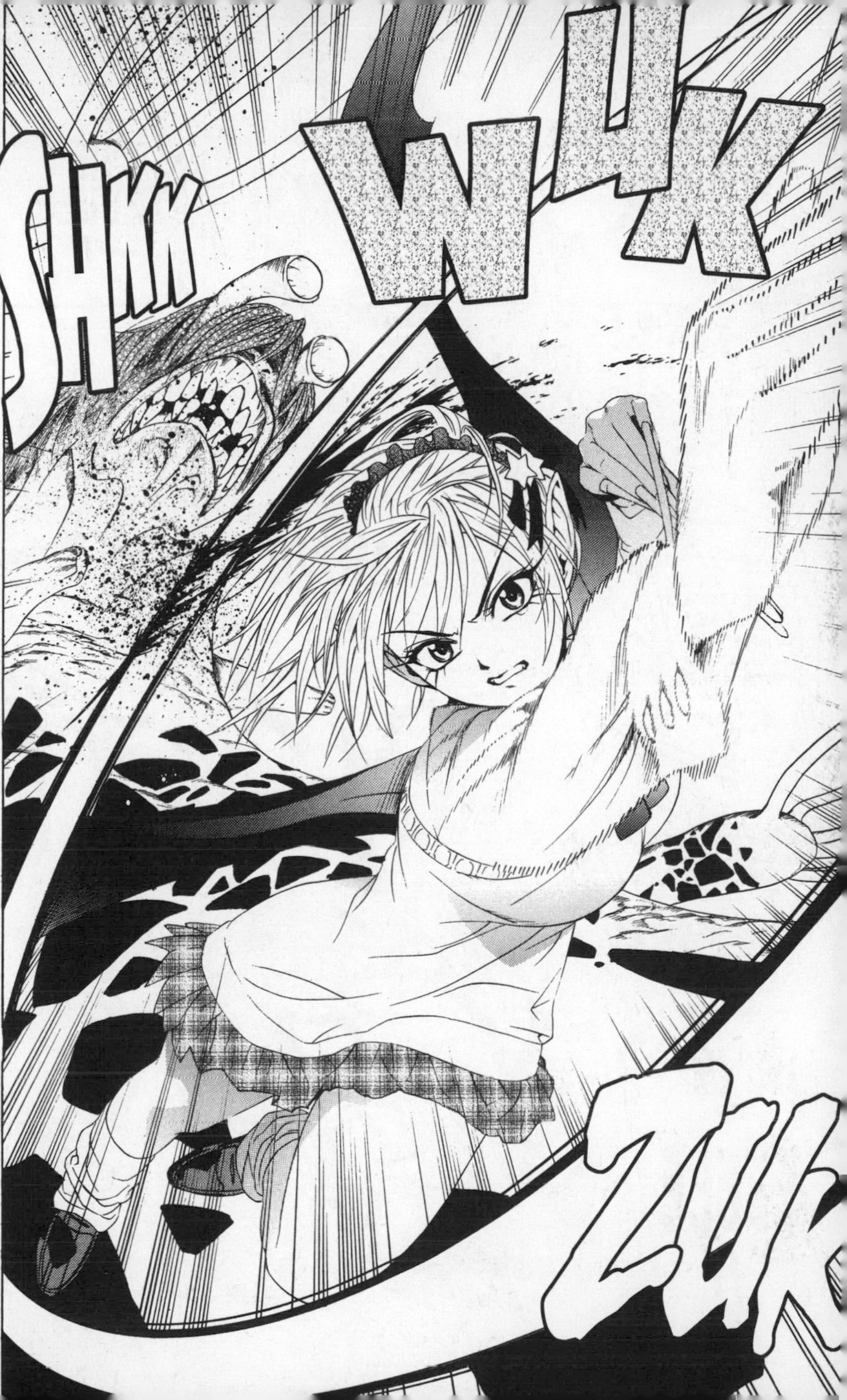
WUK
SHKK
ZUK

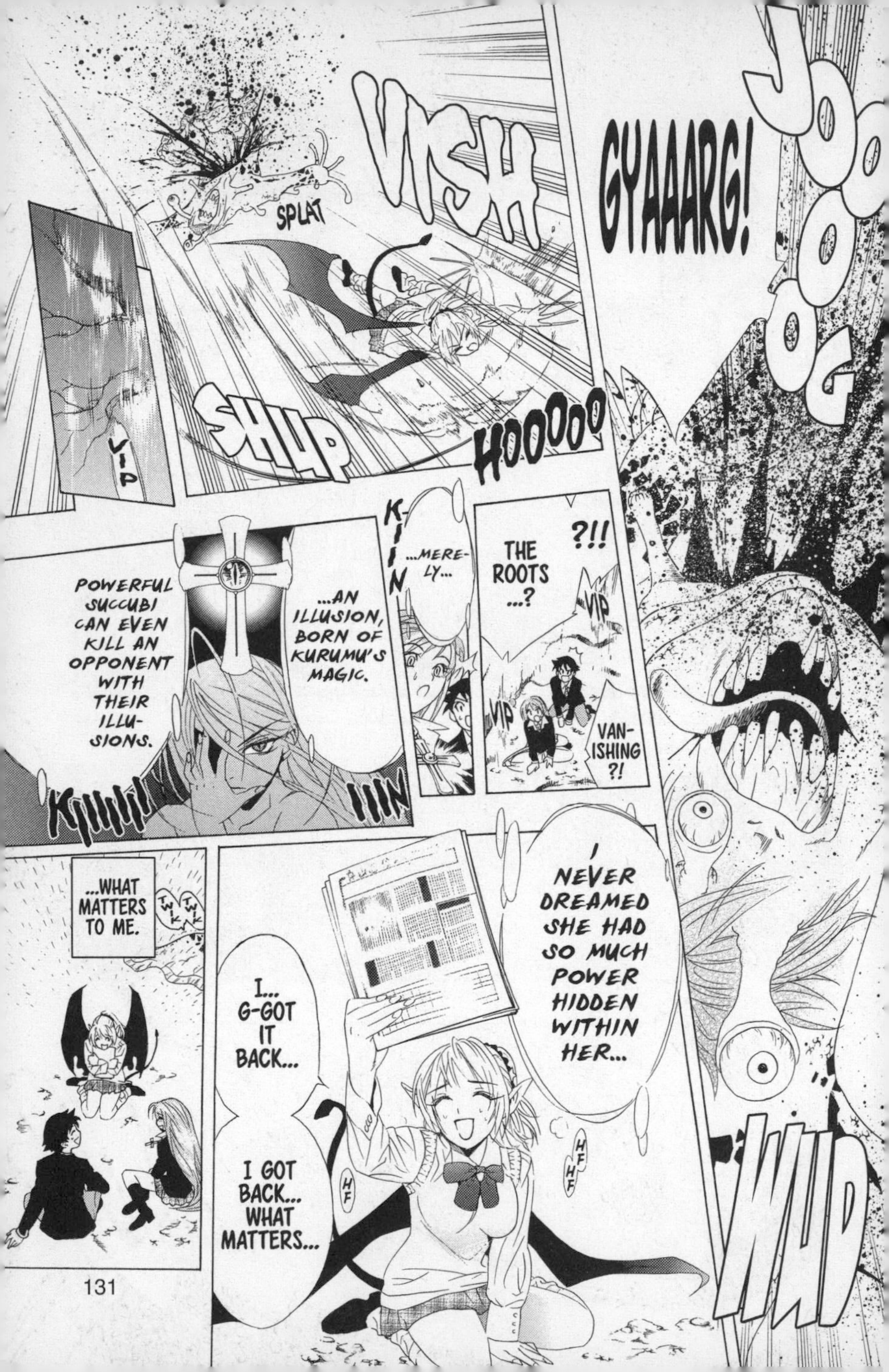

JOOOOG
GYAARG!
WHUD
VISH
SPLAT
SHUP
HOOOOO
VIP
?!!
THE ROOTS ...?
VIP
VIP
VAN-ISHING ?!
K-IIN
...MERE-LY...
...AN ILLUSION, BORN OF KURUMU'S MAGIC.
POWERFUL SUCCUBI CAN EVEN KILL AN OPPONENT WITH THEIR ILLU-SIONS.
KIIIIIIIIN
I NEVER DREAMED SHE HAD SO MUCH POWER HIDDEN WITHIN HER...
HF HF HF
I... G-GOT IT BACK...
HF
I GOT BACK... WHAT MATTERS...
...WHAT MATTERS TO ME.
TWIK TWIK

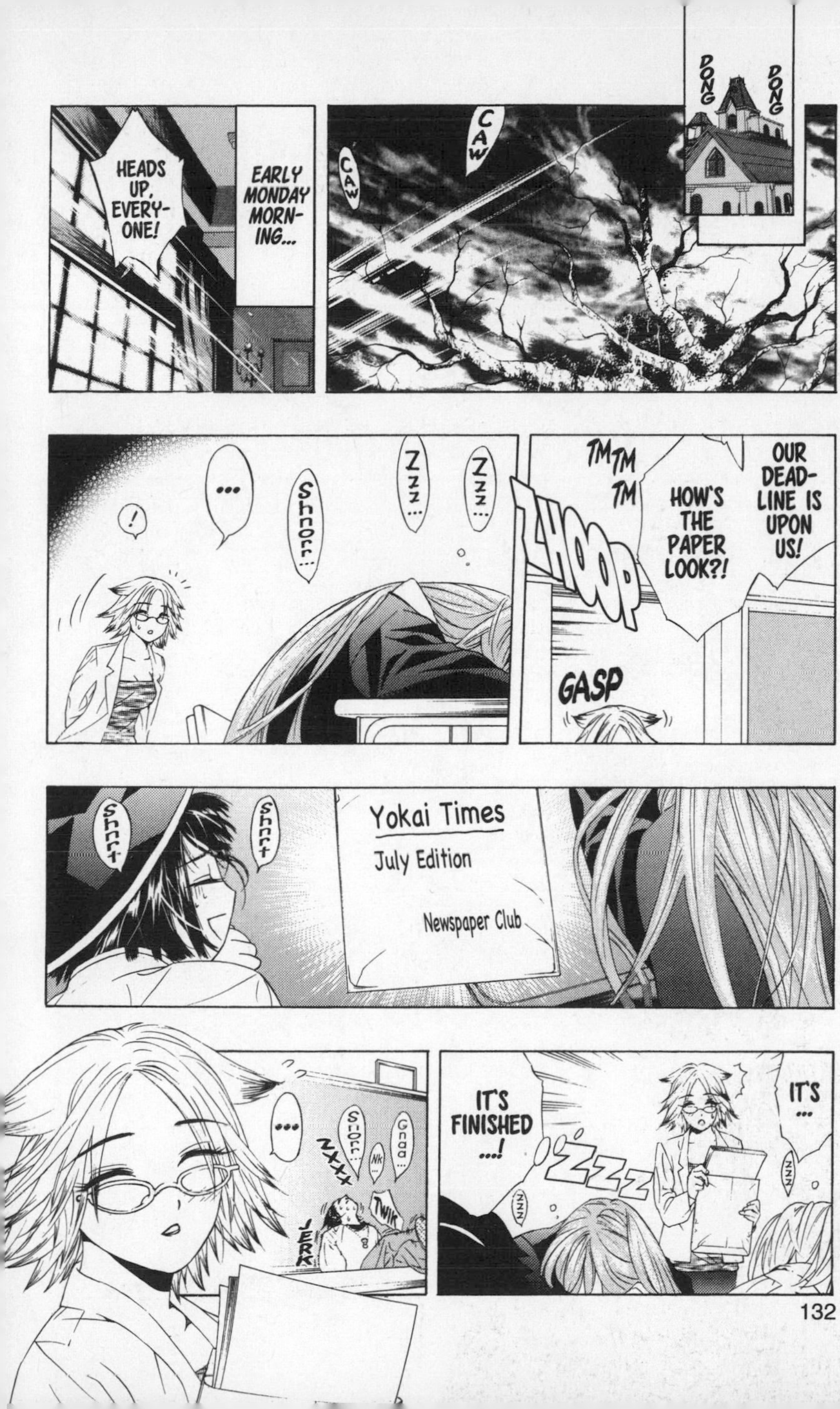
DONG
DONG
CAW
CAW
EARLY MONDAY MORNING...
HEADS UP, EVERYONE!
OUR DEADLINE IS UPON US!
HOW'S THE PAPER LOOK?!
TM TM TM
ZHOOP
GASP
Zzz...
Zzz...
Shnorr...
...
!
Shnrt
Shnrt
Yokai Times
July Edition
Newspaper Club
IT'S...
IT'S FINISHED...!
ZZZ
ZNN
ZNN
...
Gnaa...
NK...
Snorr...
ZXXX
TWIK
JERK

READ THIS WAY

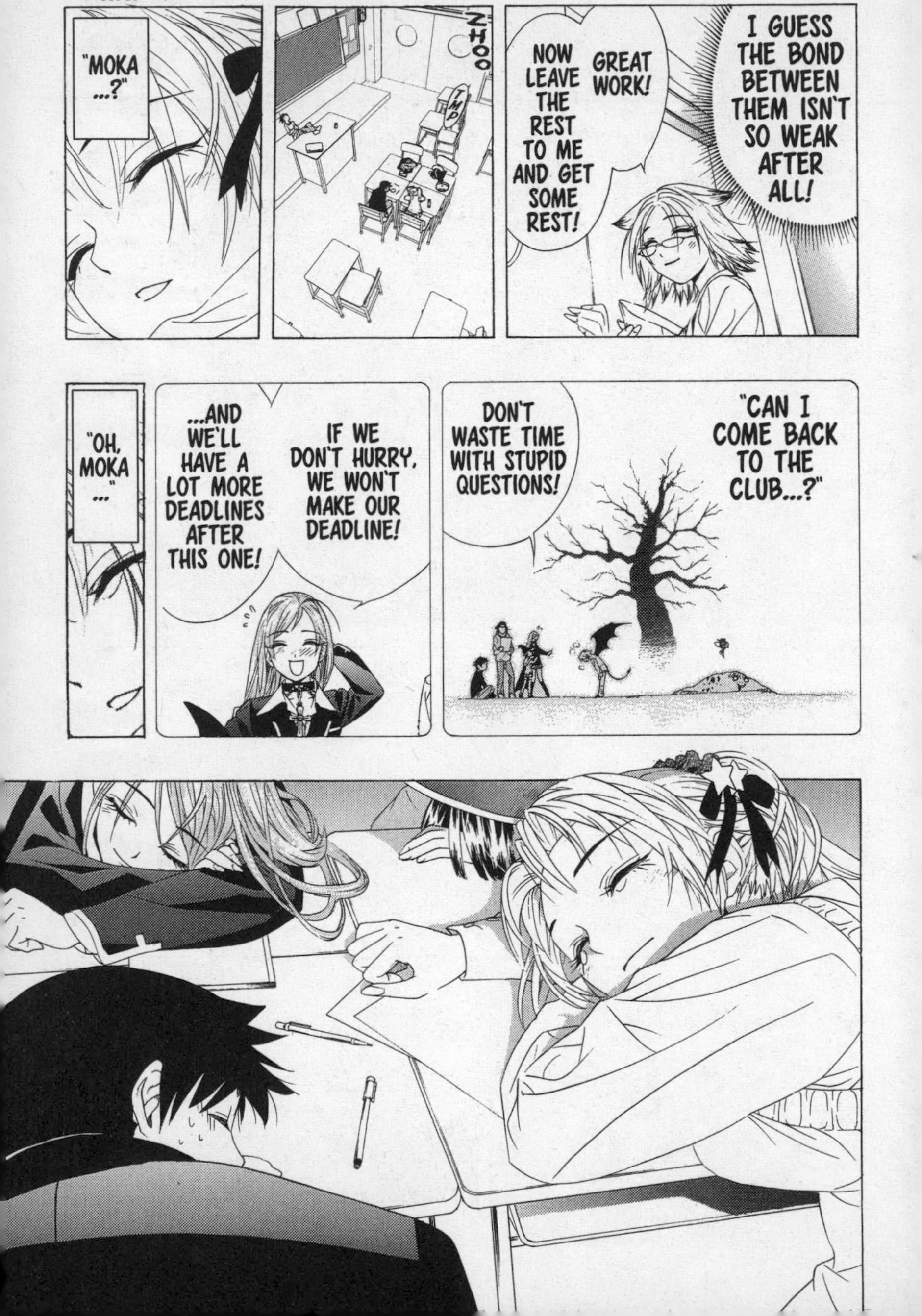
I GUESS THE BOND BETWEEN THEM ISN'T SO WEAK AFTER ALL!
GREAT WORK!
NOW LEAVE THE REST TO ME AND GET SOME REST!
ZHOO
TMP
"MOKA...?"
"CAN I COME BACK TO THE CLUB...?"
DON'T WASTE TIME WITH STUPID QUESTIONS!
IF WE DON'T HURRY, WE WON'T MAKE OUR DEADLINE!
...AND WE'LL HAVE A LOT MORE DEADLINES AFTER THIS ONE!
"OH, MOKA"...

ROSARIO+VAMPIRE

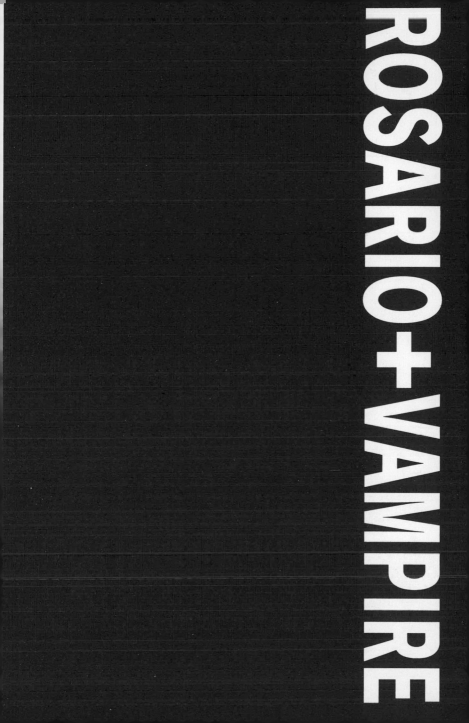

8: Wish Upon the Moon

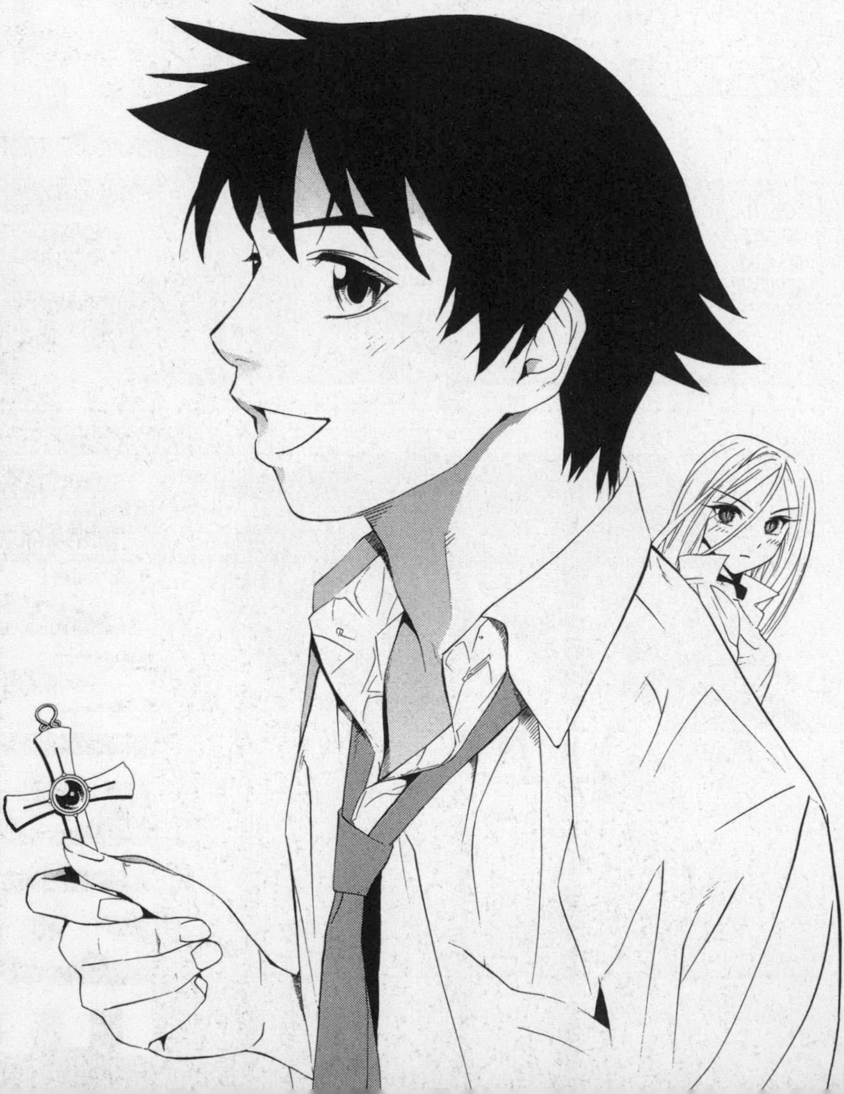

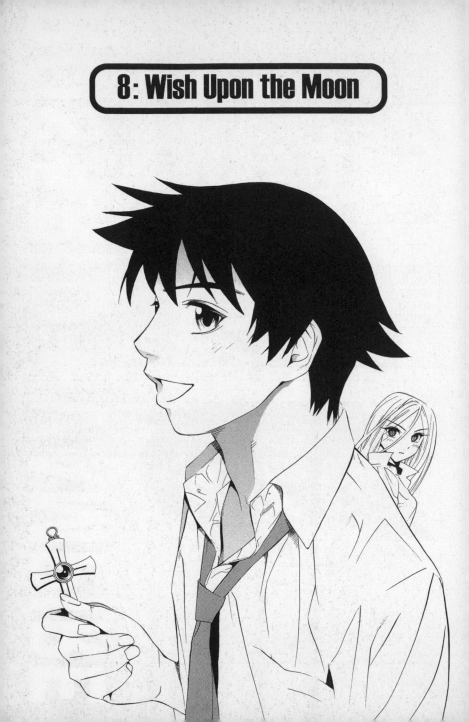

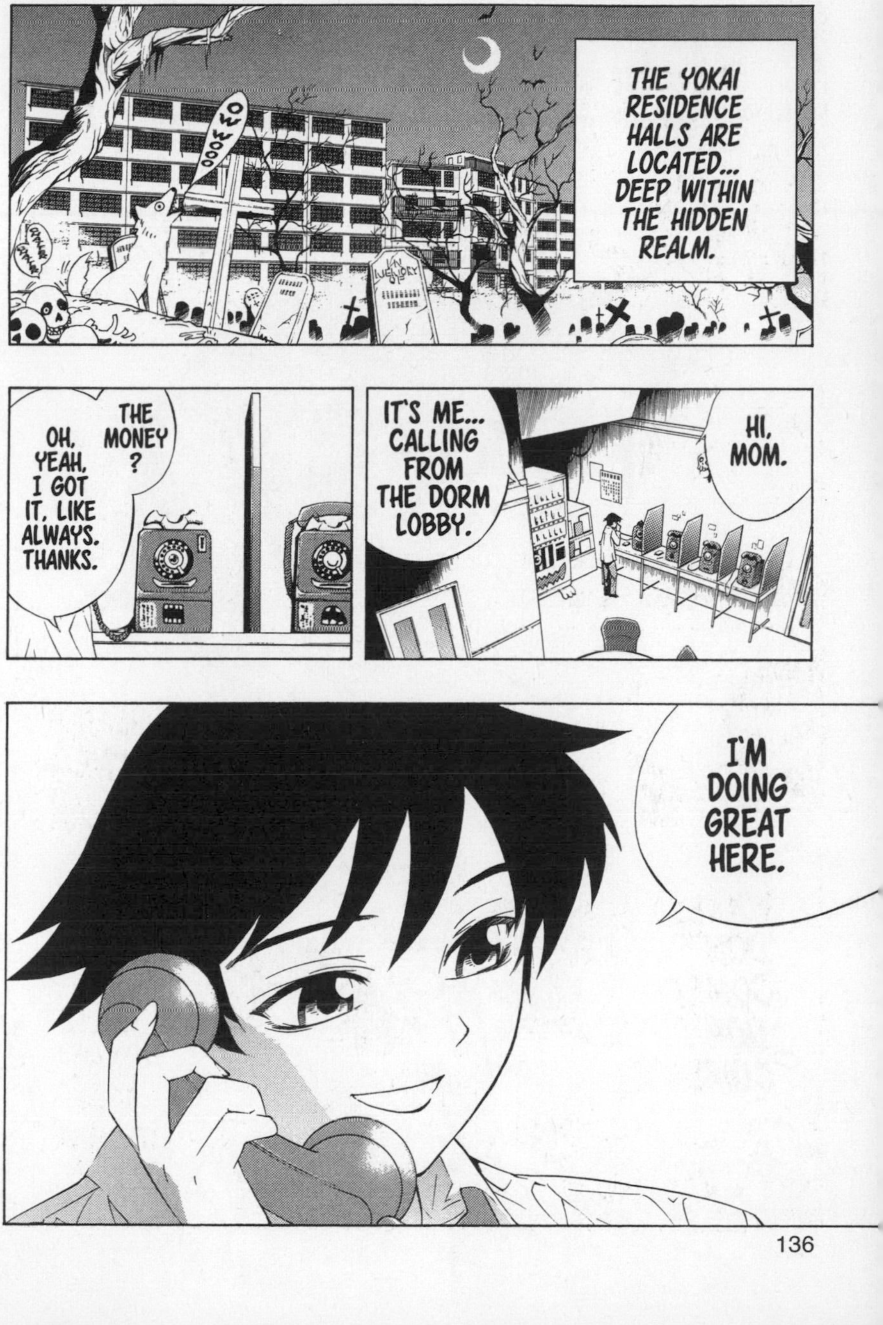

THE YOKAI RESIDENCE HALLS ARE LOCATED... DEEP WITHIN THE HIDDEN REALM.
OWOOO
HI, MOM.
IT'S ME... CALLING FROM THE DORM LOBBY.
THE MONEY?
OH, YEAH, I GOT IT, LIKE ALWAYS. THANKS.
I'M DOING GREAT HERE.

READ THIS WAY

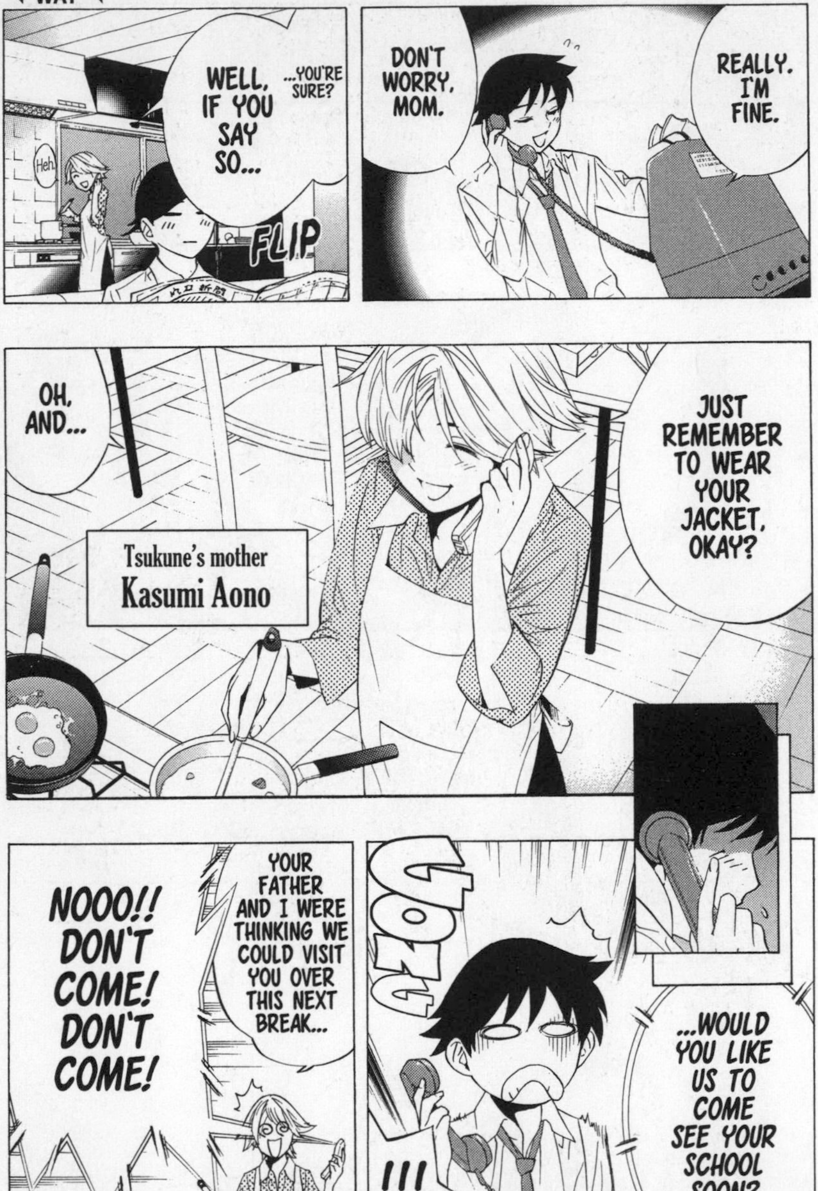
REALLY. I'M FINE.
DON'T WORRY, MOM.
...YOU'RE SURE?
WELL, IF YOU SAY SO...
Heh.
FLIP
JUST REMEMBER TO WEAR YOUR JACKET, OKAY?
OH, AND...
Tsukune's mother Kasumi Aono
...WOULD YOU LIKE US TO COME SEE YOUR SCHOOL SOON?
GONG
!!!
YOUR FATHER AND I WERE THINKING WE COULD VISIT YOU OVER THIS NEXT BREAK...
NOOO!! DON'T COME! DON'T COME!

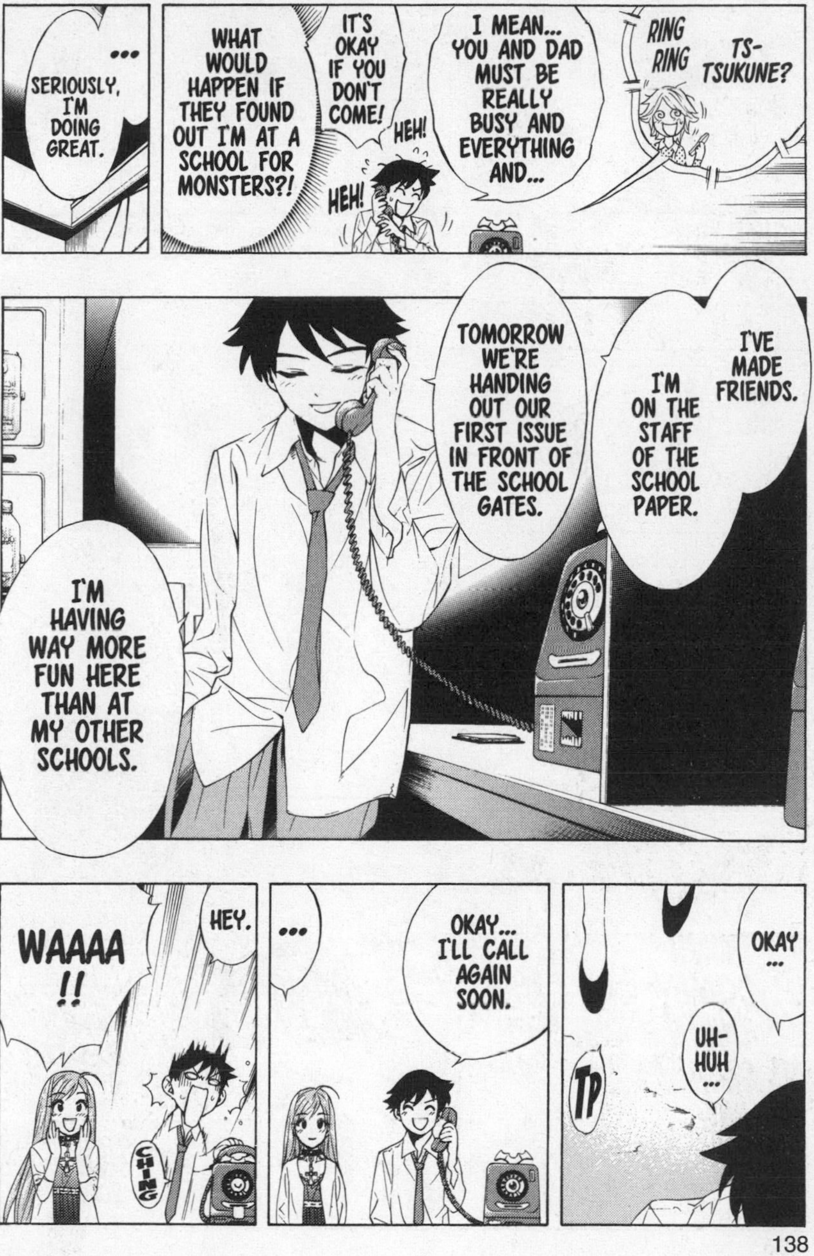
RING RING
TS-TSUKUNE?
I MEAN... YOU AND DAD MUST BE REALLY BUSY AND EVERYTHING AND...
HEH!
HEH!
IT'S OKAY IF YOU DON'T COME!
WHAT WOULD HAPPEN IF THEY FOUND OUT I'M AT A SCHOOL FOR MONSTERS?!
...
SERIOUSLY, I'M DOING GREAT.
I'VE MADE FRIENDS.
I'M ON THE STAFF OF THE SCHOOL PAPER.
TOMORROW WE'RE HANDING OUT OUR FIRST ISSUE IN FRONT OF THE SCHOOL GATES.
I'M HAVING WAY MORE FUN HERE THAN AT MY OTHER SCHOOLS.
OKAY ...
UH-HUH ...
TP
OKAY... I'LL CALL AGAIN SOON.
...
HEY.
WAAAA !!
CHING

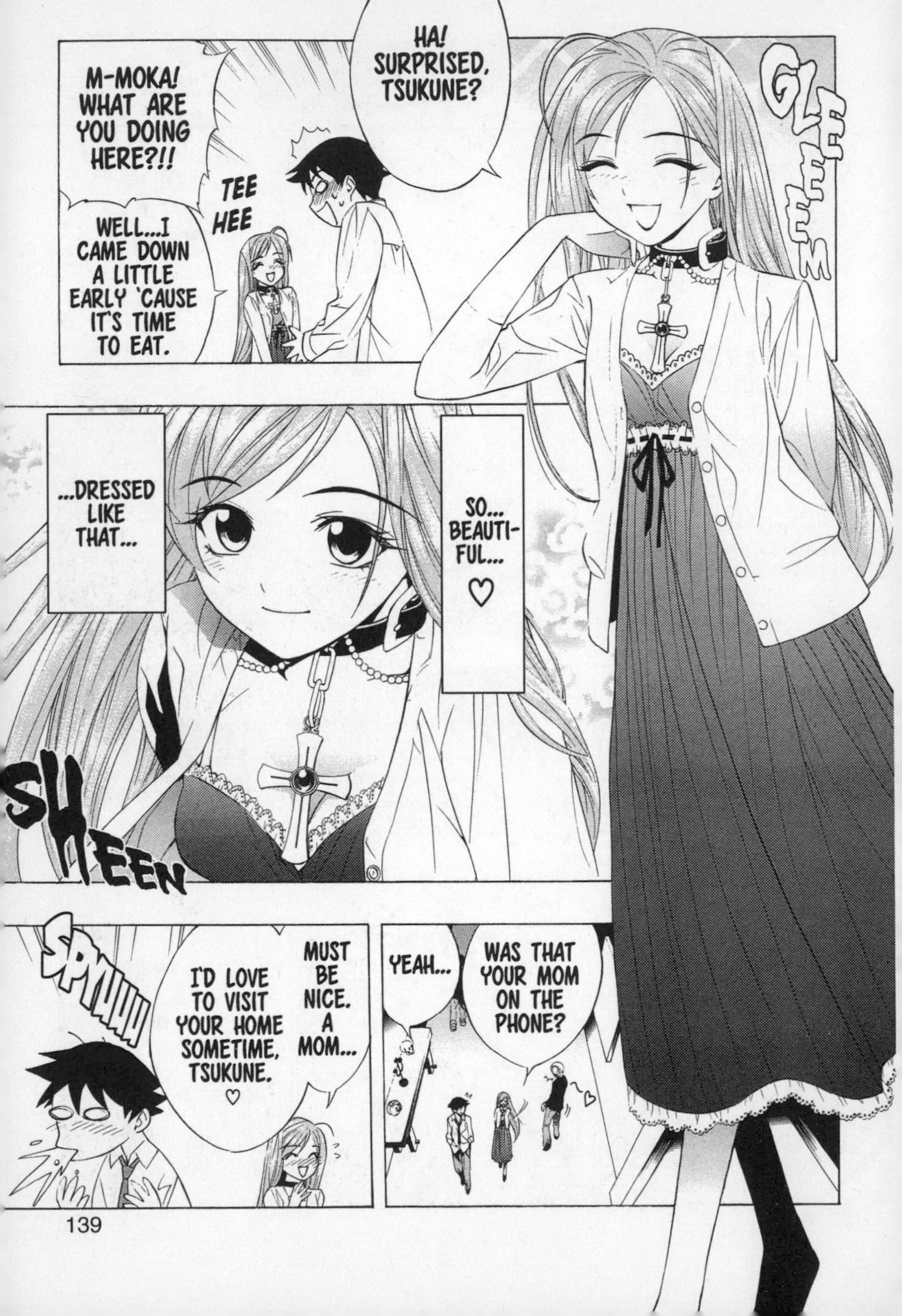
HA! SURPRISED, TSUKUNE?
GLEEEEM
M-MOKA! WHAT ARE YOU DOING HERE?!!
TEE HEE
WELL...I CAME DOWN A LITTLE EARLY 'CAUSE IT'S TIME TO EAT.
SO... BEAUTI-FUL... ♡
...DRESSED LIKE THAT...
SHEEN
WAS THAT YOUR MOM ON THE PHONE?
YEAH...
MUST BE NICE. A MOM...
I'D LOVE TO VISIT YOUR HOME SOMETIME, TSUKUNE. ♡
SPINNN

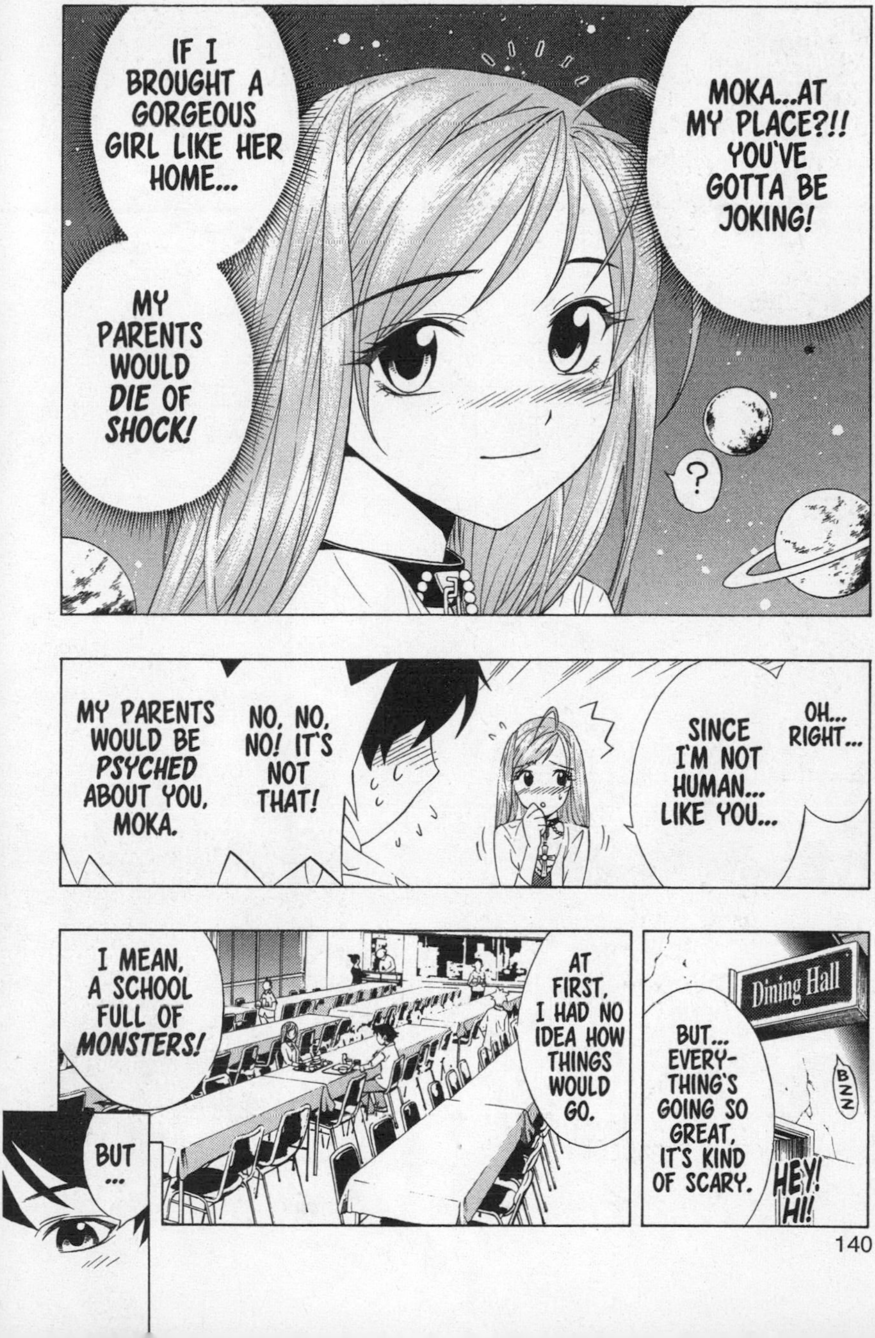
MOKA...AT MY PLACE?!! YOU'VE GOTTA BE JOKING!
IF I BROUGHT A GORGEOUS GIRL LIKE HER HOME...
MY PARENTS WOULD DIE OF SHOCK!
?
OH... RIGHT...
SINCE I'M NOT HUMAN... LIKE YOU...
NO, NO, NO! IT'S NOT THAT!
MY PARENTS WOULD BE PSYCHED ABOUT YOU, MOKA.
Dining Hall
BZZ
HEY! HI!
BUT... EVERY-THING'S GOING SO GREAT, IT'S KIND OF SCARY.
AT FIRST, I HAD NO IDEA HOW THINGS WOULD GO.
I MEAN, A SCHOOL FULL OF MONSTERS!
BUT ...

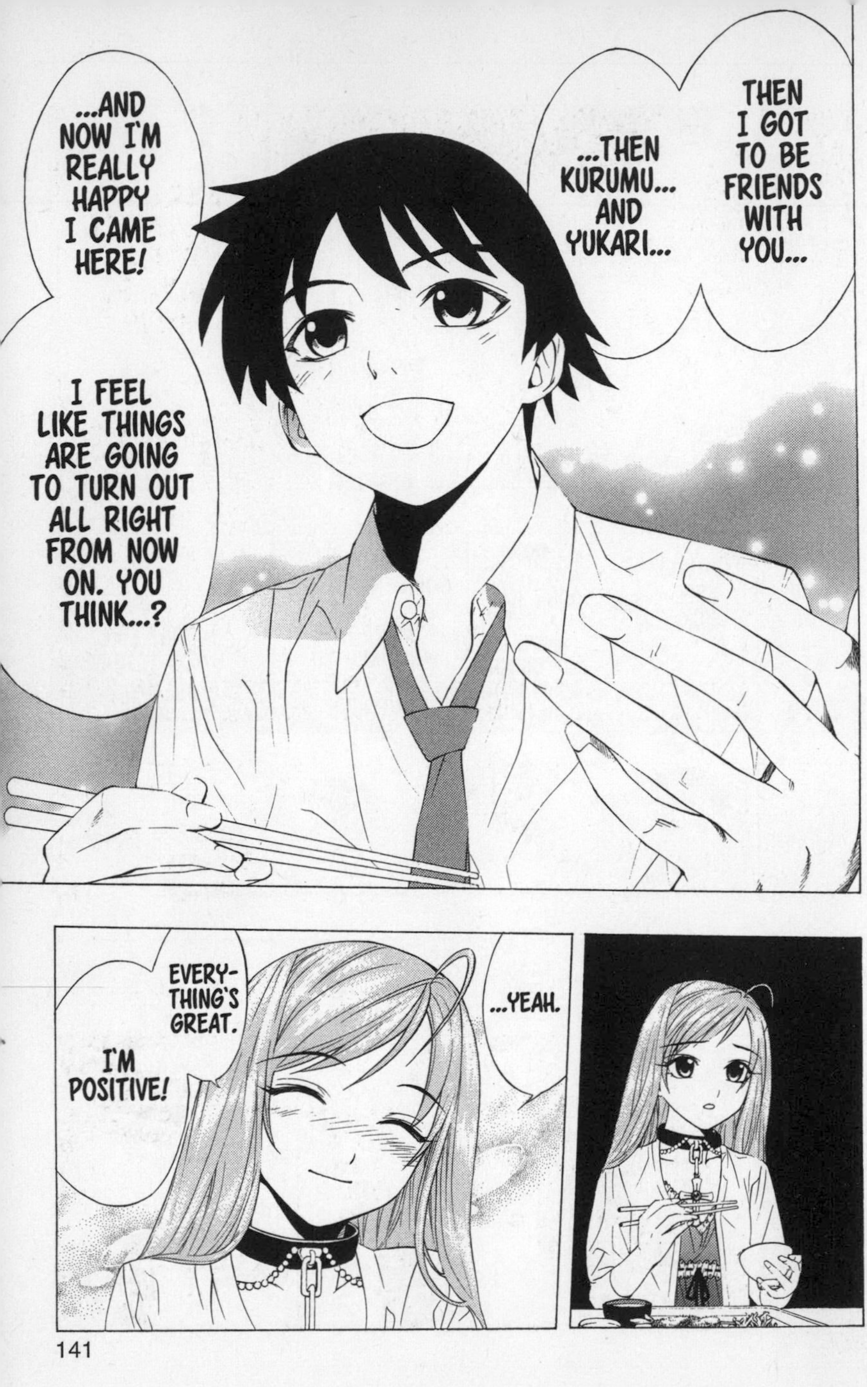
THEN I GOT TO BE FRIENDS WITH YOU...
...THEN KURUMU... AND YUKARI...
...AND NOW I'M REALLY HAPPY I CAME HERE!
I FEEL LIKE THINGS ARE GOING TO TURN OUT ALL RIGHT FROM NOW ON. YOU THINK...?
...YEAH.
EVERY-THING'S GREAT.
I'M POSITIVE!

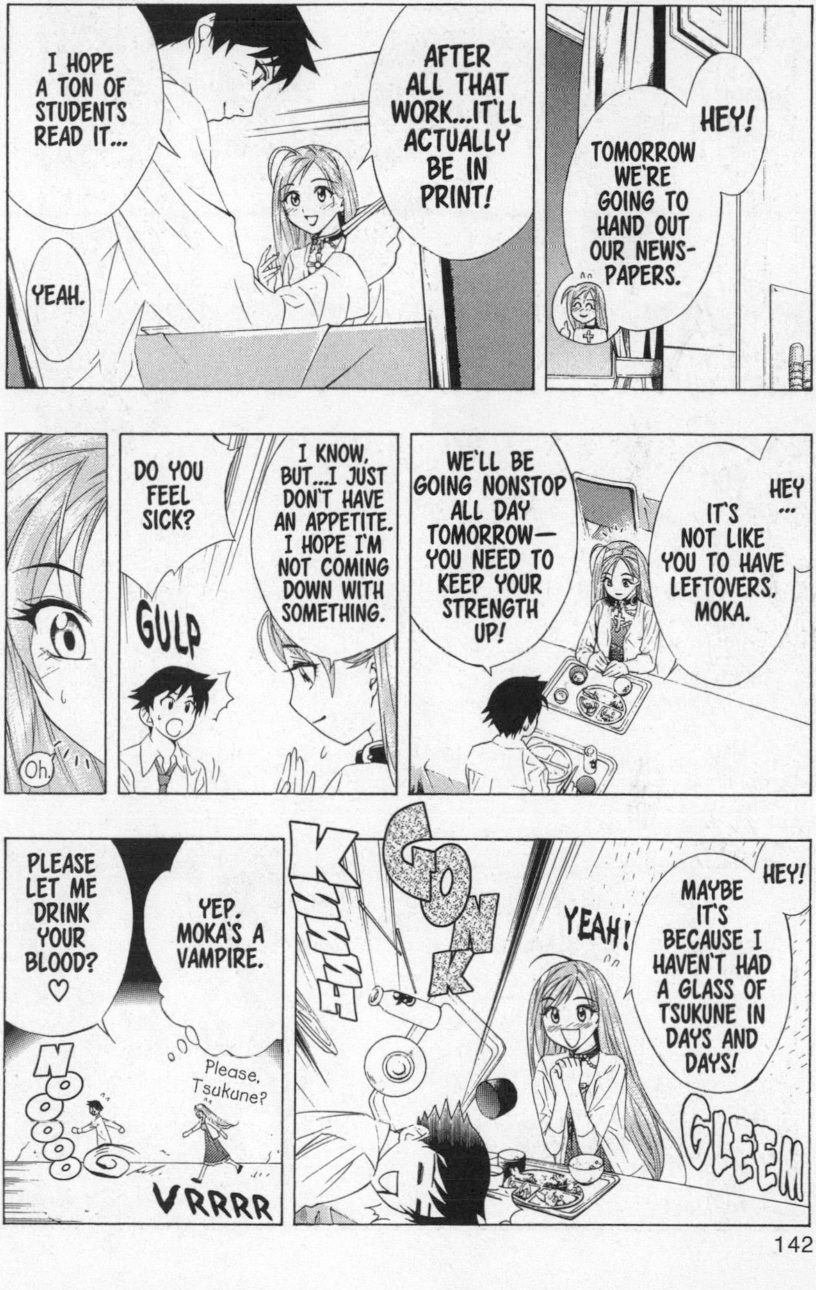
HEY!
TOMORROW WE'RE GOING TO HAND OUT OUR NEWS-PAPERS.
AFTER ALL THAT WORK...IT'LL ACTUALLY BE IN PRINT!
I HOPE A TON OF STUDENTS READ IT...
YEAH.
HEY ...
IT'S NOT LIKE YOU TO HAVE LEFTOVERS, MOKA.
WE'LL BE GOING NONSTOP ALL DAY TOMORROW—YOU NEED TO KEEP YOUR STRENGTH UP!
I KNOW, BUT...I JUST DON'T HAVE AN APPETITE. I HOPE I'M NOT COMING DOWN WITH SOMETHING.
DO YOU FEEL SICK?
GULP
Oh.
HEY!
MAYBE IT'S BECAUSE I HAVEN'T HAD A GLASS OF TSUKUNE IN DAYS AND DAYS!
YEAH!
GLEEM
GONK
KSHSH
YEP. MOKA'S A VAMPIRE.
PLEASE LET ME DRINK YOUR BLOOD? ♡
Please, Tsukune?
NOOOOOO
VRRRR

READ THIS WAY

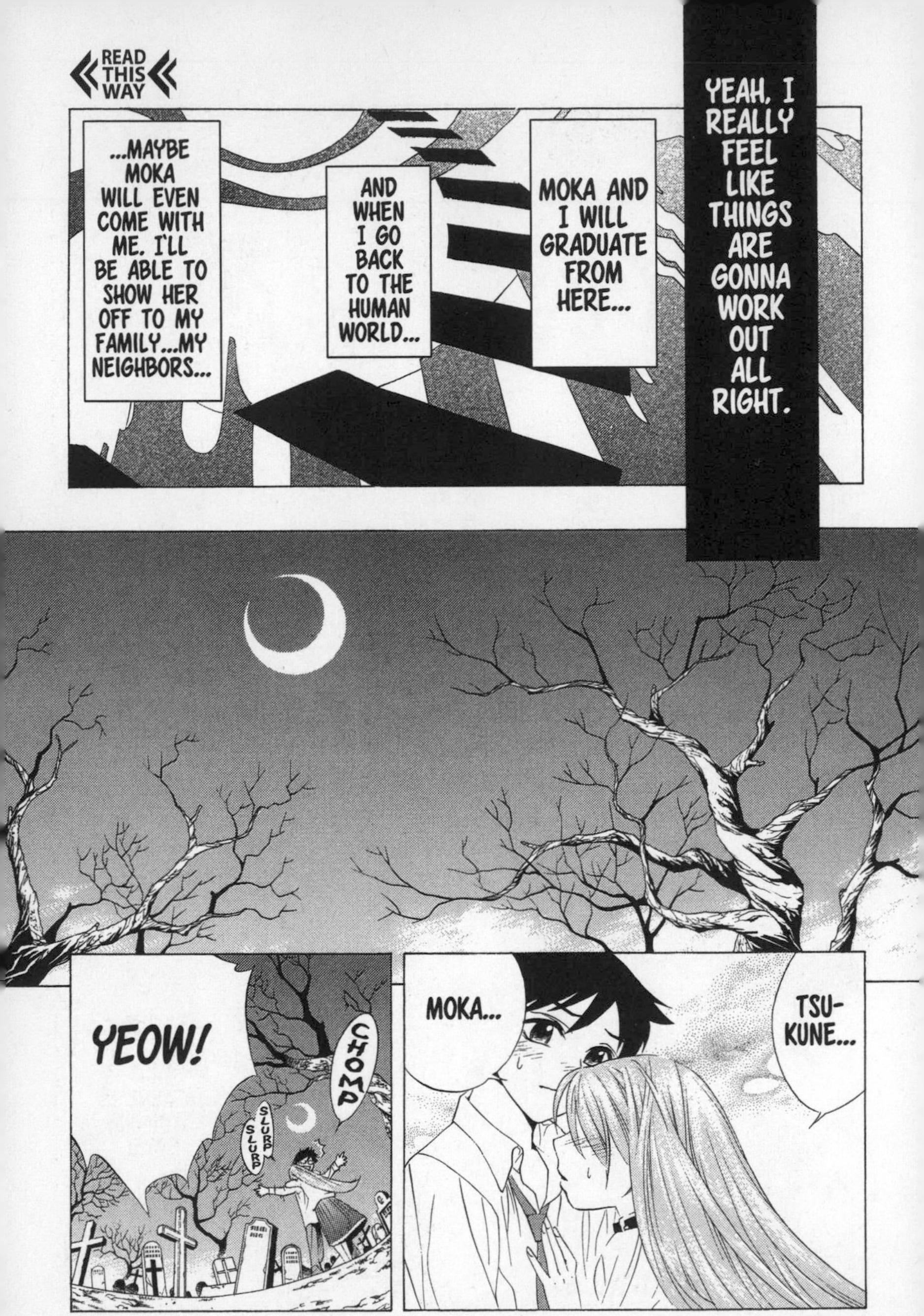

YEAH, I REALLY FEEL LIKE THINGS ARE GONNA WORK OUT ALL RIGHT.
MOKA AND I WILL GRADUATE FROM HERE...
AND WHEN I GO BACK TO THE HUMAN WORLD...
...MAYBE MOKA WILL EVEN COME WITH ME. I'LL BE ABLE TO SHOW HER OFF TO MY FAMILY...MY NEIGHBORS...
TSU-KUNE...
MOKA...
CHOMP
YEOW!
SLURP SLURP

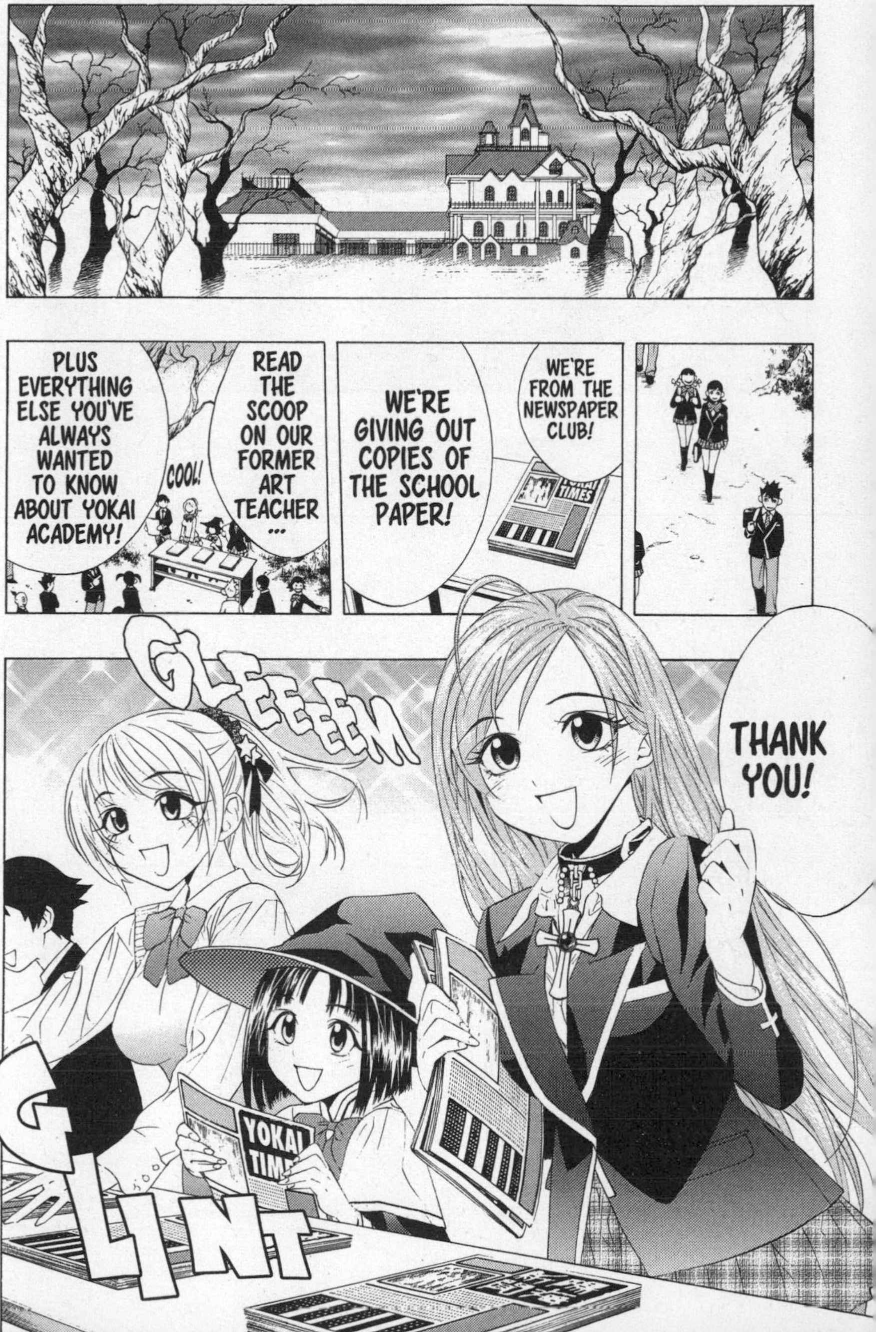
WE'RE FROM THE NEWSPAPER CLUB!
TIMES
WE'RE GIVING OUT COPIES OF THE SCHOOL PAPER!
READ THE SCOOP ON OUR FORMER ART TEACHER ...
COOL!
PLUS EVERYTHING ELSE YOU'VE ALWAYS WANTED TO KNOW ABOUT YOKAI ACADEMY!
THANK YOU!
GLEEEEM
YOKAI TIMES
GLINT

READ THIS WAY

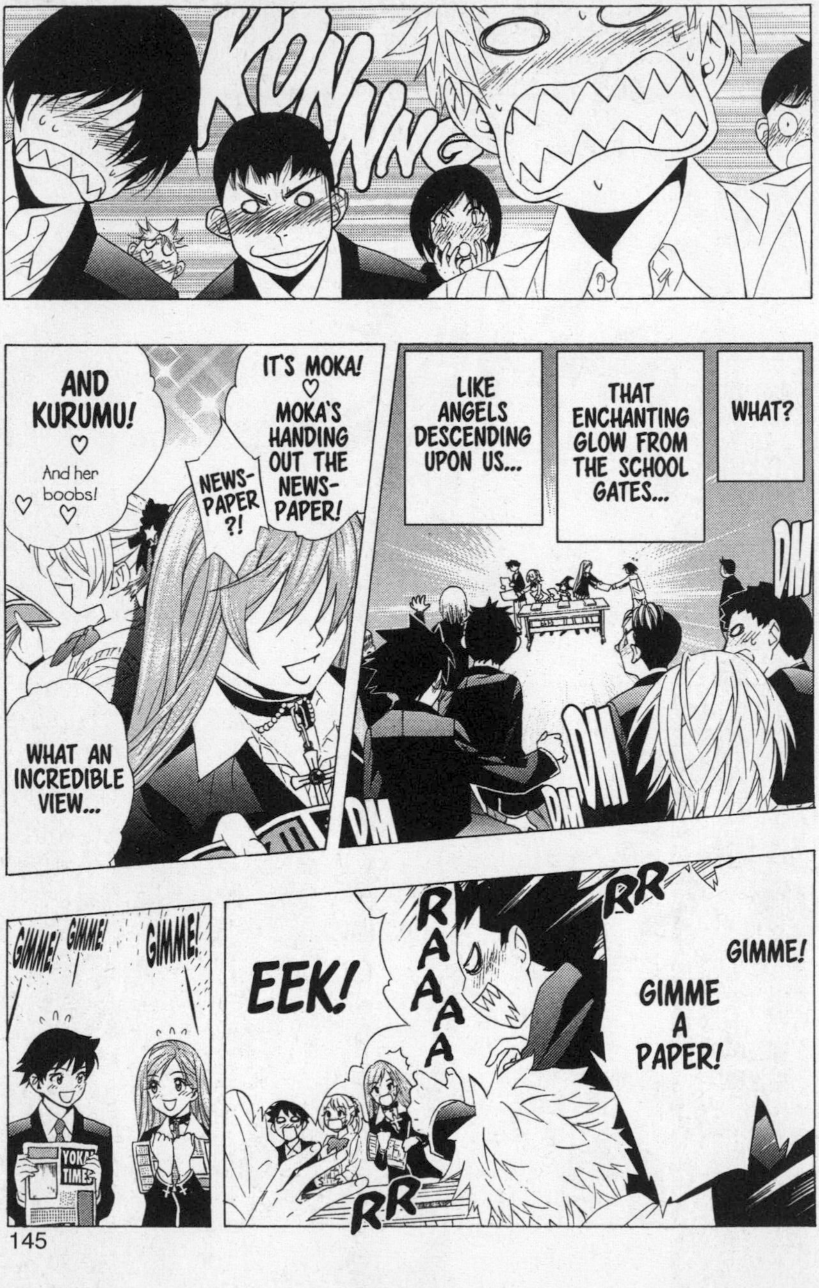
KONNNG
WHAT?
THAT ENCHANTING GLOW FROM THE SCHOOL GATES...
LIKE ANGELS DESCENDING UPON US...
DM
DM
DM
DM
IT'S MOKA! ♡
MOKA'S HANDING OUT THE NEWS-PAPER!
NEWS-PAPER?!
AND KURUMU! ♡
And her boobs! ♡ ♡
WHAT AN INCREDIBLE VIEW...
DM
RR
GIMME!
GIMME A PAPER!
RAAAAA
EEK!
RR
GIMME!
GIMME!
GIMME!

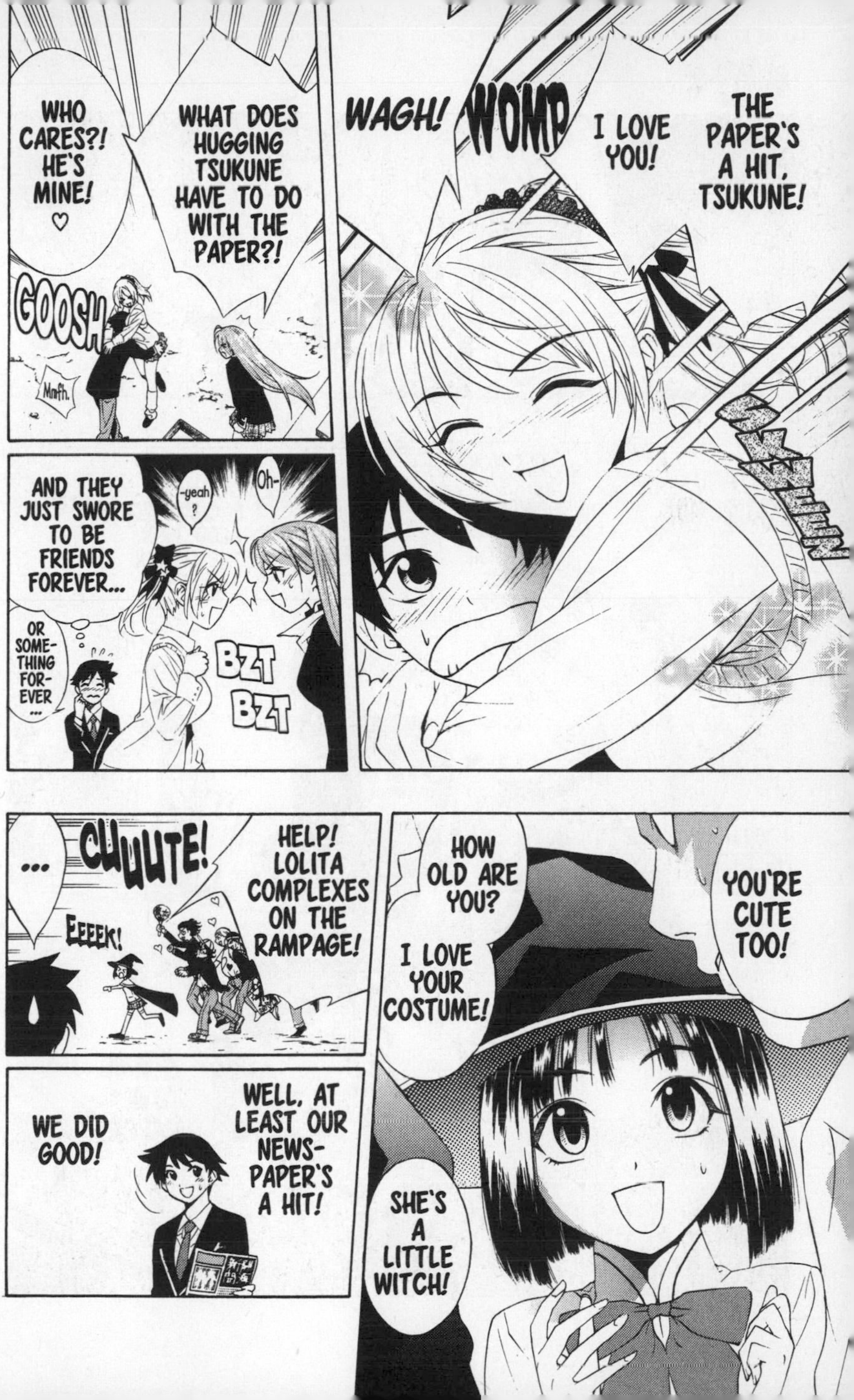
THE PAPER'S A HIT, TSUKUNE!
I LOVE YOU!
WOMP
WAGH!
SKWEEN
WHAT DOES HUGGING TSUKUNE HAVE TO DO WITH THE PAPER?!
WHO CARES?! HE'S MINE! ♡
GOOSH
Mnfh.
Oh-
-yeah?
AND THEY JUST SWORE TO BE FRIENDS FOREVER...
OR SOMETHING FOREVER...
BZT
BZT
YOU'RE CUTE TOO!
HOW OLD ARE YOU?
I LOVE YOUR COSTUME!
SHE'S A LITTLE WITCH!
HELP! LOLITA COMPLEXES ON THE RAMPAGE!
CUUUTE!
...
EEEEK!
WELL, AT LEAST OUR NEWSPAPER'S A HIT!
WE DID GOOD!

READ THIS WAY

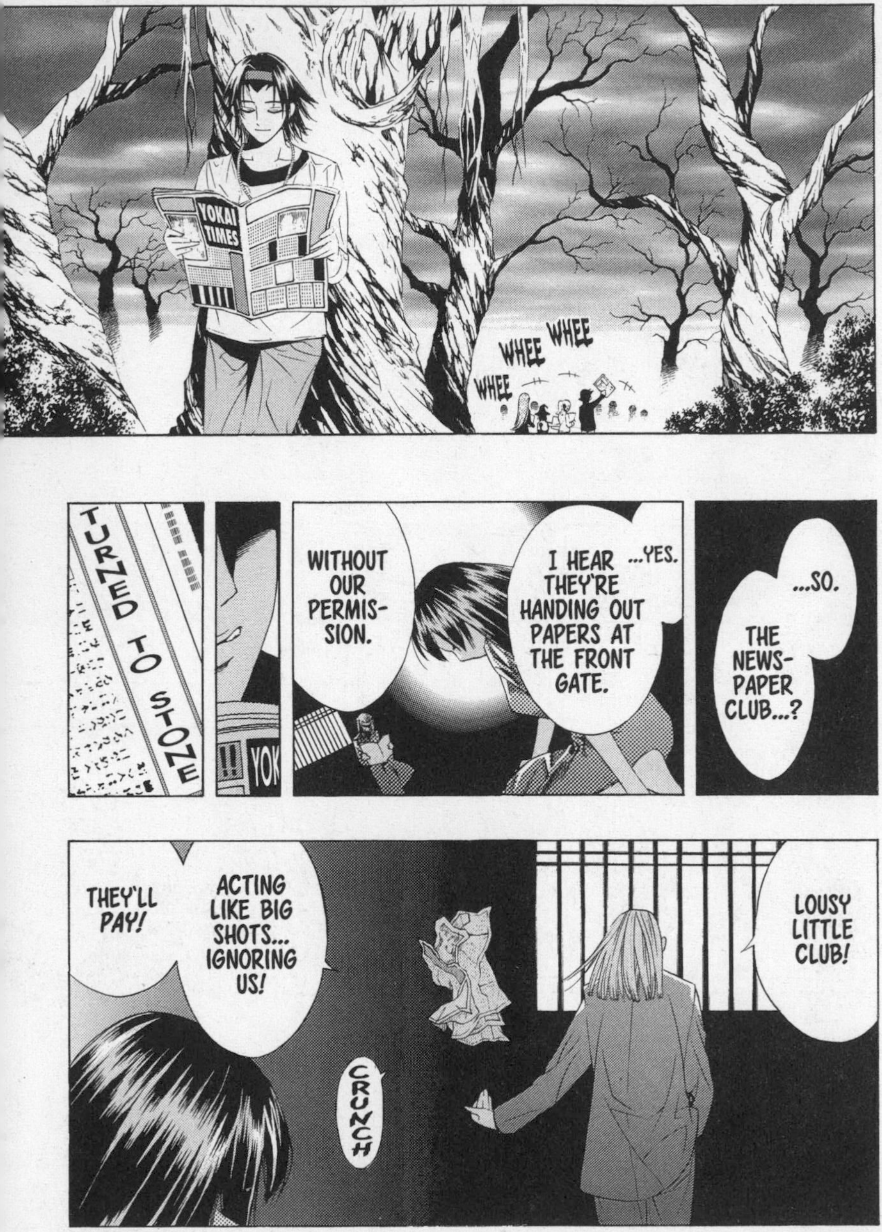

YOKAI TIMES
WHEE
WHEE
WHEE
...SO.
THE NEWS-PAPER CLUB...?
...YES.
I HEAR THEY'RE HANDING OUT PAPERS AT THE FRONT GATE.
WITHOUT OUR PERMIS-SION.
!!
YOK
TURNED TO STONE
LOUSY LITTLE CLUB!
CRUNCH
ACTING LIKE BIG SHOTS... IGNORING US!
THEY'LL PAY!

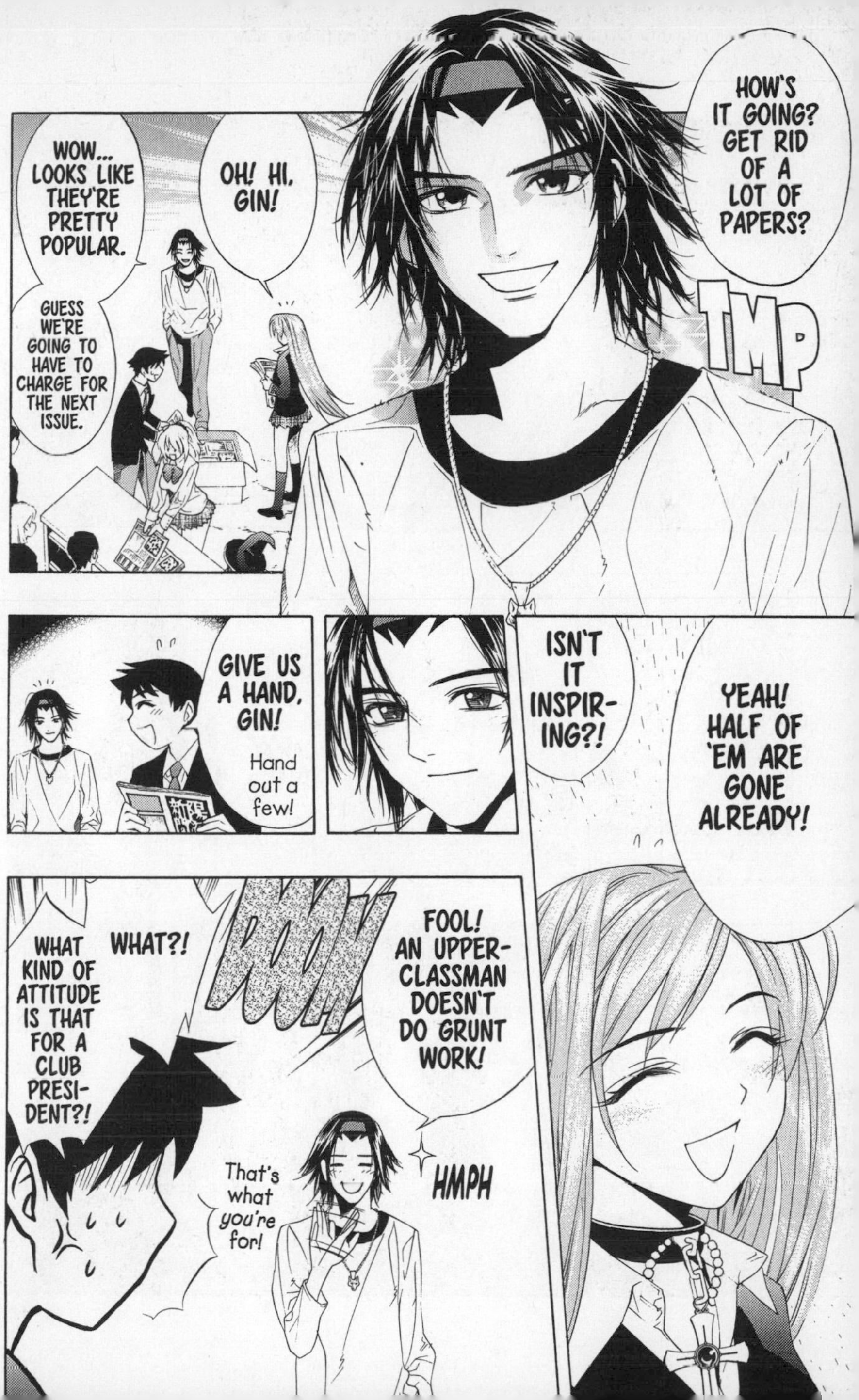

HOW'S IT GOING? GET RID OF A LOT OF PAPERS?
TMP
OH! HI, GIN!
WOW... LOOKS LIKE THEY'RE PRETTY POPULAR.
GUESS WE'RE GOING TO HAVE TO CHARGE FOR THE NEXT ISSUE.
YEAH! HALF OF 'EM ARE GONE ALREADY!
ISN'T IT INSPIRING?!
GIVE US A HAND, GIN!
Hand out a few!
FOOL! AN UPPER-CLASSMAN DOESN'T DO GRUNT WORK!
HMPH
That's what you're for!
WHAT?!
WHAT KIND OF ATTITUDE IS THAT FOR A CLUB PRESI-DENT?!

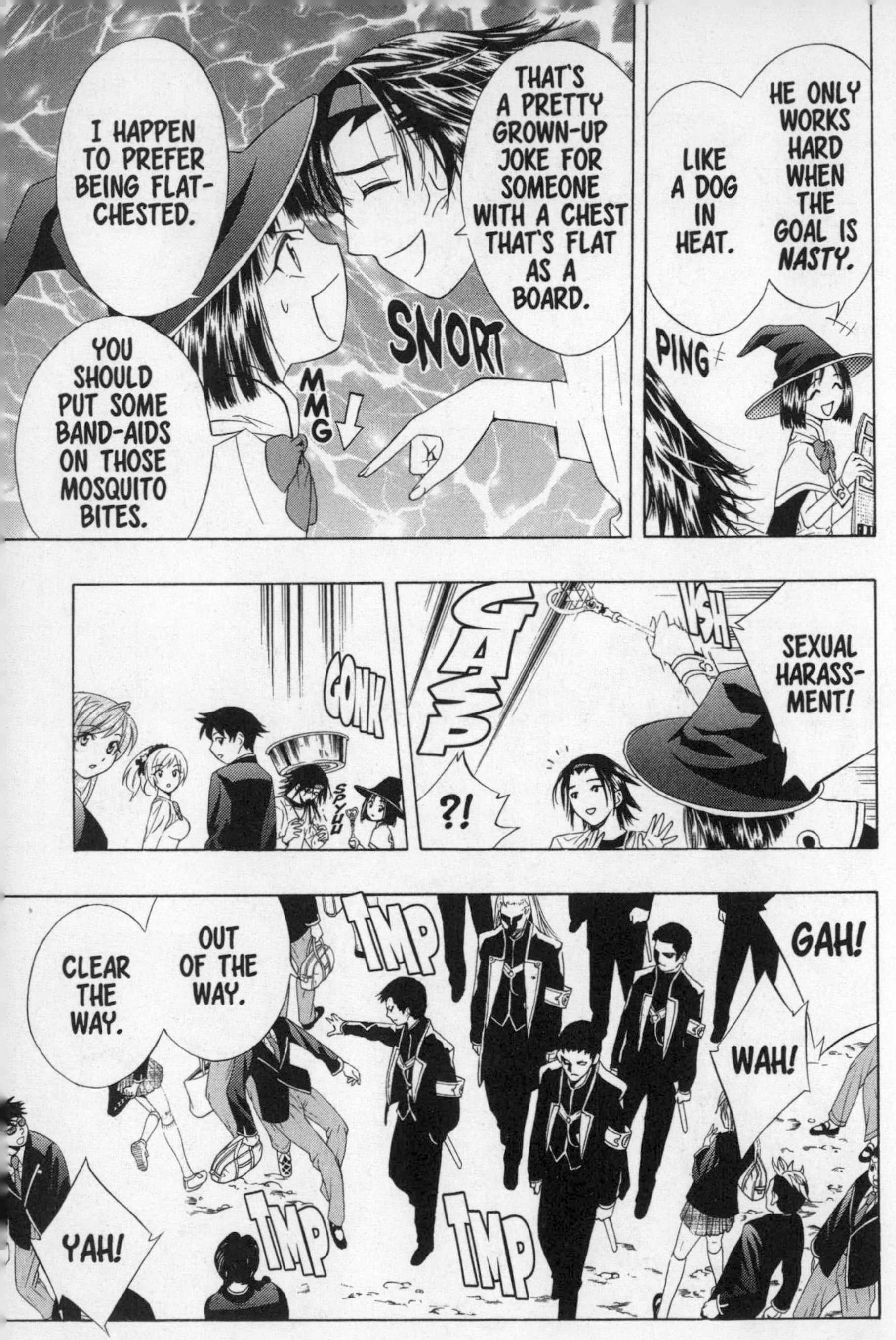
HE ONLY WORKS HARD WHEN THE GOAL IS NASTY.
LIKE A DOG IN HEAT.
PING
THAT'S A PRETTY GROWN-UP JOKE FOR SOMEONE WITH A CHEST THAT'S FLAT AS A BOARD.
SNORT
I HAPPEN TO PREFER BEING FLAT-CHESTED.
MMG
YOU SHOULD PUT SOME BAND-AIDS ON THOSE MOSQUITO BITES.
SEXUAL HARASS-MENT!
VSH
CLAMP
?!
GONK
SPYUU
GAH!
WAH!
TMP
OUT OF THE WAY.
CLEAR THE WAY.
TMP
TMP
YAH!

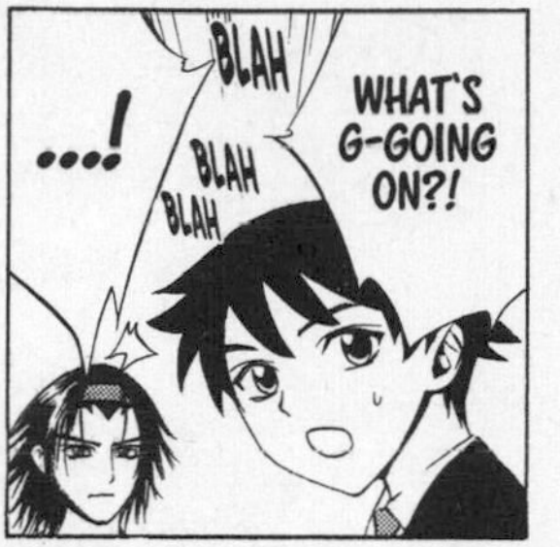
BLAH
WHAT'S G-GOING ON?!
BLAH BLAH
...!

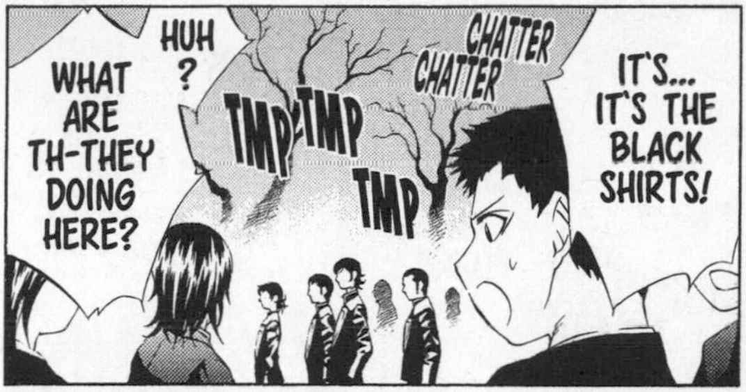
IT'S... IT'S THE BLACK SHIRTS!
CHATTER CHATTER
TMP TMP
TMP
HUH ?
WHAT ARE TH-THEY DOING HERE?

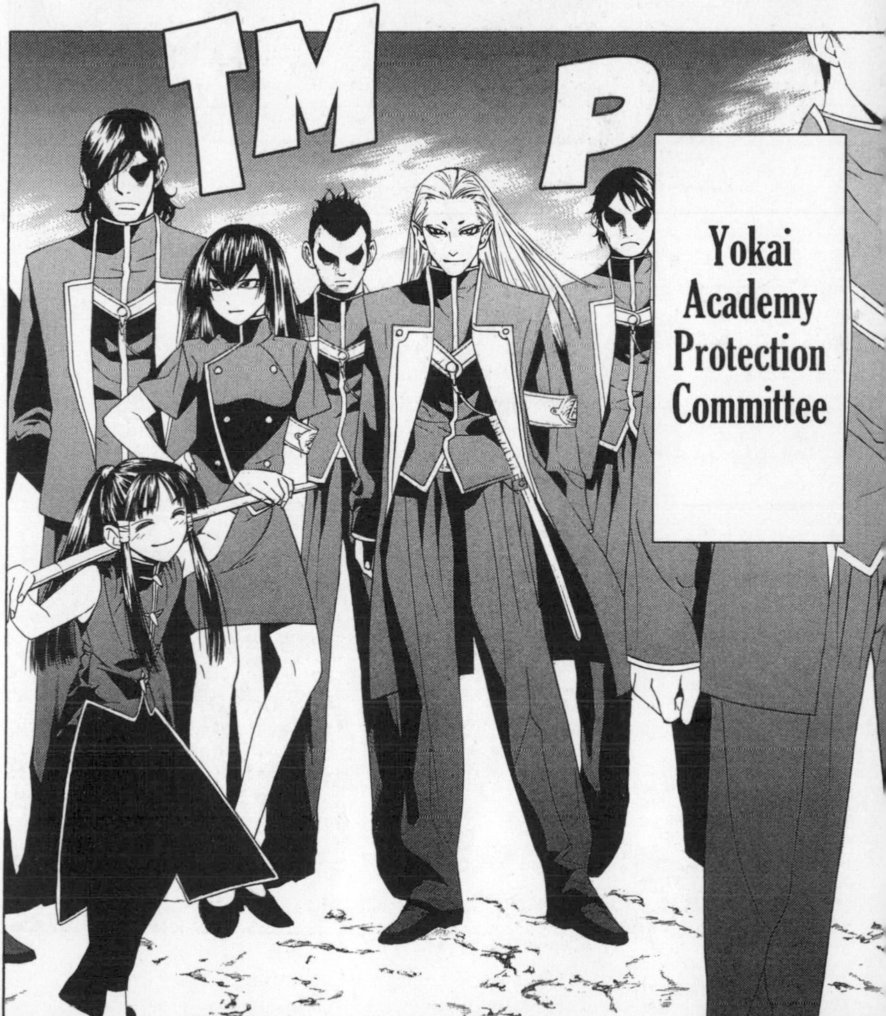
Yokai Academy Protection Committee
TMP

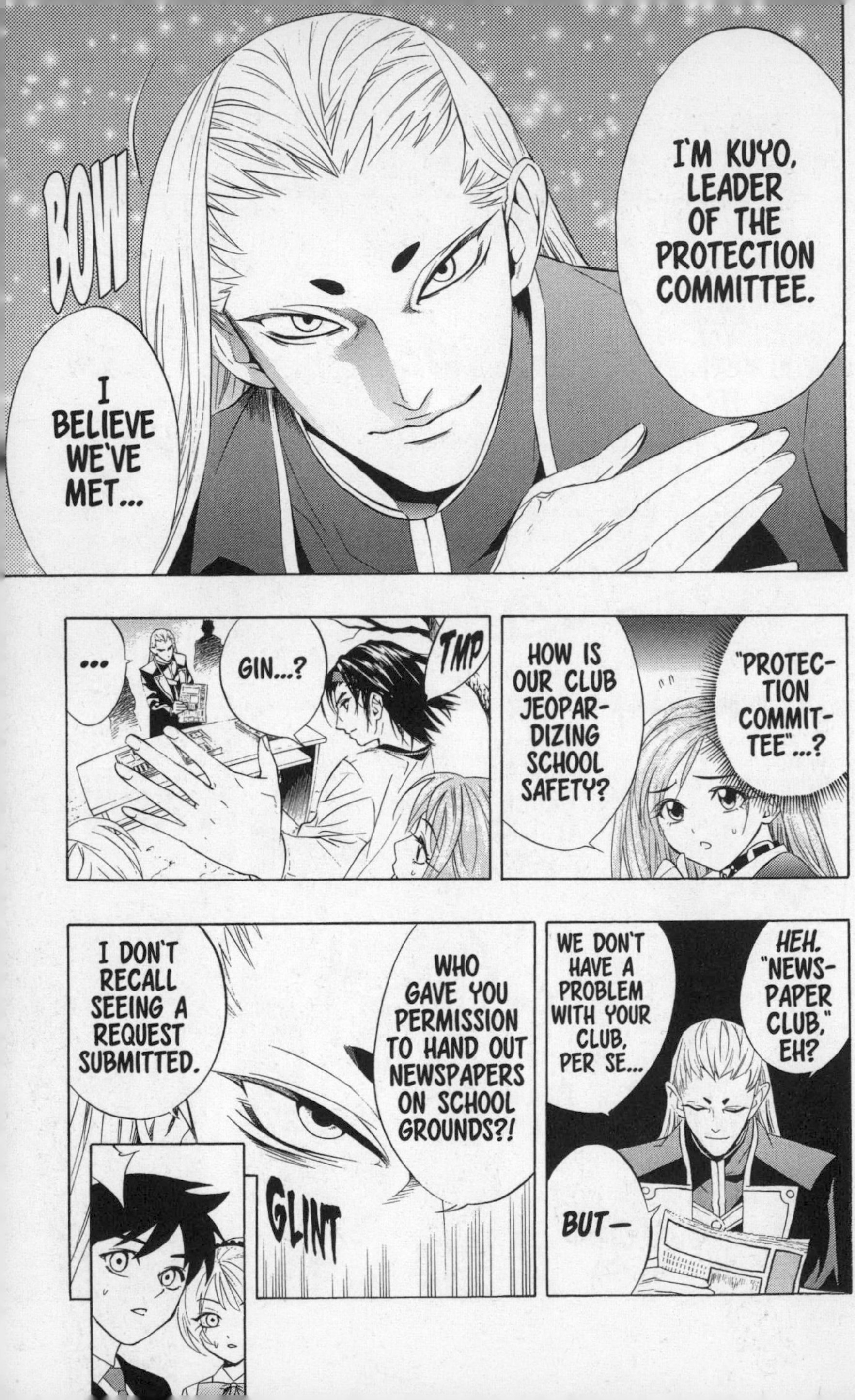
I'M KUYO, LEADER OF THE PROTECTION COMMITTEE.
BOW
I BELIEVE WE'VE MET...
"PROTECTION COMMITTEE"...?
HOW IS OUR CLUB JEOPARDIZING SCHOOL SAFETY?
TMP
GIN...?
...
HEH. "NEWSPAPER CLUB," EH?
WE DON'T HAVE A PROBLEM WITH YOUR CLUB, PER SE...
BUT—
WHO GAVE YOU PERMISSION TO HAND OUT NEWSPAPERS ON SCHOOL GROUNDS?!
I DON'T RECALL SEEING A REQUEST SUBMITTED.
GLINT

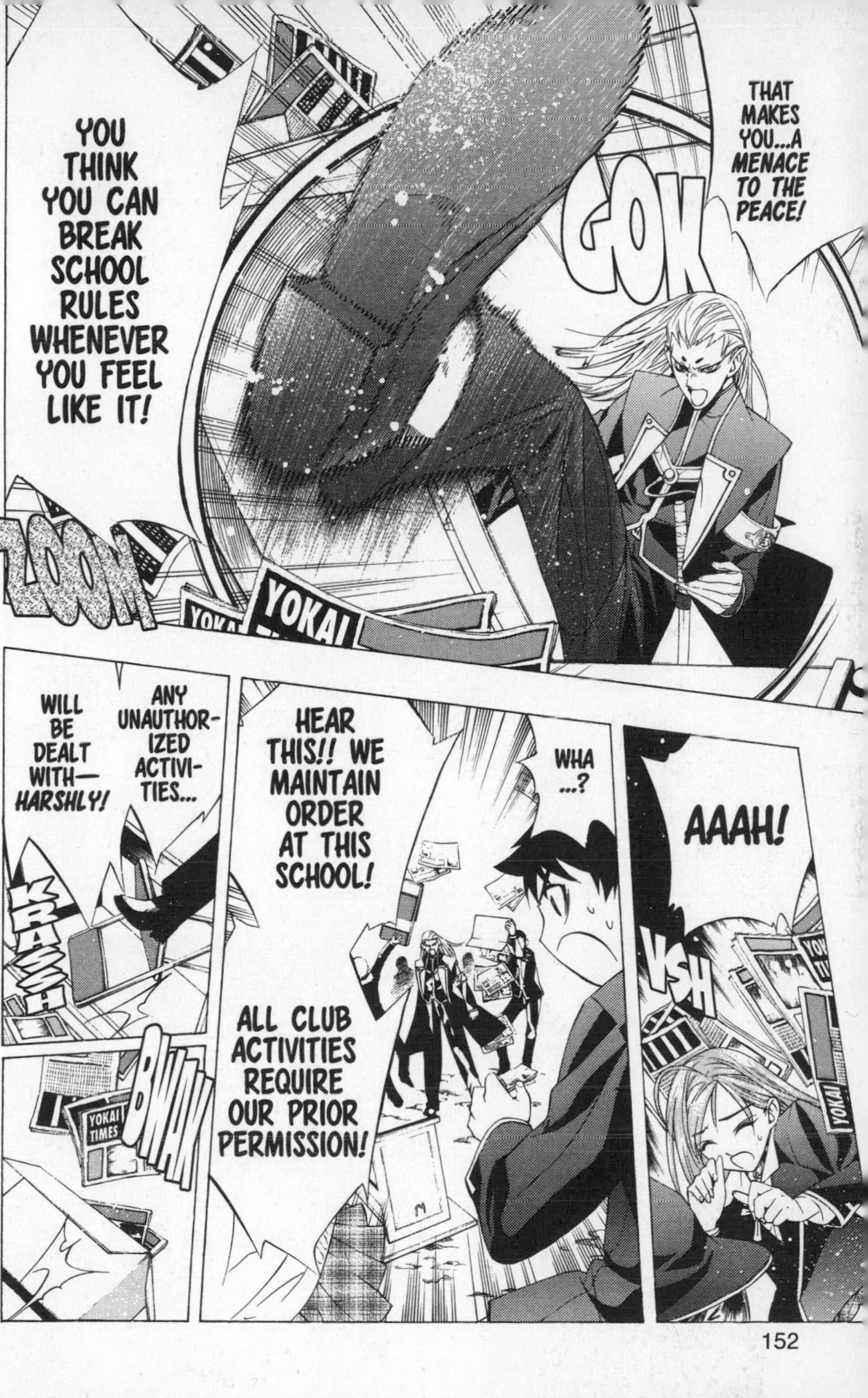
THAT MAKES YOU...A MENACE TO THE PEACE!
GOK
YOU THINK YOU CAN BREAK SCHOOL RULES WHENEVER YOU FEEL LIKE IT!
ZOOM
YOKAI
AAAH!
VSH
WHA ...?
HEAR THIS!! WE MAINTAIN ORDER AT THIS SCHOOL!
ALL CLUB ACTIVITIES REQUIRE OUR PRIOR PERMISSION!
ANY UNAUTHOR-IZED ACTIVI-TIES...
WILL BE DEALT WITH—HARSHLY!
KRASH
BWAM
YOKAI TIMES

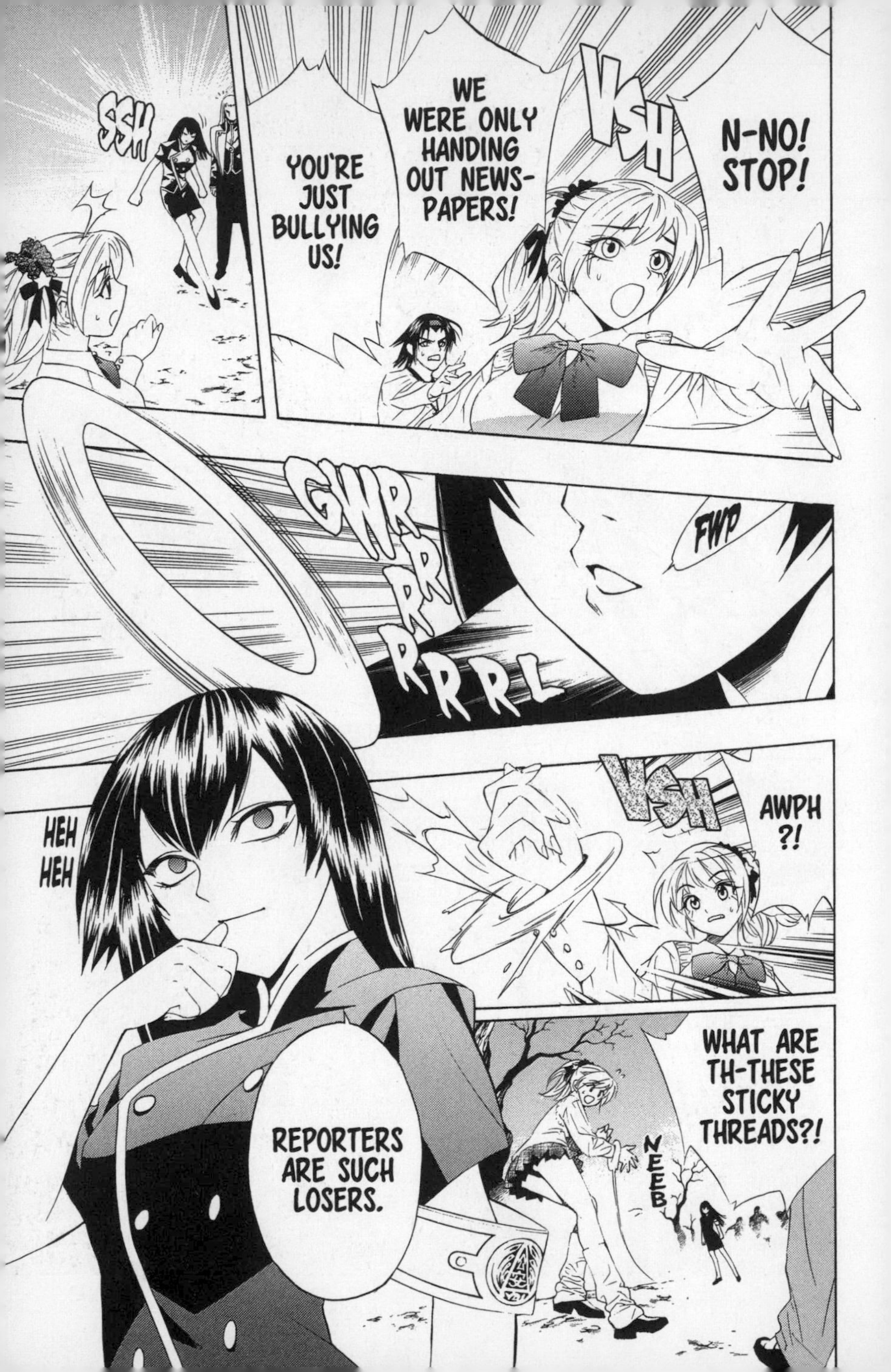
N-NO! STOP!
VSH
WE WERE ONLY HANDING OUT NEWS-PAPERS!
YOU'RE JUST BULLYING US!
SSH
FWP
GWRRRRRRL
AWPH ?!
VSH
WHAT ARE TH-THESE STICKY THREADS?!
NEEB
HEH HEH
REPORTERS ARE SUCH LOSERS.

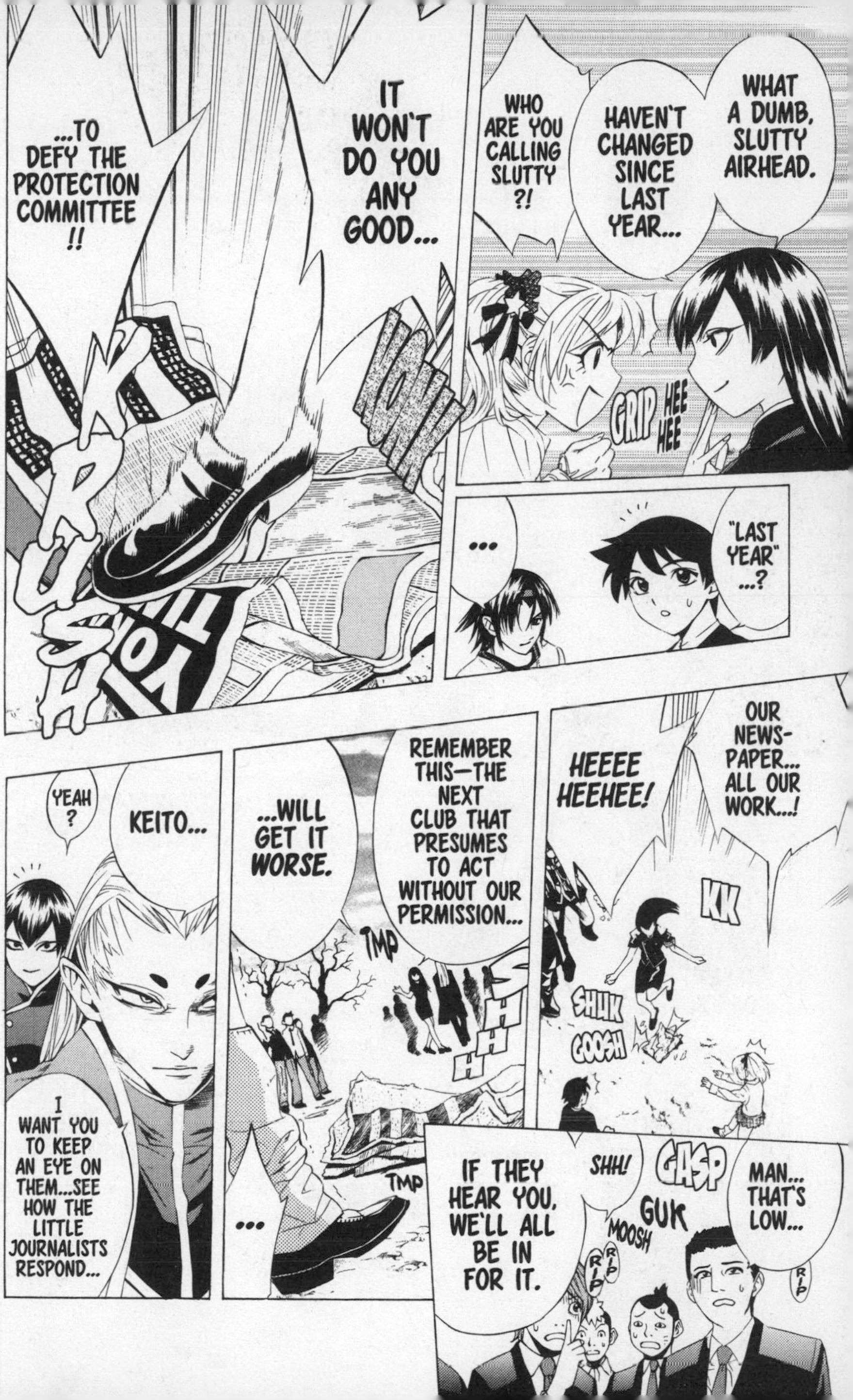
WHAT A DUMB, SLUTTY AIRHEAD.
HAVEN'T CHANGED SINCE LAST YEAR...
WHO ARE YOU CALLING SLUTTY?!
GRIP
HEE HEE
"LAST YEAR"...?
...
IT WON'T DO YOU ANY GOOD...
...TO DEFY THE PROTECTION COMMITTEE!!
OUR NEWS-PAPER... ALL OUR WORK...!
HEEEE HEEHEE!
KK
SHUK
GOOSH
MAN... THAT'S LOW...
GASP
SHH!
GUK
MOOSH
IF THEY HEAR YOU, WE'LL ALL BE IN FOR IT.
RIP
RIP
RIP
REMEMBER THIS—THE NEXT CLUB THAT PRESUMES TO ACT WITHOUT OUR PERMISSION...
...WILL GET IT WORSE.
TMP
...
TMP
KEITO...
YEAH?
I WANT YOU TO KEEP AN EYE ON THEM...SEE HOW THE LITTLE JOURNALISTS RESPOND...

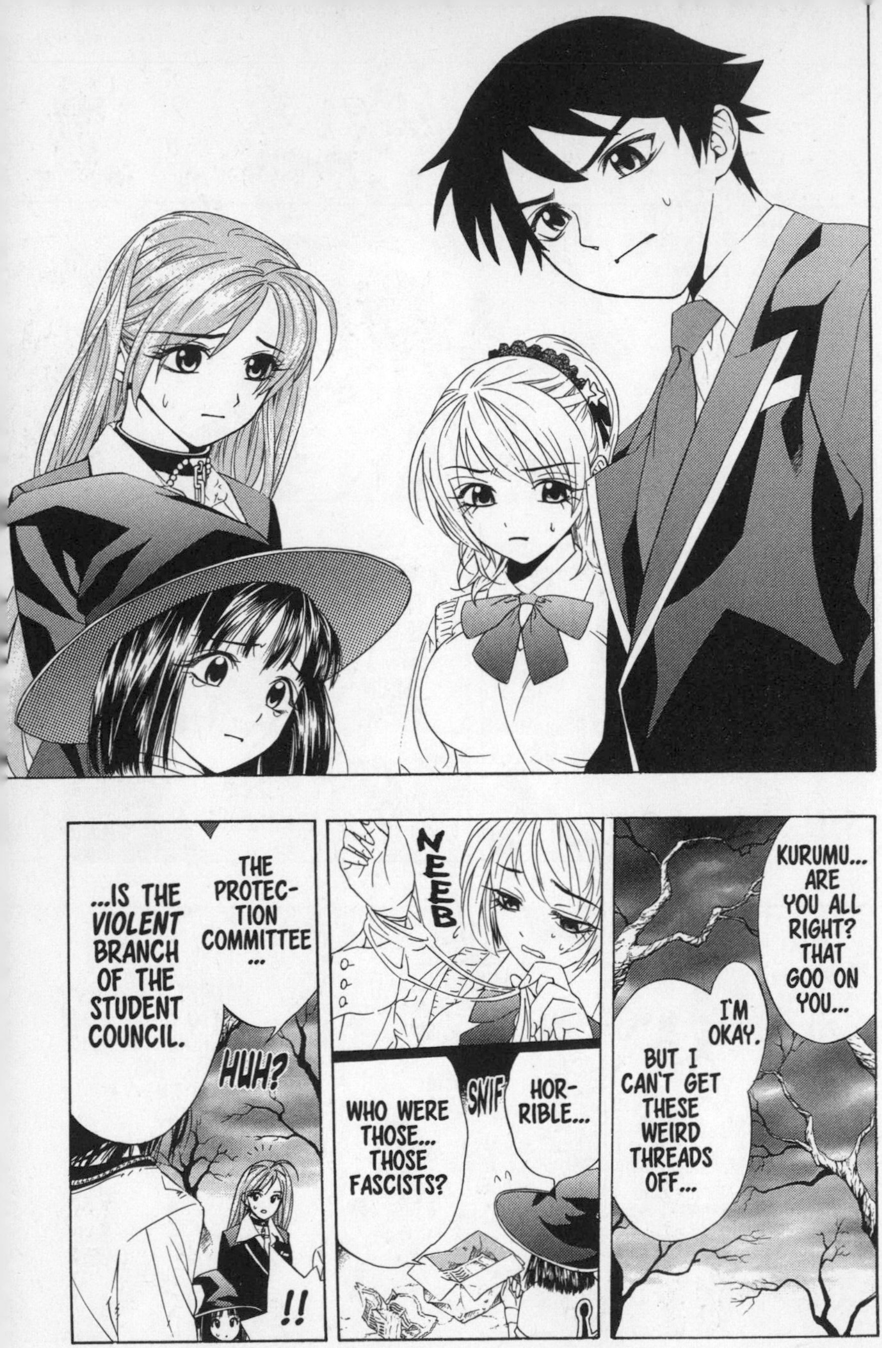

KURUMU... ARE YOU ALL RIGHT? THAT GOO ON YOU...
I'M OKAY.
BUT I CAN'T GET THESE WEIRD THREADS OFF...
NEEB
HOR-RIBLE...
SNIF
WHO WERE THOSE... THOSE FASCISTS?
THE PROTEC-TION COMMITTEE...
...IS THE *VIOLENT* BRANCH OF THE STUDENT COUNCIL.
HUH?
!!

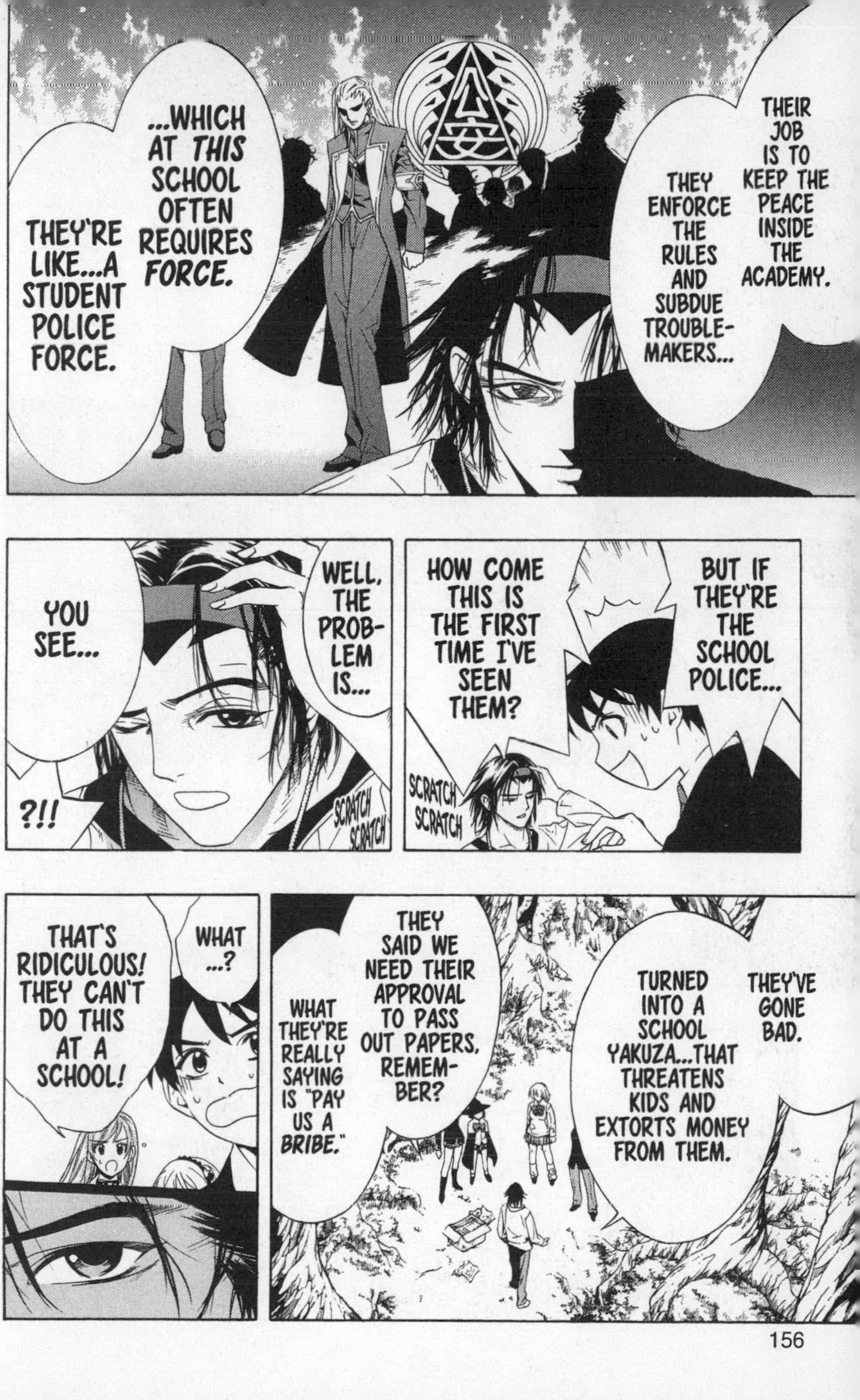

THEIR JOB IS TO KEEP THE PEACE INSIDE THE ACADEMY.
THEY ENFORCE THE RULES AND SUBDUE TROUBLE-MAKERS...
THEY'RE LIKE...A STUDENT POLICE FORCE.
...WHICH AT *THIS* SCHOOL OFTEN REQUIRES *FORCE.*
BUT IF THEY'RE THE SCHOOL POLICE...
HOW COME THIS IS THE FIRST TIME I'VE SEEN THEM?
SCRATCH SCRATCH
WELL, THE PROB-LEM IS...
SCRATCH SCRATCH
YOU SEE...
?!!
THEY'VE GONE BAD.
TURNED INTO A SCHOOL YAKUZA...THAT THREATENS KIDS AND EXTORTS MONEY FROM THEM.
THEY SAID WE NEED THEIR APPROVAL TO PASS OUT PAPERS, REMEMBER?
WHAT THEY'RE REALLY SAYING IS "PAY US A *BRIBE.*"
WHAT ...?
THAT'S RIDICULOUS! THEY CAN'T DO THIS AT A SCHOOL!

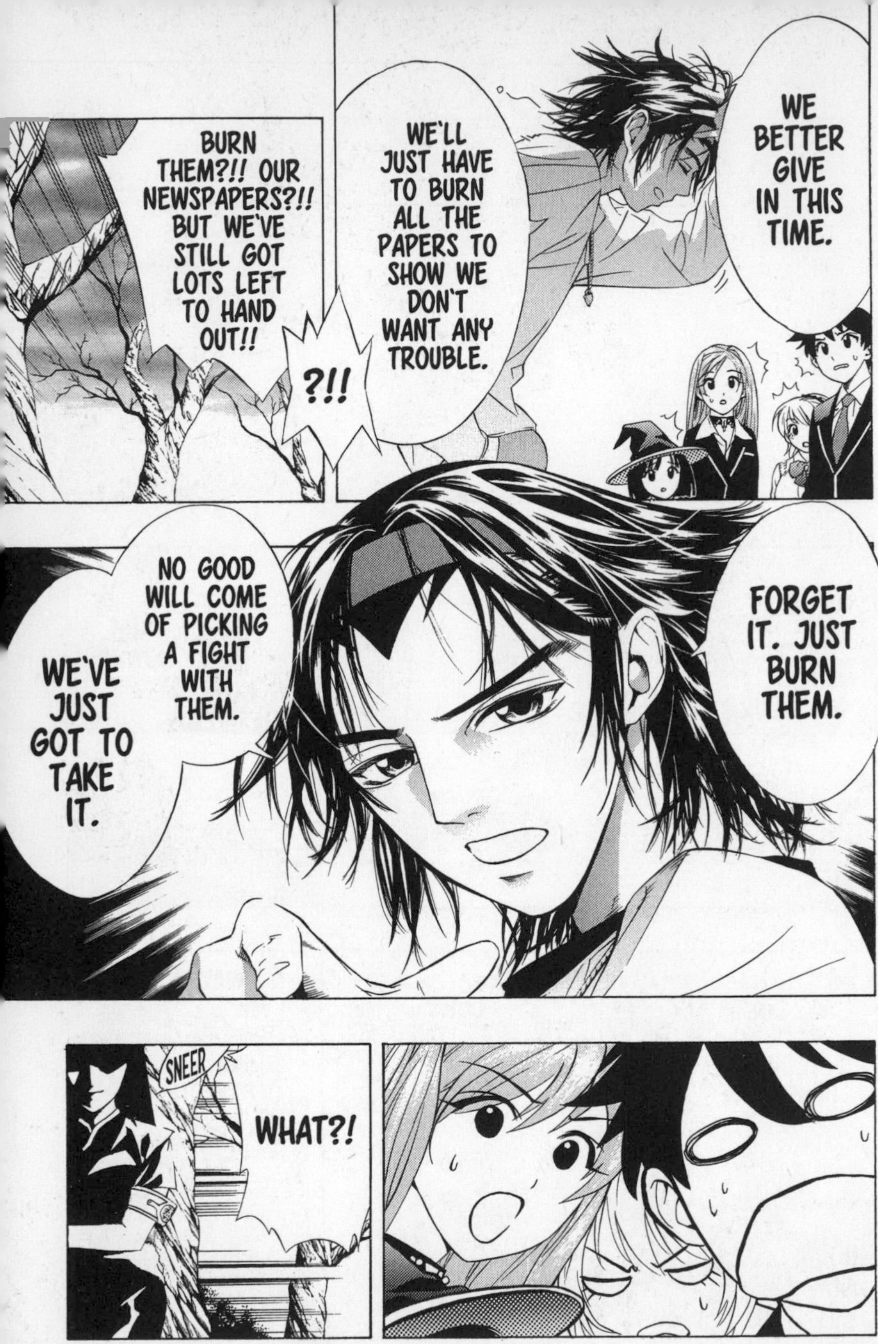
WE BETTER GIVE IN THIS TIME.
WE'LL JUST HAVE TO BURN ALL THE PAPERS TO SHOW WE DON'T WANT ANY TROUBLE.
?!!
BURN THEM?!! OUR NEWSPAPERS?!! BUT WE'VE STILL GOT LOTS LEFT TO HAND OUT!!
FORGET IT. JUST BURN THEM.
NO GOOD WILL COME OF PICKING A FIGHT WITH THEM.
WE'VE JUST GOT TO TAKE IT.
SNEER
WHAT?!

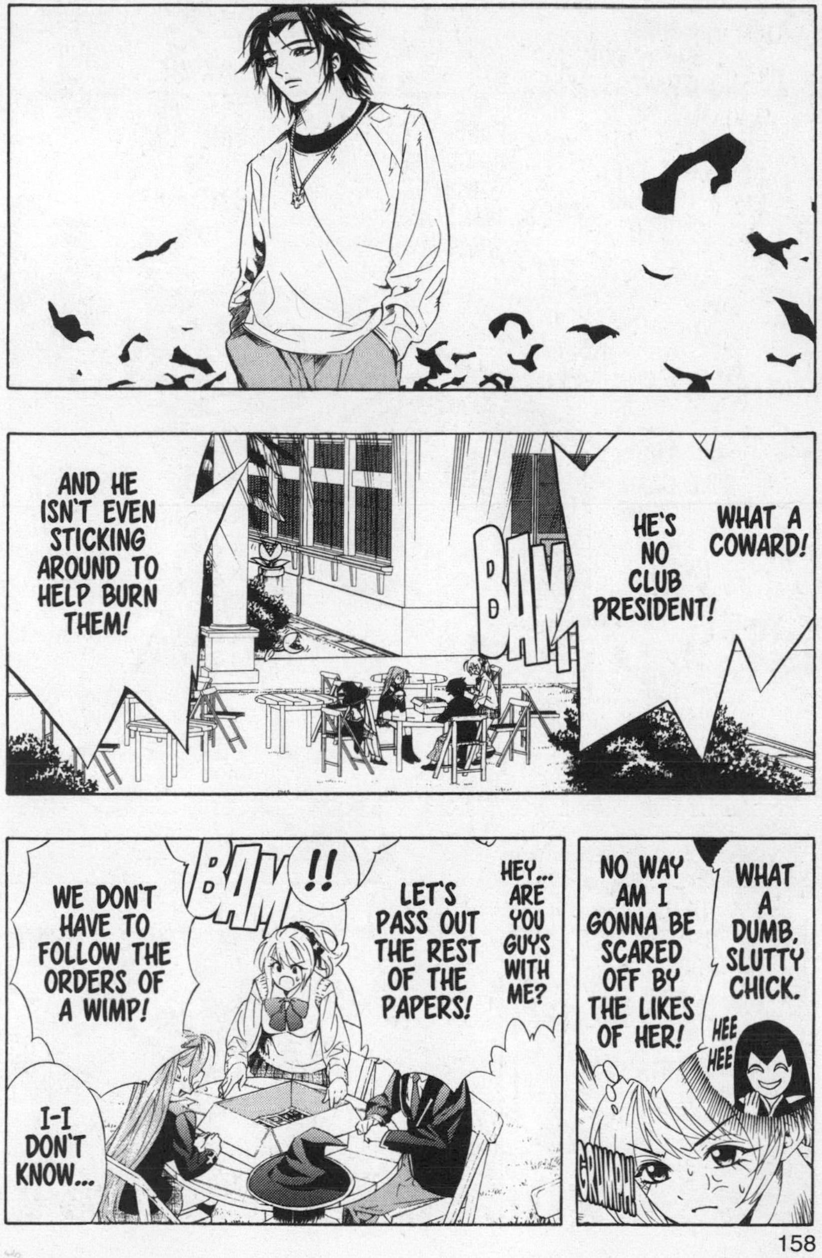
WHAT A COWARD!
HE'S NO CLUB PRESIDENT!
BAM
AND HE ISN'T EVEN STICKING AROUND TO HELP BURN THEM!
WHAT A DUMB, SLUTTY CHICK.
NO WAY AM I GONNA BE SCARED OFF BY THE LIKES OF HER!
HEE HEE
GRUMPH!!
HEY... ARE YOU GUYS WITH ME?
LET'S PASS OUT THE REST OF THE PAPERS!
BAM !!
WE DON'T HAVE TO FOLLOW THE ORDERS OF A WIMP!
I-I DON'T KNOW...

READ THIS WAY

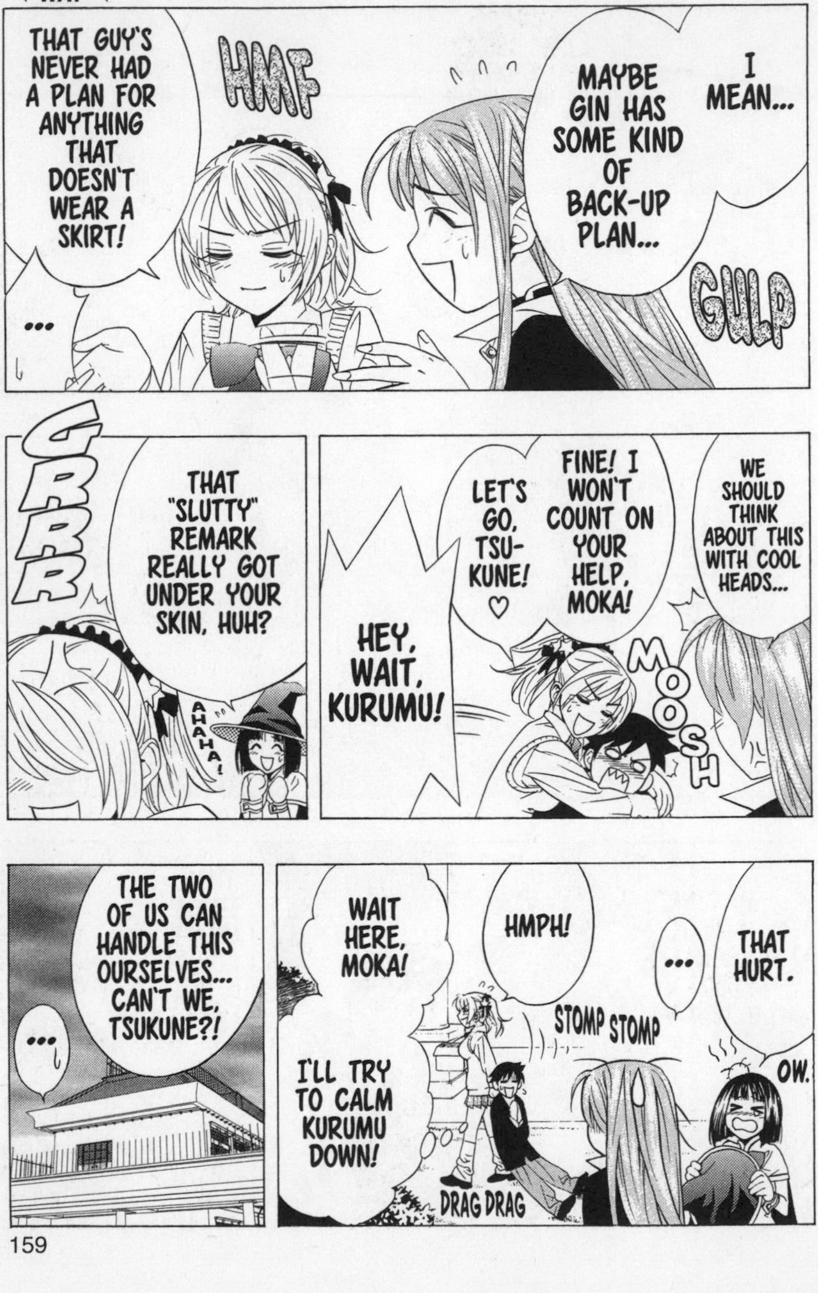
I MEAN...
MAYBE GIN HAS SOME KIND OF BACK-UP PLAN...
GULP
HMF
THAT GUY'S NEVER HAD A PLAN FOR ANYTHING THAT DOESN'T WEAR A SKIRT!
...
WE SHOULD THINK ABOUT THIS WITH COOL HEADS...
FINE! I WON'T COUNT ON YOUR HELP, MOKA!
LET'S GO, TSU-KUNE! ♡
MOOSH
HEY, WAIT, KURUMU!
GRRR
THAT "SLUTTY" REMARK REALLY GOT UNDER YOUR SKIN, HUH?
AHAHA!
THAT HURT.
...
HMPH!
WAIT HERE, MOKA!
STOMP STOMP
OW.
I'LL TRY TO CALM KURUMU DOWN!
DRAG DRAG
THE TWO OF US CAN HANDLE THIS OURSELVES... CAN'T WE, TSUKUNE?!
...

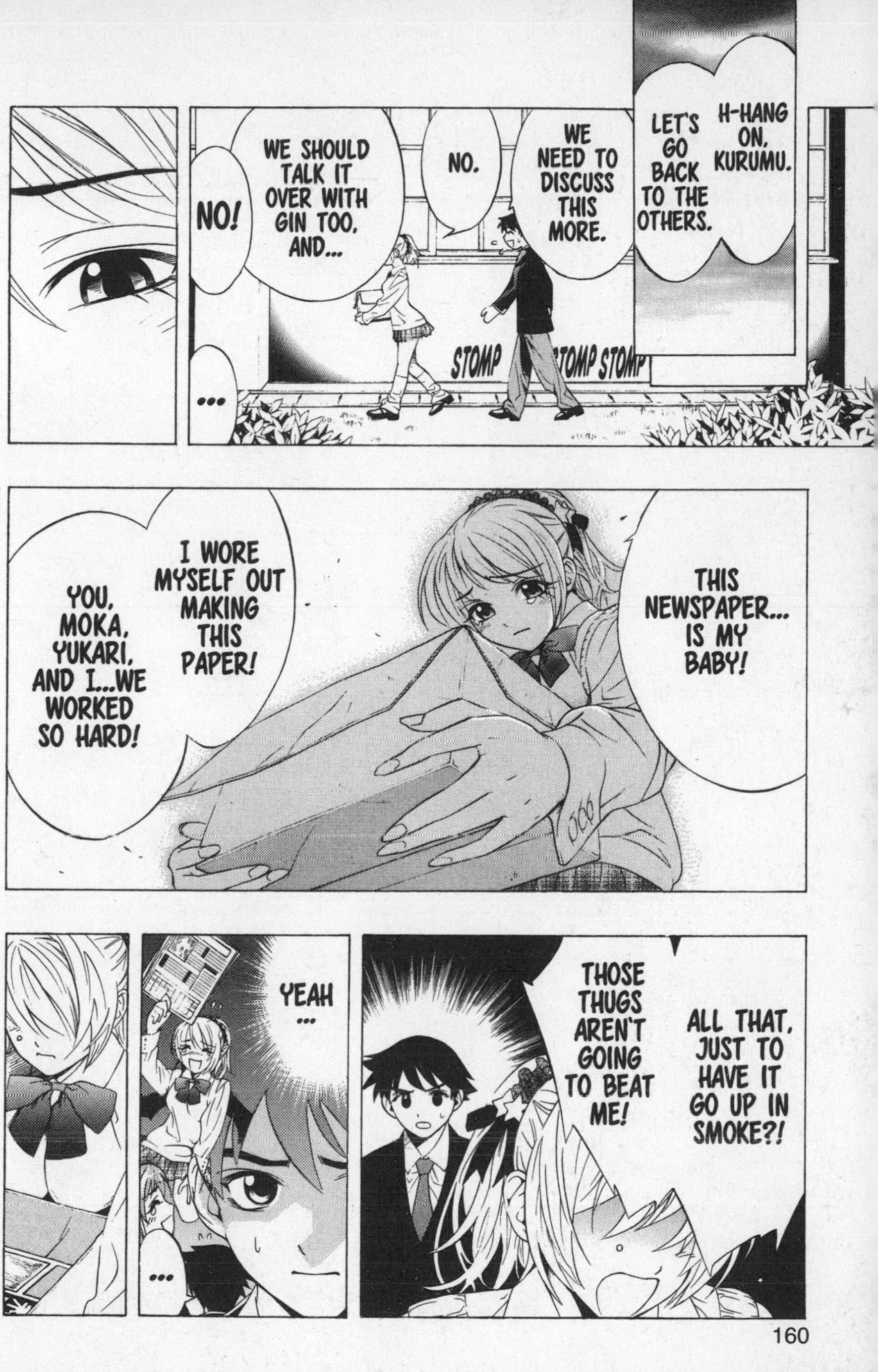
H-HANG ON, KURUMU.
LET'S GO BACK TO THE OTHERS.
WE NEED TO DISCUSS THIS MORE.
NO.
WE SHOULD TALK IT OVER WITH GIN TOO, AND...
NO!
STOMP STOMP STOMP
...
THIS NEWSPAPER... IS MY BABY!
I WORE MYSELF OUT MAKING THIS PAPER!
YOU, MOKA, YUKARI, AND I...WE WORKED SO HARD!
ALL THAT, JUST TO HAVE IT GO UP IN SMOKE?!
THOSE THUGS AREN'T GOING TO BEAT ME!
YEAH...
...

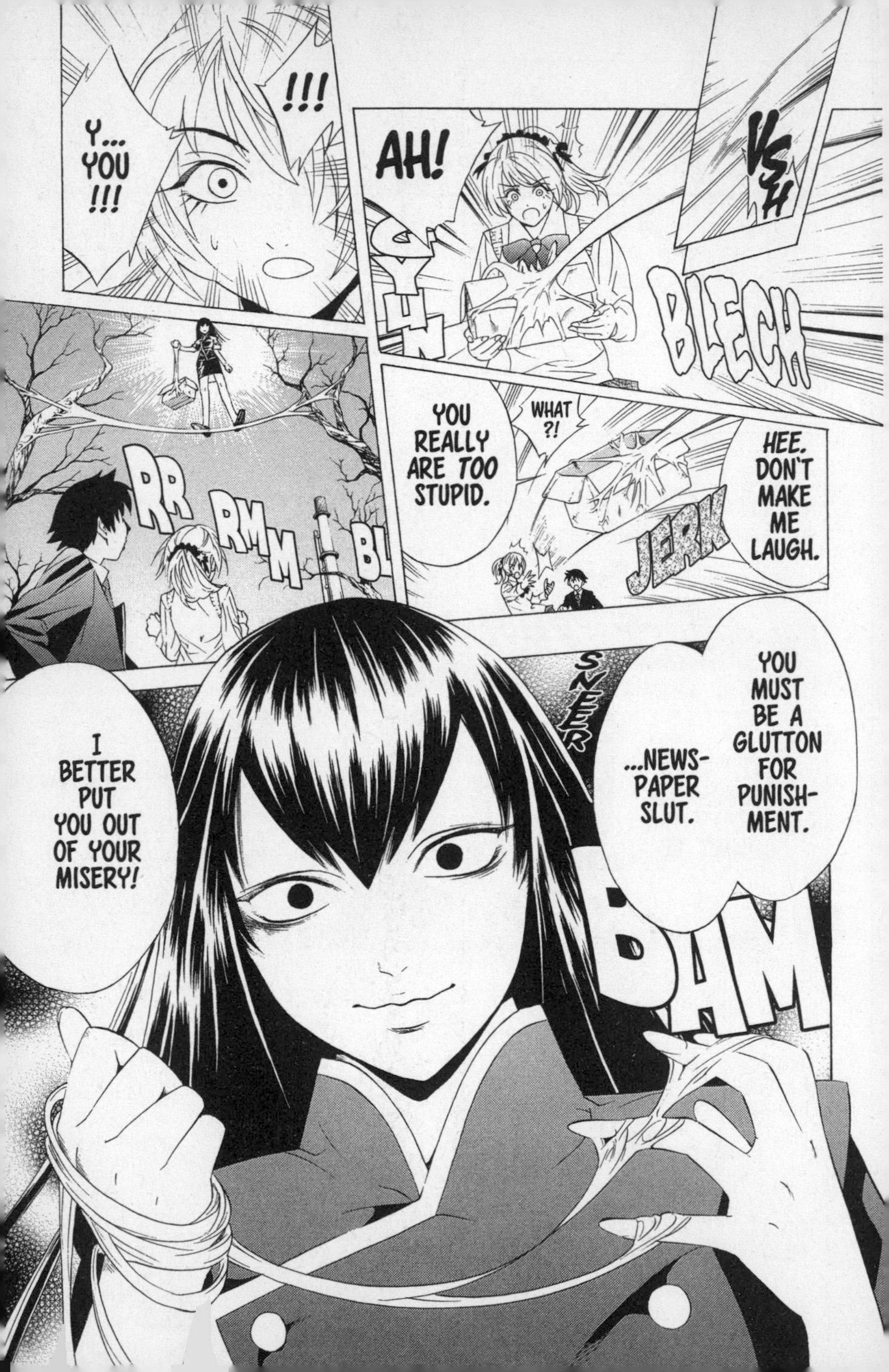
VSH
BLECH
AH!
GYUN
!!!
Y... YOU !!!
HEE. DON'T MAKE ME LAUGH.
WHAT ?!
YOU REALLY ARE TOO STUPID.
JERK
RR RMMM BL
YOU MUST BE A GLUTTON FOR PUNISH-MENT.
...NEWS-PAPER SLUT.
SNEER
BAM
I BETTER PUT YOU OUT OF YOUR MISERY!

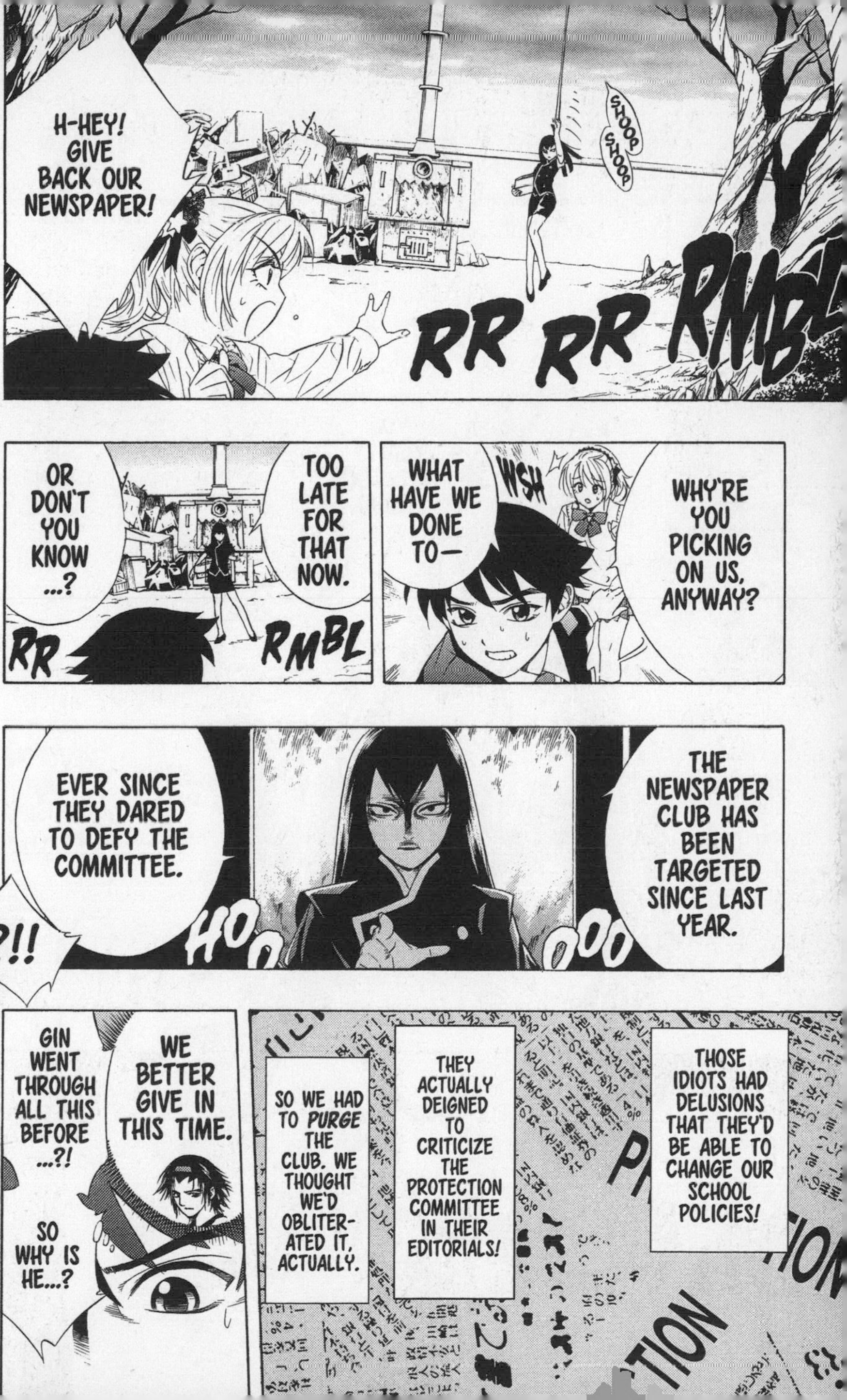
SHOOP SHOOP
H-HEY! GIVE BACK OUR NEWSPAPER!
RR RR RMBL
WHY'RE YOU PICKING ON US, ANYWAY?
WSH
WHAT HAVE WE DONE TO—
TOO LATE FOR THAT NOW.
OR DON'T YOU KNOW ...?
RR RMBL
THE NEWSPAPER CLUB HAS BEEN TARGETED SINCE LAST YEAR.
HOOOO
EVER SINCE THEY DARED TO DEFY THE COMMITTEE.
?!!
THOSE IDIOTS HAD DELUSIONS THAT THEY'D BE ABLE TO CHANGE OUR SCHOOL POLICIES!
THEY ACTUALLY DEIGNED TO CRITICIZE THE PROTECTION COMMITTEE IN THEIR EDITORIALS!
SO WE HAD TO *PURGE* THE CLUB. WE THOUGHT WE'D OBLITERATED IT, ACTUALLY.
WE BETTER GIVE IN THIS TIME.
GIN WENT THROUGH ALL THIS BEFORE ...?!
SO WHY IS HE...?

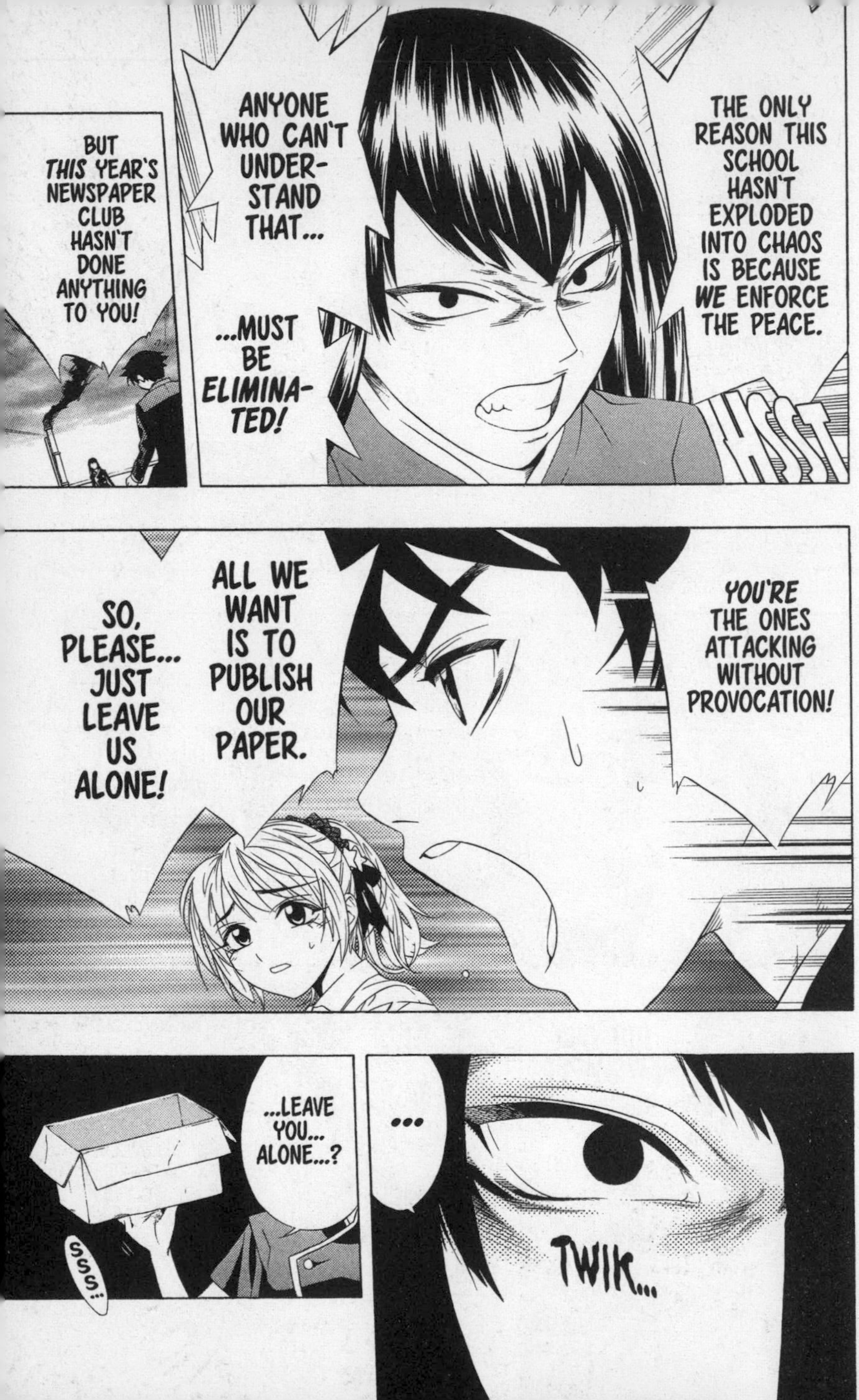
THE ONLY REASON THIS SCHOOL HASN'T EXPLODED INTO CHAOS IS BECAUSE WE ENFORCE THE PEACE.
ANYONE WHO CAN'T UNDER-STAND THAT...
...MUST BE ELIMINA-TED!
HSST
BUT THIS YEAR'S NEWSPAPER CLUB HASN'T DONE ANYTHING TO YOU!
YOU'RE THE ONES ATTACKING WITHOUT PROVOCATION!
ALL WE WANT IS TO PUBLISH OUR PAPER.
SO, PLEASE... JUST LEAVE US ALONE!
...
TWIK...
...LEAVE YOU... ALONE...?
SSS...

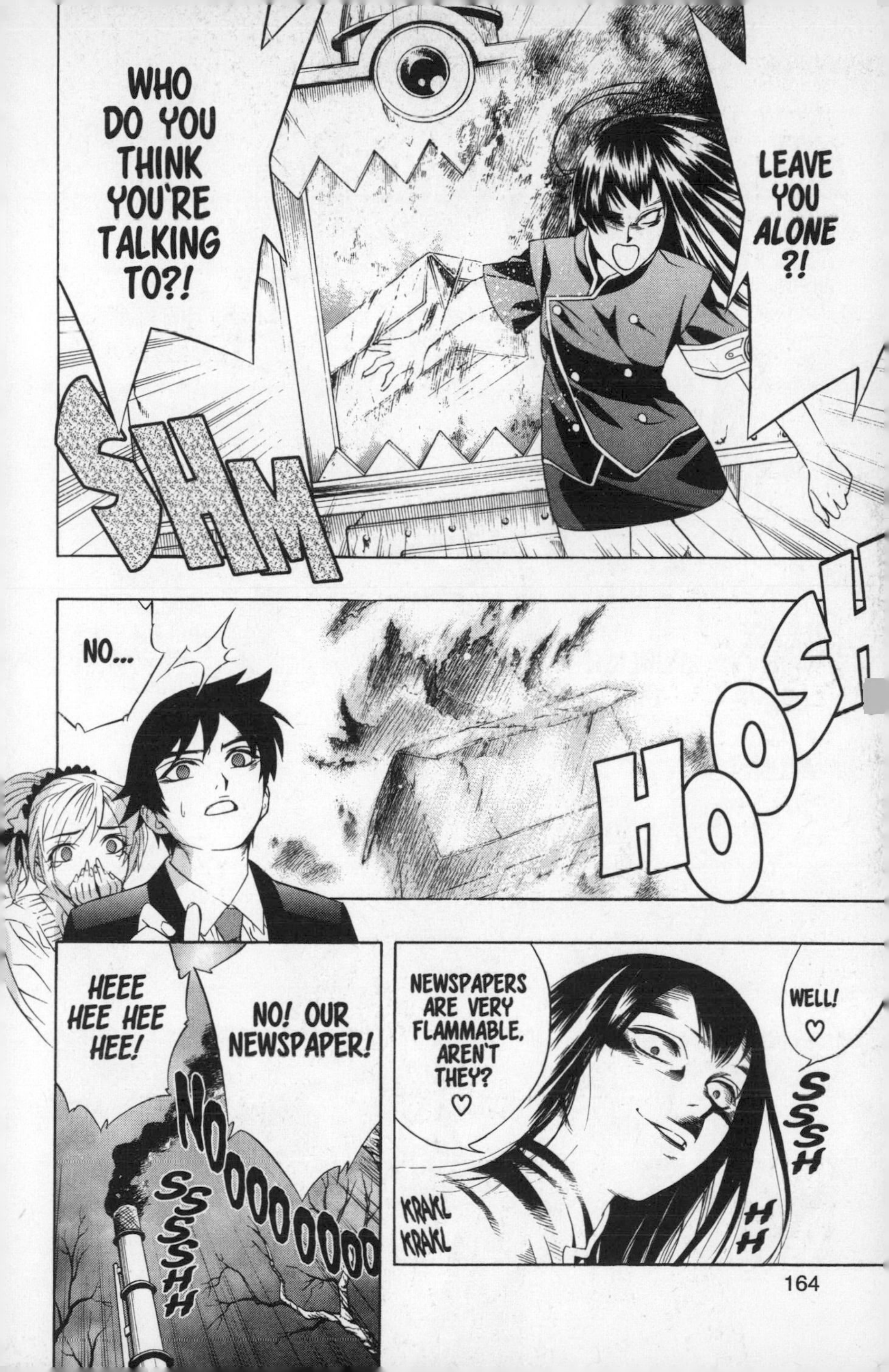
LEAVE YOU ALONE ?!
WHO DO YOU THINK YOU'RE TALKING TO?!
SHM
NO...
HOOSH
WELL! ♡
NEWSPAPERS ARE VERY FLAMMABLE, AREN'T THEY? ♡
SSSH HH
KRAKL KRAKL
NO! OUR NEWSPAPER!
HEEE HEE HEE HEE!
NOOOOOOOOO
SSSSHH

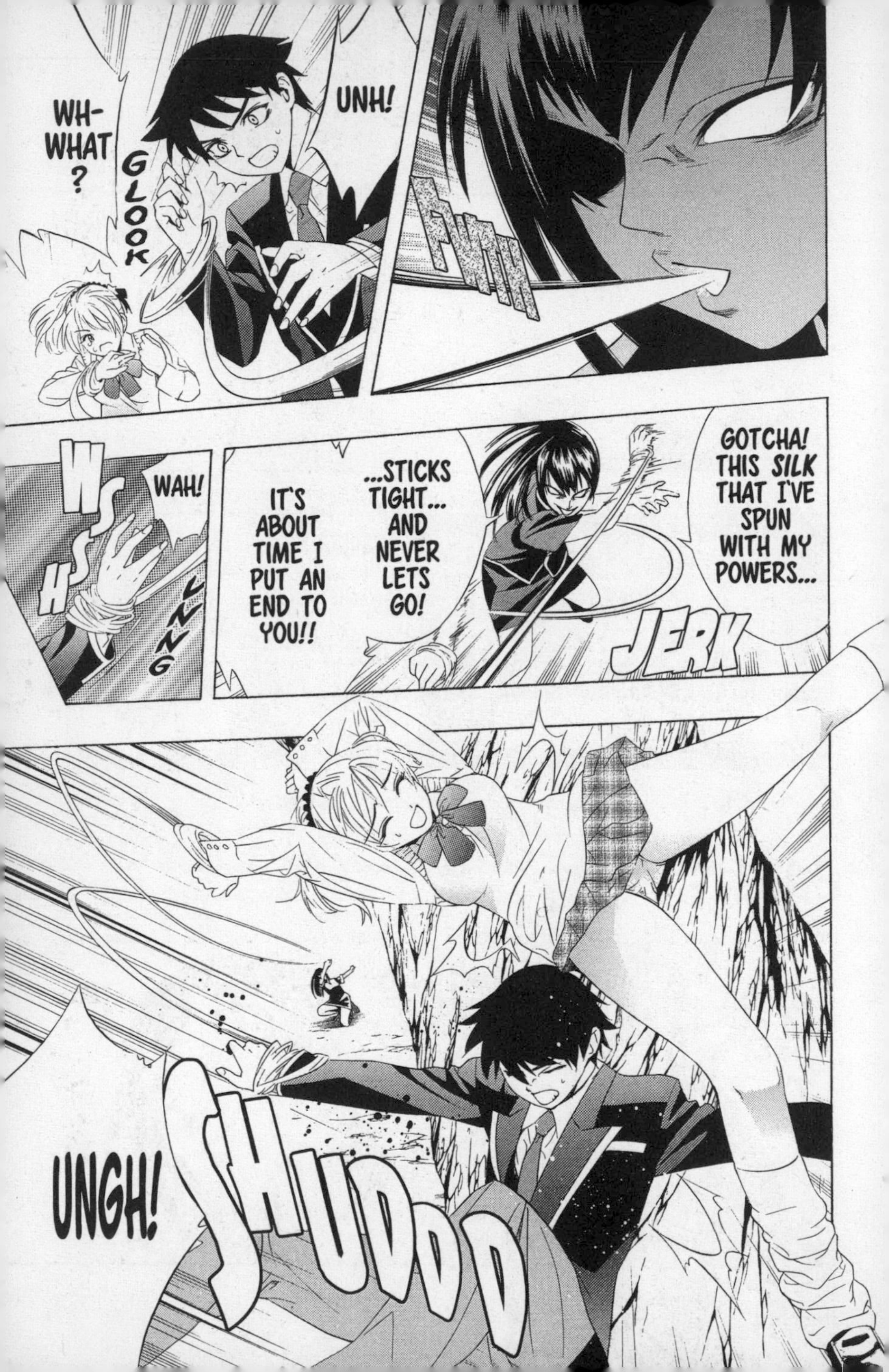
UNH!
WH- WHAT?
GLOOK
GOTCHA! THIS SILK THAT I'VE SPUN WITH MY POWERS...
...STICKS TIGHT... AND NEVER LETS GO!
IT'S ABOUT TIME I PUT AN END TO YOU!!
JERK
WAH!
UNNG
SHUDDD
UNGH!

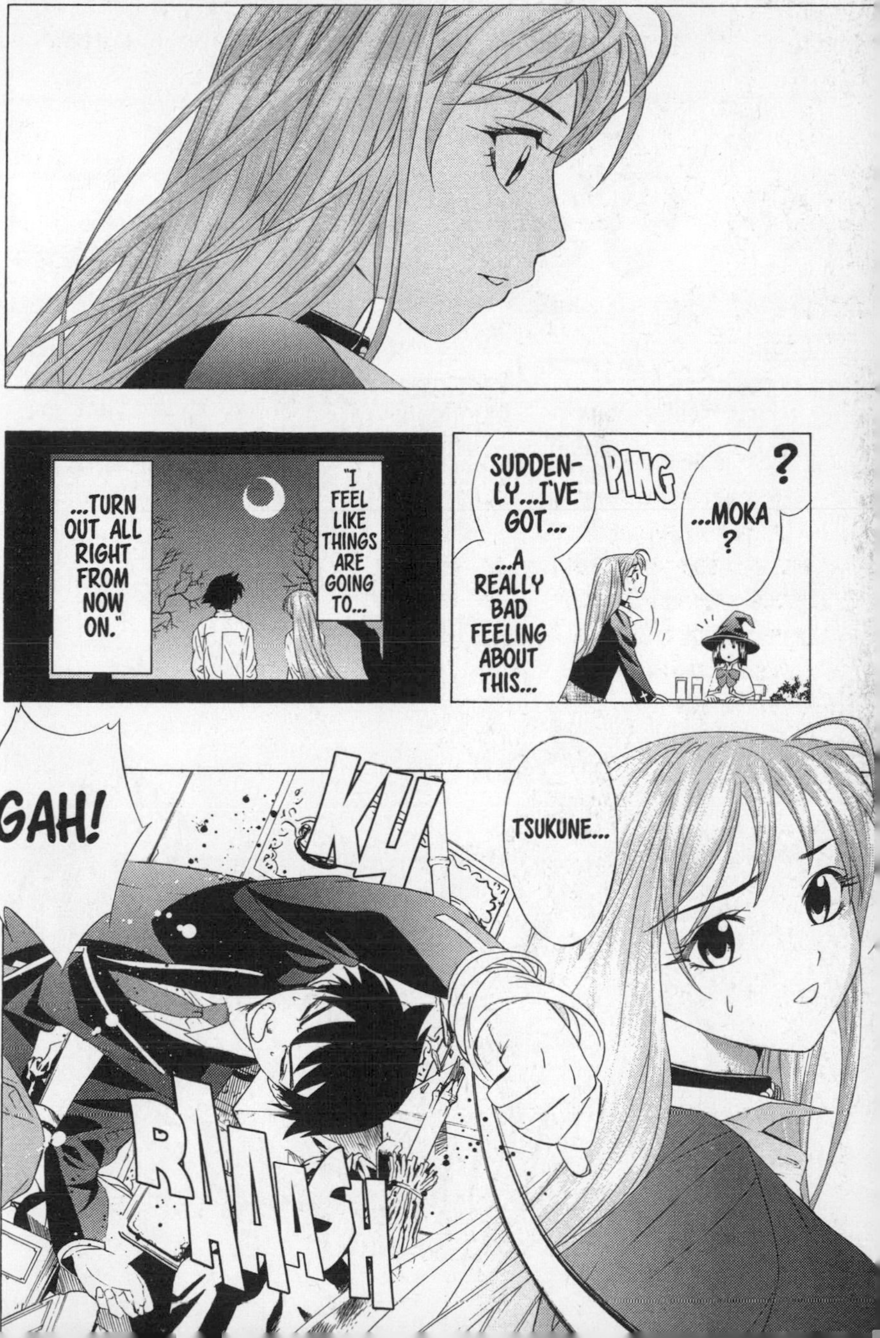
?
...MOKA ?
PING
SUDDEN-LY...I'VE GOT...
...A REALLY BAD FEELING ABOUT THIS...
"I FEEL LIKE THINGS ARE GOING TO...
...TURN OUT ALL RIGHT FROM NOW ON."
TSUKUNE...
KU
GAH!
RAAASH

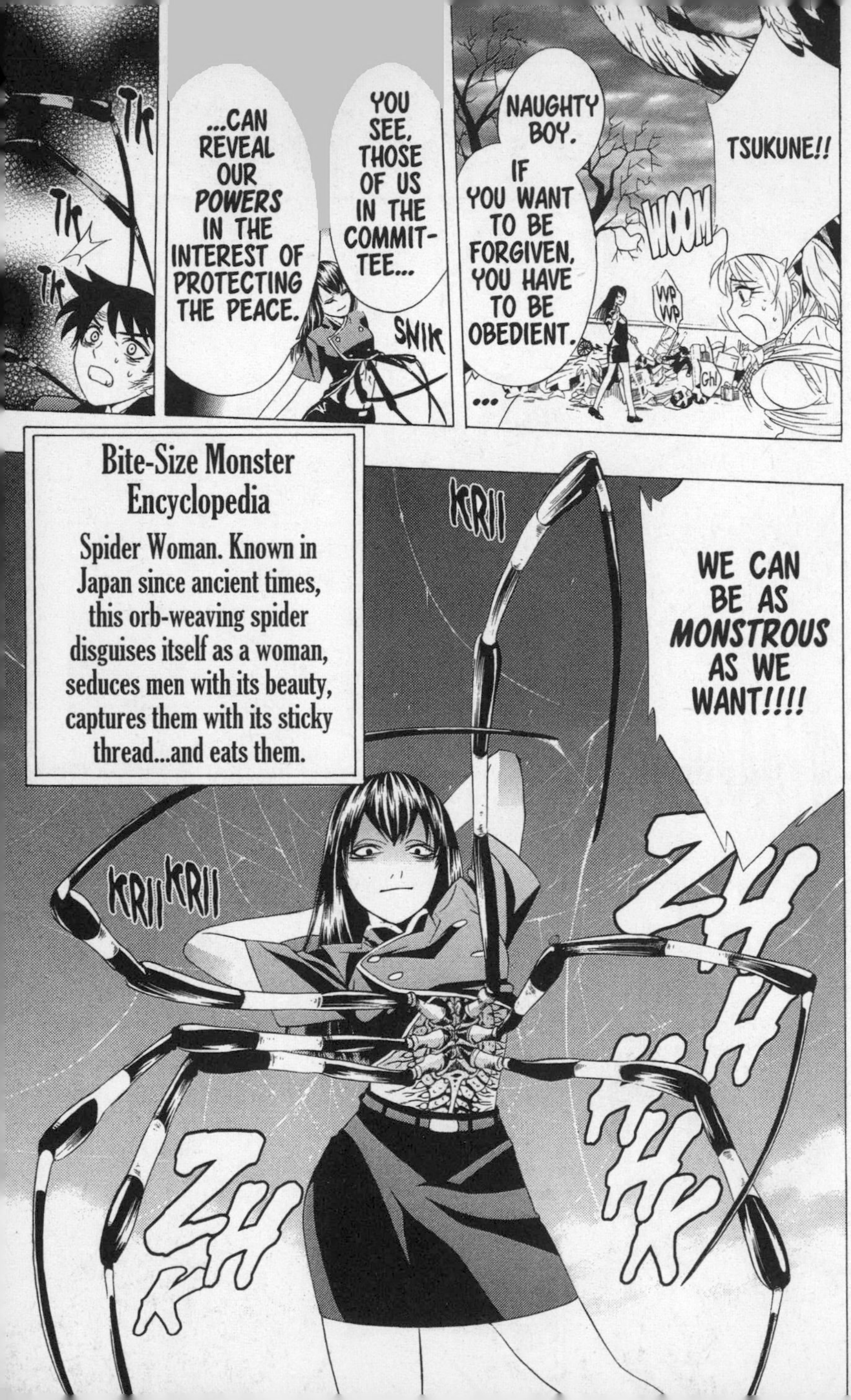

TSUKUNE!!
WOOM
NAUGHTY BOY.
IF YOU WANT TO BE FORGIVEN, YOU HAVE TO BE OBEDIENT.
...
VVP VVP
YOU SEE, THOSE OF US IN THE COMMIT-TEE...
SNIK
...CAN REVEAL OUR *POWERS* IN THE INTEREST OF PROTECTING THE PEACE.
Tk
Tk
Tk
WE CAN BE AS *MONSTROUS* AS WE WANT!!!!
KRII
ZHHHK
Bite-Size Monster Encyclopedia
Spider Woman. Known in Japan since ancient times, this orb-weaving spider disguises itself as a woman, seduces men with its beauty, captures them with its sticky thread...and eats them.
KRII KRII
ZHK

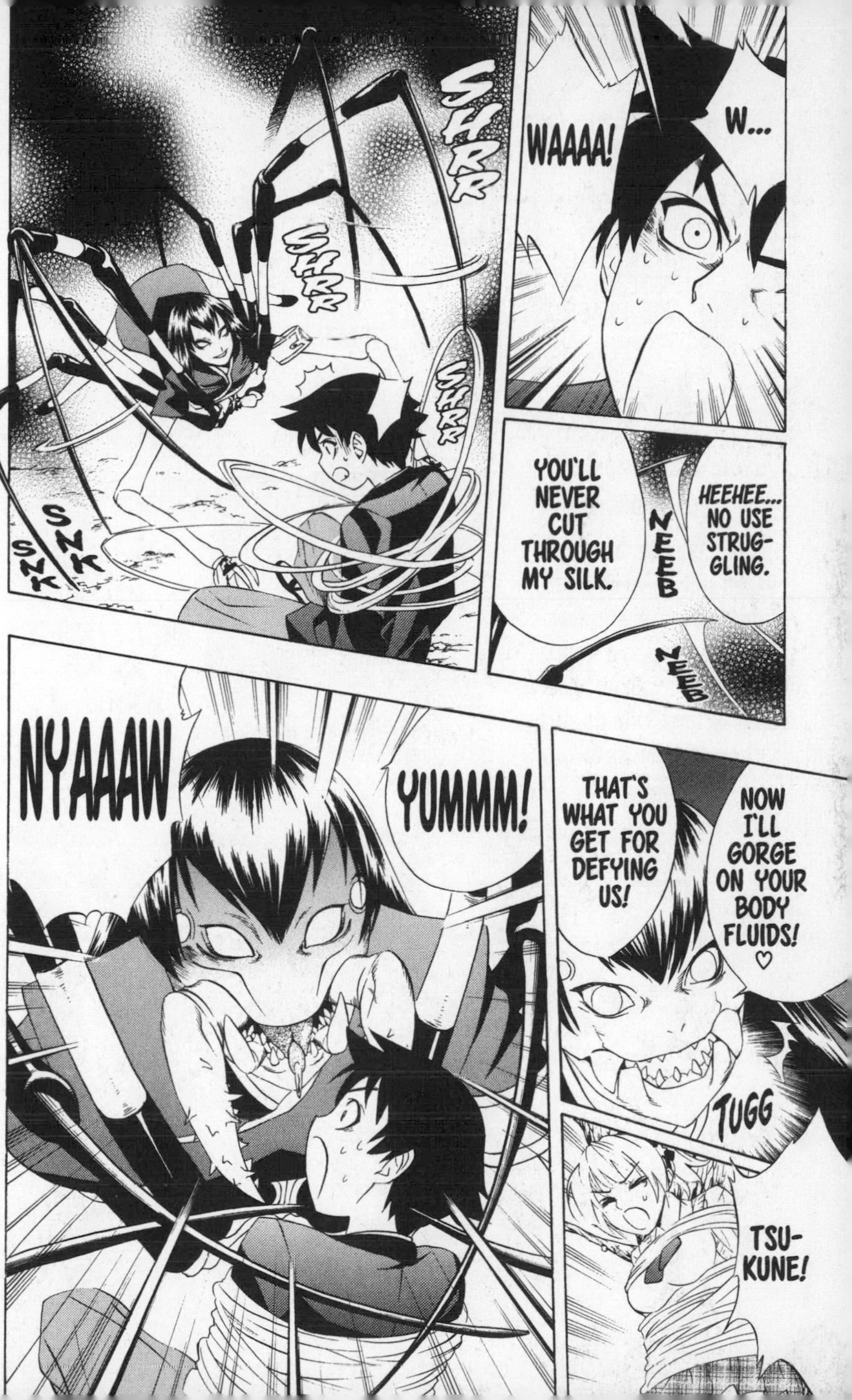
W...
WAAAA!
HEEHEE... NO USE STRUG-GLING.
NEEB
YOU'LL NEVER CUT THROUGH MY SILK.
NEEB
SHRR
SHRR
SHRR
SNK
SNK
NOW I'LL GORGE ON YOUR BODY FLUIDS! ♡
THAT'S WHAT YOU GET FOR DEFYING US!
TUGG
TSU-KUNE!
YUMMM!
NYAAAW

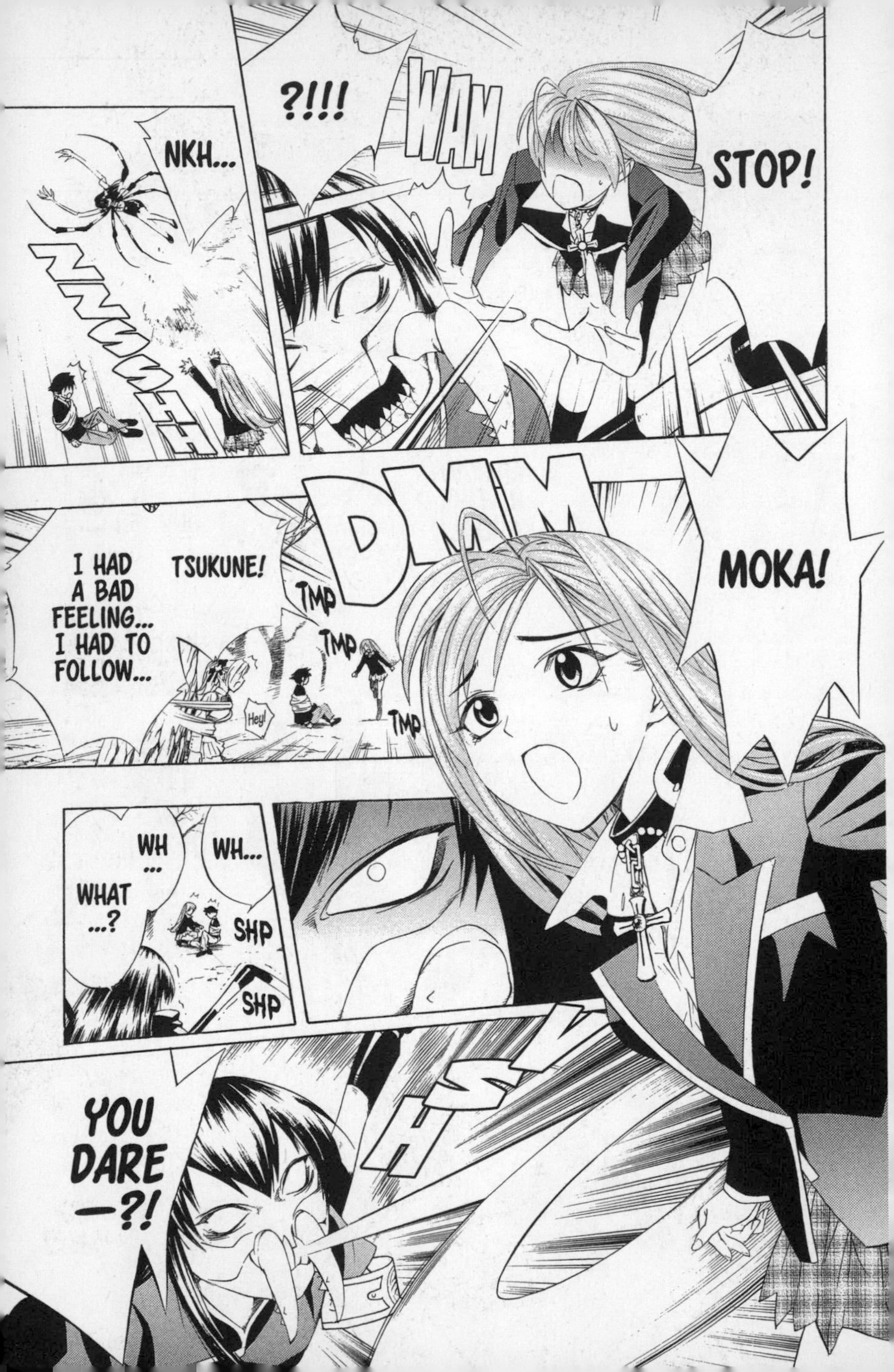
STOP!
WAM
?!!!
NKH...
MOKA!
DMM
TMP
TMP
TMP
TSUKUNE!
Hey!
I HAD A BAD FEELING... I HAD TO FOLLOW...
WH...
WH ... WHAT ...?
SHP
SHP
YOU DARE—?!

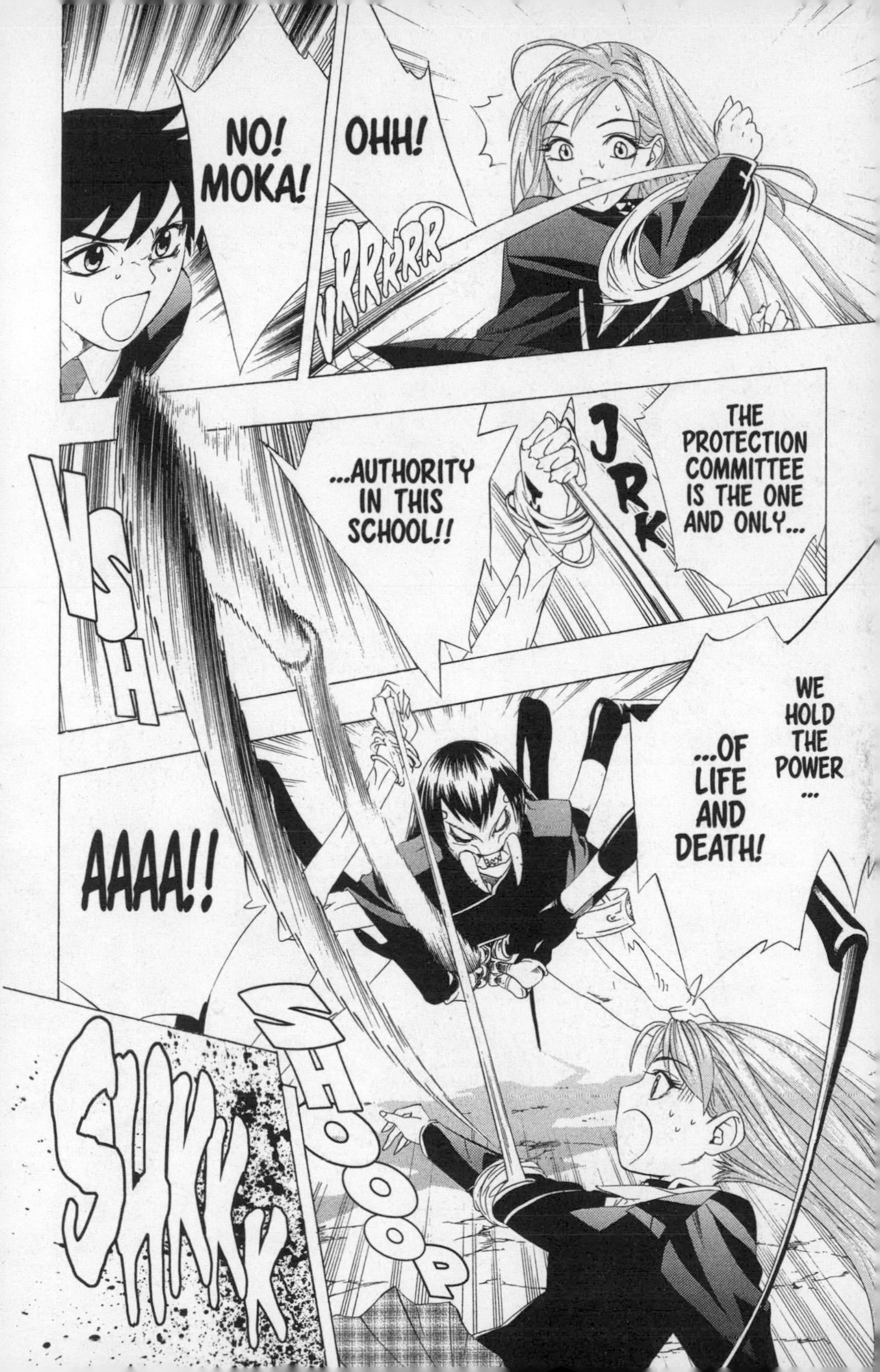
OHH!
VRRRRR
NO! MOKA!
THE PROTECTION COMMITTEE IS THE ONE AND ONLY...
JRK
...AUTHORITY IN THIS SCHOOL!!
VSH
WE HOLD THE POWER ...
...OF LIFE AND DEATH!
AAAA!!
SHOOOOP
SHNKK

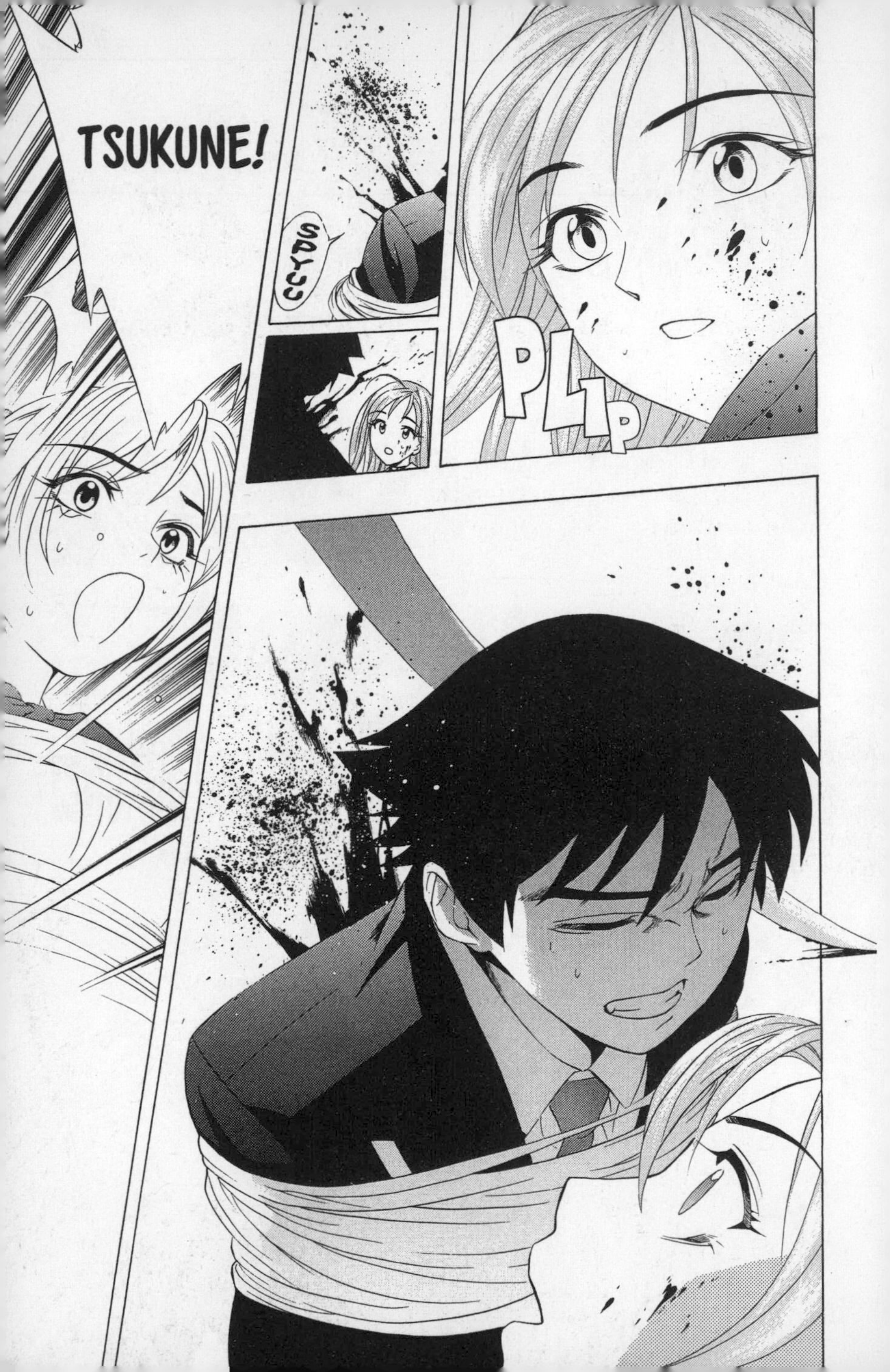

PLIP
SPYUU
TSUKUNE!

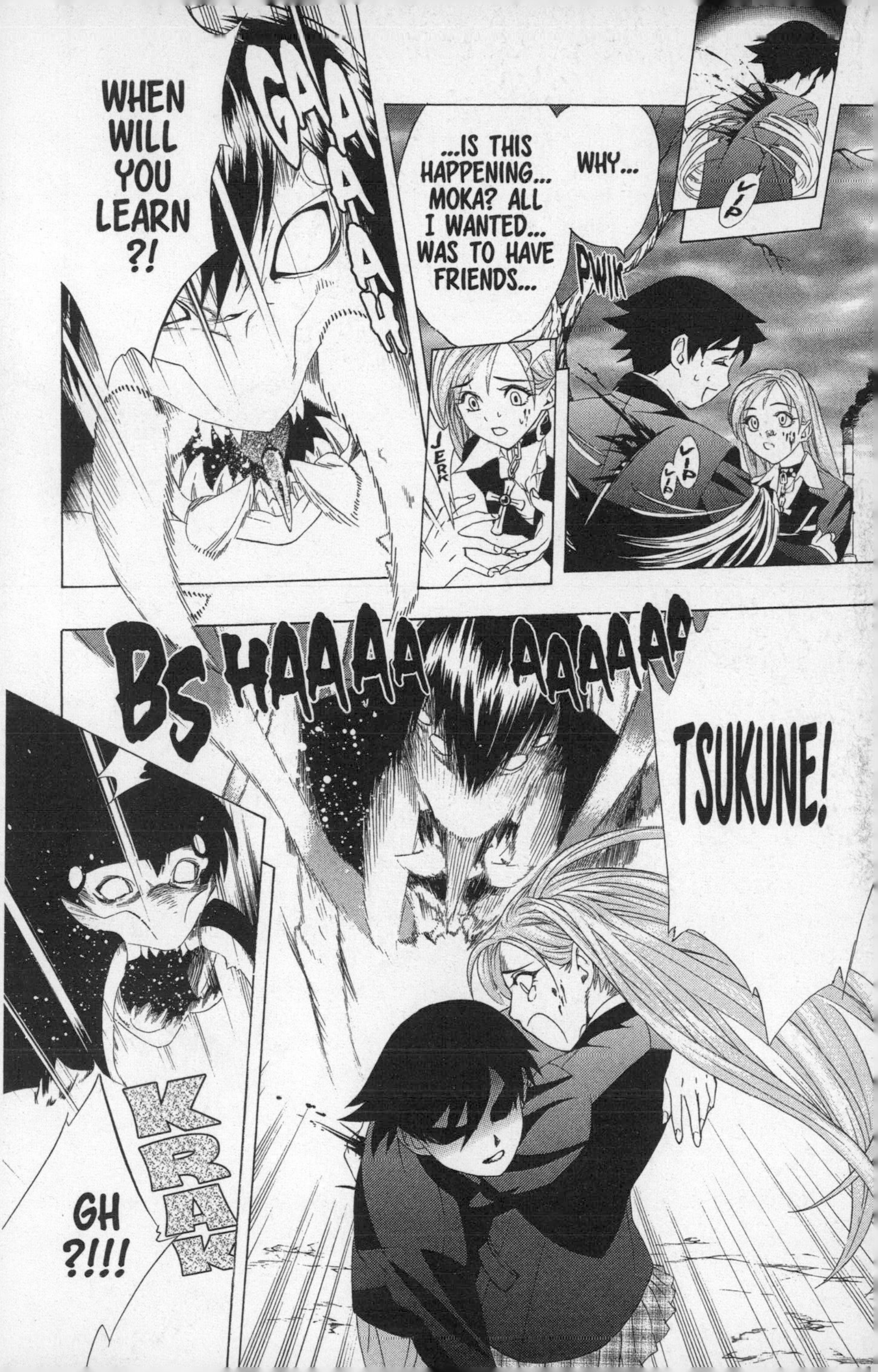
VIP
WHY...
...IS THIS HAPPENING... MOKA? ALL I WANTED... WAS TO HAVE FRIENDS...
PWIK
VIP VIP
JERK
WHEN WILL YOU LEARN ?!
GAAAAAH
BS HAAAA AAAAAA
TSUKUNE!
KRAK
GH ?!!!

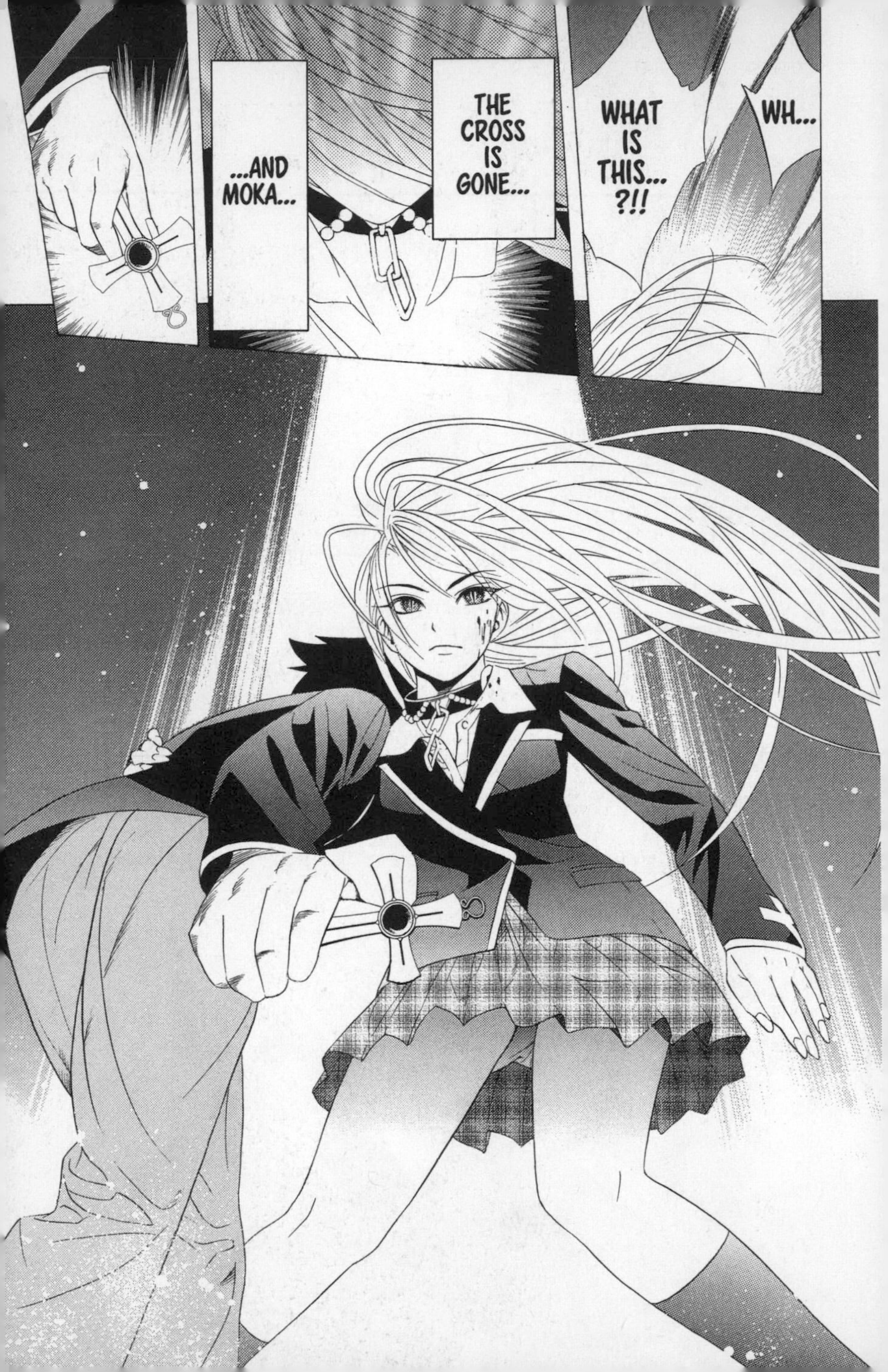
WH...
WHAT IS THIS...?!!
THE CROSS IS GONE...
...AND MOKA...

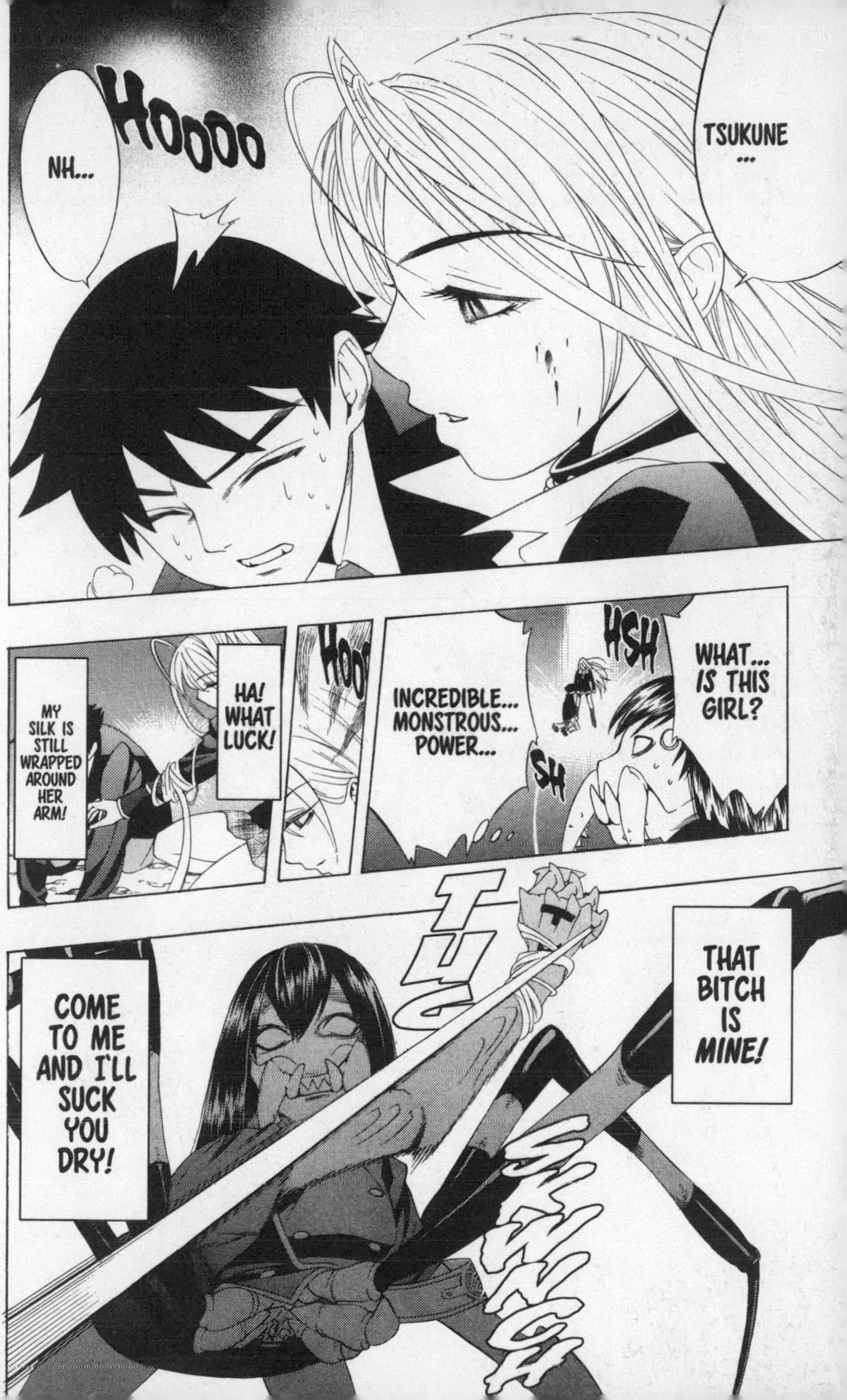
TSUKUNE ...
HOOOO
NH...
WHAT... IS THIS GIRL?
HSH
INCREDIBLE... MONSTROUS... POWER...
SH
HOO
HA! WHAT LUCK!
MY SILK IS STILL WRAPPED AROUND HER ARM!
THAT BITCH IS MINE!
TUG
COME TO ME AND I'LL SUCK YOU DRY!

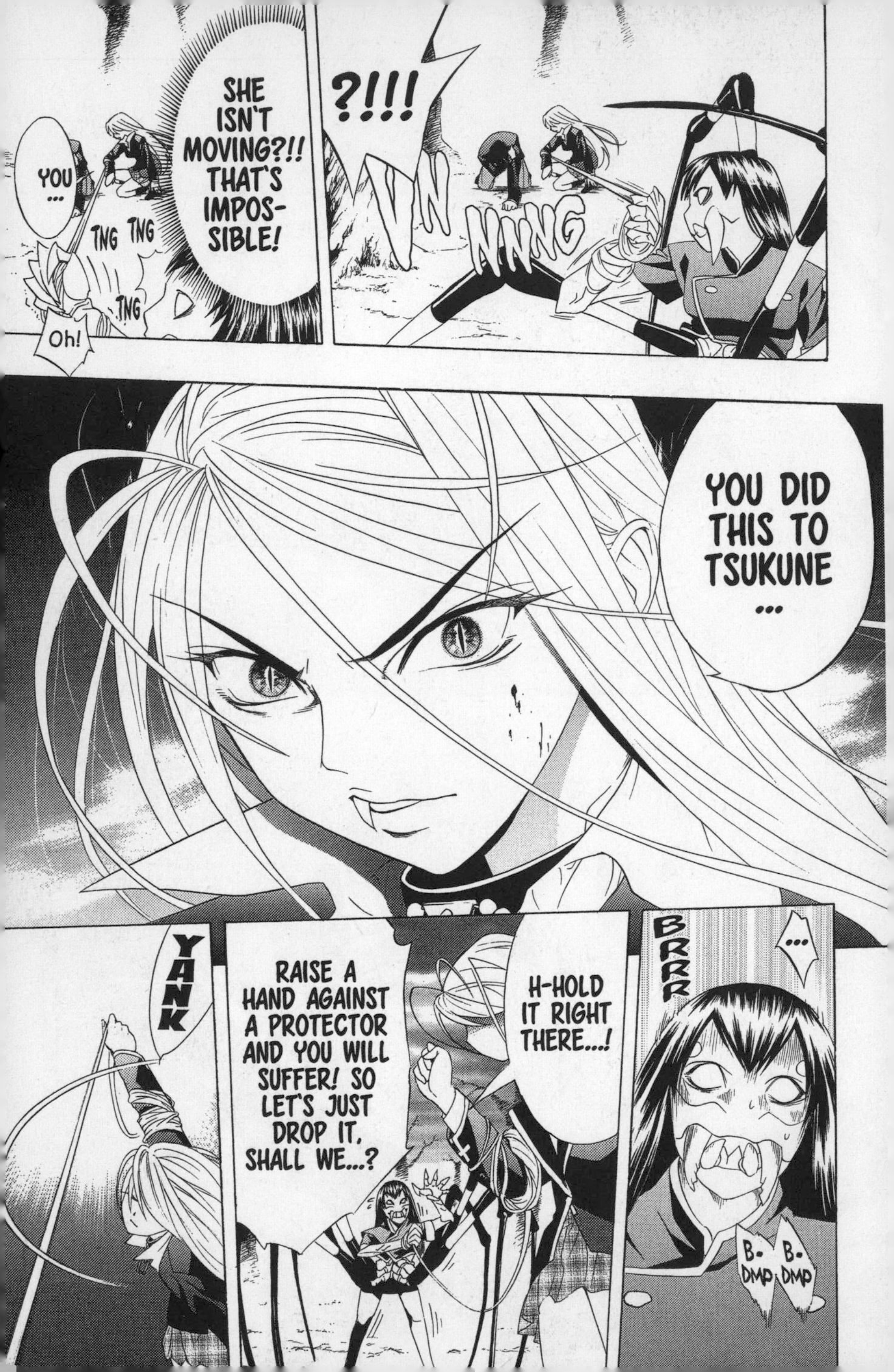
?!!!
VN NNNG
SHE ISN'T MOVING?!! THAT'S IMPOSSIBLE!
YOU ...
TNG TNG
TNG
Oh!
YOU DID THIS TO TSUKUNE ...
...
BRRR
B-DMP B-DMP
H-HOLD IT RIGHT THERE...!
RAISE A HAND AGAINST A PROTECTOR AND YOU WILL SUFFER! SO LET'S JUST DROP IT, SHALL WE...?
YANK

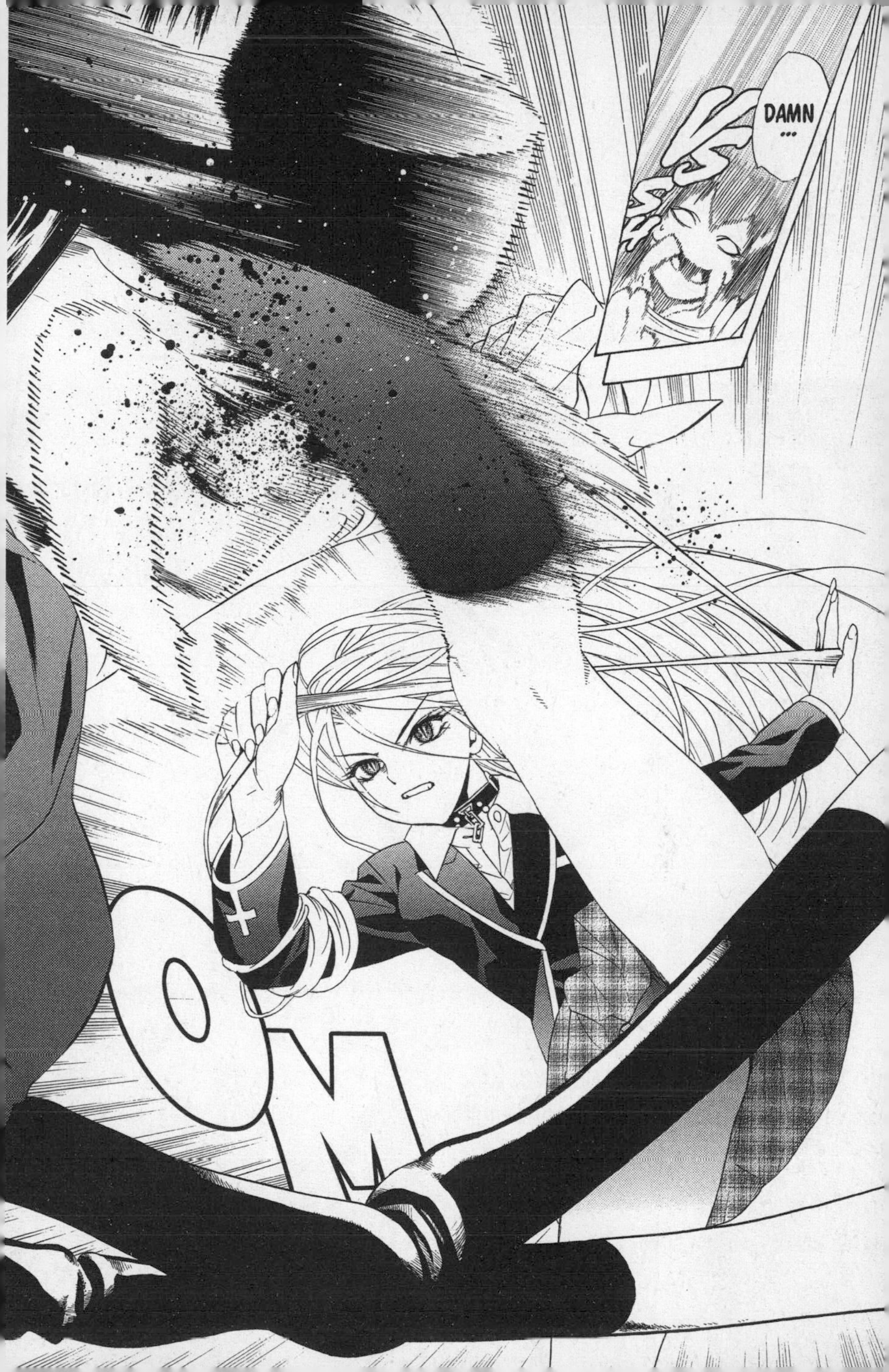
DAMN …

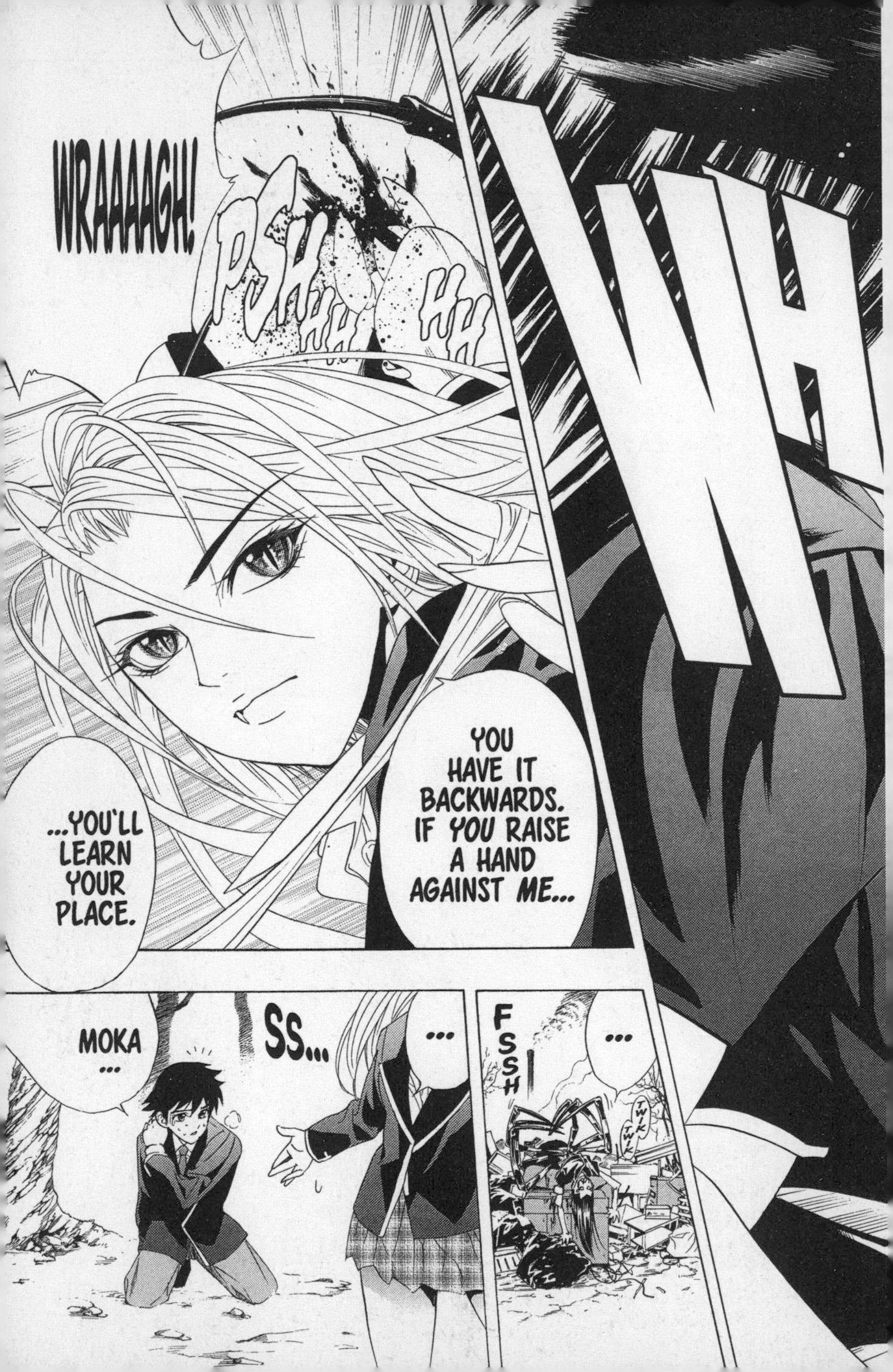
WH
PCHHH HH
WRAAAGH!
YOU HAVE IT BACKWARDS. IF YOU RAISE A HAND AGAINST ME...
...YOU'LL LEARN YOUR PLACE.
FSSH
...
TWIK TWIK
...
SS...
MOKA...

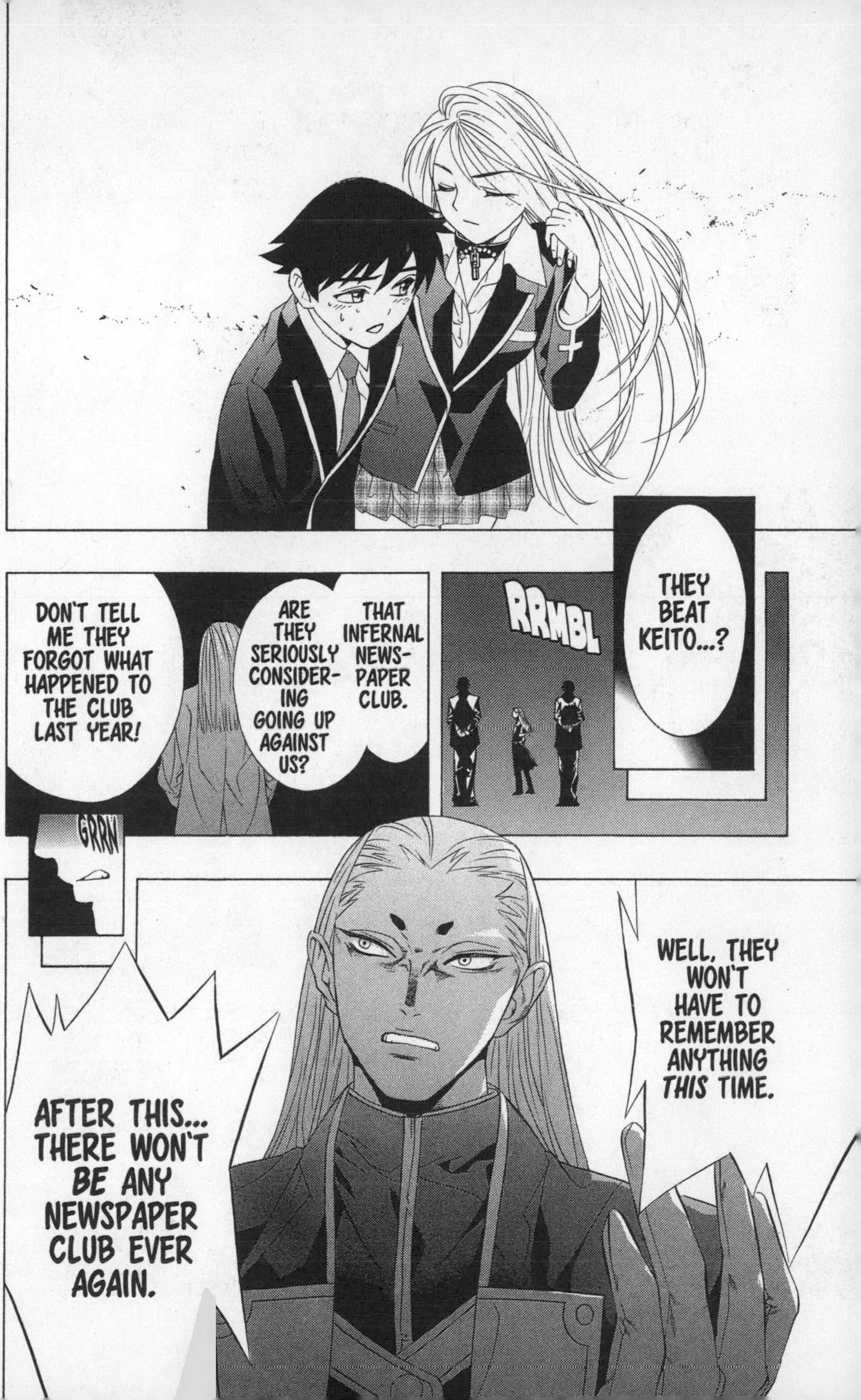

THEY BEAT KEITO...?
RRMBL
THAT INFERNAL NEWSPAPER CLUB.
ARE THEY SERIOUSLY CONSIDERING GOING UP AGAINST US?
DON'T TELL ME THEY FORGOT WHAT HAPPENED TO THE CLUB LAST YEAR!
GRRN
WELL, THEY WON'T HAVE TO REMEMBER ANYTHING *THIS* TIME.
AFTER THIS... THERE WON'T *BE* ANY NEWSPAPER CLUB EVER AGAIN.

READ THIS WAY

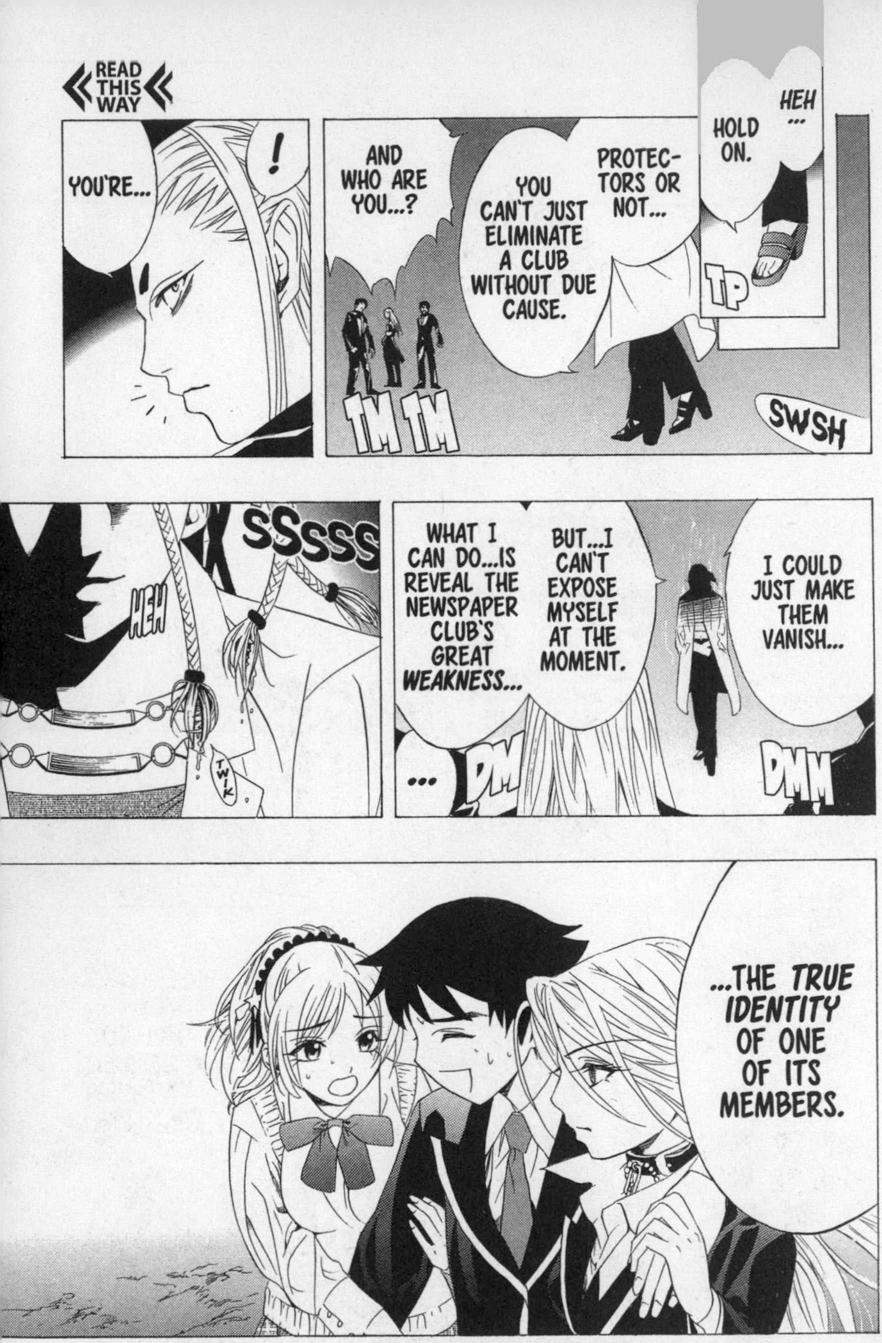

HEH...
HOLD ON.
TP
PROTECTORS OR NOT...
YOU CAN'T JUST ELIMINATE A CLUB WITHOUT DUE CAUSE.
SWSH
AND WHO ARE YOU...?
TM TM
!
YOU'RE...
I COULD JUST MAKE THEM VANISH...
DMM
BUT...I CAN'T EXPOSE MYSELF AT THE MOMENT.
WHAT I CAN DO...IS REVEAL THE NEWSPAPER CLUB'S GREAT *WEAKNESS*...
DM
...
SSSSS
HEH
TWIK
...THE *TRUE IDENTITY* OF ONE OF ITS MEMBERS.

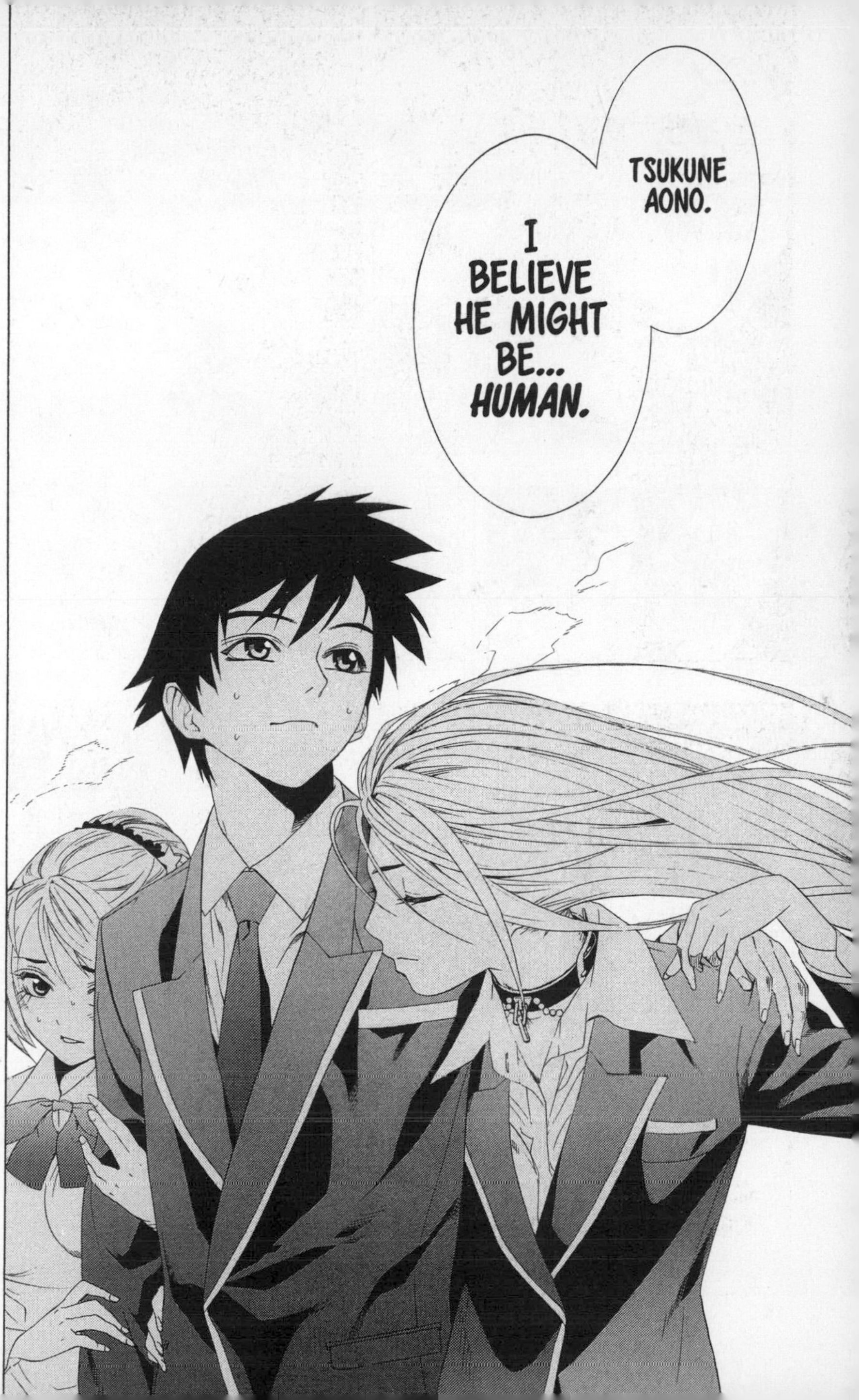
TSUKUNE AONO.
I BELIEVE HE MIGHT BE... HUMAN.

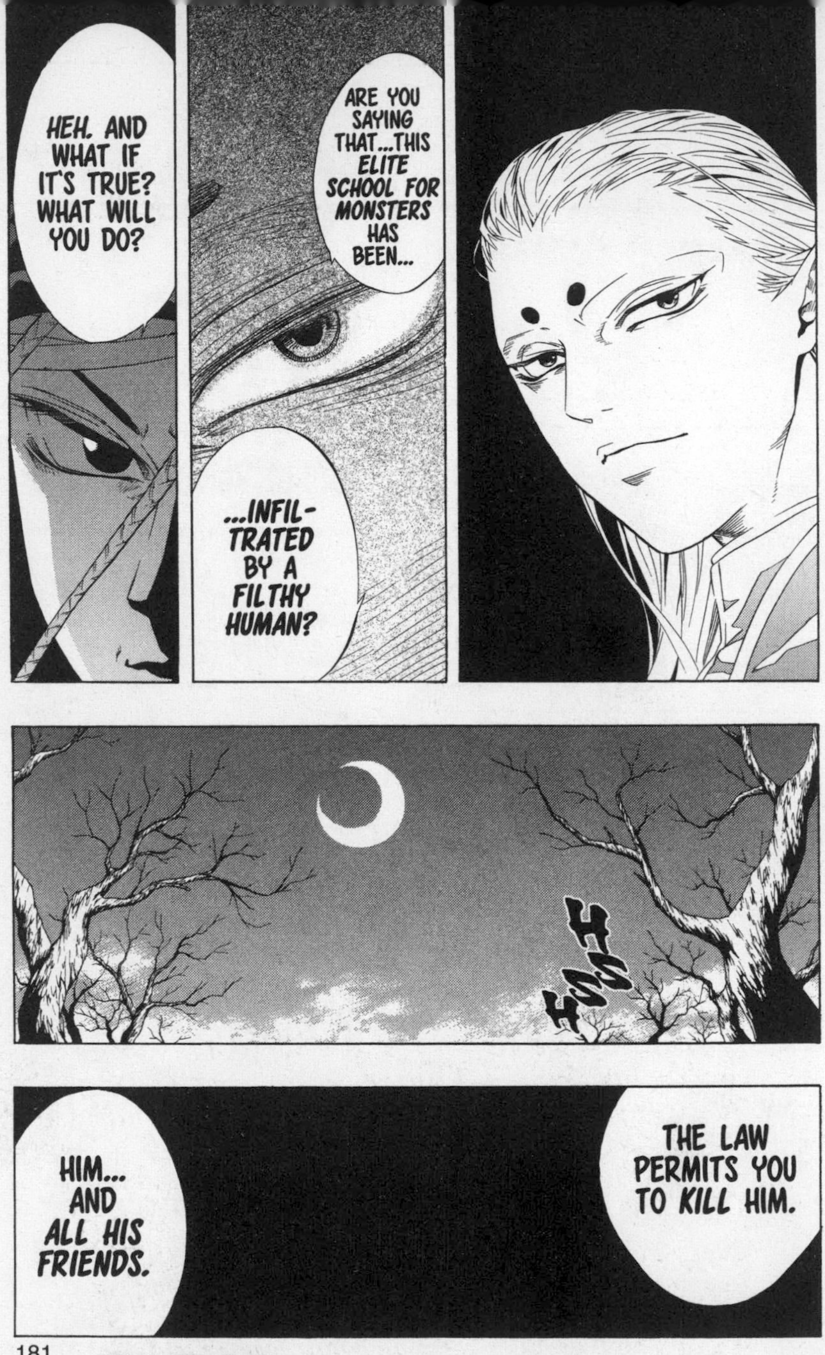
ARE YOU SAYING THAT...THIS *ELITE* SCHOOL FOR MONSTERS HAS BEEN...
...INFILTRATED BY A FILTHY HUMAN?
HEH. AND WHAT IF IT'S TRUE? WHAT WILL YOU DO?
HSSH
THE LAW PERMITS YOU TO *KILL* HIM.
HIM... AND *ALL* HIS FRIENDS.

Witch (The End)

ROSARIO + VAMPIRE

End-of-Volume Theater

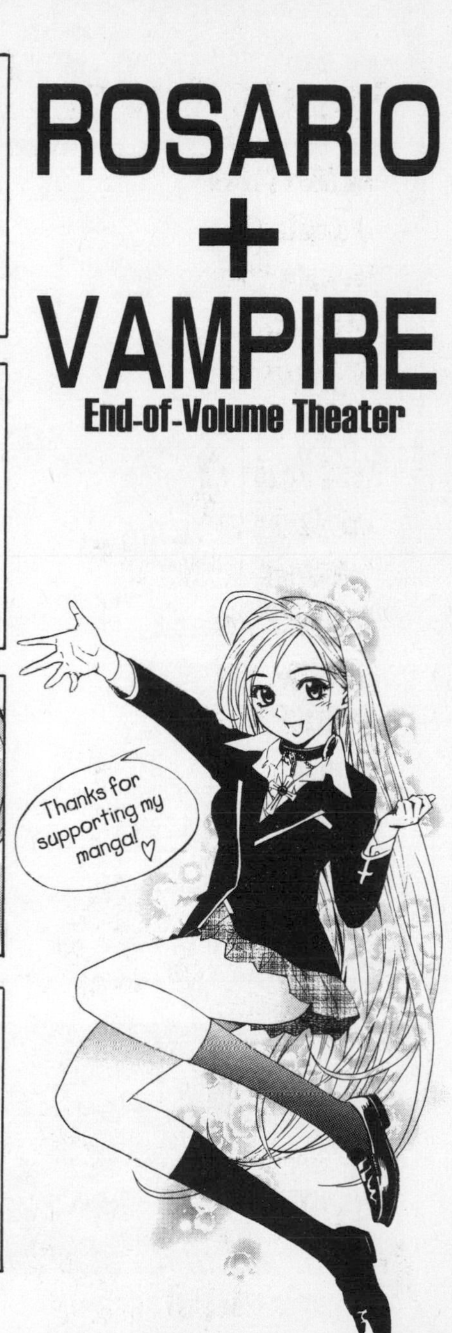
Thanks for supporting my manga! ♡

• Go Go Yukari •

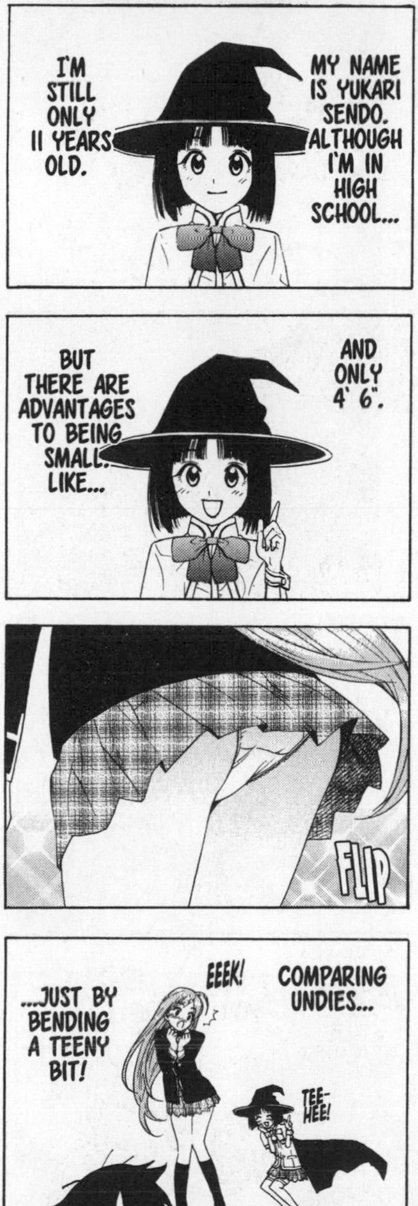
MY NAME IS YUKARI SENDO. ALTHOUGH I'M IN HIGH SCHOOL...
I'M STILL ONLY 11 YEARS OLD.
AND ONLY 4' 6".
BUT THERE ARE ADVANTAGES TO BEING SMALL. LIKE...
FLIP
COMPARING UNDIES...
EEEK!
...JUST BY BENDING A TEENY BIT!
TEE-HEE!

• Dear Yukari... •

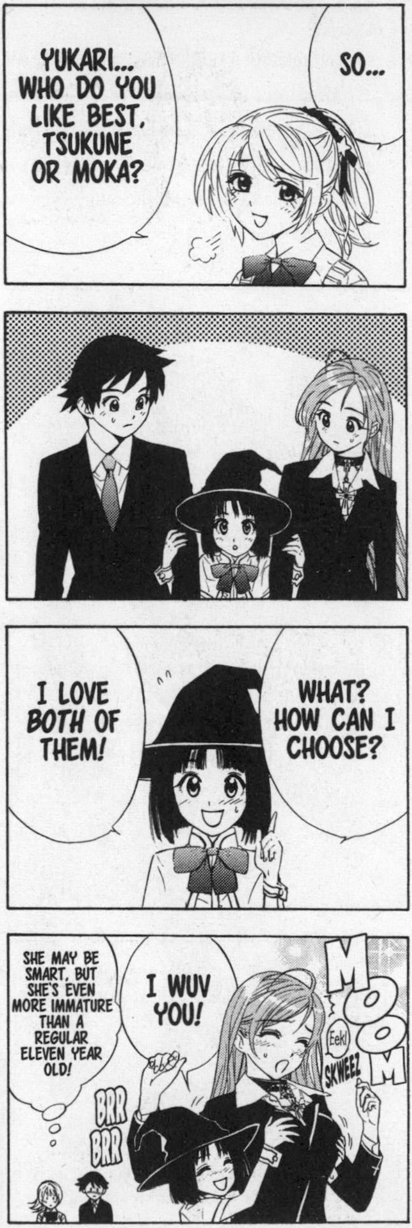
SO...
YUKARI... WHO DO YOU LIKE BEST, TSUKUNE OR MOKA?
WHAT? HOW CAN I CHOOSE?
I LOVE BOTH OF THEM!
MOOOM
I WUV YOU!
SHE MAY BE SMART, BUT SHE'S EVEN MORE IMMATURE THAN A REGULAR ELEVEN YEAR OLD!
Eek!
SKWEEZ
BRR BRR

Rosario+Vampire

Akihisa Ikeda

•Assistants•

Makoto Saito

Takafumi Okubo

Miyo Isshiki

•Help•

Beef Ogaki

•3D Modeling•

Takaharu Yoshizawa

Akihisa Ikeda

•Editing•

Satoshi Adachi

•Comic•

Mika Asada

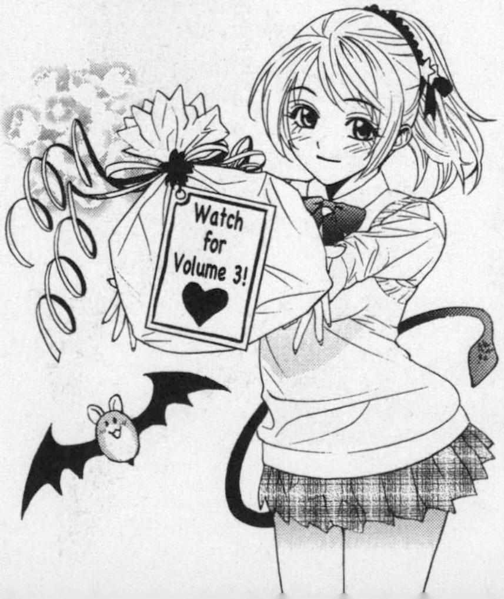
Watch for Volume 3!

CRYPT SHEET FOR VOLUME 3: TROLLS!

QUIZ 3

WHEN FIGHTING A TROLL WHO WANTS TO BE BIG MAN ON CAMPUS...

a. hide under a bridge—that's the last place he'd expect to find you

b. If you've recently received an unsolicited infusion of vampire blood, fight back—since you've probably been transformed into a powerful vampire for all eternity anyway

c. let the rude vampire girl who infused you with her vampire hemoglobin without your permission lend you a fang

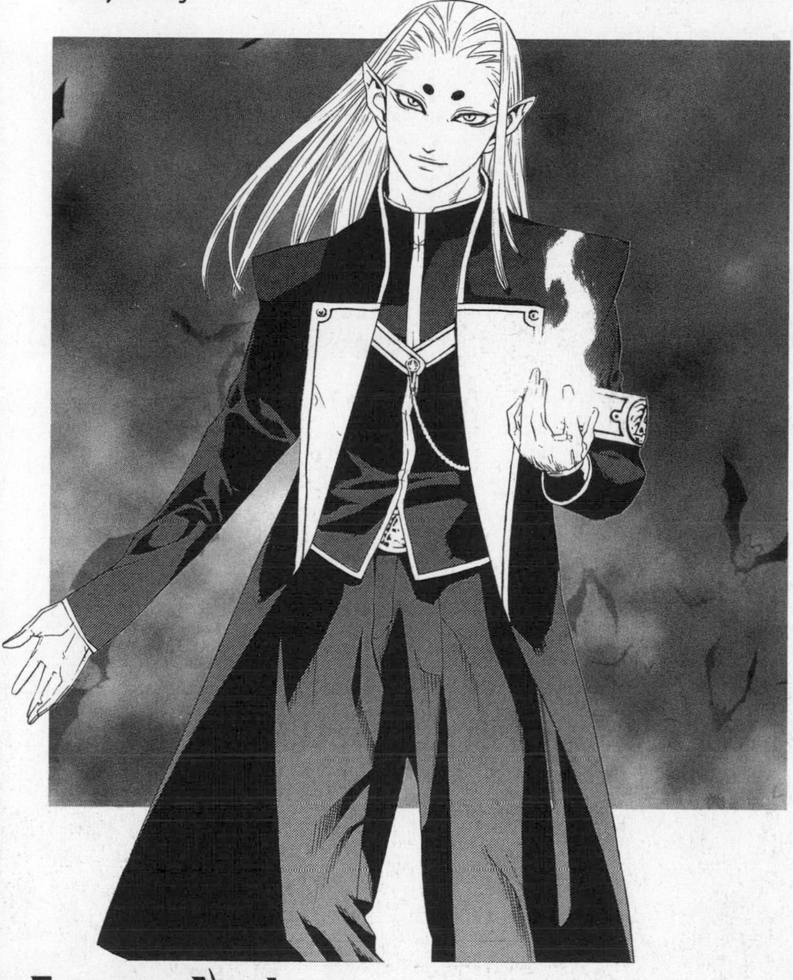

AVAILABLE NOW!

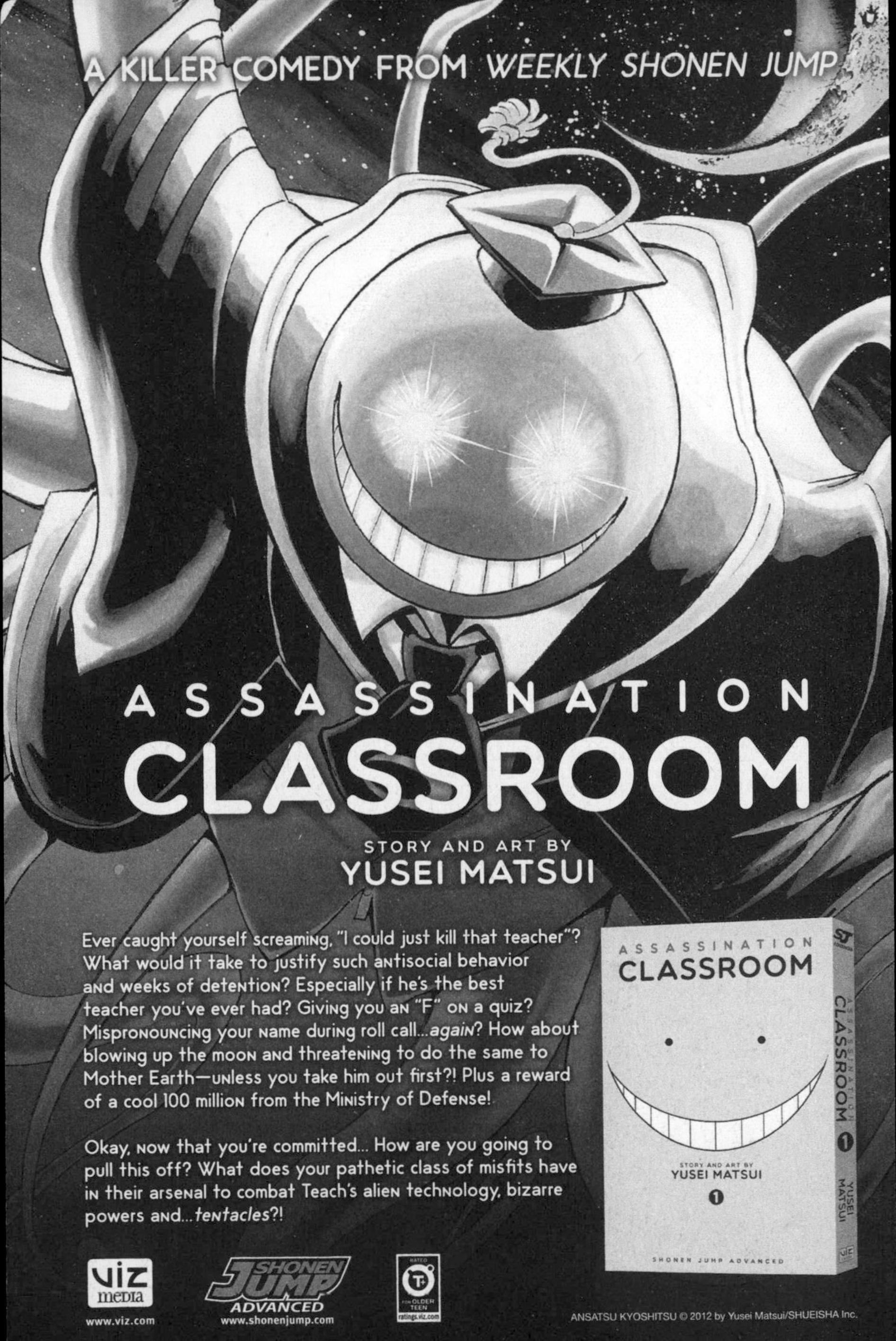
A KILLER COMEDY FROM WEEKLY SHONEN JUMP
ASSASSINATION
CLASSROOM
STORY AND ART BY
YUSEI MATSUI
Ever caught yourself screaming, "I could just kill that teacher"? What would it take to justify such antisocial behavior and weeks of detention? Especially if he's the best teacher you've ever had? Giving you an "F" on a quiz? Mispronouncing your name during roll call...again? How about blowing up the moon and threatening to do the same to Mother Earth—unless you take him out first?! Plus a reward of a cool 100 million from the Ministry of Defense!
Okay, now that you're committed... How are you going to pull this off? What does your pathetic class of misfits have in their arsenal to combat Teach's alien technology, bizarre powers and...tentacles?!
ASSASSINATION
CLASSROOM
STORY AND ART BY
YUSEI MATSUI
1
SHONEN JUMP ADVANCED
viz media
www.viz.com
SHONEN JUMP ADVANCED
www.shonenjump.com
RATED T+ FOR OLDER TEEN
ratings.viz.com
ANSATSU KYOSHITSU © 2012 by Yusei Matsui/SHUEISHA Inc.

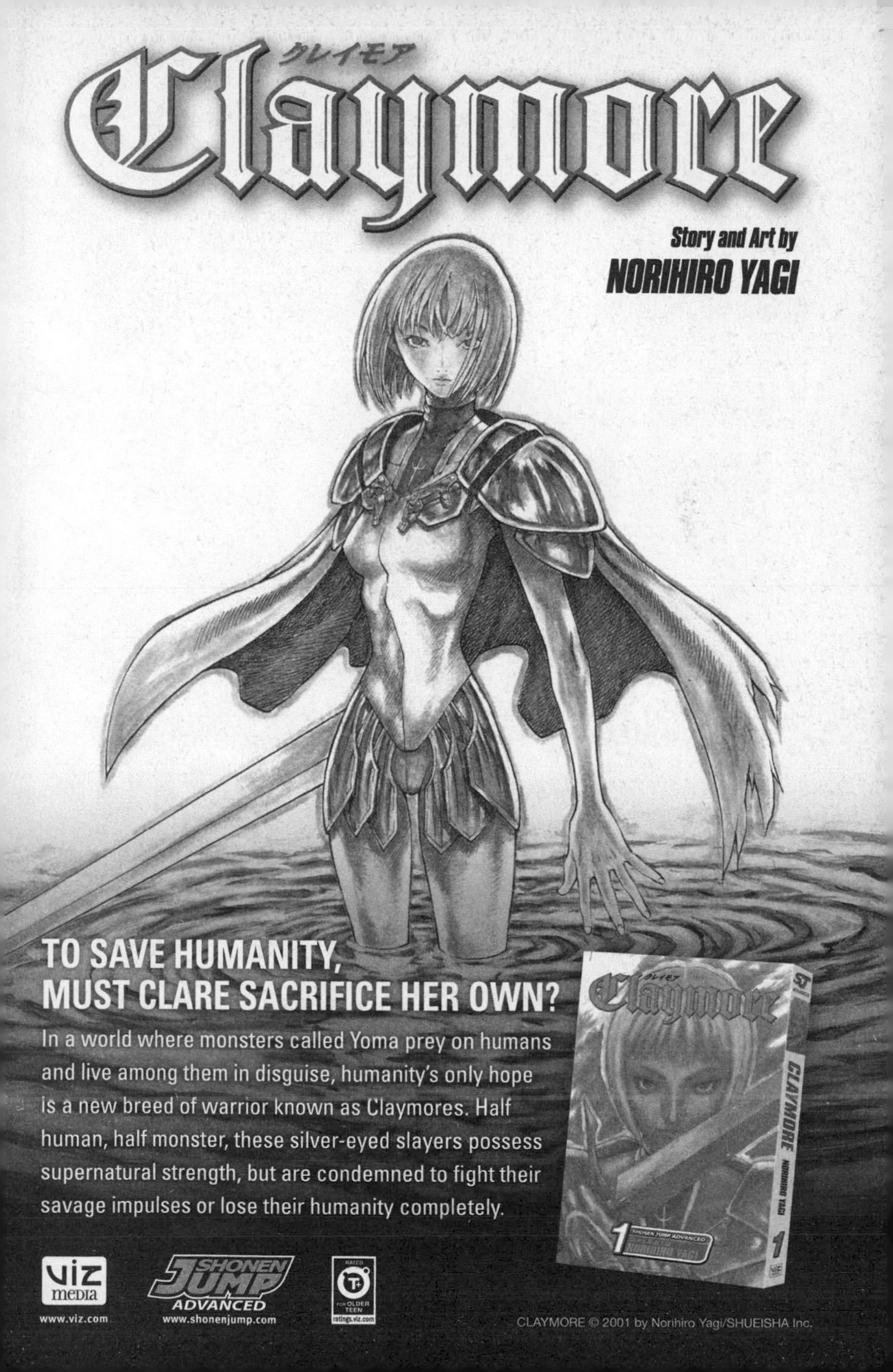
Claymore
クレイモア
Story and Art by
NORIHIRO YAGI
TO SAVE HUMANITY,
MUST CLARE SACRIFICE HER OWN?
In a world where monsters called Yoma prey on humans and live among them in disguise, humanity's only hope is a new breed of warrior known as Claymores. Half human, half monster, these silver-eyed slayers possess supernatural strength, but are condemned to fight their savage impulses or lose their humanity completely.
Claymore
CLAYMORE
NORIHIRO YAGI
1
SHONEN JUMP ADVANCED
viz media
www.viz.com
SHONEN JUMP ADVANCED
www.shonenjump.com
RATED T+ FOR OLDER TEEN
ratings.viz.com
CLAYMORE © 2001 by Norihiro Yagi/SHUEISHA Inc.

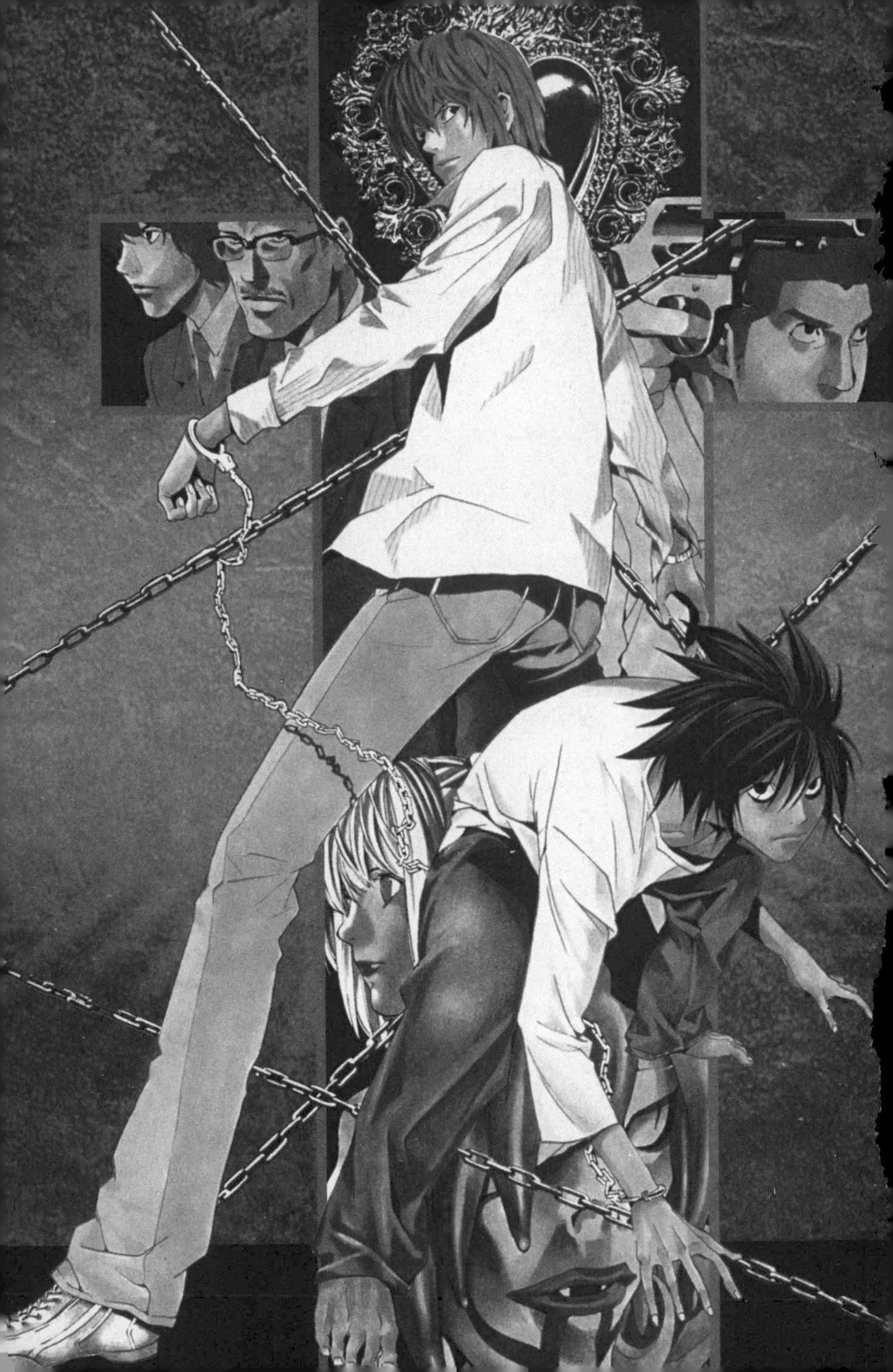

You're Reading the Wrong Direction!!

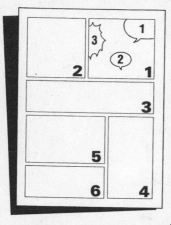

Whoops! Guess what? You're starting at the wrong end of the comic!

…It's true! In keeping with the original Japanese format, **Rosario+Vampire** is meant to be read from right to left, starting in the upper-right corner.

Unlike English, which is read from left to right, Japanese is read from right to left, meaning action, sound effects and word-balloon order are completely reversed… something which can make readers unfamiliar with Japanese feel pretty backwards themselves. For this reason, manga or Japanese comics published in the U.S. in English have sometimes been published "flopped"—that is, printed in exact reverse order, as though seen from the other side of a mirror.

By flopping pages, U.S. publishers can avoid confusing readers, but the compromise is not without its downside. For one thing, a character in a flopped manga series who once wore in the original Japanese version a T-shirt emblazoned with "M A Y" (as in "the merry month of") now wears one which reads "Y A M"! Additionally, many manga creators in Japan are themselves unhappy with the process, as some feel the mirror-imaging of their art skews their original intentions.

We are proud to bring you Akihisa Ikeda's **Rosario+Vampire** in the original unflopped format. For now, though, turn to the other side of the book and let the haunting begin…!

—Editor